HTML5 in Action

ROB CROWTHER
JOE LENNON
ASH BLUE
GREG WANISH

MANNING
SHELTER ISLAND

Manning Publications Co.	Development editor:	Renae Gregoire
20 Baldwin Road	Copyeditor:	Tiffany Taylor
PO Box 261	Proofreader:	Elizabeth Martin
Shelter Island, NY 11964	Typesetter:	Dennis Dalinnik
	Cover designer:	Marija Tudor

ISBN: 9781617290497
Printed in the United States of America
1 2 3 4 5 6 7 8 9 10 – MAL – 19 18 17 16 15 14

brief contents

contents

v

Explaining what HTML5 is can be a very daunting task. I've been doing this since its inception, and I'm still amazed by how many myths abound and how much confusion there is on the topic. With HTML5, we rebooted web development. The world of HTML4 and the nonstarter XHTML stranded those who wanted to use the web as a platform for applications. HTML4 was meant for linked documents, and XHTML was far too strict for its own good and lacked real support in browsers.

HTML5 started with a clean slate. We analyzed what was used on the web and added a lot of features we didn't have before, like Canvas for creating visuals on the fly or accessing images and videos on a pixel level, native audio and video without the need for plug-ins, and forms that validate in the browser without our having to write extra JavaScript. We also started muddying the waters by merging HTML and JavaScript functionality—a lot of HTML5 won't do anything without accessing the elements via a JavaScript API. This confuses many people. We moved on from a document-based web, and in that process we needed more technical expertise. And this meant we needed to rethink a few of our "best practices," which can annoy people so that they spread nasty rumors about the viability of HTML5 as a choice for professional development.

HTML5 is built on the robustness principle, which means that a browser will make a lot of educated guesses as to what you might have meant when you make a syntax error instead of simply giving up and showing an error. This gives it backward compatibility, and we can show pages developed for a never-to-arrive XHTML world in browsers these days. A large part of the standard is just that: it tells you how to write a browser that renders HTML5 rather than using it as a web developer. Again, this angers some people, and they shout about the verbosity of the standard.

HTML5 is also the new hotness. Much of the advertising talk, shiny demos, and promises of fidelity that matches native apps on phones makes us cynical, battle-hardened web developers think back on Java, Flash, and Silverlight and their promises, and sigh. There's a lot of buzz about HTML5, and many things that aren't part of the standard are simply declared part of it, because it makes a good punch line.

When it comes to extending the language and bringing new features into it, we're running wild right now. Every browser maker and web company comes up with great new concepts on almost a weekly level. That can be frustrating for developers who want only to get a job done. Can we rely on the functionality that's currently developed, or will the standard be changed later on? We're pushing browsers further into the OS and allowing them to access hardware directly, which comes with security and robustness issues that need to be fixed by trial and error. Can you take that risk with us when it comes to delivering your product?

These are exciting times, and when you want to be part of the ride, you can help forge the future development environment for all of us. If you don't have the time to follow the discussions on mailing lists, do a lot of browser testing in previews, and propose your own ideas, you can be left quite confused.

And this is where a book like *HTML5 in Action* comes in. Instead of promising a cornucopia of functionality that will soon be available, you get examples that work right now, based on examples that worked in the past. Instead of getting experimental demos, you'll learn how to build production code based on proven ideas, using the features in modern browsers that make it easier for developers and much more enjoyable for end users. All the examples come with a legend telling you which browsers support the features, and you'll learn how not to give features to old browsers that will choke on them.

You'll learn how to use HTML5 *now*, using secure and intelligent solutions like Modernizr and HTML5 Boilerplate, and you'll come out at the end understanding how to write things in HTML5 that currently work. This will make you a part of the movement to get HTML5 production-ready for all of us.

Those who live on the bleeding edge of defining the next browser and language features need implementations in the wild—right now. We're past the "show-and-tell" stage, and we need to get to "deliver and enhance." And you can become an integral part of this process by following the advice and applying the examples you find here. Go forth and deliver.

CHRISTIAN HEILMANN
PRINCIPAL EVANGELIST HTML5, MOZILLA

preface

Writing a book about all things HTML5 is more difficult than it sounds. Primarily because of browser and specification changes, it seemed that no matter how much we wrote every six months, browsers would adjust an implementation enough to break a few chapters. This pushed progress back and forth, making chapter revisions a constant fear, especially after we had seen so many books released on HTML5 that were outdated months later. After fighting the tides of change, we eventually nailed down solid app techniques that were resistant to change. These apps should continue to work as HTML5 continues past this book's release date.

To add to our book's track record of chaos, it originally started with just Robert Crowther (who was already writing another book) and Joe Lennon. Rob's death-defying stunt while writing the book was that he somehow managed to write another book called *Hello! HTML5 and CSS3* (Manning, 2012) at the same time. If that weren't enough, he reviewed chapters from his coauthors and provided helpful feedback (still wondering when he finds time to sleep).

Joe Lennon wrote about forms, about file storage, appendices, and an awesome general overview of the HTML5 specification. Greg Wanish (originally our editor) worked with Joe on his sections. The two tackled some of the most difficult and volatile specifications that are still being implemented in most browsers. Ash Blue came on board to tackle HTML5's massive APIs for interactive visual data.

Greg and Ash are from the United States, while Joe lives in Ireland and Rob in London. Our team's geographical makeup made meeting as a group very difficult. At almost every meeting, somebody was missing. If you've ever worked on a group project, then you know how essential meetings for something like this book can be. Even with all four of us dedicating much of our free time to work on the book, it took much longer than expected. The delay was partially because we wanted to keep the book up to date with the latest techniques and specification changes. Another time-consuming task was integrating feedback from our MEAP readers, who gave us great information on how to improve the book.

The true lesson we learned from writing *HTML5 in Action* is that you should never write on an experimental subject—just kidding! But in all honesty, HTML5's volatile state did make things both difficult and rewarding. Our hope is that our long nights of handcrafting every letter of this book will make learning HTML5 much easier for you.

acknowledgments

We'd like to thank our editor at Manning, Renae Gregoire, for putting up with us in general. Without her reviewing our thousands and thousands of lines of text, sending weekly status reports, and organizing meetings, this book would never have happened. She was dropped into our book halfway through the writing process and made quite the effort to get up to speed as quickly as she could. Also big thanks to our first editor, Maria Townsley, for getting the ball rolling.

Thanks to everyone at Manning for their extreme patience on this book's timeline. They could have released a broken book that was half-baked, but they were really true to their readers and pushed to produce a great product. Without Troy Mott's magical ability to find tech writers, we would never have finished. He staffed the book quickly and helped when he could with the feedback process.

Thanks also to our MEAP readers and peer reviewers whose comments and corrections helped make this a much better book. We would like to acknowledge the following reviewers for reading our manuscript at various stages of its development: "Anil" Radhakrishna, Alexander Esser, Arun Noronha, Chris Zimmerman, Dave Pawson, Dmitry Skylut, Donald Matheson, Federico Tomassetti, James Hatheway, Jeff Kirkell, John Ryan III, Jonas Bandi, Joseph Morgan, Julio Guijarro, Leonel Waisblatt, Lester Lobo, Lloyd S. Derbyshire, Michael Caro, Osama A. Morad PhD, Robert Williams, Sebastian Rogers, Stan Bice, Timothy Hanna, and Tyson S. Maxwell.

Finally, special thanks to Chris Heilmann at Mozilla for contributing the foreword to our book, and to Adam London for his careful technical proofread of the manuscript shortly before it went into production.

Rob Crowther

This is the second set of acknowledgments I've written in less than a year, so take it as read that all the family, friends, and people who got me started in web development and whom I thanked in my first book are just as important to me now as they were then. For this book I'd like to thank my colleagues at work over the last two years for their (sometimes inadvertent) contributions to my sanity while I was trying to write two books at once: Ade, Adriana, Alexandru, Amy, Angelique, Annie, Anusha, Boris, Carlos, Chani, Dan, Danielle, Darren, Dave, David, Delia, Denis, Don, Dorin, Dragos, Eric, Gary, Gemma, Gifty, Hazel, Indrani, Ioan, Ionel, Jack, Jhumi, Jo, Katie, Liam, Liming, Lindsay, Lisa, Louise, Marc, Marinela, Mark K., Mark R., Mark W., Martin H., Martin J., Mihai, Nancy, Natalie, Nia, Patricia, Paul, Paula, Phil, Razvan, Rhavy, Rob, Sally, Scott, Sean, Simon, Stella, Sudini, Tal, Tom H., and Tom W. (and if I forgot anyone, sorry, but you managed to avoid emailing me for two years!).

Joe Lennon

I'd like to thank my wife, Jill, for her love and support—I'd be lost without her. I'd also like to thank my parents, Jim and Maria; my sisters, Laura and Kelly; the Mac Sweeney family; and all at Core International. Finally, special thanks to Prof. Ciaran Murphy and Patricia Lynch at University College Cork and to Troy Mott for bringing me on board this project in the first place.

Ash Blue

I would like to thank my beautiful wife for contributing artwork and time to make this book happen, my family for their patience with my writing over the holidays, and also friends who let me lock myself in a room for over a year to write this thing. Despite how crazy as I got while trying to balance life and writing this book, I'm happy nobody carted me off to the funny farm.

Greg Wanish

I would like to thank my parents for supporting my dreams and ambitions throughout the years. All the adventures and experiences that I had in pursuit of those goals have given me a wealth of wisdom beyond my grandest expectations.

about this book

HTML5 is one of the fastest-growing technologies in web development. The reason for such a quick adoption is the technology's usability across desktops and mobile devices. In theory, you program an application once, and it magically works everywhere. It also gives powerful native functionality through simple API access.

Because of HTML5's dynamic nature, it's usable for far more than just mobile and desktop browsers. It can be compiled into a native mobile app through platforms such as PhoneGap and appMobi, which can save developers and companies lots of money because they don't have to maintain two completely separate code bases for apps on iOS and Android.

Most HTML5 APIs are still quite young, so we'll guide you around pitfalls developers experience while building their first HTML5 apps. In addition, you'll learn about modern fallback techniques, application-oriented JavaScript, and what is/isn't an HTML5 API.

Who should read this book?

If you're looking to build full-functioning, in-browser applications for the real world, then this book is for you. It covers everything from data storage, to messaging, and even interactive development such as video games.

This book is for developers who have a decent understanding of JavaScript and HTML syntax. If the terms *loop*, *array*, and *JSON* are completely unfamiliar to you, you should brush up on those before proceeding.

Roadmap

Part 1 Introduction

Chapter 1 covers a basic overview of HTML5's markup syntax and all the APIs this book covers.

Part 2 Browser-based apps

Chapter 2 focuses on building HTML5 forms for an ecommerce site from markup to completion. It goes in depth about calculations and input validation.

Chapter 3 walks you through creating a filesystem and managing data. It also covers drag-and-drop functionality and the Geolocation API.

Chapter 4 is one of the more complicated chapters, because it focuses on messaging with WebSockets and other technologies to build a chat system.

Chapter 5 is an in-depth look at the various HTML5 APIs for storage, such as IndexedDB and local storage. It covers building a mobile task list.

Part 3 Interactive graphics, media, and gaming

Chapter 6 covers building an HTML5 game called Canvas Ricochet with the Canvas API. The game features a simple leveling system.

Chapter 7 shows you how to use Canvas's counterpart, Scalable Vector Graphics (SVG), to create a 2D space shooter game.

Chapter 8 takes a complex look at the audio and video API to show some powerful techniques you can use in your applications. It also covers format issues, inputs, and building a video player.

Chapter 9 is one of the most complex chapters because it covers WebGL for 3D programming. By the end of this chapter, you'll have created your own 3D space shooter with complex shapes rolled from scratch.

Appendixes

There are nine appendixes in *HTML5 in Action*, further explaining ideas in the book, offering suggestions for setting up or installing programs, and listing important links and references:

Appendix A: HTML5 and related specifications
Appendix B: HTML5 API reference
Appendix C: Installing PHP and MySQL
Appendix D: Computer networking primer
Appendix E: Setting up Node.js
Appendix F: Channel messaging
Appendix G: Tools and libraries
Appendix H: Encoding with FFmpeg
Appendix I: HTML Next
Appendix J: Links and references

Chapter features

Each chapter starts with an "At a Glance" table, letting you see which topics will be covered in the chapter, with the corresponding page numbers listed for each topic. Throughout the book, we include Core API icons in the margins

Core API

that highlight the main topics and help you locate the section you need, quickly and easily.

Code conventions and downloads

Code samples are presented in a monospaced font like this. It should be noted that although we attempted to keep code snippets as small as possible, they overflow on some of the pages. Lines of code that are too wide will overflow onto the next line, and code sections that take up more than a whole page will continue on the next. To help with understanding, code sample annotations have been included. These would normally be written with JavaScript comments such as // or /* */.

Source code for all chapters in this book is available for download from the publisher's site at www.manning.com/crowther2/ or at www.manning.com/HTML5inAction, and from the GitHub repository https://github.com/html5-ia/html5-ia.

Software requirements

To complete this book's applications, you'll need the latest version of Chrome on a Mac or Windows operating system. If additional setup is required to run an app, it will be stated in the readme.txt file in the source files.

About the authors

Rob Crowther is a web developer and blogger from London, UK, and the author of Manning's *Hello! HTML5 and CSS3*. **Joe Lennon** is an enterprise mobile application developer from Ireland. **Ash Blue** is the developer for game dev studio Clever Crow Games. As an indie developer, he utilizes HTML5 to distribute games to several different platforms. In the past, he has developed robust front-end architecture and application solutions for companies such as Hasbro, Tastemaker, and Wikia. His blog is at blueashes.com. **Greg Wanish** is an independent developer of client-side web and e-commerce applications. He also designs and sells a line of graphic and message t-shirts.

Author Online

Purchase of *HTML5 in Action* incudes free access to a private web forum run by Manning Publications, where you can make comments about the book, ask technical questions, and receive help from the authors and from other users. To access the forum and subscribe to it, point your web browser to www.manning.com/HTML5inaction. This page provides information on how to get on the forum once you are registered, what kind of help is available, and the rules of conduct on the forum.

Manning's commitment to our readers is to provide a venue where a meaningful dialogue between individual readers and between readers and the authors can take place. It is not a commitment to any specific amount of participation on the part of the authors, whose contributions to the book's forum remains voluntary (and unpaid). We suggest you try asking the authors challenging questions, lest their interest stray.

The Author Online forum and the archives of previous discussions will be accessible from the publisher's website as long as the book is in print.

About the cover illustration

The figure on the cover of *HTML5 in Action* is captioned "Le touriste," which means tourist or traveler. The illustration is taken from a 19th-century edition of Sylvain Maréchal's four-volume compendium of regional dress customs published in France. Each illustration is finely drawn and colored by hand. The rich variety of Maréchal's collection reminds us vividly of how culturally apart the world's towns and regions were just 200 years ago. Isolated from each other, people spoke different dialects and languages. In the streets or in the countryside, it was easy to identify where they lived and what their trade or station in life was just by their dress.

Dress codes have changed since then and the diversity by region, so rich at the time, has faded away. It is now hard to tell apart the inhabitants of different continents, let alone different towns or regions. Perhaps we have traded cultural diversity for a more varied personal life—certainly for a more varied and fast-paced technological life.

At a time when it is hard to tell one computer book from another, Manning celebrates the inventiveness and initiative of the computer business with book covers based on the rich diversity of regional life of two centuries ago, brought back to life by Maréchal's pictures.

Part 1

Introduction

It's important that you know about HTML5's semantic markup basics and wide variety of APIs. For the introduction, we'll cover these concepts briefly, but in heavy detail, to ramp you up.

If you're already building sites with HTML5's new tag structure you could skip this section. However, you'll miss advanced markup concepts such as ARIA and microdata (if you aren't already familiar with them).

HTML5: from documents to applications

1

This chapter covers

- The basics of using HTML5
- New semantic markup and media features
- New JavaScript APIs
- Closely related web specifications

HTML5 is one of the hottest topics in web development, and with good reason. Not only is it the latest version of the markup language for the web, but it also defines a whole new standard for developing web applications. Previous iterations of HTML (and its rigid XML-based sibling, XHTML) have been centered primarily on the concept of HTML as a markup language for documents. HTML5 is the first version to embrace the web as a platform for web application development.

HTML5 defines a series of new elements that you can use to develop rich internet applications as well as a range of standard JavaScript APIs for browsers to implement natively. A good example of HTML5's new elements is `<video>`, which provides a means of playing video content in the browser without requiring an additional plug-in. HTML5 also provides the Media Element Interface that allows you to control video playback with JavaScript. It lets you create games, build mobile applications, and much more.

3

In this chapter, you'll learn

- About great new features introduced in HTML5 and how to immediately use them in your web applications.
- How to provide fallbacks and workarounds for users with older or incompatible browsers.
- How to use ARIA (Accessible Rich Internet Applications) roles and microdata to further enhance the semantics of your HTML pages.
- The wide range of JavaScript APIs available in HTML5 itself, as well as a number of closely related API specifications you can use in your applications.

By the end of this chapter, you'll have a broad sense of what HTML5 has to offer and be able to use it in your own web applications.

Documents (HTML4) versus applications (HTML5)

Initially the web was all about documents. Forms were added by the Mosaic browser in 1993, but this was merely data entry; all application logic remained on the server. The introduction of JavaScript in 1995 made browser-based applications theoretically possible, but things didn't really take off until after the arrival of the `XMLHTTPRequest` object in 1999. The last major version of the HTML specification, 4.01, only became a recommendation in 1999. So it's not surprising that the 4.01 spec still concentrated almost entirely on the use of markup to describe documents, what we now normally refer to as *semantic markup*.

The next version of HTML has been a long time coming, and the web has changed a lot in the meantime. As you'll see in the following sections, HTML5 contains improvements in the area of semantic markup. The majority of the differences and improvements in HTML5 over HTML4, however, are in facilities for building browser-based applications with JavaScript. Because of that, and because this book is focused on the new features of HTML5, we spend a lot more time dealing with JavaScript than with markup. We do cover some markup, but, as you'll see, JavaScript is the *real* big deal in HTML5.

To get started, we'll show you how to get up and running by creating an HTML5 document.

1.1   *Exploring the markup: a whirlwind tour of HTML5*

The best way to learn what's new in HTML5 is to jump right in and explore. The goal of this section isn't only to give you a high-level tour of the new features but also to give you enough knowledge to be able to update your existing applications to use HTML5 conventions, without upsetting users who don't have the latest and greatest browsers.

In this section, you'll learn

- How to create a basic HTML5 document structure.
- How to use the new semantic elements to lay out a page.
- How to deal with older versions of Internet Explorer that don't recognize the new elements.
- About the new form features you can implement immediately in HTML5.
- How to use new UI elements, such as progress bars and collapsible sections.

Let's get started by examining the basic structure of an HTML5 document. If you're not interested in the basics, you can read quickly until you reach section 1.2, which goes beyond semantic markup and into the HTML5 ecosystem.

1.1.1 Creating the basic structure of an HTML5 document

HTML5 documents are structured in the same way as older versions of HTML: you put a <!DOCTYPE> declaration at the top of the document and open and close the HTML document with matching <html> and </html> tags. Between these tags, you have a <head> section, where you place <meta> information and other noncontent items such as stylesheets, and a <body> section, where your page content should go. If you've written HTML pages or applications before, none of this will be new to you, but you need to be aware of some subtle differences, which we'll cover in this section:

- The HTML5 DOCTYPE declaration syntax.
- How to use the opening <html> element.
- How to use the shorter versions of the various elements in the <head> section.

Let's look more closely at these differences by examining hello.html, the HTML5 equivalent of a "Hello, World!" application, shown in the following listing.

Listing 1.1 hello.html—The basic structure of an HTML5 document

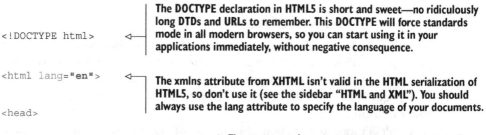

```
<!DOCTYPE html>
```
The DOCTYPE declaration in HTML5 is short and sweet—no ridiculously long DTDs and URLs to remember. This DOCTYPE will force standards mode in all modern browsers, so you can start using it in your applications immediately, without negative consequence.

```
<html lang="en">

<head>
```
The xmlns attribute from XHTML isn't valid in the HTML serialization of HTML5, so don't use it (see the sidebar "HTML and XML"). You should always use the lang attribute to specify the language of your documents.

```
    <meta charset="utf-8">

    <title>Hello, HTML5!</title>
```
The <meta> element now supports a charset attribute, allowing for a more memorable syntax than the older combination of http-equiv and content attributes for defining the page's character set (in this case we're using 8-bit Unicode). Note that in the XML serialization of HTML5 this tag is required to be self-closing (e.g., <meta charset="utf-8"/>). See the sidebar "HTML and XML" for further details.

```
<link rel="stylesheet" href="style.css">

<script src="app.js"></script>

</head>

<body>

    <h1>Hello, HTML5!</h1>

</body>

</html>
```

All modern browsers will assume that a stylesheet's <link> element will have a type of text/css by default, so you can safely omit that attribute in your HTML5 documents.

Browsers assume that <script> elements have a type of text/javascript, so you don't need to specify the attribute unless you're using it for something other than JavaScript.

That's a basic page structure. Next, we'll show you how to use the new semantic elements to construct a page—in this case, a sample blog post page.

HTML and XML

Previous versions of what we think of as the HTML specification were either HTML or XHTML. HTML markup was designed to be fairly forgiving, whereas XHTML was built around XML and a strict parsing model. XHTML required all elements to have closing tags (
 instead of <br>, for example) and all tags and attributes to be lowercase. A single error would cause the whole page to fail. Because of this draconian error handling, most websites never properly implemented XHTML. They tended to use XHTML syntax forms but send pages with a content type of text/html, causing HTML parsing of the XML markup.

HTML5 unifies everything in a single specification by allowing both HTML and XML serializations; that is, the specification provides a vocabulary that can be expressed in either HTML or XHTML. The XHTML serialization must be sent with an XML content type such as application/xml+xhtml. It also conforms to XML parsing rules rather than HTML ones, requiring an xmlns declaration, closing tags, and so on. In the code download there are two additional versions of listing 1.1 showing the same markup in valid and invalid XHTML markup: hello-invalid.xhtml, which uses HTML syntax in an XML document, and hello-valid.xhtml, which corrects the markup to valid XML.

1.1.2   Using the new semantic elements

If you've read about HTML5 before you picked up this book, chances are you've heard plenty about the new semantic elements. They're important, particularly if you want search engines and assistive technologies such as screen readers to understand your pages better, but they're no more difficult to use than the elements you know and love from HTML4.

Don't get too excited about this new set of tags. If you're expecting these new elements to do something magical in terms of how they look on your page, you're in for some disappointment. Using these new elements on your page is functionally equivalent to using a series of <div> elements; they behave as block elements by default and can be styled as required using CSS. Their importance comes from the standard semantic meaning they have.

Consider, for example, a typical blog post, in which the web page contains a series of sections. First, you'd have the site heading and navigation, maybe some sidebar navigation, a main content area, a footer area with further navigation links, and perhaps some copyright and legal links. The next listing demonstrates how such a blog post might have been marked up in HTML4 or XHTML.

Listing 1.2 html4-blog.html—HTML4 markup for a blog post

```
<div class="header">
    <h1>My Site Name</h1>
    <h2>My Site Slogan</h2>
    <div class="nav">
        <ul><!-- Main Site Nav here --></ul>
    </div>
</div>

<div class="sidebar">
    <h3>Links Heading</h3>
    <ul><!-- Sidebar links --></ul>
</div>

<div class="main">
    <h4>Blog Post Title</h4>
    <div class="meta">
        Published by Joe on 01 May 2011 @ 12:30pm
    </div>
    <div class="post">
        <!-- Actual blog post -->
    </div>
</div>

<div class="footer">
    <ul><!-- Footer links --></ul>
    <!-- Copyright info -->
</div>
```

The previous code isn't wrong. It's perfectly valid to use it in HTML5, and you can absolutely continue to use <div> elements with semantic class names if you wish. But from a semantic point of view, this approach poses a couple of problems:

- By using the old standard, you wind up separating areas of the blog post using named classes. This is fine, but the class-naming convention is up to the author. Our "header" might be your "heading"; we call the main section "main," but you might call it "body" or "article."
- Some people may prefer to use IDs instead of classes. They may use id="header" whereas others might use class="header."

In short, a search engine or other computer-controlled application has no way to reliably determine what each section represents.

This is where the new semantic elements come into play. Rather than using classes and IDs for sections like headings, navigation, and footers, you now use several different

HTML elements, shown in the following listing. Add this code between the `<body>` tags of the hello.html file.

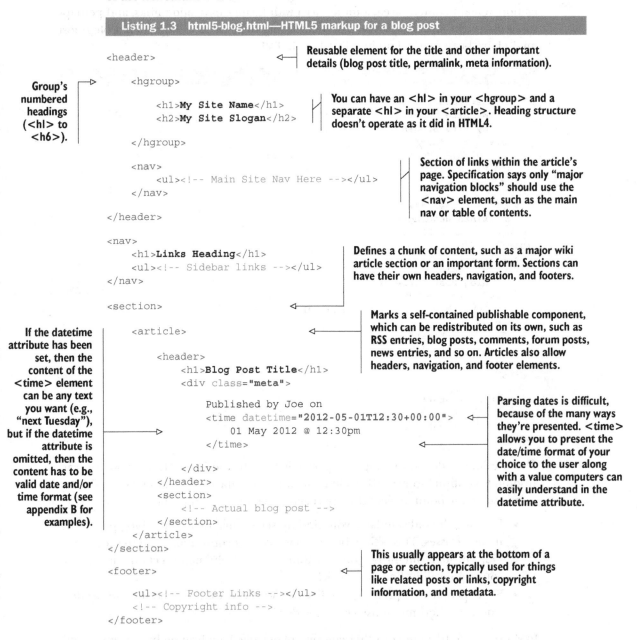

Listing 1.3 html5-blog.html—HTML5 markup for a blog post

```
<header>
```
↤ Reusable element for the title and other important details (blog post title, permalink, meta information).

Group's numbered headings (`<h1>` to `<h6>`).
```
    <hgroup>

        <h1>My Site Name</h1>
        <h2>My Site Slogan</h2>

    </hgroup>
```
You can have an `<h1>` in your `<hgroup>` and a separate `<h1>` in your `<article>`. Heading structure doesn't operate as it did in HTML4.

```
    <nav>
        <ul><!-- Main Site Nav Here --></ul>
    </nav>

</header>
```
Section of links within the article's page. Specification says only "major navigation blocks" should use the `<nav>` element, such as the main nav or table of contents.

```
<nav>
    <h1>Links Heading</h1>
    <ul><!-- Sidebar links --></ul>
</nav>

<section>
```
↤ Defines a chunk of content, such as a major wiki article section or an important form. Sections can have their own headers, navigation, and footers.

```
    <article>
```
↤ Marks a self-contained publishable component, which can be redistributed on its own, such as RSS entries, blog posts, comments, forum posts, news entries, and so on. Articles also allow headers, navigation, and footer elements.

```
        <header>
            <h1>Blog Post Title</h1>
            <div class="meta">
```

If the datetime attribute has been set, then the content of the `<time>` element can be any text you want (e.g., "next Tuesday"), but if the datetime attribute is omitted, then the content has to be valid date and/or time format (see appendix B for examples).
```
                Published by Joe on
                <time datetime="2012-05-01T12:30+00:00">
                    01 May 2012 @ 12:30pm
                </time>
```
↤ Parsing dates is difficult, because of the many ways they're presented. `<time>` allows you to present the date/time format of your choice to the user along with a value computers can easily understand in the datetime attribute.

```
            </div>
        </header>
        <section>
            <!-- Actual blog post -->
        </section>
    </article>
</section>

<footer>
```
↤ This usually appears at the bottom of a page or section, typically used for things like related posts or links, copyright information, and metadata.

```
    <ul><!-- Footer Links --></ul>
    <!-- Copyright info -->
</footer>
```

TWO OTHER IMPORTANT HTML5 ELEMENTS: `<ASIDE>` AND `<MARK>`

We don't want to move on without telling you about two other important HTML5 elements that you'll use a lot: `<aside>` and `<mark>`. You can use the `<aside>` element to define a section of a page that's separate from the content area in which it's defined.

In a book or magazine, this might be represented as a sidebar that contains information on the same topic but doesn't quite fit into the main article itself. For example, if you had a blog, you may have advertisements displaying alongside posts—these could be placed in an <aside> element. In a web application, you might use <aside> for a pop-up or a floating window that appears over the main part of the application itself.

You can use the <mark> element to represent a part of text in your document that should be marked or highlighted. A common use for this would be to highlight search terms within a document.

With the new semantic elements, not only is your page's markup easier on the eye, but search engine spiders and assistive technologies will also more easily understand your pages. Speaking of assistive technologies brings us to our next important topic: ARIA roles.

1.1.3 Enhancing accessibility using ARIA roles

When building web applications, you must ensure that your application is accessible to all users, including those who require assistive technologies such as screen readers. Ensuring that your documents are accessible requires careful consideration when it comes to the semantic meaning of your markup. Using simple HTML markup makes this relatively straightforward, and HTML5's new elements improve the semantics even further. But when you're creating web applications, it becomes much more difficult to cater to assistive technology. The increasing amount of JavaScript code used to dynamically modify web pages in modern web applications makes it far more difficult to deliver accessibility through good markup alone. This is where the Web Accessibility Initiative (WAI) and ARIA standards come into play.

The WAI-ARIA specification aims to improve web applications by expanding on the accessibility information provided by the author of an HTML document. ARIA roles, relationships, states, and properties allow you to define exactly how your web application works in a way that an assistive technology such as a screen reader can understand. If, for example, you build a drop-down list out of a text input and an unordered list, you can apply the ARIA role combobox to the input element so that it can be rendered appropriately to the user's device. The following listing shows an example of this style of markup taken directly from the WAI-ARIA 1.0 spec.

Listing 1.4 ARIA combobox example from www.w3.org/TR/wai-aria/roles#combobox

```
<input type="text"
  aria-label="Tag"
  role="combobox"
  aria-autocomplete="list"
  aria-owns="owned_listbox">
<ul role="listbox"
  id="owned_listbox">
    <li role="option">Zebra</li>
    <li role="option">Zoom</li>
</ul>
```

The element providing the autocomplete options will have this ID.

The role attribute allows you to declare what sort of widget it is.

ARIA has a number of autocomplete types; in this case, a list will provide the combo values.

The unordered list has the role listbox, to complement the type provided in the ARIA annotation.

This ID corresponds to the one given previously.

The HTML5 specification explicitly states that you may use the ARIA role and aria-* attributes on HTML elements as described in the ARIA specification; this wasn't allowed in HTML4. HTML5 also defines a set of default ARIA roles that apply to certain HTML elements. For example, it's implied that a checkbox <input> element has an ARIA role of checkbox, and you shouldn't explicitly use role or aria-* attributes that differ from those implied in these cases.

You'll also find HTML elements where the native semantics can be modified so that they behave differently. For example, you might create an <a> element that behaves like a button and use it to submit a form after performing some validation. The HTML5 specification defines a list of valid semantics for these elements. When you use the <a> element to create a hyperlink, it assumes the link role by default, and if this is modified, its role can only be changed to one of the following: button, checkbox, menuitem, menuitemcheckbox, menuitemradio, tab, or treeitem.

For a complete list of the default, implied ARIA semantics, and the restrictions on how you can modify the semantics of certain elements, see the WAI-ARIA section of the HTML5 specification at http://mng.bz/6hb2.

1.1.4   *Enabling support in Internet Explorer versions 6 to 8*

A subject you may wonder about as you consider HTML5 elements is compatibility with older browsers, and rightly so. Each new version of HTML brings with it new elements that you can use in your documents. HTML5 is no different. Most modern browsers are more than capable of rendering these elements, even versions that don't specifically support them. The way that most browsers handle unrecognized elements is by rendering them like normal in-line <span> elements. All that is required is to set them to display: block with CSS. Unfortunately, Internet Explorer (IE) is the one exception. In versions prior to IE9, the browser would render unrecognized elements but wouldn't allow you to style them using Cascading Style Sheets (CSS). As you can imagine, this makes it difficult to start using the new HTML5 elements in a production application, because your users may still be using IE6, 7, or 8.

RENDERING NEW ELEMENTS PROPERLY IN IE

Fortunately, this problem has a simple remedy. If you want to use the element <header> on your page and need to apply CSS styles, include the following snippet in the <head> section of your page. This will force IE to apply the CSS rules to the tag, even if the version of IE used doesn't support a particular element natively:

```
<!--[if lte IE 8]>
<script>document.createElement("header");</script>
<![endif]-->
```

You'll need to execute an equivalent of this JavaScript statement for every HTML5-specific element you wish to use in your page. As you're doing this, it will cause IE versions 6 to 8 to render the style correctly, with the problem persisting if you attempt to print the page.

RENDERING NEW ELEMENTS PROPERLY ON PAGES PRINTED FROM IE

Fortunately, a solution known as IE Print Protector fixes the printing issue. But rather than reinvent the wheel, we recommend you use an HTML shiv script. The most popular HTML5 shiv was originally created by Remy Sharp and has since been improved by many others. For more information and to get the latest version of the script, see http://mng.bz/50dt.

> **WARNING**　The HTML5 shiv solution requires JavaScript. If you want a JavaScript-free solution, you can use HTML5's XML-based sibling, XHTML5, instead. See Eric Klingen's post on the subject at http://mng.bz/QBIw.

What else can you do to boost the presence of your existing applications using HTML5? How about integrating easy features that jazz up your forms? Even though forms are ubiquitous, in HTML5 that doesn't mean they have to be boring and plain.

1.1.5　Introducing HTML5's new form features

It rarely receives acclaim, but the humble web form has played a major role in the emergence of the web as a platform for application development. HTML5's focus on web applications led to many improvements in web forms, all of which you can use today, without breaking compatibility with older web browsers.

IMPROVING THE SEMANTICS OF DATA INPUT USING NEW FORM INPUT TYPES

The basic text field has been used far beyond its primitive capabilities. In the same way that the <div> element was used in HTML4 for all sorts of block content, the text input is used for all sorts of textual input. HTML5 aims to ease its burden by offering a number of new and backward-compatible types, each of which provides enhancements over the simple text field. Table 1.1 identifies the new input types in HTML5.

Table 1.1　The new form input types introduced in HTML5

color	date	datetime	datetime-local	email
month	number	range	search	tel
time	url	week		

You can use these new input types in your web pages immediately because older browsers will fall back to a standard text input type when they find a type they don't understand. Some of the new input types will also allow browsers to provide standard widget controls for given types of form fields. Figure 1.1 shows examples of these new widgets.

In chapter 2, you'll learn about Modernizr, an HTML5 feature-detection script. Using Modernizr, you'll be able to detect if a browser supports a given input type, providing a fallback JavaScript-powered widget if required.

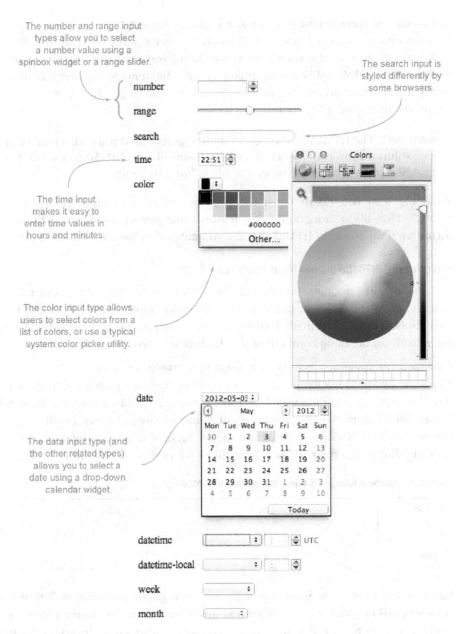

Figure 1.1 Examples of some of the new form input widgets introduced in HTML5. Note that not all browsers provide support for widgets yet.

NEW ATTRIBUTES FOR ALTERING THE BEHAVIOR OF FIELDS

In addition to new form field types, HTML5 introduces ten common attributes, shown in table 1.2, that allow you to alter the behavior of a given field. The placeholder

Placeholder text: What are you looking for?   After user input: HTML5 books

Figure 1.2   **You can use the new** `placeholder` **attribute to provide a piece of text that should be displayed in a field when it's empty. This text is typically gray and will be removed when you populate the field with a value.**

attribute is an example of one of these new attributes, and it allows you to define text that will appear in the field before it contains a value. This is illustrated in figure 1.2.

Table 1.2 provides a list of the new input attributes introduced in HTML5. You'll look at which attributes apply to which input types in chapter 2.

Table 1.2   HTML5's new input element attributes

autocomplete	autofocus	list	max	min
multiple	pattern placeholder	required	step	

NEW ATTRIBUTES FOR PERFORMING CLIENT-SIDE VALIDATION

Some of these attributes allow the browser to perform client-side validation without JavaScript. For example, the `required` attribute specifies that a field must be populated, or the browser will produce an error. The `pattern` attribute allows you to define a regular expression that the input value will be tested against. The `max` and `min` attributes allow you to restrict the maximum and minimum values on `number` and `date` field types.

In addition, the browser will perform validation on some of the new input types to warn users when they have entered values in an incorrect format. If the user enters an invalid email address in an `email` input field, for example, the browser will flag an error and prevent the form from being submitted to the server.

> **WARNING**   You should never rely solely on client-side validation, whether it's the new native browser validation in HTML5 or JavaScript validation code. It's easy to bypass client-side validation, so you should always check input on the server side. Client-side validation should be used to improve the user experience, not as application security.

You'll learn much more about the new input types and attributes in chapter 2. First we'll show you other new elements introduced in HTML5 that you can easily, and immediately, integrate into your applications.

1.1.6   *Progress bars, meters, and collapsible content*

HTML5 defines a series of new elements that you can use to convey information to the user. These include widgets that developers would previously have relied on third-party JavaScript libraries for, such as progress bars, meters, and collapsible sections.

Figure 1.3   The left-hand progress bar is an example of a determinate progress bar. In this example, the value of the bar is set to 50 percent, and the appearance of the bar reflects this because it's half filled. The right-hand progress bar is an indeterminate bar and doesn't have a value. It displays an animated full bar to indicate that something's happening, but the percentage complete isn't known.

USING PROGRESS BARS TO SHOW PERCENTAGE COMPLETION

The `<progress>` element allows you to present the user with either a determinate or indeterminate progress bar. A determinate progress bar has a given value, and the bar will fill up to that value—this is useful for displaying the progress of a file upload, where you dynamically update the value of the progress bar as the file is uploaded. An indeterminate progress bar has no particular value, and the bar will be full but animated—this is useful for informing the user that the application is loading when you're unsure of the exact progress of the operation. An example of both types of progress bar is shown in figure 1.3.

The code to create the progress bars in figure 1.3 is as follows:

```
<progress value="50" max="100"></progress>
<progress></progress>
```

Determinate progress bar must have a value and optionally a max attribute.

Indeterminate progress bar has no value.

USING METERS TO SHOW USERS MEASURES WITHIN KNOWN RANGES

Following along the same path as the `<progress>` element is the `<meter>` element. You'd use the `<progress>` element primarily to show the percentage of completion of a task and you'd use the `<meter>` element to give a representation of a scalar measurement within a known range. In addition to showing the value using a filled bar graphic, the `<meter>` element allows you to define low, high, and optimum ranges that you can use to give further meaning. When the value is in the low range, the meter will display in red; in the medium range, it'll display in yellow; and in the high and optimum ranges, it'll display in green. Figure 1.4 illustrates the appearances the `<meter>` element can have.

The code for the `<meter>` element in figure 1.4 is as follows:

Define the ranges of a meter using the min, max, low, high, and optimum attributes.

```
<meter min="0" max="10" low="3" high="7" optimum="9" value="0"></meter>
<meter min="0" max="10" low="3" high="7" optimum="9" value="1"></meter>
<meter min="0" max="10" low="3" high="7" optimum="9" value="4"></meter>
<meter min="0" max="10" low="3" high="7" optimum="9" value="7"></meter>
<meter min="0" max="10" low="3" high="7" optimum="9" value="10"></meter>
```

USING DETAILS AND SUMMARY TO CREATE COLLAPSIBLE CONTENT WITHOUT JAVASCRIPT

In the past, the only way to create collapsible content sections was to use JavaScript to toggle the display CSS property of the section so it would show or hide. HTML5

Figure 1.4 A screenshot of the states in which you can represent a <meter> element: empty, low, medium, high, and full.

introduces the <details> and <summary> elements to provide a script-free method for providing such functionality. Figure 1.5 illustrates these new elements in action.

The code to create the <details> and <summary> example is as follows:

```
<details>
    <summary>Section Heading</summary>
    This is an example of using &lt;details&gt; and &lt;summary&gt;
    to create collapsible content without using JavaScript.
</details>
```

Unfortunately, browser support for these new elements has been rather slow to date. Fortunately, it's simple to provide a fallback for this using JavaScript, several of which are provided at http://mng.bz/cJhc.

Using the techniques you learned in this section, you should now be able to update your existing applications to use HTML5 conventions, without having a negative impact on users who lack the latest and greatest browser. In the next section, you'll learn how you can take things further by going beyond HTML markup and using related concepts such as CSS3 and JavaScript to improve the style and interactivity of your documents.

1.2 Beyond the markup: additional web standards

As we mentioned, the web is no longer all about documents; it's a platform for application development. As a result, HTML5 doesn't include only markup for outlining document structure; it also encompasses many more features and associated specifications

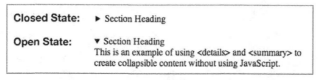

Figure 1.5 An example of the <details> and <summary> elements in action, first in the closed state, where only the code inside the <summary> element is visible, and second in the open state, where the entire contents of the <details> element are visible.

for ensuring that your applications look great and provide the best possible experience to the user. One example of this is microdata and the associated Microdata API, which enable you to provide additional semantics in your documents and then retrieve and modify them. Another example is CSS3; its evolved stylesheets allow you to apply the latest innovations in styling and effects—without relying on external images and JavaScript hacks.

In this section, you'll learn

- How to use microdata and microdata vocabularies to provide search engines with better information about your pages.
- The microdata DOM API that lets you dynamically retrieve and modify microdata items using JavaScript.
- Several of the new features in CSS3 that allow you to enhance the visual appeal of your applications while providing better user interactions and feedback.
- How HTML5 treats JavaScript as a first-class citizen with detailed specifications and advanced APIs.

To begin, let's look at microdata.

1.2.1   *Microdata*

Microdata in HTML5 allows you to add semantic information to a web page, which in turn could be used by applications such as search engines and web browsers to provide additional functionality to the user based on that data. An example of how Google uses microdata to provide smart search results is illustrated in figure 1.6.

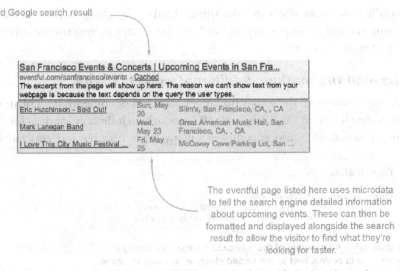

Figure 1.6   Google reads microdata from HTML documents to provide improved search results to users. By using microdata in your pages, you enable Google to provide similar search result listings for your website or application.

To use microdata, you need a vocabulary, which defines the semantics you'll use. You can define your own vocabularies, but more likely you'll want to use a published vocabulary, such as those provided by Google at www.data-vocabulary.org/, including Event, Organization, Person, Product, Review, Review-aggregate, Breadcrumb, Offer, and AggregateOffer. By using a published vocabulary, you can be sure search engines and other applications will interpret your microdata consistently.

Listing 1.5 illustrates microdata in action using an event item that adheres to Google's Event microdata vocabulary at www.data-vocabulary.org/Event. This code creates a snippet of HTML code for an event, with defined microdata properties that will allow a search engine to unambiguously interpret the event information and use it to enhance search results, perhaps by showing the event date in a calendar or as a location on a map.

Listing 1.5   html5-microdata.html—Microdata in action

The itemprop attribute indicates the name of the microdata property that the content of the element should be assigned to. This attribute is the one you'll likely use the most when working with microdata.

The itemscope attribute tells the parser that this element and everything contained inside it describes the entity being referenced. The value of this attribute is Boolean and is usually omitted. The itemtype attribute defines the URL at which the vocabulary for the item being specified is found.

```
<div itemscope itemtype="http://data-vocabulary.org/Event">
    <a href="http://example.com/event/1" itemprop="url">
        <span itemprop="summary">John's 40th Birthday Party</span>
    </a>
    <span itemprop="description">To celebrate John turning 40,
    we're throwing a BBQ party in his honour this Friday evening
    at close of business. Please come and bring your friends and
    family!</span>

    Location:
    <span itemprop="location"
        itemscope
        itemtype=http://data-vocabulary.org/Address>
        <span itemprop="street-address">500 Market Way</span>
        <span itemprop="locality">Ballincollig</span>
        <span itemprop="region">Cork</span>
    </span>

    Date and Time:
    <time itemprop="startDate" datetime="2011-05-06T18:00+00:00">
        Fri, May 6th @ 6pm
    </time>
</div>
```

The HTML5 specification also defines a DOM API that you can use to dynamically retrieve and modify microdata items using JavaScript. Descriptions of the API are provided in table 1.3.

Table 1.3   The microdata DOM API

Method/property	Description
document.getItems([types])	Gets all elements that are top-level microdata items (elements with an itemscope attribute). You can use the types argument to filter by one or more itemtype attribute values.

Table 1.3 The microdata DOM API *(continued)*

Method/property	Description
`element.properties`	Gets all item properties (those elements with an `itemprop` attribute) for a given microdata item (`element`).
`element.itemValue [= value]`	Gets or sets the value of an item property.

Using microdata is an excellent way to improve how your application (or document) looks in search results. In the next section, you'll learn how you can use CSS3 to make your application visually stunning with the new styles and effects it has to offer.

1.2.2 CSS3

If you've been developing on the web for a long time, you may remember when styling HTML documents was facilitated by the use of elements like <font> and the clever use of <table> elements. Thankfully, the introduction of Cascading Style Sheets has meant that such approaches are no longer necessary.

As the web has evolved, developers have come up with innovative ways to present content, using effects like drop shadows, rounded corners, and gradients to improve their application's visual appeal. Even more impressive has been the use of transition and animation to provide better feedback to and interaction with the user. The main issue with all of these wonderful enhancements is that they've traditionally required a degree of trickery to implement using images and JavaScript (or at least required the use of a JavaScript library). CSS3 sets out to change that. Table 1.4 lists some of the new style features available in CSS3—all without JavaScript or the clever use of images.

Table 1.4 A partial list of the new features in CSS3

New selectors	New pseudo-classes	Rounded borders	Border images
Gradients	Box shadow	Box sizing	Background sizing
Text shadow	Word wrapping	Multiple columns	Web fonts
Multiple backgrounds	Alpha color channels	Media queries	Speech style
Transitions	Animations	3D transforms	2D transforms

As you work through the samples in this book, you'll learn to build applications primarily using HTML and JavaScript. We do use CSS3 throughout for styling, but we won't be covering it in the chapters themselves. You can download the CSS source for all the examples from the book's web page. If you're looking for detailed insight into CSS3, check out *Hello! HTML5 and CSS3* (Manning, 2012). Rob Crowther, the author of that book, is one of this book's coauthors.

1.2.3 JavaScript and the DOM

JavaScript and the Document Object Model (DOM) play a hugely important role in modern web applications. The ability to dynamically interact with elements on the page has enabled developers to provide rich functionality and interactivity previously found only in desktop applications. The advent of Asynchronous JavaScript and XML (AJAX) has removed the burden of page refreshes, allowing server-side actions to be updated inline, providing a much-improved user experience. JavaScript Object Notation (JSON) has become the de facto data interchange format for web applications, with most server-side languages and frameworks now supporting it natively. In addition, a range of powerful JavaScript frameworks and libraries has risen to provide an abstraction of JavaScript that allows developers to worry less about the cross-browser inconsistencies that plagued earlier web development, concentrating their efforts more on crafting highly functional applications.

> **WARNING** Each and every chapter in this book shows you to how to build powerful applications using HTML5 and JavaScript. But this isn't a book for JavaScript beginners. At the least, you should be familiar with JavaScript syntax and the basics like variable declarations, conditional statements, functions, closures, callbacks, and scopes as well as other concepts like AJAX, JSON, and interacting with the DOM. If you have experience using JavaScript libraries such as jQuery, you should be able to follow along. To learn more about JavaScript or if you're feeling rusty, check out *Ajax in Action* (Manning, 2005) by David Crane and Eric Pascarello with Darren James and *Secrets of the JavaScript Ninja* (Manning, 2012) by John Resig and Bear Bibeault.

In previous versions of the HTML (and XHTML) specification, the only coverage of JavaScript was a minor section on use of the `<script>` element and some of the attributes that could be added to HTML elements to provide event-handling functionality. In HTML5, JavaScript is treated as a first-class citizen, with each section of the specification detailing what DOM API methods and properties are available for any given element. In addition, HTML5 defines advanced APIs that allow you to develop applications that use audio and video, work offline, store data locally on the client, and do much more. We'll cover these APIs briefly later in this chapter and in greater detail throughout the book.

HTML5 vs. HTML Living Standard vs. HTML5 for web developers

The HTML5 specification has a long history. Without getting caught up in the details, the end result is that the specification has two versions, both with the same editor: Ian Hickson of Google. The HTML5 specification is published by the W3C, whereas the HTML Living Standard specification is published by WHATWG (Web Hypertext Application Technology Working Group). To make things even more confusing, WHATWG also published a document, "HTML5: A technical specification for web developers," which is more concise and easier to read.

(continued)

The specifications are similar in many respects, but you'll find considerable differences. For example, the HTML Living Standard specification includes several APIs that are published as completely separate specifications by the W3C, such as Microdata, Web Storage, and Web Workers. For the latest differences between the specifications, see "Is this HTML5?" in the HTML Living Standard specification at http://mng.bz/PraC.

In this chapter, we treat the APIs that exist in the HTML Living Standard as "part of HTML5 itself" and any APIs outside of that specification as separate. As you progress in the book, you'll see that we're much less concerned about the differences and treat any of the new specifications as "HTML5." For further discussion of the differences between the WHATWG and W3C versions as well as the differences in approach between the WHATWG and W3C themselves, see appendix A.

In the next section, we'll take a look at the DOM APIs currently included in the HTML5 specification itself.

1.3   The HTML5 DOM APIs

DOM APIs exist for nearly everything in HTML5. In fact, many have been around for a long time but have never been defined in the HTML specification itself. These include features that enable you to get a DOM element by its ID attribute and that allow you to manipulate form element values. All of this is included in HTML5 and the specification also defines new DOM APIs for developing advanced applications, many of which aren't at all associated with HTML elements.

This section provides an overview of the new DOM APIs in HTML5:
- 2D Canvas
- Audio and Video
- Drag and Drop
- Cross-document Messaging
- Server-sent Events
- WebSockets
- Document Editing
- Web Storage
- Offline Web Applications

We cover all of these topics in great detail throughout the book, with full working examples that often integrate multiple APIs at once. In this chapter, you'll get a glimpse of what's to come, starting with the new <canvas> element and its associated API.

1.3.1 Canvas

HTML5 provides numerous elements that allow you to present information on a web page. You can style these in many different ways, and you can use JavaScript to animate them and apply dynamic effects. If you're comfortable with complex JavaScript code (and expect your users to be running high-performance browsers), you can do amazing things with HTML and JavaScript.

The problem is, designers and developers have many things they may want to implement that HTML doesn't cater to. What if you want to insert a circle, square, or other shape? What if you want to display an image and dynamically alter it based on user selections, on the fly? You could use static images or a server-side solution, but these aren't optimal. The only viable solution had been to use a third-party plug-in such as Adobe Flash.

HTML5 introduces the <canvas> element and a series of related drawing APIs that will allow you to do amazing things, without requiring the user to install a plug-in. The <canvas> element's name describes this new feature well: it's a canvas for your web pages. Figure 1.7 depicts a game, "Canvas Break," which we created entirely in HTML5 and JavaScript, with the game's visuals output on a <canvas> element. Neat, huh? You'll learn how to use the Canvas API as you build this game yourself in chapter 6.

The Canvas API defines a 2D context, which provides a series of methods for drawing on the canvas. These include methods to create shapes, define paths, use color and gradients, provide text, and much more. The API also provides developers with a way to export the current content of the canvas as a PNG or JPG format image using data URLs or Blob objects.

1.3.2 Audio and video

The majority of internet bandwidth in recent years has been driven by the delivery of multimedia content: video and audio. Today, the majority of web video is deployed in Flash video (FLV) format, an Adobe Flash container for various types of video codec. If users have a Flash plug-in installed, they can view the video. Some developers have raised questions about the security and performance of Flash as a platform for video

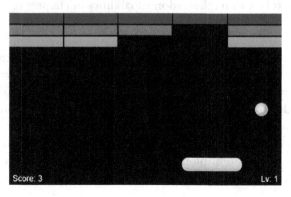

Figure 1.7 The <canvas> element allows developers to present information in more creative ways. You'll learn how to build this game in chapter 6.

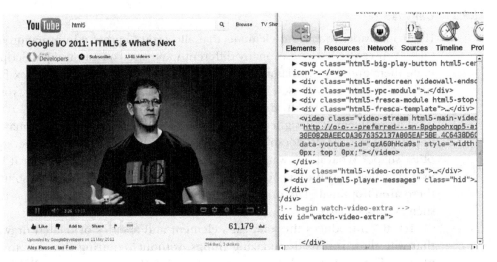

Figure 1.8   YouTube HTML5 video in action. As you can see from the code in the inspector, the YouTube video in this screenshot doesn't use the Adobe Flash plug-in but is fully implemented using the HTML5 `<video>` element and related APIs.

delivery and are looking for alternative solutions. In addition, the lack of support for Flash on mobile devices has meant that if you want your multimedia content to be available on devices such as the iPad, you're out of luck.

HTML5 provides a solution for this with the new `<video>` and `<audio>` elements, which allow supported multimedia files to be played back natively by the browser, with no third-party plug-ins required. An example is shown in figure 1.8.

The `<video>` and `<audio>` elements both support the `<track>` element, which you can use to deliver accompanying text content such as subtitles. You can use the `<source>` element to provide a variety of file formats, ensuring that visitors can consume the content, regardless of what OS or browser they're using.

HTML5 also defines an API with a series of methods for controlling the playback of a video or audio file. These include methods for playing, pausing, fast-forwarding, rewinding, adjusting the volume, and more. You'll learn about these APIs in detail as you build a working video jukebox with telestration capabilities in chapter 8.

1.3.3   Drag and drop

Lack of drag-and-drop interactivity had been an issue that has plagued web application developers for a long time. This type of functionality has been prevalent in desktop applications for as long as graphical UIs have been around. As a result, users have come to expect to be able to drag objects around applications and are sometimes shocked to learn that their favorite web applications can't do it.

Attempts at implementing drag and drop in the browser began in the late 1990s, with Netscape 4.0 providing a basic implementation and Microsoft following up with a more complete offering in IE 5.0. At the time, it was seen as a nonstandard,

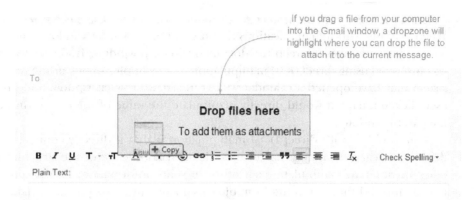

If you drag a file from your computer into the Gmail window, a dropzone will highlight where you can drop the file to attach it to the current message.

Figure 1.9 Gmail allows you to drag files into the browser window and drop them into a designated area to add them as attachments to your messages.

browser-specific extension to IE, but over time other browser vendors adopted the same API, leading to its eventual inclusion in HTML5.

The great news is that HTML5 drag and drop is supported on all modern browsers, including IE from version 5.0 up. The bad news is that the original Microsoft implementation used is, quite frankly, terrible. Ian Hickson, the editor of the HTML5 specification, once tweeted, "The drag-and-drop API is horrible, but it has one thing going for it: IE6 implements it, as do Safari and Firefox."

To use drag and drop in HTML5, you can use the draggable attribute on an element to explicitly define that element as draggable. (Many elements, such as images, are draggable by default.) You can then use a series of events to listen for changes as the user drags the element into and out of other elements and indeed when the user drops the element. The API allows you to set the data you want to associate with the drag operation and then to read this back when dropped.

A new feature of HTML5 drag and drop is the ability to drag files from your computer and drop them into a web application. An example of this functionality can be seen in Gmail, as shown in figure 1.9.

You'll learn how to use drag and drop to import and export files from an application in chapter 3.

1.3.4 *Cross-document messaging, server-sent events, and WebSockets*

Web applications work on a request-response model, where the client issues a request to the server, and the server in turn sends a response to the client. After this, if the client requires further information from the server, the client needs to initiate another request. This makes it difficult to send changes from the server to the client, without frequently sending requests to check for these changes. In this section, you'll learn about some of the new messaging features in HTML5 that allow the server to communicate with the client. Before that, let's look at how to use messaging to send updates between documents.

ENABLING COMMUNICATION BETWEEN CLIENTS WITH CROSS-DOCUMENT AND CHANNEL MESSAGING

When working with web applications that use multiple browser windows, you'll often want to pass messages between the documents in each window. Traditionally, this was accomplished using direct DOM manipulation. For example, an old airline reservation system may have opened a calendar widget in a new browser window, and when the user clicked a date, it would directly manipulate the value of the date form field on the parent window.

One problem with direct DOM manipulation is that it directly connects the two documents; each document has to have detailed knowledge of the structure of the other in order to manipulate each other to share information. HTML5 provides a much-improved solution in the form of cross-document messaging and channel messaging, illustrated in figure 1.10.

Cross-document messaging enables documents to communicate with each other via messages—one document posts a message, and the other document has an event handler registered to listen for any messages posted by the other document.

Another issue with direct DOM manipulation surfaces when you consider the security of including remote script files in your application—a common use case for implementing the likes of Google Analytics and Facebook "Like" buttons in your applications. These scripts have complete access to your entire DOM—it's not possible to give them only partial access when they're loaded this way. Cross-document messaging works cross-domain, enabling messages to be sent between separate applications without exposing each application's DOM.

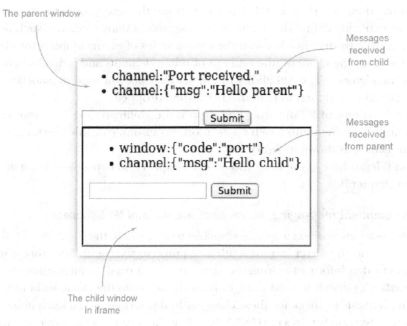

Figure 1.10   A simple application demonstrating channel messaging. You'll build this in appendix J, one of the companion appendices to chapter 4.

ENABLING ONE-WAY COMMUNICATIONS FROM SERVER TO CLIENT WITH SERVER-SENT EVENTS

Cross-document messaging is a great way to communicate between two clients—but what if you want to allow your web server to send messages that can be read by the browser? Server-sent events are designed to do that. Using the EventSource interface, your application can subscribe to a server-side event stream, which will only receive messages when the server sends an update. This is a considerable improvement over approaches like AJAX long polling, which can be cumbersome to implement. This works well for a chat application, where you can post new chat messages using AJAX and receive any chat messages from other users over the event stream. Figure 1.11 is a screenshot of such an application, which you'll build later on.

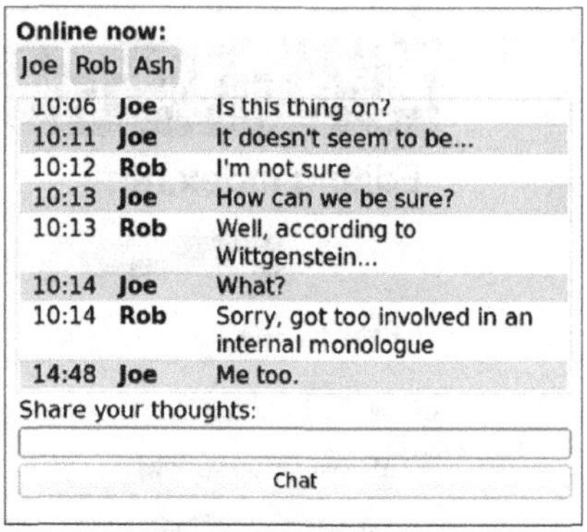

Online now:		
Joe Rob Ash		
10:06	**Joe**	Is this thing on?
10:11	**Joe**	It doesn't seem to be...
10:12	**Rob**	I'm not sure
10:13	**Joe**	How can we be sure?
10:13	**Rob**	Well, according to Wittgenstein...
10:14	**Joe**	What?
10:14	**Rob**	Sorry, got too involved in an internal monologue
14:48	**Joe**	Me too.

Share your thoughts:

Chat

Figure 1.11   A chat application implemented using server-sent events

ENABLING TWO-WAY COMMUNICATIONS BETWEEN SERVER AND CLIENT WITH WEBSOCKETS

The obvious drawback with server-sent events is that they only facilitate one-way communication—messages can only be sent from the server to the client, not vice versa. If you need two-way communication, HTML5 provides WebSockets—bare-bones networking between clients and servers, without the overhead associated with HTTP. WebSockets are great for passing small amounts of data quickly, which is critical in applications like online multiplayer games and time-sensitive financial systems.

In chapter 4, you'll learn how to use all three of these new messaging technologies as you build a simple chat application and a multiuser planning board, using server-sent events and WebSockets via Node.js, and then allow them to communicate with each other through cross-document messaging.

1.3.5   Document editing

Earlier in this chapter, we talked about the new forms features in HTML5. Web forms are a great means of capturing simple plain-text user input, but they don't allow the user to edit HTML content. Sure, you could load HTML source code in a <textarea> element and allow the user to edit that, but wouldn't it be great if you could allow the user to edit the content using a series of rich-text editing controls?

HTML5 defines two new attributes that allow you to enable rich-text editing in your HTML documents. The first, contenteditable, can be set on any HTML element in your page to make that element editable. The second, designMode, can be set on the HTML document itself to make the entire document editable.

These attributes are supported by all modern browsers and were first introduced by Microsoft in IE 5.5.

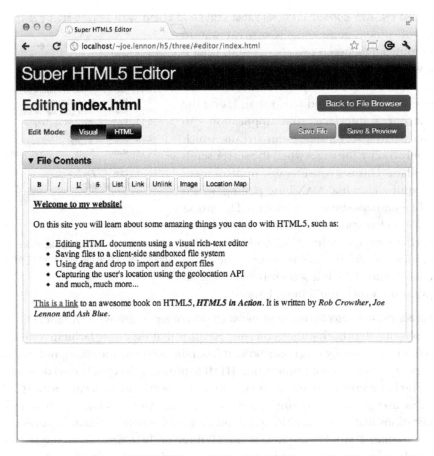

Figure 1.12   The Super HTML5 Editor application that you'll learn to build in chapter 3 uses the `designMode` attribute and the Editing DOM API to allow users to edit HTML markup using a set of rich-text editing controls. The toolbar in this screenshot allows you to use Bold, Italic, Underline, Strikethrough, List, Link, and Image formatting commands on the contents of the area below the toolbar.

When an element or document is editable, you can manipulate its content using the API method `document.execCommand`, part of the Editing DOM API in HTML5. This method accepts a wide selection of commands that will be applied to the current selection or block, such as Bold, Italic, CreateLink, and many others. An example of the type of editor you can create with this functionality is shown in figure 1.12; even better, you'll learn how to use these new features as you build that rich-text editor in chapter 3.

1.3.6   Web storage

For many years, web applications have used cookies to store small chunks of data in the client that persist for the session or between multiple sessions. This is the technology underlying web authentication systems—they store on the client a cookie that holds some form of identifier used to tell the application who's logged in. Cookies present a number of issues, making them less useful for storing all but the smallest chunks of data.

The first issue is that most browsers limit the size of cookies to 4 kilobytes, and the number of cookies stored per domain to 20. After reaching these limits, the browser will start discarding older cookies to make way for the newer ones, which means there's no guarantee it'll keep them. Another issue is that when an application uses cookies, those cookies are sent in every HTTP request made for the session, adding overhead to each and every transaction. This might not be an issue if you're using one or two cookies, but what if you use several? And consider that the cookies will be sent along with every HTTP request—slowing down every page load and AJAX request your application makes.

The Web Storage DOM API provides a JavaScript alternative to cookies for web applications. It defines two interfaces:

- `sessionStorage`—Client-side data storage that persists for the length of the current session only
- `localStorage`—Client-side data storage that persists for multiple sessions

These APIs expose methods that allow developers to store simple key/value pair data in a client-side store. The data items stored using these interfaces are accessible only by pages in the same domain. In chapter 5 you'll build the application shown in figure 1.13, which stores user settings and preferences in local storage.

Although the Web Storage API can store megabytes of data (5 megabytes is the limit imposed by most browsers), it's not ideal for storing complex data structures that would typically be stored in a database. Later in this chapter, you'll learn about IndexedDB, which defines a full indexed database API for storing data locally on the client.

Figure 1.13 In chapter 5, you'll learn how to use the `localStorage` interface to persist user settings in a mobile task-management application.

1.3.7 Offline web applications

These days, it seems we're permanently online—our internet connections are always on, our mobile devices have data plans that work over cellular data networks, and now we can even get connected as we travel by air. That said, we may still have times when we need to make do with working offline. Maybe your network connection is down, or you're abroad and don't want to pay exorbitant data roaming fees. Or you're using one of the few devices that doesn't have a wireless data connection.

Solutions have long existed for saving HTML documents for offline use. As useful as these are for reading static content like news articles, they're useless when it comes to web applications. HTML5 goes a step beyond saving documents, by providing developers the ability to define a cache manifest file that defines how their applications' files should be cached for offline use.

The cache manifest file can also define those files that shouldn't be cached for offline use. In this case, a fallback can be provided that will be loaded by the browser when the user is offline. This enables you to provide separate files for online and offline use.

An example use case might be where your application saves data to a database on a server. When online, the application may perform AJAX requests to retrieve and update data on this database. In the background, the application may be storing data locally in an IndexedDB database, which we'll talk more about in an upcoming section. Now, when the user is offline, the application could load a JavaScript file specifically designed for use in offline mode. Instead of firing AJAX requests to the server, it would retrieve and modify the data in the local IndexedDB database. The next time the user connects to the network, the application can then submit the data from the local database to the server-side database.

You'll learn how to develop the offline-capable web application shown in figure 1.14 in chapter 5.

1.4   Additional APIs and specifications

As you learned earlier, the HTML5 family doesn't stop at the HTML5 specification itself. A host of other technologies and specifications exist that define new functionality,

Figure 1.14   A screenshot of the mobile application with offline capabilities that you'll create in chapter 5

which modern browser vendors are steadily including in their latest offerings, such as the Geolocation API; the IndexedDB API; the File Reader, File Writer, and File System APIs; and SVG and WebGL.

In this section, you'll learn

- The Geolocation API and how you can use it to determine a user's geographic location
- The IndexedDB API and how it allows you to store an entire database on the client side
- File-oriented specifications and how you can use them to work with and store files locally on the user's filesystem
- SVG and WebGL and how they're enabling developers to produce impressive high-quality vector graphics and 3D animations on the web

---

We'll talk about each ancillary yet important specification, starting with Geolocation.

1.4.1 Geolocation API

As mobile device usage has surged in recent years, so has the use of location-aware applications. The Global Positioning System (GPS) sensors found on modern smartphones enable applications to locate users to a high degree of accuracy. If GPS isn't available (if the device doesn't have a sensor, or if the user is out of satellite line of sight), devices can fall back to other means of tracking location, using information such as your cellular network, Wi-Fi network, or IP address.

The Geolocation API defines methods that allow web applications to find a user's location. When these methods are called, the browser will notify the user that the application is requesting access to their location. The user can then choose to accept or reject this request, ensuring that applications don't track user location without their express prior permission. If the user accepts the request, the API then provides the application with a series of data about the user's location including coordinates (latitude and longitude), altitude, heading, and speed, as well as the level of accuracy of the result.

You'll learn how to use geolocation in chapter 3, where you'll use it to get the user's current location and include a map of that location in an HTML document (figure 1.15).

1.4.2 Indexed database (IndexedDB API)

The IndexedDB API provides developers with a means of storing complex data structures in a full client-side database. The main advantage of the IndexedDB API over the Web Storage API is that in Web Storage the only index is the key of the key/value pair, whereas in IndexedDB the values are fully indexable too, making it a more viable solution for any application where you need to search or filter data. The trade-off is that the API for IndexedDB is much more complex, and it can be difficult to get to grips with initially.

Figure 1.15   Adding maps showing your current location in the chapter 3 application

IndexedDB is a relative newcomer to the HTML5 specification family. There had been a different proposed solution, Web SQL (Structured Query Language), a specification that defined a relational client-side database that used SQL statements for query and data manipulation. In the end, it was dropped because all the browsers that had adopted it were using the same implementation (an SQLite database) so it could never meet the WHATWG's and W3C's standardization criteria of having "two independent, interoperable implementations of each feature." When it was dropped, support had already been included in several browsers, including mobile browsers like Mobile Safari and Android. Browser support for IndexedDB has been slow-moving, and as a result, most applications that use IndexedDB also use Web SQL as a fallback.

In chapter 5, you'll learn how to use IndexedDB (with a Web SQL fallback) to store task data in a mobile task-management application, as illustrated in figure 1.16.

1.4.3   *File, File Reader, File Writer, and File System APIs*

Working with files in web applications has traditionally been a pain. The only native means of allowing users to select files from their computers was to use the file input type, which is well known for being cumbersome, particularly when it comes to styling the UI of the widget. When the user selected the file, the application would have to upload the entire file to the server in order to do anything with it. Although Flash- and Java-based offerings are available that provide improved functionality, these aren't ideal given that they require a third-party plug-in.

The HTML5 family includes a number of related file-based specifications that promise to make working with files in web applications much easier. The File API allows developers to get a reference to a file object in JavaScript, reading properties such as its name, size, and MIME type. You can use the File Reader API to read a file object, either in its entirety or partially in chunks. Similarly, you can use the File Writer API to output data to a file. The File System API allows developers to manipulate file objects in a sandboxed local filesystem on the client. This enables you to perform much of the file interaction on the client, significantly saving the load on the server. No longer do you have to upload the entire file to the server, only to discover it's of the wrong MIME type, and then have to tell the user that the file wasn't of the correct type. You can imagine how annoying this would be to users after they've uploaded a large file.

Figure 1.16 The chapter 5 application will use IndexedDB to store a list of tasks and allow fast sorting and searching.

You'll use all of these APIs to provide a full local filesystem, and we'll cover where HTML files will be stored in chapter 3. A screenshot of how you can use some of this functionality is illustrated in figure 1.17.

1.4.4 *Scalable Vector Graphics*

Scalable Vector Graphics (SVG) is an XML language that allows you to create impressive vector graphics using markup that can be styled using CSS and interacted with via the DOM using JavaScript. One of the primary issues with bitmap graphics is that as you scale their dimensions up, the quality of the graphic degrades and produces a "pixelated" result. Vector graphics are constructed using math equations rather than pixels, and as a result they can scale up to look impressive even at large sizes.

In chapter 7, you'll learn how to use SVG as you build the app SVG Aliens (figure 1.18), an exercise that illustrates how to create shapes and complex objects using SVG, implement collision detection, and understand the pros and cons of using SVG rather than the <canvas> element.

Figure 1.17　The Super HTML5 Editor you'll build in chapter 3 will allow you to perform file operations such as creating a new blank file and importing an existing file either by selecting it or dragging it into the application. It'll store these files in a sandboxed local filesystem, from which you can view, edit, and delete the files or export them to your computer by dragging them out of the application.

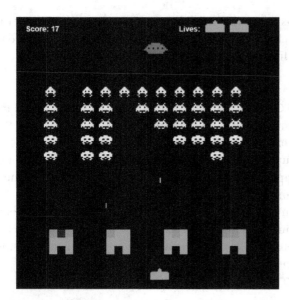

Figure 1.18　The SVG Aliens game in action. You'll learn to build this game in its entirety later in this book.

Figure 1.19 The 3D Geometry Destroyer game in all its glory. Building this game is covered in chapter 9.

1.4.5 *Web Graphics Library*

Last but not least is the Web Graphics Library (WebGL), a JavaScript API for creating 3D graphics using the <canvas> element. WebGL is based on the Open Graphics Library for Embedded Systems (OpenGL ES) standard, which was designed for implementing 3D on embedded devices including mobile phones. It provides developers with an API that allows them to control graphics hardware at a low level using shader, buffer, and drawing methods.

In chapter 9, you'll learn not only about the WebGL API but also about 3D graphics programming in general, including how to create shaders, work with data using buffers, assemble 3D data onto the screen using matrix manipulation, and more. You'll do these tasks through the lens of our sample application, which has you building an entire 3D game, Geometry Destroyer, a screenshot of which you can see in figure 1.19.

1.5 *Summary*

HTML5 is the most important revision of HTML since its inception in 1991. Although HTML began as a relatively straightforward markup language, it has since become a platform for complex web page design and web application development, particularly when coupled with its close relations CSS and JavaScript. HTML5 is the first version of the language to acknowledge this significance and include a number of application-oriented JavaScript APIs within the specification.

Over the course of the next eight chapters, you'll learn how to build eight separate applications, everything from mobile applications that work offline to 3D games. In the next chapter, you move away from introductory concepts and delve deep into the vast improvements in web forms that HTML5 has to offer, including the new input types that allow guided entry of a much wider variety of data types, new attributes such as `autofocus` and `placeholder`, and the out-of-the-box features that simplify client-side validation.

Part 2

Browser-based apps

For a very long time developers were processing everything—form validation, file management, storage, messaging, and other vital application functionality—on the server. Server-side processing was a great idea for security reasons, lack of user processing power, and many other issues. There were workarounds through technologies such as Flash and Java, but the mobile market explosion revealed unanticipated limitations that HTML5 is aiming to fix.

Thanks to major advances in JavaScript processing power and new W3C standards, you can now perform server-side tasks through a user's browser (aka client-side). Performing complex tasks through browsers saves tons of money on server costs, allows startups to easily create complex apps, and creates seemingly instant application responses during heavy load times. It also opens up a completely different thought process on application development and deployment to mobile and desktop. And they can both be done at the same time if you play your cards right.

Many popular web applications use HTML5's application features. Google Drive, for example, uses a new storage technology known as the Indexed Database API. You've probably also used HTML5's WebSockets, forms, and many other features that we'll be covering throughout this section. By the time you've completed part 2 (chapters 2–5), you'll know enough to put together a small application with minimal server usage.

Chapter 2 at a glance

Topic	Description, methods, and so on	Page
New input types[1]	HTML5 `<input>` element types	
	• `email`	42
	• `tel`	42
	• `number`	46
	• `month`	49
New input attributes[1]	HTML5 attributes on `<input>` elements	
	• `required`	42
	• `pattern`	49
	• `autofocus`	43
	• `placeholder`	42
	• `min` and `max`	46
`data-*` attributes	Storing key/value data in attributes on elements	46
`valueAsNumber` property	Reading input values in numeric format	54
`<output>` element	Displaying the output of calculations	47
Preventing validation	Providing means of bypassing client-side validation	
	• `formnovalidate` attribute	51
	• `formaction` attribute	51
Constraint Validation API	Client-side API for validation	
	• `setCustomValidity` method	59
	• `validationMessage` property	59
	• `invalid` event	60
CSS3 pseudo-classes	Styling invalid elements with CSS3	61
Backward compatibility	Feature detection and unsupported browsers	
	• Modernizr.js	63
	• Polyfills	64
	• Validation	65

[1] Only the input types and attributes used or discussed in this chapter are listed here. For comprehensive coverage, visit mng.bz/wj56.

Look for this icon ⟶ Core API throughout the chapter to quickly locate the topics outlined in this table.

Form creation: input widgets, data binding, and data validation

This chapter covers

- New HTML5 input types and attributes
- `data-*` attributes, `valueAsNumber` property, and the `<output>` element
- Constraint Validation API
- Ways to bypass validation
- CSS3 pseudo-classes
- HTML5 feature detection with Modernizr and backward compatibility with polyfill

As the web has matured, the need for a much richer set of form field types and widgets has emerged. Today's users expect a consistent standard between web applications, particularly when it comes to data validation. HTML5 meets this requirement with 13 new form input types, ranging from number spinners and sliders to date- and color-pickers.

The standard also defines new attributes you can apply to `<input>` elements to enhance the functionality of your forms, including presentational attributes like `placeholder` and `autofocus`, as well as validation attributes such as `required` and `pattern`. You can even use a set of new CSS3 pseudo-classes to style valid or invalid form elements with zero JavaScript. And if you have advanced validation requirements you can't provide natively, the new Constraint Validation API offers a standardized

JavaScript API that can test for the validity of form fields, along with a new event you can use to detect an invalid data entry.

In this chapter, you'll implement all of these new features by building an order form for computer products. The form will use HTML5 validation to "sanitize" the input on the client side before it's submitted.

> **Why build this chapter's order form?**
> While working through this chapter's sample application, you'll learn to use:
> - New *input types* to provide more widgets with less coding
> - New *input attributes* to provide validation with less coding
> - *data-* attributes* to bind data to HTML elements
> - *Constraint Validation API* features to create custom validation tests

We'll get started by showing you a preview of the form and helping you get your prerequisites in order.

2.1 Previewing the form and gathering prerequisites

The order form you'll build in this chapter, shown in figure 2.1, allows users to enter personal data, login details, and order and payment information.

The form makes use of several new HTML5 features:

- *Form* `<input>` *element types* (`email`, `tel`, `number`, and `month`) and *attributes* (`required`, `pattern`, `autofocus`, `placeholder`, and `max` and `min`) to provide users with better widgets and data validation when appropriate.
- The `data-*` *attributes* to hold the price of each product, the `valueAsNumber` *property* to read input values in numeric format, and the `<output>` *element* to present subtotals and grand totals.
- The `formnovalidate` and `formaction` *attributes* to bypass data validation and save an incomplete form.
- The *Constraint Validation API* to perform custom validation and detect when the user attempts to submit the form with elements that are invalid, and *CSS3 pseudo-class selectors* to style invalid elements.
- The *Modernizr.js JavaScript library* and *polyfills* to serve users whose browsers don't support various HTML5 features. (Although we admit that Modernizr and polyfills aren't strictly HTML5 features, we recommend that you use them if you're serious about developing HTML5 applications.)

When you've finished, the order form will be functional in the latest versions of all the major browsers, although you may find varying levels of support for some features such as widgets for new input types and inline error messages for the Constraint Validation API. But browser hiccups will become less and less an issue as support for the new features increases.

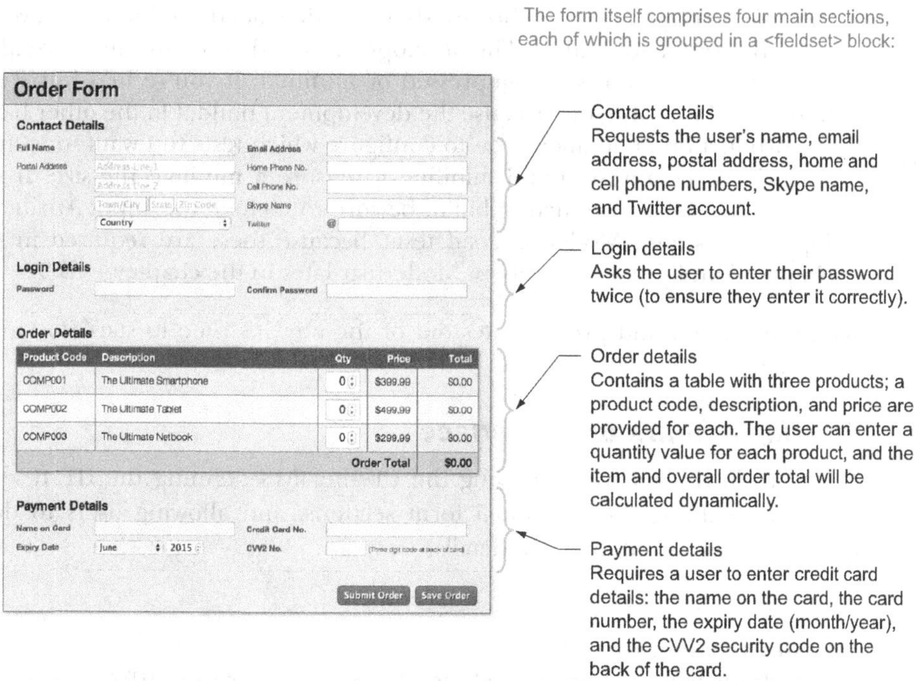

The form itself comprises four main sections, each of which is grouped in a <fieldset> block:

Contact details
Requests the user's name, email address, postal address, home and cell phone numbers, Skype name, and Twitter account.

Login details
Asks the user to enter their password twice (to ensure they enter it correctly).

Order details
Contains a table with three products; a product code, description, and price are provided for each. The user can enter a quantity value for each product, and the item and overall order total will be calculated dynamically.

Payment details
Requires a user to enter credit card details: the name on the card, the card number, the expiry date (month/year), and the CVV2 security code on the back of the card.

Figure 2.1 The order form running in Google Chrome. The user is given two options when submitting the form: Submit Order or Save Order. The Submit Order button performs validation and processes a user's order, whereas the Save Order button bypasses the validation and saves the details, so users can come back later and finish filling out their order.

NOTE This chapter covers only the client-side portion of the order form. When the form is submitted, it makes a request to a URL. To perform further processing, you'll need to implement the form on the server side using your choice of server-side language or framework (such as PHP or Ruby on Rails). The server-side aspect is outside the scope of this book.

2.1.1 Gathering the application prerequisites

You'll work with five files in this chapter:

- An HTML document
- A JavaScript source file
- A CSS stylesheet
- The Modernizr library
- The month-picker polyfill script

The stylesheet and polyfill are part of the chapter's source code archive, but you'll need to download the Modernizr library from its website at http://modernizr.com/. Rename the .js file to modernizr.js and place it, along with both the CSS file and monthpicker.js, in the application's directory.

TIP   Modernizr offers two choices when you download the library—development or production builds. The development build contains the entire Modernizr test suite and isn't compressed or minified. If you're in a hurry and don't mind the large file size, use the development build. On the other hand, the production build allows you to configure which tests you want to include and will be compressed and minified to ensure a minimal file size. If you choose to use the production build, be sure to include the Input Attributes, Input Types, and Modernizr.load tests, because these are required in this chapter. You'll learn more about Modernizr later in the chapter.

With the preview and prerequisites out of the way, it's time to start working on the form's UI.

2.2   Building a form's user interface

The work in this section—building the UI—involves defining the HTML document structure, building the individual form sections, and allowing users to determine whether to save or submit form details.

> **In this section, you'll learn**
> - How to provide users with widgets and data validation using HTML5 form `<input>` element types and attributes
> - How to store the price of each product with `data-*` attributes
> - How to present subtotals and grand totals using the `<output>` element
> - How to bypass form validation and save an incomplete form using the form attribute properties, `formnovalidate` and `formaction`

We'll walk you through the UI work in seven steps:

- Step 1: Create index.html and load external files.
- Step 2: Create the Contact Details form section.
- Step 3: Build the Login Details form section.
- Step 4: Build the Order Details form section.
- Step 5: Build the Payment Details form section.
- Step 6: Bypass form validation and save form data.
- Step 7: Change the form action in older browsers.

First up, the HTML document.

2.2.1   Defining a form's basic HTML document structure

Before you begin, we recommend that you create a new directory on your system. Ideally, it would be a location on a web server, but that's not a requirement for the example.

STEP 1: CREATE INDEX.HTML AND LOAD EXTERNAL FILES

Create a new file named index.html and place it in the new directory. Then, add the contents of the following listing to that file. The code loads external dependencies (CSS and JavaScript files) and defines the <form> element with the heading at the top and the buttons at the bottom.

Listing 2.1   index.html—HTML document structure

```
<!DOCTYPE html>
<html lang="en">
<head>
    <meta charset="utf-8">
    <title>Order Form</title>
    <link rel="stylesheet" href="style.css">
    <script src="modernizr.js"></script>
    <script src="app.js"></script>
</head>
<body>
    <form name="order" method="post" action="/submit">
        <h1>Order Form</h1>

        <div class="buttons">
            <input type="submit" value="Submit Order">
            <input type="submit" id="saveOrder" value="Save Order">
        </div>
    </form>
</body>
</html>
```

Load the Modernizr library. You may wonder why we don't include the monthpicker.js file—later we'll use the Modernizr.load method to dynamically load that file, but only if it's needed by the user's web browser.

The order form is split into four sections, which we'll work on sequentially: Contact Details, Login Details, and Payment Details in this section, and Order Details in the section that follows.

2.2.2   Using the form input types email and tel and the input attributes autofocus, required, and placeholder

Before you actually start building the order form, we'd like to give you more details about the new input types and attributes and show you how to use these types and attributes to build your forms in less time. As we proceed, we'll improve the example form with the email and tel (for telephone) input types and also make use of the autofocus, required, and placeholder attributes.

`email` **input type**	10.0	4.0	10.0	10.6	5.0*
`tel` **input type**	10.0	4.0	10.0	10.6	5.0

* Indicates partial support

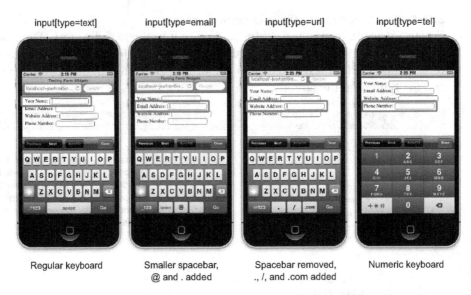

input[type=text]   input[type=email]   input[type=url]   input[type=tel]

Regular keyboard   Smaller spacebar,   Spacebar removed,   Numeric keyboard
                    @ and . added   ., /, and .com added

Figure 2.2   Different virtual keyboards are displayed on an iPhone for different input types—from left to right: `text`, `email`, `url`, **and** `tel`. **Notice how symbols are added and removed for the** `email` **and** `url` **input types. An entirely different keyboard is displayed for the** `number` **input type.**

Core API

Both the `email` and `tel` input types look identical to the standard text input element. But if the user is browsing on a mobile device that supports these input types, it can display different virtual keyboard layouts depending on what type of data the user is entering. See figure 2.2 for an example of this in action.

In the case of the `email` input type, the browser will also check that the user inputs a valid email address. If not, it will raise an error when the user submits the form. The error style is defined by the browser, which means it will look somewhat different depending on the user's browser. Figure 2.3 illustrates this.

Core API

Now, let's look at three additional attributes: `autofocus`, `required`, and `placeholder`.

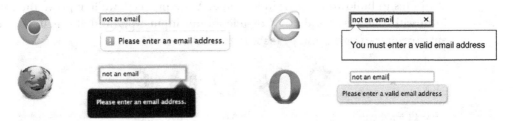

Figure 2.3   Each web browser vendor implements a different style when presenting input validation errors to the user. As more websites begin to use HTML5 form validation, users will become more familiar with the standard style of error message displayed by their browser of choice.

THE AUTOFOCUS, REQUIRED, AND PLACEHOLDER ATTRIBUTES

autofocus attribute	6.0	4.0	10.0	11.0	5.0
required attribute	10.0	4.0	10.0	10.0	5.0*
placeholder attribute	4.0	4.0	10.0	11.6	5.0

* Indicates partial support

The autofocus attribute is self-explanatory; it allows you to define which input element should receive focus when the page loads. The required attribute is also straightforward—it allows you to define that a field must contain input from the user in order to be valid. You'll learn much more about HTML5 form validation later in the chapter. The placeholder attribute allows you to define a piece of text that will appear in a field when it's empty and inactive. As soon as the user types in the field, the placeholder text will be cleared and replaced with the user's input. This is illustrated in figure 2.4.

Placeholder text: (What are you looking for?)   **After user input:**   [HTML5 books| ⊘]

Figure 2.4   Demonstration of the placeholder attribute. This example displays a search input field, with the placeholder text "What are you looking for?" When the user enters a value, the placeholder text is replaced with that value.

STEP 2: CREATE THE CONTACT DETAILS FORM SECTION

Let's integrate those new features into the Contact Details section of the form, the markup for which is shown in the next listing. You should add this code to the index.html file, immediately after the line `<h1>Order Form</h1>` from the previous listing.

Listing 2.2   index.html—The Contact Details form section

```
<fieldset>
    <legend>Contact Details</legend>
    <ul>
        <li>
            <label class="required">
                <div>Full Name</div>
                <input name="name" required autofocus>
            </label>
        </li>
        <li>
            <label class="required">
                <div>Email Address</div>
                <input type="email" name="email" required>
            </label>
        </li>
        <li>
```

The name field is the first in the form, so it makes sense to autofocus it. It's also a required field.

The email field uses the new email input type. It's also a required field.

```
                        <label>
                            <div>Postal Address</div>
                            <input name="address1" placeholder="Address Line 1">
                        </label>
                        <div> </div>
                        <input name="address2" placeholder="Address Line 2">
                        <div> </div>
                        <input name="city" class="city" placeholder="Town/City">
                        <input name="state" class="state" placeholder="State">
                        <input name="zip" class="zip" placeholder="Zip Code">
                        <div> </div>
                        <select name="country">
                            <option value="0">Country</option>
                            <option value="US">United States</option>
                            <option value="CA">Canada</option>
                        </select>
                    </li>
                    <li>
                        <label>
                            <div>Home Phone No.</div>
                            <input type="tel" name="homephone">
                        </label>
                    </li>
                    <li>
                        <label>
                            <div>Cell Phone No.</div>
                            <input type="tel" name="cellphone">
                        </label>
                    </li>
                    <li>
                        <label>
                            <div>Skype Name</div>
                            <input name="skype">
                        </label>
                    </li>
                    <li>
                        <label>
                            <div>Twitter</div>
                            <span class="twitter_prefix">@</span>
                            <input name="twitter" class="twitter">
                        </label>
                    </li>
                </ul>
            </fieldset>
```

Each of the lines in the address field uses the placeholder attribute to indicate what type of information is relevant for each of the fields.

The homephone and cellphone fields both use the tel input type. Although this will make no apparent difference on a regular browser, visitors using mobile browsers will benefit from a virtual keyboard that's designed specifically for entering telephone numbers.

2.2.3   *Using the form input attribute required*

The Login Details form section is the most unremarkable part of the form. It asks the user to enter an account password and to enter it a second time to confirm. The markup doesn't introduce any new HTML5 features, but later in this chapter you'll learn how to use the Constraints Validation API to provide password confirmation.

STEP 3: BUILD THE LOGIN DETAILS FORM SECTION

At this point, you need only to add the code from the following listing to index.html, after the end of the previous listing; then we'll move on to a more interesting section.

Listing 2.3   index.html—The Login Details form section

```
<fieldset>
    <legend>Login Details</legend>
    <ul>
        <li>
            <label class="required">
                <div>Password</div>
                <input type="password" name="password" required>
            </label>
        </li>
        <li>
            <label class="required">
                <div>Confirm Password</div>
                <input type="password" name="confirm_password" required>
            </label>
        </li>
    </ul>
</fieldset>
```

Both the password and confirm_password fields are required fields.

2.2.4   *Building a calculator-style form using the input type number, the input attributes min/max and data-*, and the element <output>*

If you look at figure 2.5, you'd be forgiven for thinking there's not much HTML5 form functionality in the Order Details section.

However, several HTML5 features are at work in the Order Details section of the form:

- The number input type for the quantity input fields
- The min and max attributes for validating the quantity inputs
- The data-* attributes for storing price data
- The <output> element for displaying totals

The fields for entering quantity values are <input> elements with the type "number."

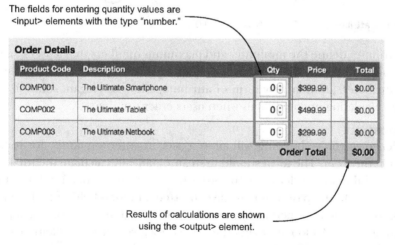

Results of calculations are shown using the <output> element.

Figure 2.5   There's more going on here than meets the eye. This simple-looking form uses several HTML5 features: the number input type, min and max attributes, data-* attributes, and the <output> element.

THE NUMBER INPUT TYPE

number **input type**	10.0	N/A	10.0*	11.0**	5.2

* Indicates partial support; although IE10 does support validation of the number
input type, it doesn't display a spinbox widget for the field.
** Opera 11 correctly displays a spinbox widget for picking a number but doesn't
enforce numeric validation on the field.

Core API   The number input type should display a new UI widget on supported browsers—a spin-box component that allows the user to change the value by pressing the up button to increase the value and the down button to decrease the value. An example of this is shown in figure 2.6.

Before increment: 100   **After increment:**   101

Figure 2.6   The number input type allows the user to increment and decrement the field value using the up and down buttons in the spinbox on the right-hand side of the field. The user can also change the value by typing a numeric value into the text field itself.

Core API   Two other new attributes that go hand in hand with the number input type are the min and max attributes.

THE MIN AND MAX ATTRIBUTES

min **and** max **attributes**	6.0	N/A	10.0	10.6	5.0

These attributes define the minimum and maximum numbers that a user can enter in a number input field (or the bounds of a slider input using the range input type). Yet data-* attributes, another new form of attribute, allow an elegant solution for automatically calculating updated totals when users enter numbers.

DATA-* ATTRIBUTES

Core API   The order form you're building will allow a user to enter a quantity for each of the products in the form. The form should then automatically calculate the total price for this item and the total order price. In order to do this, you'll need to know the price of a given item. In the past, you may have inserted a hidden field in each row to hold the price for that item, or perhaps you would have stored the price data in a JavaScript array and performed a lookup to get the price for a given product. Neither solution is elegant—that's where HTML5 data-* attributes come into play.

data-* attributes	7.0	6.0	N/A	11.1	5.1

HTML5 data-* attributes allow you to bind arbitrary key/value pair data to any element. JavaScript can then read this data to perform calculations and further client-side manipulation.

Using data-* attributes is simple: prefix the key with data- to form the attribute name and assign it a value. In this example, you're binding a price to a quantity input field:

```
<input type="number" data-price="399.99" name="quantity">
```

You can then listen to this field for changes and multiply the value of the user's input (the quantity) by the value of the data-price attribute to calculate the total price of the item. You'll see how to retrieve data-* attribute values a little later. First, we want to talk about the final feature we're introducing in this section: the new <output> element.

THE <OUTPUT> ELEMENT

Core API

The name of this element explains its purpose—it's used to display output to the user. A typical use case for the <output> element is displaying the result of a calculation based on some data, such as that entered by a user in an <input> element. You'll learn how to update the value of the <output> element later on, as the work progresses. For now, you'll add these new features to your application code.

STEP 4: CREATE THE ORDER DETAILS FORM SECTION

The following listing contains the code for the Order Details section. Let's put the number input type, min/max attributes, data-* attribute, and <output> element to work. Notice how these new features can simplify programming tasks for HTML5-compatible browsers. Add this code directly after the code from the previous listing.

Listing 2.4 index.html—The Order Details form section

```
<fieldset>
    <legend>Order Details</legend>
    <table>
        <thead>
        <tr>
            <th>Product Code</th><th>Description</th><th>Qty</th>
            <th>Price</th><th>Total</th>
        </tr>
        </thead>
        <tbody>
        <tr>
            <td>
                COMP001
                <input type="hidden" name="product_code" value="COMP001">
```

Use a number
input type to
allow the user to
enter a quantity
for each product
in the order form.
The minimum
value is set to zero
using the min
attribute, whereas
the max is set to
99. Each field has
a data-* attribute,
data-price, which
holds the price of
the product.

```
        </td>
        <td>The Ultimate Smartphone</td>
        <td>
            <input type="number" data-price="399.99" name="quantity"
              value="0" min="0" max="99" maxlength="2">
        </td>
        <td>$399.99</td>
        <td>
            <output name="item_total" class="item_total">$0.00</output>
        </td>
    </tr>
    <tr>
        <td>
            COMP002
            <input type="hidden" name="product_code" value="COMP002">
        </td>
        <td>The Ultimate Tablet</td>
        <td>
            <input type="number" data-price="499.99" name="quantity"
              value="0" min="0" max="99" maxlength="2">
        </td>
        <td>$499.99</td>
        <td>
            <output name="item_total" class="item_total">$0.00</output>
        </td>
    </tr>
    <tr>
        <td>
            COMP003
            <input type="hidden" name="product_code" value="COMP003">
        </td>
        <td>The Ultimate Netbook</td>
        <td>
            <input type="number" data-price="299.99" name="quantity"
              value="0" min="0" max="99" maxlength="2">
        </td>
        <td>$299.99</td>
        <td>
            <output name="item_total" class="item_total">$0.00</output>
        </td>
    </tr>
    </tbody>
    <tfoot>
    <tr>
        <td colspan="4">Order Total</td>
        <td>
            <output name="order_total" id="order_total">$0.00</output>
        </td>
    </tr>
    </tfoot>
</table>
</fieldset>
```

The <output> element will store
the line total for each product and
has a default value of $0.00.

2.2.5 Using the form input type month and input attribute pattern

The Payment Details section of the form asks users to enter their credit card details—the name on the card, the card number, the expiry date, and the CVV2 security code, found on the back of most cards. These fields use some of the HTML5 form features introduced in the Contact Details section: `required` and `placeholder` input attributes. The Payment Details section also uses some new features: the `pattern` input attribute and the `month` input type.

THE MONTH INPUT TYPE

| month **input type** | N/A | N/A | N/A | 9.0 | N/A |

 Core API The `month` type allows the user to select a month and year combination from a date-picker widget. HTML5 defines a number of date-related types: `date`, `datetime`, `datetime-local`, `month`, `week`, and `time`. Browser support for these widgets and validation has been slow moving—with the exception of Opera, which has had good support for these types for quite some time, albeit with an ugly date-picker widget, as shown in figure 2.7.

Figure 2.7 The Opera date-picker widget is used for all date/time input types, including `month`, as shown in this screenshot. When the date picker is used to select a month, clicking any day in the month will select that month.

Later in the chapter you'll learn how to provide a fallback for the `month` input type, which gives users something a little more intuitive than a plain text box to enter a month value.

THE PATTERN ATTRIBUTE

| pattern **attribute** | 10.0 | 4.0 | 10.0 | 11.0 | N/A |

 Core API The `pattern` attribute allows you to specify a regular expression pattern to test against data input in a field. In the order form, we'll use the `pattern` attribute on both the card_number and card_cvv2 fields to ensure they're numeric and of appropriate length.

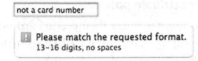

Figure 2.8   When the pattern matching fails, the browser will pick up extra information about the format required from the `title` **attribute. If it's provided, tag it onto the end of the error message displayed to the user.**

When using the `pattern` attribute, you can give a hint to your users about what format your data field requires by using the `title` attribute. This hint will be shown to users in a tooltip when they move their mouse over the field, but it will also be appended to the error message if users enter an invalid value in the field, as shown in figure 2.8.

STEP 5: BUILD THE PAYMENT DETAILS FORM SECTION

Let's add those two new features: the month-picker to give the user a quick and easy way to enter dates and the `pattern` attribute to define valid data patterns. Add the code from the following listing to index.html, directly after the code from the previous listing.

Listing 2.5   index.html—The Payment Details form section

```
<fieldset>
    <legend>Payment Details</legend>
    <ul>
        <li>
            <label class="required">
                <div>Name on Card</div>
                <input name="card_name" required>
            </label>
        </li>
        <li>
            <label class="required">
                <div>Credit Card No.</div>
                <input name="card_number" pattern="[0-9]{13,16}"
                    maxlength="16" required title="13-16 digits, no spaces">
            </label>
        </li>
        <li>
            <label class="required">
                <div>Expiry Date</div>
                <input type="month" name="card_expiry" maxlength="7"
                    placeholder="YYYY-MM" required value="2015-06">
            </label>
        </li>
        <li>
            <label class="required">
                <div>CVV2 No.</div>
                <input name="card_cvv2" class="cvv" maxlength="3"
                    pattern="[0-9]{3}" required title="exactly 3 digits">
                <span>(Three digit code at back of card)</span>
            </label>
        </li>
    </ul>
</fieldset>
```

The regular expression in the card number field specifies that the value should be numeric and between 13 and 16 characters in length. The title attribute is used to give users more detail about the field's requirements, should they attempt to submit an invalid value.

The expiry date for the card uses the month input type, which displays a date-picker widget on supported browsers and should validate based on the format mask YYYY-MM.

The CVV2 security code uses a pattern attribute and title hint to specify that the field value should contain exactly three numeric characters.

TRY IT OUT!

You should be able to use the form now. In browsers with good support for HTML5's form features, you'll be able to see the new input types, attributes, and validation functionality in action. In the next section, we'll allow users to choose whether they want to save the data in the form for later completion or to submit it right away.

2.2.6 Allowing users to choose whether to save or submit a form: Using the input attributes formnovalidate and formaction

When users are filling out a form, they may not be able to complete the form in one session; you need to provide them with a means of saving their progress and returning to the form later. Because a user may need to leave the form quickly, forcing them to correct any validation errors before saving doesn't make sense; this is required only when the form is finally submitted. Therefore, you need to give the user a way to bypass validation.

 Core API

You can force an entire form to bypass validation using the new `novalidate` attribute on the form itself. This is useful only if you want to use the new HTML5 form widgets but don't want to use any of the new validation features. An alternative approach is to have a separate button for saving progress, which uses the `formnovalidate` attribute to prevent the form from being validated when it's used. In addition, you may want to change the `formaction` property of the form to call a different URL when saving the data rather than submitting it. You can do this in HTML5 with the `formaction` attribute.

STEP 6: BYPASS FORM VALIDATION AND SAVE FORM DATA

Let's change the order form's Save Order button to make use of these new attributes:

- Find the line in index.html that reads

  ```
  <input type="submit" id="saveOrder" value="Save Order">
  ```

  Replace that line with the following:

  ```
  <input type="submit" id="saveOrder" value="Save Order" formnovalidate
      formaction="/save">
  ```

- Open the Order Form page in IE10 (and higher) and leave all the fields blank.
- Click the Submit Order button, and an error message will pop up on the Name field telling you that this field must be filled out.
- Click the Save Order button, and you'll notice that the validation will no longer be performed, and the URL the form has been submitted to will be /save rather than /submit.

That was easy, huh? Unfortunately, it's not all that simple, because this won't work on browsers that don't support these new attributes. Thankfully, with a little bit of Java-Script you can fix this problem.

STEP 7: CHANGE THE FORM ACTION IN OLDER BROWSERS

On older browsers, the application should also be able to change the form action. When the user submits the form, it should call a different URL than when saving the data.

Create a new file named app.js in the same directory as the index.html file. Add the contents of the next listing to this file.

Listing 2.6   app.js—Changing the form action in older browsers

```
(function() {
    var init = function() {
        var orderForm = document.forms.order,
            saveBtn = document.getElementById('saveOrder'),
            saveBtnClicked = false;

        var saveForm = function() {
            if(!('formAction' in document.createElement('input'))) {
                var formAction = saveBtn.getAttribute('formaction');
                orderForm.setAttribute('action', formAction);
            }
            saveBtnClicked = true;
        };

        saveBtn.addEventListener('click', saveForm, false);
    };

    window.addEventListener('load', init, false);
})();
```

When users click the Save button, check if their browser supports the formaction attribute. *(arrow points to the if statement)*

If the browser doesn't support formaction, manually set the action attribute on the form using the setAttribute method. *(arrow points to the saveForm function)*

This flag will be used later in the chapter when you provide fallback validation for browsers that don't support HTML5 validation. *(arrow points to saveBtnClicked = true)*

If you open the page in a browser that doesn't support the formaction attribute, such as IE9, clicking the Submit Order button submits the form to the /submit URL. Under the same initial conditions, clicking the Save Order button submits the form to the /save URL. You'll also notice that the validation doesn't work; don't worry, you'll add a fallback for that later in the chapter.

PROGRESS CHECK

To this point, you've created the major pieces of the form: the Contact Details, Login Details, Order Details, and Payment Details sections. Using new HTML5 input types, such as email or tel, the new input attributes such as required, and the general data-* attribute and <output> element, can simplify coding for some browsers. Another tedious task, the implementation of bypassing data validation when saving an incomplete form, can be simplified for browsers that support the new input attributes formnovalidate and formaction.

In the next section, you'll implement the computational logic behind the Order Details section, taking the quantity values entered by the user, then calculating and displaying the total values for each item and the entire order.

2.3 Calculating totals and displaying form output

In the previous section, you used data-* attributes to associate key/value pair data with the quantity field, and you added <output> elements to the totals for each product and for the order total. Yet, in its present state, the order form doesn't seem to care what values you enter for the quantity fields—the total amounts are always $0.00.

In this section, you'll learn
- How to read input values in numeric format using the valueAsNumber property
- How to access data from HTML5 data-* attributes
- How to update the <output> element

In this section, you'll use the data-* attributes and <output> element to calculate the totals and output the results to the user's browser. Four steps will get you there:

- Step 1: Add functions to calculate total values.
- Step 2: Retrieve the value of quantity input fields.
- Step 3: Retrieve price values and calculate line and form totals.
- Step 4: Display updated totals on the order form.

2.3.1 Building calculation functions

We'll start by building the functions that will perform the calculations in the order form example.

STEP 1: ADD FUNCTIONS TO CALCULATE TOTAL VALUES

The code in listing 2.7 gets the relevant fields (quantity, item total, and order total) from the DOM and sets up an event listener on each of the quantity fields to calculate the totals whenever the user modifies the quantity value. The calculation code isn't shown in the listing; you'll add that later in the chapter.

Open app.js and add the following code to the end of the init function, below the line saveBtn.addEventListener('click', saveForm, false);.

Listing 2.7   app.js—Functions to calculate total values

```
var qtyFields = orderForm.quantity,
    totalFields = document.getElementsByClassName('item_total'),
    orderTotalField = document.getElementById('order_total');

var formatMoney = function(value) {
    return value.toString().replace(/\B(?=(\d{3})+(?!\d))/g, ",");
}

var calculateTotals = function() {
    var i = 0,
        ln = qtyFields.length,
```

Returns a number formatted for currency, using a comma as a 1,000 separator character.

Calculates the totals for each item and the overall order total.

```
            itemQty = 0,
            itemPrice = 0.00,
            itemTotal = 0.00,
            itemTotalMoney = '$0.00',
            orderTotal = 0.00,
            orderTotalMoney = '$0.00';

        for(; i<ln; i++) {
        }
    };

    calculateTotals();

    var qtyListeners = function() {
        var i = 0,
            ln = qtyFields.length;

        for(; i<ln; i++) {
            qtyFields[i].addEventListener('input', calculateTotals, false);
            qtyFields[i].addEventListener('keyup', calculateTotals, false);
        }
    };

    qtyListeners();
```

You'll add calculation code in this for loop later in the section.

Perform an initial calculation, just in case any fields are prepopulated. Because the init function is called on page load, any prepopulated data will be ready for access.

Calls the qtyListeners function to add event listeners to fields.

The input event doesn't detect backspace or delete keystrokes or cut actions in IE9, so bind to the keyup event as well.

We'll now look at valueAsNumber, a new HTML5 property that allows you to get a numeric representation of the value of an input field element.

THE VALUEASNUMBER PROPERTY

 Core API The value property of an input element like qtyFields[i] allows you to read the current value of that element in JavaScript. But this value is always returned as a string. If you needed to convert the value to a floating-point number, you likely used parse-Float, but HTML5 has provided a new solution, the valueAsNumber property.

When you read the valueAsNumber property of a number input type, the property returns the number as a floating-point number. If you assign a floating-point number to the valueAsNumber property of a number input type, the property will convert the floating-point number to a string-based value.

> **Using valueAsDate for date and time fields**
> In the case of date/time fields, there is a property, valueAsDate, that works much like the valueAsNumber property. When you use it to retrieve the value of a date-oriented field, it will return a Date object. Similarly, you can use the property to set the value of the field to a Date object.

The valueAsNumber property should be available on browsers that support the new number input type—but what if the browser doesn't support this and has fallen back to a regular text input? In this case, you can fall back on the JavaScript parseFloat function. The following statements are equivalent for reading the floating-point value of a field:

```
value = field.valueAsNumber;       //HTML5 version
value = parseFloat(field.value);   //Fallback version
```

Similarly, the following statements provide the same result when modifying the floating-point value of a field:

```
field.valueAsNumber = value;       //HTML5 version
field.value = value.toString();    //Fallback version
```

Why use valueAsNumber instead of parseFloat?

At this point, you may be wondering why you'd use `valueAsNumber` at all, when you can use `parseFloat` instead, and it'll work consistently across all browsers. `valueAsNumber` offers a more concise way to convert values between string and floating-point. Also, using `valueAsNumber` over `parseFloat` could lead to a tiny increase in performance, but this is unlikely to be noticeable in most web applications. When the usefulness of `valueAsNumber` was questioned on a W3C mailing list, HTML5 editor Ian Hickson provided a use case where the `valueAsNumber` property was much more concise than `parseFloat`—incrementing the value of a field programmatically. Here's an example:

```
field.valueAsNumber += 1;                                  //HTML5 version
field.value = (parseFloat(field.value) + 1).toString()     //Fallback
                                                             version
```

STEP 2: RETRIEVE THE VALUE OF QUANTITY INPUT FIELDS

In the order form example, you'll use the `valueAsNumber` property to get the value of the quantity fields for each product row in the Order Details section. Inside the empty `for` loop from listing 2.7, add the following code.

Listing 2.8   app.js—Getting the value of the quantity input fields

valueAsNumber isn't available in older browsers, so fall back to use parseFloat.

```
if(!!qtyFields[i].valueAsNumber) {
    itemQty = qtyFields[i].valueAsNumber || 0;
} else {
    itemQty = parseFloat(qtyFields[i].value) || 0;
}
```

Testing for existence of valueAsNumber property. The !! is used to cast the property valueAsNumber to a Boolean type. The first ! negates the truthness of the property and converts it to a Boolean. The second ! converts the Boolean to its original truth state.

Next you'll learn how to read HTML5 data-* attribute values to get the prices for each of the items, and then you'll implement it in the sample application.

2.3.2 Accessing values from HTML5 data-* attributes

Earlier, you learned how to bind key/value pair data to elements using the new data-* attributes in HTML5. This information is useful when you want to add extra data to an element that can be easily picked up and used in your JavaScript code. It's straightforward to read data-* attributes—each element has a dataset property that contains all of the data-* attributes for that element. Each of the items in the dataset property has a key name that matches the key name in the element markup, with the data- prefix dropped. In listing 2.4 you defined the item's price using the data-price attribute. To retrieve that value, you can use the following code:

```
var price = element.dataset.price;
```

> **WARNING**   If you hyphenate your data-* attribute names, they'll be camelcased in the dataset property. For example, if you use the attribute name data-person-name, you'd read this using element.dataset.personName rather than element.dataset.person-name.

The dataset *property* is new in HTML5, but it's not yet supported in all browsers. Thankfully, we can show you an easy fallback that'll work on all modern browsers (yes, even IE6)—the getAttribute *method*. To get the value of the data-price attribute using this fallback, you'd use the following code:

```
var price = element.getAttribute('data-price');
```

STEP 3: RETRIEVE PRICE VALUES AND CALCULATE LINE AND FORM TOTALS
In the order form example, let's add some code to get the price of each item and use it to calculate the total cost for each line by multiplying the quantity by the price, as well as the total cost for the entire order. Add the code from the following listing right below the code from the previous listing and before the terminating bracket of the for loop.

> Listing 2.9   app.js—Getting the price values using data-* attributes

```
if(!!qtyFields[i].dataset) {
    itemPrice = parseFloat(qtyFields[i].dataset.price);
} else {
    itemPrice = parseFloat(qtyFields[i].getAttribute('data-price'));    ⟵  Fall back to getAttribute
}                                                                          if the dataset property
                                                                           isn't available.
itemTotal = itemQty * itemPrice;
itemTotalMoney = '$'+formatMoney(itemTotal.toFixed(2));
orderTotal += itemTotal;
orderTotalMoney = '$'+formatMoney(orderTotal.toFixed(2));
```

Now that you've calculated the totals for each item and the overall order total, all that's left is to display these values on the form using <output> elements. By writing values to the <output> element in browsers that support the <output> element, you can access it through the form, for example:

```
var element = document.forms.formname.outputname;
```

Figure 2.9 When the user enters a quantity for an item, the application multiplies it by the price for that item to get the total, then adds up all totals to get the overall order total.

To update the value of an <output> element, you can set the value property:

```
element.value = newValue;
```

What to do for browsers that don't support <output>

To access the element in browsers that don't support <output>, you'll need to give the element an ID and use document.getElementById instead:

```
var element = document.getElementById('outputid');
```

To update the value of the element, set the innerHTML property:

```
element.innerHTML = newValue;
```

Let's add the code you need to update the totals in your order form example.

STEP 4: DISPLAY UPDATED TOTALS ON THE ORDER FORM

Add the code from the next listing to app.js, right after the code from the previous listing and before the terminating bracket of the for loop.

Listing 2.10 app.js—Displaying updated totals using the <output> element

```
if(!!totalFields[i].value) {                          ◁─┐  Test if the <output>
    totalFields[i].value = itemTotalMoney;               │  element is supported
    orderTotalField.value = orderTotalMoney;             │  by the user's browser.
} else {
    totalFields[i].innerHTML = itemTotalMoney;
    orderTotalField.innerHTML = orderTotalMoney;
}
```

TRY IT OUT!

At this point, the calculation of item line and overall order total values should be working. Load the page in a modern browser and try changing the value of the quantity fields—you should notice the totals change accordingly. This is demonstrated in the screenshot in figure 2.9.

Your form now has the ability to compute totals and validate data, but what if you want to provide additional validation functions with custom error messages? In the next section, you'll extend the validation of the form to perform custom validation using the Constraint Validation API and to style invalid fields using CSS3.

2.4   Checking form input data with the Constraint Validation API

Earlier in the chapter, you learned about some of HTML5's new validation features—the `required`, `pattern`, and `min` and `max` attributes—that enable the browser itself to perform native validation on form input fields without requiring any additional Java-Script. These attributes are only the beginning when it comes to HTML5 validation—the Constraint Validation API offers many more possibilities.

In this section, you'll learn
- How to use validation properties and methods to design custom validation tests
- How to use the `invalid` event to detect invalid fields on a submitted form
- How to use the new pseudo-class selectors in CSS3 to apply styling to invalid fields without adding redundant class names to your input elements

The Constraint Validation API defines new properties and methods you can use to detect and modify the validity of a given element. Using this API, you can provide additional validation functionality and use custom error messages. The API allows you to detect whether a field has an error and, if so, what type of error and what error message you'll display. It also provides a method that allows you to set your own custom validation message that will be displayed natively by the browser.

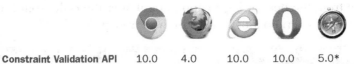

| Constraint Validation API | 10.0 | 4.0 | 10.0 | 10.0 | 5.0* |

* Indicates partial support; although Safari 5.0 supports the Constraints Validation API, it doesn't currently enforce it automatically and display inline error messages like other browsers do.

In this section, as you continue working on this chapter's sample application, you'll walk through two steps:

- Step 1: Add custom validation and error messages to input fields.
- Step 2: Detect form validation failure.

Also, although you won't have to do any coding because we've already provided the full CSS file for the sample application, at the end of the section we'll show you how to style invalid fields using CSS so you'll be prepared to do so in your own apps. First up, let's explore and use some of the Constraint Validation API's properties and methods.

2.4.1 Creating custom validation tests and error messages with the setCustomValidity method and the validationMessage property

Core API

When a validation function isn't supported by a browser or by HTML5, the application will have to implement a custom validation test. In these cases, you'll have to write some JavaScript to test the validity of the entered data and provide a custom error message when the validation fails. The Constraint Validation API simplifies the implementation of custom error messages by providing a setCustomValidity method and a validationMessage property. Both constructs allow the application to assign an error message to the <input> element's validationMessage attribute. Determining which construct to use will depend on the browser's support for setCustomValidity.

STEP 1: ADD CUSTOM VALIDATION AND ERROR MESSAGES TO INPUT FIELDS

The order form example will perform custom validation for a number of tests using the setCustomValidity method:

- Full Name must be at least four characters long.
- Password must be at least eight characters long.
- Password and Confirm Password must match.
- Name on Card must be at least four characters long.

Let's add this custom validation to the app.js file. Add the code from this listing to the end of the init function, directly after the call to qtyListeners.

Listing 2.11 app.js—Performing custom validation

```
var doCustomValidity = function(field, msg) {
    if('setCustomValidity' in field) {              ◁┐  Check if the browser supports
        field.setCustomValidity(msg);                  │  the setCustomValidity method;
    } else {                                           │  if not, manually set the value
        field.validationMessage = msg;                 │  of validationMessage.
    }
};

var validateForm = function() {
    doCustomValidity(orderForm.name, '');
    doCustomValidity(orderForm.password, '');
    doCustomValidity(orderForm.confirm_password, '');
    doCustomValidity(orderForm.card_name, '');

    if(orderForm.name.value.length < 4) {
        doCustomValidity(
            orderForm.name, 'Full Name must be at least 4 characters long'
        );
    }
    if(orderForm.password.value.length < 8) {
        doCustomValidity(
            orderForm.password,
            'Password must be at least 8 characters long'
        );
    }
```

Perform custom validation check; if that fails, call the doCustomValidity function.

Perform custom validation check; if that fails, call the doCustom-Validity function.

```
if(orderForm.password.value != orderForm.confirm_password.value) {
    doCustomValidity(
        orderForm.confirm_password,
        'Confirm Password must match Password'
    );
}

if(orderForm.card_name.value.length < 4) {
    doCustomValidity(
        orderForm.card_name,
        'Name on Card must be at least 4 characters long'
    );
}
};

orderForm.addEventListener('input', validateForm, false);
orderForm.addEventListener('keyup', validateForm, false);
```

The keyup event binding is required to detect backspace, delete, and cut actions in IE9.

TRY IT OUT!

If you load the form in a compatible browser and try to break the custom validation rules described previously, you'll notice that the custom error message will be displayed to the user, as illustrated in figure 2.10.

Next you'll use the invalid event, which fires any time the user tries to submit a form with one or more fields that are marked as invalid.

2.4.2 *Detecting a failed form validation with the invalid event*

 Core API

When the user attempts to submit a form that uses HTML5 validation features, the submit event will only fire if the entire form has passed the validation tests. If you need to detect when form validation has failed, you can listen for the new invalid event. This event is fired when one of the following occurs:

- The user attempts to submit the form and validation fails.
- The checkValidity method has been called by the application and has returned false.

STEP 2: DETECT ORDER FORM VALIDATION FAILURE

Let's add a listener to the invalid event in the order form. Add the following code directly after the code from the previous listing.

Login Details

| Password | •••••••• | Confirm Password | ••• |

⚠ Confirm Password must match Password

Figure 2.10 A demonstration of custom validation in action. In this case, the user has entered a valid password (at least eight characters in length), but they've entered a value in the Confirm Password field that doesn't match the value in the Password field. This causes the error "Confirm Password must match Password" to be displayed.

Listing 2.12   app.js—Listening to the `invalid` event

```
var styleInvalidForm = function() {
    orderForm.className = 'invalid';      ◁─┤
}
```
Add a class invalid to the <form> element.
You'll use this in the next section to style
invalid fields on a submitted form.

```
orderForm.addEventListener('invalid', styleInvalidForm, true);      ◁──┐
```
Listens to the invalid event on the form
and all other elements in the form.

The `invalid` event is useful if you want to apply styling to erroneous form fields on a submitted form. You'll learn how to do that next.

2.4.3   Styling invalid elements using CSS3 pseudo-classes

One way to style invalid elements would be to iterate over the fields, checking if each one is invalid and applying CSS classes to those that have errors. But this is a bit cumbersome, and you can do this much more elegantly using a bit of CSS3 magic.

 Core API

CSS3 introduces a range of new pseudo-classes for styling form fields based on their validity. These styles will be applied only if the condition defined by the pseudo-class is true. The following self-explanatory pseudo-classes are available:

- `:valid`
- `:invalid`
- `:in-range`
- `:out-of-range`
- `:required`
- `:optional`

As you can probably guess, pseudo-classes make styling invalid fields easy. For example, the following code would style any element declared invalid by the Constraint Validation API with a light red background and a maroon border:

```
:invalid {
    background-color: #FFD4D4;
    border: 1px solid maroon;
}
```

But this declaration has a problem: Any field that uses validation attributes like `required` or `pattern` will be initially invalid because these order form fields are blank. As a result, those fields that apply validation attributes will display a red background and maroon border, which isn't nice.

Fortunately, you can easily get around this by applying a class to the parent form when the `invalid` event has fired and adding the pseudo-class selector, `:invalid`, to the CSS rules for the input and selector elements in the form.

NOTE   Please don't change the CSS file that you included in your application's directory when you started the chapter. In this section, we're walking through the theoretical changes you might make rather than directing you to make changes.

In the previous section, you applied a class to the parent form. So, now add the pseudo-class selector, :invalid, to the CSS:

```
form.invalid input:invalid, form.invalid select:invalid,
form.invalid input.invalid, form.invalid select.invalid {
    background-color: #FFD4D4;
    border: 1px solid maroon;
}
```

The order form also uses the :required pseudo-class to style required fields with a light yellow background:

```
input:required, select:required {
    background-color: lightyellow;
}
```

A screenshot of the required and invalid field styling is shown in figure 2.11.

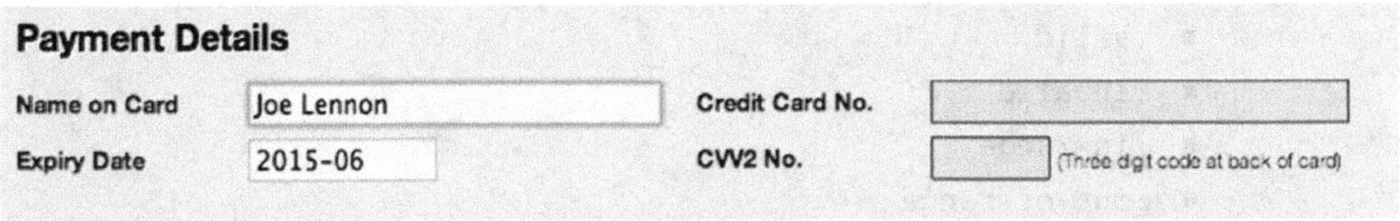

Payment Details

| Name on Card | Joe Lennon | Credit Card No. | |
| Expiry Date | 2015-06 | CVV2 No. | (Three digit code at back of card) |

Figure 2.11   The required fields are styled with a light yellow background (left), as you can see in the Name on Card and Expiry Date fields. The invalid fields are styled with a light red background and a maroon border (right), as shown in the Credit Card No. and CVV2 No. fields.

At this point, the form is more or less fully functional for most recent versions of all browsers (with the exception of Safari). In the next section, you'll learn how to perform rock-solid feature detection using the Modernizr library and how to plug feature gaps using polyfills.

2.5   *Providing fallbacks for unsupported browsers*

One of the main drawbacks to using HTML5's new features is that browser support isn't uniform. Thus, you need to find ways to allow those with the latest and greatest browsers to make use of HTML5 features while ensuring that those using slightly older versions aren't left behind.

In this section, you'll learn

- How Modernizr simplifies detection of browser support for various features of HTML5 and conditionally loads fallbacks
- How to plug gaps in browser support with polyfills, a JavaScript fallback, that will only deploy if the browser lacks native support
- How to use JavaScript to implement basic fallback validation for those browsers that don't yet fully support the Constraint Validation API

You'll learn about these topics as you build out your form using these three steps:

- Step 1: Build feature detection and conditionally deploy a fallback for month-picker.
- Step 2: Build fallback constraint validation for Safari 5.1.
- Step 3: Build fallback constraint validation for IE9.

First up, though, we'd like to give you an overview of feature detection with Modernizr.

2.5.1 Detecting features and loading resources with Modernizr: an overview

An important concept when you're working with HTML5's new APIs is that of feature detection—testing to see if the browser supports a given feature. Unfortunately, the approaches for detecting feature support vary widely, making it difficult to remember how to test for each individual feature. Another issue with feature detection is that you may wish to load certain external resources only if the user's browser supports (or doesn't support) a given feature. We don't see a point, for example, to loading a large WebGL support framework if the user's browser doesn't support WebGL. In a similar way, why should we load a color-picker widget library if the user's browser includes a native widget that will be used instead? Dynamic loading of external resources is possible, but the JavaScript for doing so is hardly straightforward.

 Enter Modernizr, a purpose-built JavaScript library for performing bulletproof feature detection and dynamic loading. When you include Modernizr in a web page, you can detect support for a feature using a much easier syntax. For example, to check to see if the user's browser supports the Canvas element, you'd use the following:

```
if(Modernizr.canvas) {
    //Canvas is supported, fire one up!
} else {
    //Canvas is not supported, use a fallback
}
```

To detect Canvas support without Modernizr, you'd need to use the following:

```
if(!!document.createElement('canvas').getContext) {
    //Canvas is supported, fire one up!
} else {
    //Canvas is not supported, use a fallback
}
```

It's also simple to use Modernizr to dynamically load resources (either .js or .css files) based on a feature test. Consider this example, in which Modernizr will determine if the browser supports the localStorage API. If supported, it will load the localstorage.js file, which would likely contain code that interacts with this API. Otherwise, it will load the localstorage-polyfill.js file, which contains a fallback.

```
Modernizr.load({
    test: Modernizr.localstorage,
    yep: 'localstorage.js',
    nope: 'localstorage-polyfill.js'
});
```

Moving on, let's explore the concept of a polyfill and how you can use it to plug features that aren't supported by a given browser.

2.5.2 *Using polyfills and Modernizr to plug the gaps*

Core API

The term *polyfill* was coined by Remy Sharp and refers to a piece of code (or shim) that aims to implement missing parts of an API specification. The origin of the term is from a product named Polyfilla, which builders use to fill gaps or cracks in walls. Likewise, we developers can use polyfills to fill the gaps or cracks in various web browsers' support for HTML5.

> **TIP**   Paul Irish, one of the key contributors to the Modernizr library, edits and maintains a comprehensive list of polyfills, shims, and fallbacks for a wide variety of HTML5 features. This list is available on Modernizr's GitHub wiki at: http://mng.bz/cJhc.

STEP 1: BUILD FEATURE DETECTION AND CONDITIONALLY DEPLOY A FALLBACK FOR MONTH-PICKER
Let's look at how to use Modernizr to load a month-picker polyfill into those browsers without a built-in month-picker. We expect that you've already placed the monthpicker.js file from this chapter's source code (available at http://manning.com/crowther2) in the same directory as the files you've been building in this chapter. Now add the code from the next listing to the end of the `init` function, directly after the code you added from the previous listing.

> **Listing 2.13   app.js—Using the month-picker polyfill**

```
Modernizr.load({
    test: Modernizr.inputtypes.month,
    nope: 'monthpicker.js'
});
```
If the user's browser doesn't support the month input type, load the monthpicker.js file.

Before Polyfill:	Expiry Date	2015-06	After Polyfill:	Expiry Date	June ⇕	2015 ⇕

Figure 2.12 Before the polyfill has been loaded, the Expiry Date field is represented merely by a text input. After the polyfill has been loaded, the field has been replaced with a month drop-down and a year number input field. The polyfill listens for changes to these fields and populates a hidden field, which stores the month in YYYY-MM format. This hidden field will be sent to the server when the form is submitted.

If you load the order form in any browser that doesn't natively support the month input type, you should see the standard text input replaced with a month drop-down and a year number input field. This is illustrated in the side-by-side screenshots in figure 2.12.

You can apply the same technique to most of the HTML5 form's functionality. In fact, several projects are in the works that aim to polyfill the entire set of forms features in HTML5. These projects include

- Webshims Lib by Alexander Farkas (http://afarkas.github.com/webshim/demos/)
- H5F by Ryan Seddon (https://github.com/ryanseddon/H5F)
- Webforms2 by Weston Ruter (https://github.com/westonruter/webforms2)
- html5Widgets by Zoltan "Du Lac" Hawryluk (https://github.com/zoltan-dulac/html5Forms.js)

Let's wrap up this chapter by performing some basic validation, even on browsers that don't support the Constraint Validation API.

2.5.3 *Performing validation without the Constraint Validation API*

 Core API

If you run the order form example in Safari 5.1 or older versions of other browsers (such as IE9), you'll notice that the validation functionality doesn't work—the form will submit without performing any validation. In this section, you'll learn how to use JavaScript to perform this validation and, if any errors are found, prevent submission of the form.

STEP 2: BUILD FALLBACK CONSTRAINT VALIDATION FOR SAFARI 5.1

In the case of Safari 5.1, the Constraint Validation API is partially supported. This means if you have an <input> element in your form with the required attribute set, the element wouldn't pass validation in Safari 5.1. But Safari doesn't implement any of the UI features, such as displaying error messages next to invalid fields, nor does it prevent the form from submitting if errors exist in the form. Let's start off by reversing this and displaying an error message to the user if there are errors. Add the code from the following listing to your app.js file, right after the code from the previous listing.

Listing 2.14   app.js—Preventing an invalid form from submitting in Safari 5.1

This function retrieves the label for a field using either the labels property or by checking if the field's parent element is a label.

```
var getFieldLabel = function(field) {
    if('labels' in field && field.labels.length > 0) {
        return field.labels[0].innerText;
    }
    if(field.parentNode && field.parentNode.tagName.toLowerCase()=== 'label')
    {
        return field.parentNode.innerText;
    }
    return '';
}

var submitForm = function(e) {
    if(!saveBtnClicked) {
        validateForm();
        var i = 0,
            ln = orderForm.length,
            field,
            errors = [],
            errorFields = [],
            errorMsg = '';

        for(; i<ln; i++) {
            field = orderForm[i];
            if((!!field.validationMessage &&
                field.validationMessage.length > 0) || (!!field.checkValidity
                && !field.checkValidity())
            ) {
                errors.push(
                    getFieldLabel(field)+': '+field.validationMessage
                );
                errorFields.push(field);
            }
        }

        if(errors.length > 0) {
            e.preventDefault();

            errorMsg = errors.join('\n');

            alert('Please fix the following errors:\n'+errorMsg, 'Error');
            orderForm.className = 'invalid';
            errorFields[0].focus();
        }
    }
};

orderForm.addEventListener('submit', submitForm, false);
```

You previously added an event to the Save Order button. When it's clicked, a saveBtnClicked flag is marked as true. This flag is used to determine whether or not the form should be validated.

Loop through the fields in the order form and check if each field is valid.

If the checkValidity method is available and returns false, or if the validationMessage property is populated, then the field contains an error and should be pushed into the errors and errorFields arrays.

If there are errors, this stops the form from submitting and alerts the user with the errors that have been found. Also, this adds the class invalid to the order form to ensure invalid fields are styled correctly and sets the focus on the first invalid field.

If you load the form in Safari and try to submit with invalid fields, you'll get an error message like the one shown in figure 2.13, and the invalid fields will highlight in red. This isn't the prettiest way to inform your users of errors—in practice you'd probably try to mimic the behavior of one of the other browsers by showing an error bubble next to the first error that's encountered.

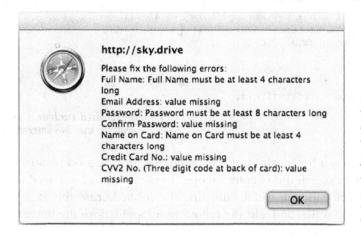

Figure 2.13 Safari now validates the form, displaying a generic alert dialog box with a list of errors that the user needs to correct. You'll notice that for each invalid field, the field's label has been picked up along with the relevant error message that's to be displayed to the user.

STEP 3: BUILD CONSTRAINT FALLBACK VALIDATION FOR IE9

You need to solve one last issue. If you try to submit the form in IE9, you'll see error messages if any input fields don't pass the custom validation tests you wrote earlier. This is great, but IE9 doesn't support the standard attribute-based validation parameters or the `email` input type. To fix this, you need to create a function to scan the form for the input field attributes `required` and `pattern` and input type `email`. When the app has collected those fields, you'll test their validity. Add the code from the next listing to app.js, directly after the code from the previous listing.

Listing 2.15   app.js—Fallback validation in IE9

```
var fallbackValidation = function() {
    var i = 0,
        ln = orderForm.length,
        field;

    for(;i<ln;i++) {
        field = orderForm[i];
        doCustomValidity(field, '');

        if(field.hasAttribute('pattern')) {
            var pattern = new
                RegExp(field.getAttribute('pattern').toString());
            if(!pattern.test(field.value)) {
                var msg = 'Please match the requested format.';
                if(field.hasAttribute('title') &&
                    field.getAttribute('title').length > 0) {
                    msg += ' '+field.getAttribute('title');
                }
                doCustomValidity(field, msg);
            }
        }
        if(field.hasAttribute('type') &&
            field.getAttribute('type').toLowerCase() === 'email') {
```

If the pattern attribute is set, this matches its regular expression against the field's value.

If the input type is email, validate it with the defined pattern.

```
        var pattern = new RegExp(/\S+@\S+\.\S+/);
        if(!pattern.test(field.value)) {
            doCustomValidity(field, 'Please enter an email address.');
        }
    }
    if(field.hasAttribute('required') && field.value.length < 1) {
        doCustomValidity(field, 'Please fill out this field.');
    }
}
};
```

If the required attribute is set, verify that the user has entered a value.

var pattern was chosen for brevity, not reliability. Designing a good pattern depends on many issues and exceeds this chapter's scope. To use this code, you need to call the fallbackValidation function when validating the form. Locate the validateForm function in your app.js file, and add the following snippet before the line if(order-Form.name.value.length < 4) {.

```
if(!Modernizr.input.required || !Modernizr.input.pattern) {
    fallbackValidation();
}
```

The snippet uses Modernizr to test whether the required and pattern attributes are supported, and if not, it calls the fallbackValidation function. If you run the example in IE9, you should see that the validation includes checking required, pattern, and email, as well as custom validation.

This fallback, Modernizr, and the month-picker polyfill are only a sample of the tools you can use to quickly provide backward compatibility in your HTML5 applications. You could easily expand on these to provide support for even older browsers such as IE6 (hint: use a library like jQuery to help with things like event handlers and DOM traversal). You shouldn't let a lack of browser support stop you from using HTML5 form features—it's easy to fill any gaps.

2.6   Summary

HTML5 gives you a lot of functionality for improving web forms. New input types like email and tel provide more widgets with less coding. Using the new input attribute, pattern, enables many validation tasks to be done with no JavaScript. Creating custom validation tests and error message is now much easier with the Constraint Validation API. Also, binding data to HTML elements can be done more efficiently with the data-* attribute.

Unfortunately, browser support is spotty, and browser vendors have been relatively slow to implement these features. Slow and partial implementation of form features appears unlikely to change anytime soon. But this shouldn't stop you from adding HTML5 form functionality to your web apps. When you have a powerful tool like Modernizr for detecting feature support and a growing list of polyfills, you have an efficient way to add HTML5 form support to your applications.

During the development of this form, you had to provide the form with a save feature. The application had no way to save the form on the client, so the application had to save the form on the server. Saving the form on the client's local system would have been a better solution; it would have delivered a faster response and required little or no server resources. And that's what you'll learn in the next chapter: how to create and save files on the client side with the File System API.

You'll also learn how to augment a form's editing functions with the Editing and Geolocation APIs. Sometimes, forms require users to add more than just plain numbers and names. For instance, text entered into a blog posting form will need special formatting (for example, **bolding** or *italics*). The Editing API has powerful constructs to quickly build in this kind of rich media support. If you need to insert a map, the next chapter will show you how to use the Geolocation API to add a localized mapping service to a web-based editor.

Chapter 3 at a glance

Topic	Description, methods, and so on	Page
Editing API	Allowing users to compose and edit HTML content ■ `execCommand()` ■ File Editor view markup	81 77
Geolocation API	Providing geographic data about the user's location ■ `getCurrentPosition()`	82
Quota Management API	Querying local storage about availability and usage; requesting a local storage quota ■ File System API	85
File API	Reading file objects ■ `readAsText()`	89
File Writer API	Writing data to files stored with the File System API ■ Editing files ■ `CreateFormSubmit`	89 91
Drag and Drop API	Using the mouse to select files for import and export ■ Importing files using the `drop` and `dragover` events ■ Saving files using the `draggable` attribute and `dragstart` event	97 98

Core API

Look for this icon ➡ throughout the chapter to quickly locate the topics outlined in this table.

File editing and management: rich formatting, file storage, drag and drop

This chapter covers

- Rich-text HTML editing
- Location awareness with geolocation
- Working with files in a local filesystem
- Implementing drag and drop

The web is no longer merely a set of interconnected documents that people use to find information; it's also an application platform that allows developers to build web apps that anyone with a computer and browser can use. In HTML5, new standardized JavaScript APIs enable web apps to present an application interface similar to current desktop apps. Features such as rich-text editing, drag/drop interactions, local file management, and geolocation are now possible.

This chapter teaches you how to use all of these new features and APIs by walking you through the build of the Super HTML5 Editor, an HTML editor application that runs entirely on the client side, with no server-side requirements. The application allows users to manipulate HTML documents using one of two editor modes:

- A visual WYSIWYG editor for formatting text, inserting hyperlinks, adding images, and inserting maps
- An HTML markup editor for changing, adding, and deleting markup elements, useful when you need formatting or a layout feature not supported in the visual editor

---

Why build the Super HTML5 Editor?

While working through this chapter's sample application, you'll learn to use the following:

- The HTML Editing API to allow users to edit HTML markup using rich-text controls
- The Geolocation API to capture the user's current location for use in a map
- The File System API to provide a client-side sandbox to store the user's files
- Drag and drop to simplify the importation and exportation of files

---

To make things more fun, the application also offers a client-side sandboxed filesystem where the user can create, import, export, edit, view, and delete files. To put icing on the cake, users will also be able to import and export files using drag and drop.

Let's jump right in with a high-level overview of the sample application you're going to build, followed by work on prerequisites and first steps.

3.1   *The Super HTML5 Editor: application overview, prerequisites, and first steps*

As you can see in figure 3.1, the final application will be split into two major views, the File Browser view and the File Editor view.

File Browser view   File Editor view

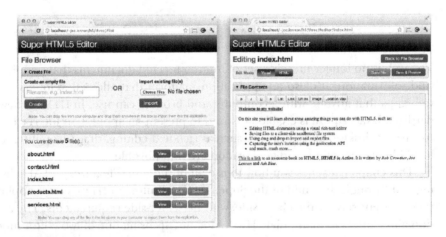

Figure 3.1   The two views of the Super HTML5 Editor application are shown. The File Browser view (left) allows users to manipulate the files stored in the app; the File Editor view (right) enables the file to be modified using rich-text editing controls or directly using HTML markup.

The File Browser view allows users to create empty files, import files from their computers, view a list of existing files, and perform an action on one of these files such as View, Edit, Delete, and Export. This view also provides drag-and-drop support for working with files.

The File Editor view provides two editors for manipulating the file's contents: a visual WYSIWYG editor and a raw HTML markup editor. This view also allows the user to save their changes, preview the file, and return to the File Editor view. It will also warn the user if they try to navigate away from the File Editor view when they have unsaved changes.

Before you begin: important browser notes

The File System API (also known as the File Directories and System API) is a relatively late addition to the HTML5 specification and thus hasn't yet been implemented by most browser vendors. Although most have provided partial support for the accompanying File API, which you can use to read the contents of local files that the user selects or drops into the application, only Google Chrome currently supports the File System and File Writer APIs that are used to actually create and store files on the client side. The sample application has been written to include vendor prefixes that will probably be used when the other browsers start to include support for these features, but we can't guarantee that their actual implementation will follow this path.

Also, if you're using Chrome and plan to test this application in your local directory instead of on a server, you'll need to start Chrome with the following option:

–Allow-File-Access-From-Files

If you don't, your application's client-side filesystem will be inaccessible and the Geolocation API won't be able to access your location.

In this section, you'll build the HTML document for the application and implement basic navigation and state management functionality using JavaScript. The work happens in five steps:

- Step 1: Create index.html.
- Step 2: Add markup for the File Browser view.
- Step 3: Add markup for the File Editor view.
- Step 4: Initialize the application.
- Step 5: Enable navigation between views and manage the state of documents being edited.

Prerequisites

Before you create the index page, you need to handle a couple of prerequisites:

1 Create a directory, and put the style.css file from this chapter's source code in it.
2 Create an empty app.js file, and put it in the same directory as the style.css file.

Note that all files for the book are available at the book's website: http://www.manning.com/crowther2.

At this stage you're probably itching to get started, so let's do just that.

3.1.1 Defining the HTML document structure

The initial code you need loads in the CSS and JavaScript resources for the application and defines the `<section>` elements for each of the two views.

STEP 1: CREATE INDEX.HTML

Begin by creating a file named index.html, and add the contents of the following listing to it.

Listing 3.1   index.html—Application HTML structure

```html
<!DOCTYPE html>
<html lang="en">
<head>
    <meta charset="utf-8">
    <title>Super HTML5 Editor</title>
    <link rel="stylesheet" href="style.css">
    <script src="app.js"></script>
</head>
<body class="browser-view">
    <header><h1>Super HTML5 Editor</h1></header>
    <section id="list">

    </section>
    <section id="editor">

    </section>
</body>
</html>
```

The value of class will determine the currently displayed view. Navigating between views will be implemented later in the section.

The File Browser view markup should be inserted here.

The File Editor view markup should be inserted here.

STEP 2: ADD MARKUP FOR THE FILE BROWSER VIEW

The File Browser view is split into two zones. The first zone contains two forms:

- A form for creating an empty file
- A form for importing a file from the user's computer

The second zone includes a list of files that the user has created or imported. To build these zones you'll use the `<details>` and `<summary>` *elements*, both of which are new in HTML5. The `<details>` element allows you to create a collapsible section in your code, which would previously have only been possible using a combination of JavaScript and CSS. Adding a `<summary>` element within `<details>` will put a label on the expanded `<details>` content. Add the code from the next listing to the index.html file, inside the `<section>` element with the ID attribute value `list`.

Listing 3.2   index.html–File Browser view markup

```html
<h1>File Browser</h1>
<details open id="filedrop">
    <summary>Create File</summary>
    <form name="create">
        <div>
```

This zone will be a target drop zone for files later in this chapter. The open attribute on the `<details>` element sets it to be expanded by default.

The create form allows users to create a new empty file.

```
            <h2>Create an empty file</h2>
            <input type="text" name="name" placeholder=" e.g. index.html">
            <input type="submit" value="Create">
        </div>
    </form>
    <div class="spacer">OR</div>
    <form name="import">
        <div>
            <h2>Import existing file(s)</h2>
            <input type="file" name="files" multiple accept="text/html">
            <input type="submit" value="Import">
        </div>
    </form>

    <div class="note">
        <strong>Note</strong>: You can drag files from your computer and
        drop them anywhere in this box to import them into the application.
    </div>
</details>

<details open>
    <summary>My Files</summary>
    <div class="note top">
        You currently have <span id="file_count">0</span> file(s):
    </div>
    <ul id="files"></ul>
    <div class="note">
        <strong>Note</strong>: You can drag any of the files in the list
        above to your computer to export them from the application.
    </div>
</details>
```

> The import form allows users to import files from their computer.

> This will be populated later with a list of files.

STEP 3: ADD MARKUP FOR THE FILE EDITOR VIEW

This File Editor view features a switch button that allows the user to change between Visual edit mode and HTML edit mode. In Visual mode, the editor will behave much like a basic word processor, and it includes buttons for formatting the content in bold, italic, and so forth. Each button has an attribute named data-command, which is an example of an HTML5 data attribute. These attributes make it easy to associate primitive data with an HTML element, and an accompanying JavaScript API makes it a breeze to get back this data when it's needed. The code for the File Editor view is shown in the following listing and should be added to index.html, inside the <section> element with the ID attribute value editor.

Listing 3.3   index.html–File Editor view markup

```
<h1>Editing <span id="file_name"></span><a href="#list">Back to File
    Browser</a></h1>
<div class="mode-toolbar">
    <div class="left">
        <div>Edit Mode:</div>
        <button id="edit_visual" class="split_left active">Visual</button>
        <button id="edit_html" class="split_right">HTML</button>
    </div>
```

> Two buttons allow the user to switch between Visual and HTML edit modes.

```
<div class="right">
    <button id="file_save" class="green">Save File</button>
    <button id="file_preview">Save &amp; Preview</button>
</div>
</div>

<details open>
    <summary>File Contents</summary>
    <div id="file_contents">
        <div id="file_contents_visual">
            <div id="file_contents_visual_toolbar">
                <button data-command="bold"><strong>B</strong></button>
                <button data-command="italic"><em>I</em></button>
                <button data-command="underline"><u>U</u></button>
                <button data-command="strikethrough"><del>S</del></button>
                <button data-command="insertUnorderedList">List</button>
                <button data-command="createLink">Link</button>
                <button data-command="unlink">Unlink</button>
                <button data-command="insertImage">Image</button>
                <button data-command="insertMap">Location Map</button>
            </div>
            <iframe id="file_contents_visual_editor"></iframe>
        </div>
        <div id="file_contents_html">
            <textarea id="file_contents_html_editor"></textarea>
        </div>
    </div>
</details>
```

Contains several buttons that allow the user to format the currently selected content in the editor window.

The visual editor is an <iframe> element, which will later be made editable using the designMode property.

The HTML markup editor is a regular <textarea> element.

With the two views defined, you can now implement JavaScript code to enable navigation between them.

3.1.2 *Implementing navigation and state management in JavaScript*

First, let's create an anonymous function block to ensure that the application doesn't pollute the global JavaScript namespace. This block will initialize the application when the DOM has finished loading.

STEP 4: INITIALIZE THE APPLICATION

Create a new file named app.js and save it in the same directory as the index.html file you created previously. Add the contents of the following listing to this file.

Listing 3.4   app.js–Application initialization code

```
(function() {
    var SuperEditor = function() {

    };

    var init = function() {
        new SuperEditor();
    }

    window.addEventListener('load', init, false);
})();
```

This constructor function is where the rest of the app's code should be inserted.

STEP 5: ENABLE NAVIGATION BETWEEN VIEWS, MANAGE THE STATE OF DOCUMENTS BEING EDITED

With the code to initialize the application out of the way, let's add code to keep track of whether the user has made changes to a document and to switch between the File Browser and File Editor views. The code in the next listing should be added inside the SuperEditor constructor function that you created in the previous listing.

Listing 3.5   app.js—View navigation and state management code

```javascript
var view, fileName, isDirty = false,                                    ◄─┐
    unsavedMsg = 'Unsaved changes will be lost. Are you sure?',
    unsavedTitle = 'Discard changes';
                                            These variables will store the current
var markDirty = function() {                view and filename (if in the File Editor
    isDirty = true;                         view) and a marker to indicate if the
};                                          document has been modified (isDirty).

var markClean = function() {
    isDirty = false;
};                                          If the user tries to close the window or
                                            navigate to another page, you'll check
var checkDirty = function() {               to see if they've made unsaved changes
    if(isDirty) { return unsavedMsg; }      and warn them first if necessary.
};

window.addEventListener('beforeunload', checkDirty, false);            ◄─┘

var jump = function(e) {                         ◄─┐  The jump event handler uses hashes in
    var hash = location.hash;                       │  the URL to switch between the two views.

    if(hash.indexOf('/') > -1) {                 ◄─┐  If the URL hash
        var parts = hash.split('/'),                │  contains a forward
            fileNameEl = document.getElementById('file_name');   slash, it should
                                                    │  show the File
        view = parts[0].substring(1) + '-view';     │  Editor view for the
        fileName = parts[1];                        │  file after the slash
        fileNameEl.innerHTML = fileName;            │  (if it exists).
    } else {
        if(!isDirty || confirm(unsavedMsg, unsavedTitle)) {
            markClean();
            view = 'browser-view';
            if(hash != '#list') {
                location.hash = '#list';
            }
        } else {                                    Use the class attribute on the
            location.href = e.oldURL;               <body> element to indicate
        }                                           which is the current view—the CSS
    }                                               will take care of showing/hiding
                                                    the views as necessary.
    document.body.className = view;      ◄─
};

jump();                                             │  The jump function is called
                                                    │  on page load and whenever
window.addEventListener('hashchange', jump, false);  ◄─┘  the URL hash changes.
```

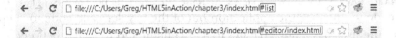

**Figure 3.2   When you load the application right now, a hash value #list will
be appended to the end of the URL. To navigate to the editor view manually,
change this to #editor/index.html as shown.**

TRY IT OUT

At this point, you should be able to navigate around the application. One slight incon-
venience is that you won't be able to easily get to the File Editor view just yet, because
you haven't added any of the File System functionality. To cheat your way around this,
modify the URL manually, changing the #list at the end to #editor/index.html, as
illustrated in figure 3.2.

With a modest amount of effort, you've roughed out the basic HTML structure,
navigation functions, and state management for the application. In the next section,
you'll discover how to enable the visual editor and connect it to the HTML editor, how
to implement the formatting buttons, and how to use geolocation to insert a map of
the user's current position coordinates.

3.2   *Rich-text editing and geolocation*

The visual editor in this chapter's sample application will allow users to write and edit
rich-text content using formatting buttons that are similar to those in most word-
processing applications. After formatting the document, users may need to see the
underlying HTML markup to make adjustments, so the application will enable them to
switch between the visual editor and the HTML editor. Also, so that you can at least get
your hands dirty with the Geolocation API, we'll have you add into the application a
button that inserts a location map.

> **In this section, you'll learn**
> - To use the designMode property to signal to the browser that an HTML docu-
>   ment is editable
> - To use the Editing API's execCommand method to provide rich-text editing controls
> - To use the Geolocation API

The work happens in three steps:

- Step 1: Turn designMode on and synchronize the content of both editors.
- Step 2: Implement the rich-text editing toolbar in the visual editor.
- Step 3: Use geolocation to insert a map of the user's location.

3.2.1 *Using designMode to make an HTML document editable*

To facilitate the visual editor mode in your app, you need to allow users to directly edit the HTML document without needing to use HTML markup. In order to make this work, you need to take advantage of a JavaScript object property, designMode. When you set this property's value to on for a given document, the entire document becomes editable, including its <!DOCTYPE> declaration, and <head> section. You'll use this property with our visual editor's <iframe> to make the entire contents of the <iframe> editable.

> **NOTE** If you need to edit the contents of only a specific HTML element, then use the contenteditable attribute. Although contenteditable is new in HTML5, it started out as a proprietary extension in IE and was later adopted by other browser vendors. As a result, browser support for it is widespread, so you can use it without fear of leaving anyone behind.

Setting designMode to on is straightforward, but you also need to build logic that will connect the visual editor to the HTML markup editor so that any changes are synced across them when appropriate. You also need to implement the switch button to allow the user to switch between the two editor modes. Enough chat about what you need to do—let's go ahead and do it.

STEP 1: TURN DESIGNMODE ON AND SYNCHRONIZE THE CONTENT OF BOTH EDITORS
In the app.js file, add the following code immediately after the line window.addEvent-Listener('hashchange', jump, false).

Listing 3.6 app.js—Enabling designMode and connecting the two editors

```
var editVisualButton = document.getElementById('edit_visual'),
    visualView = document.getElementById('file_contents_visual'),
    visualEditor = document.getElementById('file_contents_visual_editor'),
    visualEditorDoc = visualEditor.contentDocument,
    editHtmlButton = document.getElementById('edit_html'),
    htmlView = document.getElementById('file_contents_html'),
    htmlEditor = document.getElementById('file_contents_html_editor');

visualEditorDoc.designMode = 'on';

visualEditorDoc.addEventListener('keyup', markDirty, false);
htmlEditor.addEventListener('keyup', markDirty, false);

var updateVisualEditor = function(content) {
    visualEditorDoc.open();
    visualEditorDoc.write(content);
    visualEditorDoc.close();
    visualEditorDoc.addEventListener('keyup', markDirty, false);
};

var updateHtmlEditor = function(content) {
    htmlEditor.value = content;
};
```

Enable editing of the visual editor iframe by switching on its designMode property.

Mark the file as dirty whenever the user makes changes to either editor.

This function updates the visual editor content. Every execution of updateVisual-Editor constructs a new document, so you must attach a new keyup event listener.

This function updates the HTML editor content.

```
var toggleActiveView = function() {
    if(htmlView.style.display == 'block') {
        editVisualButton.className = 'split_left active';
        visualView.style.display = 'block';
        editHtmlButton.className = 'split_right';
        htmlView.style.display = 'none';
        updateVisualEditor(htmlEditor.value);
    } else {
        editHtmlButton.className = 'split_right active';
        htmlView.style.display = 'block';
        editVisualButton.className = 'split_left';
        visualView.style.display = 'none';

        var x = new XMLSerializer();
        var content = x.serializeToString(visualEditorDoc);
        updateHtmlEditor(content);
    }
}

editVisualButton.addEventListener('click', toggleActiveView, false);
editHtmlButton.addEventListener('click', toggleActiveView, false);
```

> This event handler toggles between the visual and HTML editors. When updating the HTML editor, the XMLSerializer object is used to retrieve the HTML content of the iframe element.

PROGRESS CHECK: TRY IT OUT

At this point, you should be able to type text in the visual editor. You'll notice that if you switch to the HTML editor, the contents should match. Similarly, if you make changes in the HTML editor and switch back to the visual editor, your changes should be shown. Try putting some arbitrary HTML styling markup in the HTML editor and notice the impact it has in the visual editor.

> **NOTE** If you try to use the formatting toolbar to style the contents of the visual editor, you'll notice that none of these buttons work. Don't fret; you'll fix that in the next section.

After you've made changes, try closing the window. You should see a warning message like the one shown in figure 3.3.

Because the saving function hasn't been implemented yet, you can ignore this warning and leave the page. You'll add the saving function in a later section.

Now that you have the basic visual and HTML editors working, let's move on and add some formatting functions to those do-nothing toolbar buttons.

Figure 3.3 The `isDirty` variable we created earlier allows the application to keep track of whether the user has made changes to the document. If they've made changes and try to close the window without saving, they'll be shown this warning message to confirm they want to leave the page.

3.2.2 Providing rich-text editing controls with execCommand

Core API

As you've already seen, the contenteditable attribute and designMode property allow developers to make any HTML element editable by the user. But up until now, all users have been able to do is type and edit text, which is hardly exciting; they've been able to do that with HTML form elements for ages! It'd be much more impressive if users could format the text using rich-text editing controls, as they would in a word processing application. That's where the Editing API method execCommand comes in.

| Editing API | 4.0 | 3.5 | 5.5 | 9.0 | 3.1 |

EXECCOMMAND: FORMATTING AND EDITING ELEMENTS VIA CODE

Invoking the execCommand method of an editable element applies a selected formatting command to the current selection or at the current caret position. This includes basic formatting like italicizing or bolding text and block changes like creating a bullet list or changing the alignment of a selection. ExecCommand can also be used to create hyperlinks and insert images. Basic editing commands like copy, cut, and paste can also be used by execCommand if the browser implements these features. Although the HTML5 standard specifies these editing commands, it doesn't require the browser to support them. For a full list of commands standardized in HTML5, see appendix B.

To initiate a formatting or editing action, you must pass one to three arguments to execCommand:

- The first argument, command, is a string. command contains the name of the editing or formatting action.
- The second argument, showUI, is a bool. showUI determines whether the user will see the default UI associated with command. (Some commands don't have a UI.)
- The third argument, value, is a string. execCommand will invoke command with value as its argument.

The number of required arguments for an execCommand depends on the command passed to the first argument. See appendix B or http://dvcs.w3.org/hg/editing/raw-file/tip/editing.html for a list of argument specifications for each formatting and editing command.

STEP 2: IMPLEMENT THE RICH-TEXT EDITING TOOLBAR IN THE VISUAL EDITOR

To use execCommand, the application will use a click event handler to pass the function name of a pressed toolbar button to execCommand's command argument. This function name will be retrieved from the button's data-command attribute. Add the code from the following listing to app.js, directly after the code you added in the previous section.

Listing 3.7 app.js–Implementing the rich-text editing toolbar in the visual editor

```
var visualEditorToolbar =
    document.getElementById('file_contents_visual_toolbar');

var richTextAction = function(e) {
    var command,
        node = (e.target.nodeName === "BUTTON") ? e.target :
        e.target.parentNode;

    if(node.dataset) {
        command = node.dataset.command;
    } else {
        command = node.getAttribute('data-command');
    }

    var doPopupCommand = function(command, promptText, promptDefault) {
        visualEditorDoc.execCommand(command, false, prompt(promptText,
        promptDefault));
    }

    if(command === 'createLink') {
        doPopupCommand(command, 'Enter link URL:', 'http://www.example.com');
    } else if(command === 'insertImage') {
        doPopupCommand(command, 'Enter image URL:',
        'http://www.example.com/image.png');
    } else {
        visualEditorDoc.execCommand(command);
    }
};

visualEditorToolbar.addEventListener('click', richTextAction, false);
```

RichTextAction is the event handler for all buttons on the visual editor toolbar. When a user clicks a toolbar button, the event handler determines which button the user clicked.

The dataset object offers convenient access to the HTML5 data-* attributes. If the browser doesn't support this, the app falls back to the getAttribute method.

Because this app will require a customized UI, showUI will be set to false. The third argument, value, is passed a prompt method (of the Window object). It contains a string prompting the user for an input value and another string containing a default input value.

TRY IT OUT—AND CHALLENGE YOURSELF!

 Core API

With the exception of the Location Map button, which you'll implement in the next section, you should be able to format the text in the visual editor to your heart's content using the rich-text editing toolbar. A few easy enhancements you could include here would be to provide support for more commands, to bind a keyboard event to a command (for example, Ctrl-B or Cmd-B could be mapped to bold), and to indicate the current selection state of the toolbar (for example, the Bold button should be depressed when the selected text is bold). To implement the latter, you can use the Editing API method `queryCommandState`, which is covered in more detail in appendix B.

3.2.3 *Mapping a user's current location with the Geolocation API*

 Core API

To enable your application to insert a map based on the user's position, you'll need to use the Geolocation and Google Maps APIs. The Geolocation API provides the method `getCurrentPosition`, which will enable the application to obtain the user's geographic coordinates. The Google Maps API provides a querying function to return a static map from a set of submitted coordinates.

When Google Maps returns the selected map, your application will paste the map into the visual editor using the execCommand's insertImage function.

| Geolocation API | 5.0 | 3.5 | 9.0 | 10.6 | 5.0 |

Before you dive in, we want you to know that although this sample application doesn't explore all of the features of geolocation, it does show you how simple it is to acquire a user's position and integrate it with a mapping service. If you're looking to build a more dynamic mapping app, you'll be glad to know that the Geolocation API can also support features like:

- Tracking user movement over set time intervals
- Obtaining the user's altitude, heading, and speed
- Limiting GPS use when battery life is a concern

To find out more about these geolocation features, see appendix B.

STEP 3: USE GEOLOCATION TO INSERT A MAP OF THE USER'S LOCATION
To implement geolocation in your application, in the app.js file locate the if block that checks whether the command is createLink, insertImage, or something else. Add the following code before the last else and after the }.

Listing 3.8 app.js—Using geolocation to insert a map of the user's location

```
else if(command === 'insertMap') {              Check to see if the user's
    if(navigator.geolocation) {          ◁─┤    browser supports geolocation.
        node.innerHTML = 'Loading';
        navigator.geolocation.getCurrentPosition(function(pos) {     ◁─
            var coords = pos.coords.latitude+','+pos.coords.longitude;
            var img = 'http://maps.googleapis.com/maps/api/staticmap?markers='
                +coords+'&zoom=11&size=200x200&sensor=false';
            visualEditorDoc.execCommand('insertImage', false, img);
            node.innerHTML = 'Location Map';
        });
    } else {
        alert('Geolocation not available', 'No geolocation data');
    }
}
```

Use execCommand to insert a static Google Maps image of the user's location.

The getCurrentPosition method will trigger the browser to ask the user for access to the user's location. If permission is granted, getCurrentPosition executes a callback function, passing the user's location data in the form of a Position object.

When the user clicks the Location Map button on the rich-text editor toolbar, the browser will request permission for the application to access their location data, as shown in figure 3.4.

Figure 3.4   The browser will request the user's permission to enable the Geolocation API. If access is denied, the browser will behave as though it doesn't support geolocation.

Figure 3.5   A map of the user's location will be added to the editor. This map is actually an image generated by the Google Maps Static API. Easy, huh?

If the user chooses to allow access to their location, a map with a marker on their position will be added to the editor, as illustrated in the screenshot in figure 3.5. In order for the map to appear, you must click inside the editor's text box before clicking the Location Map button.

Now that users can see their location on a map and manipulate HTML documents, you need to provide a way of saving their work in actual files. In the next section, you'll learn how to use the HTML5 File System API to do just that.

3.3   Managing files locally: the File System, Quota Management, File, and File Writer APIs

Working with files in web applications has always been tricky. If you wanted to save a file, you'd select it using a file `<input>` element, then the browser would upload the file to the server for storage. Downloading a previously stored file was a similarly slow and cumbersome process. In addition, you were burdened with the tedious task of developing yet another file management system using one set of tools and languages on the server and another on the browser side. Suffice it to say, files and web applications have always been a bit of a bitter cocktail. Thankfully, HTML5 is going to greatly speed up this development process with the File System API.

| File System API | 13.0 | N/A | N/A | N/A | N/A |

The File System API offers web applications access to a sandboxed storage space on the client's local filesystem. For security purposes, applications can only access the files in their own sandbox on the client, preventing malicious apps from accessing and manipulating data stored by other applications. The File System API also offers applications a choice between a temporary or persistent filesystem. Data in a temporary filesystem can be removed at any stage by the browser, and the data's continued existence shouldn't be relied on, whereas data in a persistent filesystem can only be removed if specifically requested by the user. Because we want the Super HTML5 Editor to save a user's work for later use, we'll show you how to build a persistent filesystem.

> **WARNING**   The File System API was added to HTML5 much later than most APIs, and so browser support for it is far less mature. Because Chrome is the only browser currently offering any implementation of the API, the code in this section has been tested only on Chrome. Every effort has been made to ensure that it will work in other browsers at a later stage, but unfortunately we can't guarantee anything on that front.

The File System API offers almost all the needed functionality to create and manage a sandboxed filesystem except the ability to request local storage and analyze local storage availability. To do this, you need the Quota Management API.

| Quota Management API | 13.0 | N/A | N/A | N/A | N/A |

The Quota Management API enables the application to determine if enough local file storage exists to save data. If sufficient space exists, the application can use the Quota Management API to request storage via a request for quota.

> **NOTE** The File System API makes use of other file-related APIs such as the File Writer and File APIs. This section will be making calls to these underlying APIs and pointing them out as the sandboxed filesystem is built.

You'll walk through seven steps to create the filesystem:

- Step 1: Create a persistent filesystem.
- Step 2: Retrieve and display a file list.
- Step 3: Load files in the File Editor view using the File API.
- Step 4: View, edit, and delete files in the filesystem.
- Step 5: Create new, empty files in the filesystem.
- Step 6: Import existing files from the user's computer.
- Step 7: Implement the Save and Preview buttons.

3.3.1 Creating an application filesystem

Using the File System and Quota Management APIs, the process of creating the first part of the filesystem, the base persistent filesystem, becomes relatively straightforward and is accomplished in a single listing, listing 3.9. To help you navigate the code, look out for the following implementation process within the code:

- Assign a filesystem object to the window `fileSystem` field.
- Assign a storage and quota management object to the window `storageInfo` field.
- Set the filesystem as persistent.
- Request a quota from the local storage system.

STEP 1: CREATE A PERSISTENT FILESYSTEM

Core API With the process in mind, review the following listing to see the detailed implementation. Then add the code after the call to `addEventListener('click', richTextAction, false)`.

Listing 3.9 app.js–Creating a persistent filesystem

For convenience, point the filesystem objects to possible vendor prefixes. If the browser doesn't support these objects, the objects will have a false value.

```
window.requestFileSystem = window.requestFileSystem ||
    window.webkitRequestFileSystem
    || window.mozRequestFileSystem || window.msRequestFileSystem || false;
window.storageInfo = navigator.persistentStorage ||
    navigator.webkitPersistentStorage || navigator.mozPersistentStorage ||
    navigator.msPersistentStorage || false;

var stType = window.PERSISTENT || 1,
    stSize = (5*1024*1024),
    fileSystem,
    fileListEl = document.getElementById('files'),
    currentFile;
```

Define basic variables for use in the app: storage type and size, filesystem object, the file list element, and the currently selected file (when editing).

```
var fsError = function(e) {                                    Standard error
    if(e.code === 9) {                                         function for all
        alert('File name already exists.', 'File System Error');   File System API
    } else {                                                   method calls.
        alert('An unexpected error occured. Error code: '+e.code);
    }
};
var qmError = function(e) {           Standard error function for all Quota
    if(e.code === 22) {               Management API method calls.
        alert('Quota exceeded.', 'Quota Management Error');
    } else {
        alert('An unexpected error occurred. Error code: '+e.code);
    }
};                                                  Check to see if the browser
                                                    supports the File System API and
if(requestFileSystem && storageInfo) {              the Quota Management API (also
    var checkQuota = function(currentUsage, quota) {  known as StorageInfo).
        if(quota === 0) {
            storageInfo.requestQuota(stType, stSize, getFS, qmError);

                                   Because this app has a persistent filesystem, the request
                                   for quota will trigger a message asking the user's
        } else {                   permission to access the browser's filesystem.
            getFS(quota);
        }
    };
    storageInfo.queryUsageAndQuota(stType, checkQuota, qmError);

                        If queryUsageAndQuota successfully executes, it passes usage and quota
                        info to the callback function, checkQuota; otherwise, qmError is called.
                        CheckQuota determines if sufficient quota exists to store files; if not, then
                        it needs to request a larger quota.
    var getFS = function(quota) {
        requestFileSystem(stType, quota, displayFileSystem, fsError);
    }
    var displayFileSystem = function(fs) {                     You'll implement
        fileSystem = fs;                                       updateBrowser-
        updateBrowserFilesList();                              FilesList and
        if(view === 'editor') {                                displayBrowserFile-
            loadFile(fileName);        You'll implement loadFile in a   List in a later section.
        }                             later section. If the editor       These functions will
    }                                 view is the current view, then     retrieve and display
} else {                              load the file into the editor.     files in the app's
    alert('File System API not supported', 'Unsupported');    filesystem.
}
```

The request-FileSystem method is used to get the filesystem object.

You'll implement updateBrowser-FilesList and displayBrowserFile-List in a later section. These functions will retrieve and display files in the app's filesystem.

Unfortunately, you aren't quite ready to test your filesystem. You need to implement some functions to retrieve and display any existing files in the app's filesystem.

3.3.2 Getting a list of files from the filesystem

In listing 3.9, the `displayFileSystem` function receives a reference to the filesystem object and then calls a function named `updatebrowserFilesList`. In this section, you'll create this function, which will retrieve a list of files in the app's filesystem directory and display it in the My Files zone of the File Browser.

Step 2: Retrieve and display a file list

You'll need the next two listings for this work: one to create the `updateBrowser-FilesList` function, another to create the `displayBrowserFileList` function. First, `displayBrowserFileList` will accept a complete list of files as an argument and update the UI to display each of these files with View, Edit, and Delete buttons. Right after the `displayFileSystem` function you created previously, add the code from the next listing.

Listing 3.10   app.js—Building the file list UI from an array of files

```
var displayBrowserFileList = function(files) {
    fileListEl.innerHTML = '';
    document.getElementById('file_count').innerHTML = files.length;
    if(files.length > 0) {
        files.forEach(function(file, i) {
            var li = '<li id="li_'+i+'" draggable="true">'+file.name
                + '<div><button id="view_'+i+'">View</button>'
                + '<button class="green" id="edit_'+i+'">Edit</button>'
                + '<button class="red" id="del_'+i+'">Delete</button>'
                + '</div></li>';
            fileListEl.insertAdjacentHTML('beforeend', li);

            var listItem = document.getElementById('li_'+i),
                viewBtn = document.getElementById('view_'+i),
                editBtn = document.getElementById('edit_'+i),
                deleteBtn = document.getElementById('del_'+i);

            var doDrag = function(e) { dragFile(file, e); }
            var doView = function() { viewFile(file); }
            var doEdit = function() { editFile(file); }
            var doDelete = function() { deleteFile(file); }

            viewBtn.addEventListener('click', doView, false);
            editBtn.addEventListener('click', doEdit, false);
            deleteBtn.addEventListener('click', doDelete, false);
            listItem.addEventListener('dragstart', doDrag, false);
        });
    } else {
        fileListEl.innerHTML = '<li class="empty">No files to display</li>'
    }
};
```

Update the file counter with the number of files in the filesystem.

Iterate over each file in the filesystem using the forEach array function.

Draggable will be discussed in a later section on drag-and-drop interactivity.

Attach event handlers to the View, Edit, and Delete buttons and the list item itself.

Later in the chapter, you'll implement doDrag to support drag-and-drop functions.

If there are no files, show an empty list message.

Now, to execute the `displayBrowserFileList` function you just created, you need to pass an array of all the files in the app's directory. The `updateBrowserFilesList` function will do just that, using a `DirectoryReader` object and reading the list of files one set of files at a time until all files in the app's directory have been read. Add the code from the next listing right after the `displayBrowserFileList` function.

Listing 3.11   app.js—Reading the file list using the directory reader

```
var updateBrowserFilesList = function() {
    var dirReader = fileSystem.root.createReader(),
        files = [];
```

Create a directory reader. Later in the listing, you'll use it to get the complete list of files.

| **The directory listing is read in one set of files at a time, so you'll use a recursive function to keep reading until all files have been retrieved.** | ```
var readFileList = function() {
    dirReader.readEntries(function(fileSet) {
        if(!fileSet.length) {
            displayBrowserFileList(files.sort());
        } else {
            for(var i=0,len=fileSet.length; i<len; i++) {
                files.push(fileSet[i]);
            }
            readFileList();
        }
    }, fsError);
}
readFileList();
};
``` |

When the end of the directory is reached, call the displayBrowserFileList function, passing the alphabetically sorted files array as an argument.

If you're not at the end of the directory, push the files just read into the files array and recursively call the readFileList function again.

Next, you'll discover how to implement the View, Edit, and Delete buttons displayed for each of the files in the filesystem.

3.3.3 Loading, viewing, editing, and deleting files

Back in the `displayFileSystem` function in listing 3.9, you may have noticed an `if` block that called a function named `loadFile` if the current view was the editor view. Let's go ahead and implement that function now, as well as some small functions that will allow users to view, edit, and delete files in the filesystem.

STEP 3: LOAD FILES IN THE FILE EDITOR VIEW USING THE FILE API

Core API

The `loadFile` function uses the File System API method `getFile` to retrieve the FileEntry from the filesystem. In order to read the file contents, `loadFile` uses the File API method `readAsText`. Lastly, `loadFile` displays the file contents to the visual and HTML editors. Add the code from the following listing to app.js right after the `updateBrowserFilesList` function you added previously.

File API	13.0	3.6	N/A	11.1	N/A

Listing 3.12 app.js—Loading files in the File Editor view

A FileReader object, reader, is used to read the contents of the file. When reader is done, it triggers the onloadend event handler to update the visual and HTML editors.	**The getFile method takes four arguments: (I) relative or absolute path to filename, (2) options object ({create: boolean, exclusive: boolean}—both default to false), (3) success callback function, and (4) error callback function. If a FileEntry is found, getFile passes the selected FileEntry to the fileEntry argument of the success callback function. See table 3.I for a list of possible options arguments and their effect on getFile behavior.**

```
var loadFile = function(name) {
    fileSystem.root.getFile(name, {}, function(fileEntry) {
        currentFile = fileEntry;
        fileEntry.file(function(file) {
            var reader = new FileReader();
            reader.onloadend = function(e) {
                updateVisualEditor(this.result);
```

The file method of the File System API is used to retrieve the file from the fileEntry and pass the file to the callback function.
```

```
            updateHtmlEditor(this.result);
        }
        reader.readAsText(file);
    }, fsError);
}, fsError);
};
```

◁─┤ **With a new FileReader created and its onloadend event defined, call readAsText to read the file and load it into reader's `result` attribute.**

Table 3.1 reviews the behavior of the File System API method getFile when passed different values of the options object. The object consists of two Boolean fields. The first, create, determines if getFile should try to create a new FileEntry object (create:true) or retrieve an existing FileEntry object (create:false). The second field, exclusive, determines if getFile should check for the existence of a FileEntry object with the same file path name as getFile's filename argument (exclusive:true).

Table 3.1 A list of getFile's responses to various configurations of the options argument[a]

FileEntry state	options object	getFile response
FileEntry found at given file path name	create: false exclusive ignored	FileEntry is returned
	create: true exclusive: true	Error is thrown
FileEntry found at given file path name, but the FileEntry is a directory	create: false exclusive ignored	Error is thrown
No FileEntry found at given file path name	create: false exclusive ignored	Error is thrown
	create: true exclusive ignored	FileEntry created exclusive ignored and returned[b]

a. http://www.w3.org/TR/file-system-api/ .
b. You cannot create a FileEntry if its immediate parent directory doesn't exist.

We know that at this point you may be thinking, "When am I going to be able to test this code?" Just a few more sections, we promise.

STEP 4: VIEW, EDIT, AND DELETE FILES IN THE FILESYSTEM

Core API

The code to view, edit, and delete files in the filesystem is quite straightforward. The three functions in listing 3.13 use two File System API methods: toURL and remove.

- The toURL method retrieves a URL location at which the file resource can be accessed. Using toURL is really convenient for viewing files. It saves you from having to read the contents of the file and display it using JavaScript. Instead, you can invoke a popup window and pass the URL location to it.
- The remove method deletes the file and executes a callback when it's done.

To implement the view, edit, and delete functionality, add the code from the next listing to app.js right after the loadFile function.

Listing 3.13   app.js—Viewing, editing, and deleting files

```
var viewFile = function(file) {
    window.open(file.toURL(), 'SuperEditorPreview', 'width=800,height=600');
};

var editFile = function(file) {
    loadFile(file.name);
    location.href = '#editor/'+file.name;
};

var deleteFile = function(file) {
    var deleteSuccess = function() {
        alert('File '+file.name+' deleted successfully', 'File deleted');
        updateBrowserFilesList();
    }

    if(confirm('File will be deleted. Are you sure?', 'Confirm delete')) {
        file.remove(deleteSuccess, fsError);
    }
};
```

> The toURL method makes it a breeze to view the contents of a file, because you can simply launch it in a new browser window.

> To edit the file, you load the file into the visual and HTML editors and make the File Editor view active by changing the URL hash.

> When the remove function has completed, it will execute the deleteSuccess callback function, which calls the updateBrowserFilesList function to ensure the listing is updated.

If you've been trying to test this functionality as you made your way through the section, you may have found it difficult given that there are no files to load, view, edit, or delete! Next, you'll learn how to create new empty files and how to allow users to import existing files from their computer using a traditional file <input> element.

3.3.4   Creating new files

There are two ways of creating new files in the File System API. The first is to create a new, empty file. The second is to allow the user to import an existing file from their computer using a file <input> element. You'll now implement both of these options, starting with creating empty files.

STEP 5: CREATE NEW, EMPTY FILES IN THE FILESYSTEM
In listing 3.12 you saw how the getFile method returns a FileEntry object for a given filename if it exists:

```
var loadFile = function(name) {
    fileSystem.root.getFile(name, {}, function(fileEntry) {...
```

You can also use getFile to create a new FileEntry, if it doesn't exist, by passing a configuration object to the method. The code in listing 3.14 shows how to do this. The logic for creating a new file will be placed in the event handler, createFormSubmit, and attached to the File Browser create button. CreateFormSubmit will perform basic validation to ensure that the user is creating an HTML file and that the file doesn't already exist, and if all validation passes, it will create the file. Add this code directly after the deleteFile function.

Listing 3.14   app.js—Creating a new empty file

```
var createFile = function(field) {
    var config = {
        create: true,
        exclusive: true
    };
    var createSuccess = function(file) {
        alert('File '+file.name+' created successfully', 'File created');
        updateBrowserFilesList();
        field.value = '';
    };
    fileSystem.root.getFile(field.value, config, createSuccess, fsError);
};

var createFormSubmit = function(e) {
    e.preventDefault();
    var name = document.forms.create.name;
    if(name.value.length > 0) {
        var len = name.value.length;
        if(name.value.substring(len-5, len) === '.html') {
            createFile(name);
        } else {
            alert('Only extension .html allowed', 'Create Error');
        }
    } else {
        alert('You must enter a file name', 'Create Error');
    }
};

document.forms.create.addEventListener('submit', createFormSubmit, false);
```

The config object is passed to the getFile method, telling getFile to create a FileEntry, but only if a FileEntry with that name doesn't exist.

When the getFile method returns successfully, display a confirmation message, reload and display the files list, and clear the form field.

This is the event handler for the File Browser create button. When the create form is submitted, perform validation, and if it passes, call the createFile function.

PROGRESS CHECK: TRY IT OUT!

Finally! You can test the code! You should be able to create empty files using the form on the File Browser view, as illustrated in figure 3.6. When the file has been created, you should be able to view it (it will be just an empty document, of course), edit it (although you won't be able to save changes just yet), and delete it.

The app is finally starting to take shape! Next, let's see how you can allow a user to import existing files on their computer into the application.

STEP 6: IMPORT EXISTING FILES FROM THE USER'S COMPUTER

 Core API   **Importing** files from the user's computer is a little more complicated than creating an empty file. You need to create a FileEntry and then write the contents of the imported file to the FileEntry using the File Writer API.

| File Writer API | 13.0 | N/A | N/A | N/A | N/A |

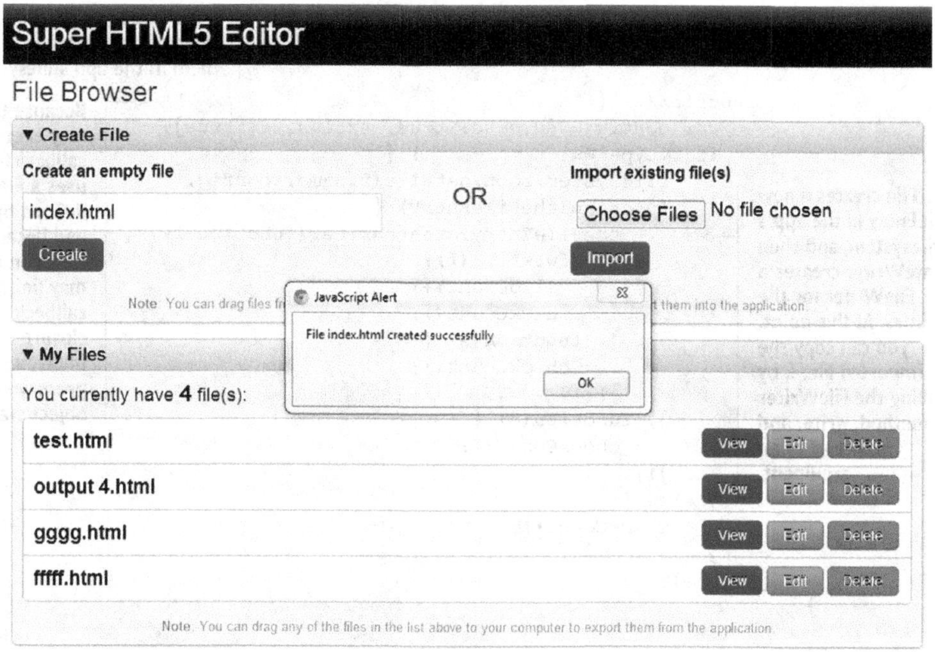

Figure 3.6   The file index.html has been successfully created!

In addition, because you added the `multiple` attribute to the File Browser Import form,

```
...<form name="import">
    <div>
        <h2>Import existing file(s)</h2>
        <input type="file" name="files" multiple accept="text/html">
        <input type="submit" value="Import">
    </div>...
```

you must handle the possibility of importing multiple files at one time. Although implementing this isn't difficult, the validation process becomes more complicated, as you'll see. Copy the following code, and insert it right after the event listener you added to the create form in the previous section.

Listing 3.15   app.js—Importing files from the user's computer

```
var importFiles = function(files) {
    var count = 0, validCount = 0;
    var checkCount = function() {                    ◁─── If all of the files have been
        count++;                                          checked, show how many were
        if(count === files.length) {                      imported and how many failed
            var errorCount = count - validCount;          and update the file list.
            alert(validCount+' file(s) imported. '+errorCount+'
            error(s) encountered.', 'Import complete');
            updateBrowserFilesList();
        }
    };
```

```
        for(var i=0,len=files.length;i<len;i++) {
            var file = files[i];

        (function(f) {
            var config = {create: true, exclusive: true};
            if(f.type == 'text/html') {
                fileSystem.root.getFile(f.name, config,
                function(theFileEntry) {
                    theFileEntry.createWriter(function(fw) {
                        fw.write(f);
                        validCount++;
                        checkCount();
                    }, function(e) {
                        checkCount();
                    });
                }, function(e) {
                    checkCount();
                });
            } else {
                checkCount();
            }
        })(file);
        }
    };

    var importFormSubmit = function(e) {
        e.preventDefault();
        var files = document.forms.import.files.files;
        if(files.length > 0) {
            importFiles(files);
        } else {
            alert('No file(s) selected', 'Import Error');
        }
    };

    document.forms.import.addEventListener('submit', importFormSubmit, false);
```

Loop through the files the user has selected and attempt to create them in the app's filesystem.

Because this for loop may execute a callback function that uses a file object, f, defined by the loop, and because an iteration of the loop may finish before the callback has fired, a closure was implemented to preserve the file object state.

GetFile creates a new FileEntry in the app's filesystem, and then createWriter creates a FileWriter for the FileEntry. At this point, you can copy the imported file, f, by calling the FileWriter method, write, and passing f as an argument.

Read the files from the file's <input> element and call the importFiles function if at least one file has been selected.

At this point you should be able to import existing HTML files from your computer into the application. You should also be able to view, edit (well, you can view in the File Editor view; you won't be able to save changes just yet), and delete files. Figure 3.7 illustrates the dialog window that pops up when you click the Choose Files button.

3.3.5 Saving files using the File Writer API

The final part of the filesystem functionality you need to add to the application is saving files in the File Editor view using the File Writer API. You've already seen the File Writer API in action; in the previous section when importing files from the user's computer, you used the File Writer API to save the contents of existing files into the newly created files in the application's filesystem. Now you'll use a similar approach to implement the Save and Preview buttons in the File Editor view of the application.

STEP 7: IMPLEMENT THE SAVE AND PREVIEW BUTTONS

To implement the Save and Preview buttons, add the code from the next listing just after the event listener you added to the import form in the previous section.

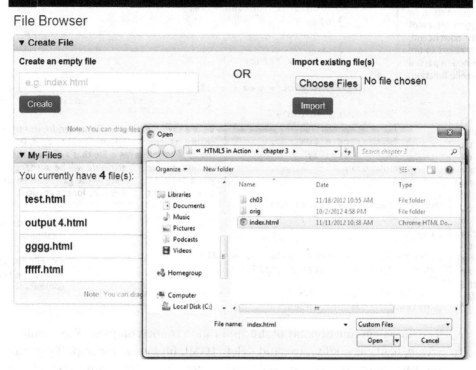

Figure 3.7   After the user clicks the Choose Files button, a dialog window pops up.

Listing 3.16   app.js—Saving files using the File Writer API

```
var saveFile = function(callback) {
    var currentView = function() {
        if(htmlView.style.display === 'block') {
            return 'html';
        } else {
            return 'editor';
        }
    }

    var content;

    if(currentView() === 'editor') {
        var x = new XMLSerializer();
        content = x.serializeToString(visualEditorDoc);
    } else {
        content = htmlEditor.value;
    }

    currentFile.createWriter(function(fw) {
        fw.onwriteend = function(e) {
```

Check if the currently displayed view is the visual or HTML editor.

Get the contents of the relevant editor.

When the file writer, fw, finishes resetting the file's length to zero, fw triggers the onwriteend event handler. This event handler redefines fw's onwriteend event handler and then saves the file by calling write.

When file writer, fw, has finished writing content to the currentfile, fw triggers the event handler for onwriteend. Callback refers to the callback function passed to the saveFile function.

Use the endings parameter to specify what type of end-of-line marker should be used. A value of native instructs a Blob constructor to use an end-of-line marker native to the browser's underlying OS.

```
    fw.onwriteend = function(e) {
        if(typeof callback === 'function') {
            callback(currentFile);
        } else {
            alert('File saved successfully', 'File saved');
        }
        isDirty = false;
    };
        var blob = new Blob([content],
                    {text: 'text/html', endings:'native'});
        fw.write(blob);
    };
    fw.onerror = fsError;
    fw.truncate(0);
  }, fsError);
};

var previewFile = function() {
    saveFile(viewFile);
};

var saveBtn = document.getElementById('file_save');
var previewBtn = document.getElementById('file_preview');

saveBtn.addEventListener('click', saveFile, false);
previewBtn.addEventListener('click', previewFile, false);
```

Use a Blob to construct a blob object from content, a string-based representation of the editor's content.

Before saving data with file writer, fw, use truncate(0) to ensure its length attribute is set to zero. Otherwise, when the application saves a file that's shorter than its previous version, the length attribute will be unchanged. As a result, you'd see old text filling in the gap between the new shorter file and its previous longer version.

SaveFile has been passed a callback function, viewFile. It's called when saveFile has finished writing the editor contents to currentFile.

The filesystem functionality of the application is now complete. You should be able to create, load, view, edit, save, and delete HTML files using the app. If you want to take the application further, you could easily extend it so that it supports multiple directories, allows editing of additional file types (CSS and JavaScript support would be nice), and provides syntax highlighting of the HTML markup. There are a plethora of opportunities for expansion.

We'll wrap up this chapter in the next section by adding a jazzy extra—drag-and-drop support.

3.4   Adding drag-and-drop interactivity

Drag-and-drop interactions are a popular feature in computer applications. For example, consider the GUIs of current OSes. They allow you to move files, documents, and applications around by dragging them from one location and dropping them to another. In Mac OS X, if you have an external hard drive plugged into your computer, you can eject it by dragging it to the trash icon in the dock.

In recent years, web applications have started to provide drag-and-drop support. Common examples are copying/moving items from one list to another; rearranging the order of a list; moving regions of the page around for a customized experience; and moving images, files, or documents to virtual directories in content management systems. Up until now, developers had to rely on using JavaScript frameworks to provide web apps with decent drag-and-drop features. In HTML5, however, a full Drag and Drop API has been specified to supplant these JavaScript frameworks.

Drag and Drop API	4.0	3.5	5.5	12.0	3.1

In this section, you'll use the Drag and Drop API to enhance the Super HTML5 Editor application by

- Enabling users to import files into the application by dragging them in from their computer
- Allowing users to export files from the application by dragging them to their computer

3.4.1 Dragging files into an application for import

Core API

To allow users to drag files into the application, you need to create a target zone or drop zone where the user can drag the files and expect them to be imported. If you've already loaded the application in your browser, you'll probably have noticed a note at the bottom of the Create File zone in the File Browser view. The note informs users to import files by dropping them anywhere in this zone. Let's stay true to our word and provide this functionality.

To enable the Create File zone, you need to implement two event handlers for the zone: one for the `drop` event and another for the `dragover` event. The `drop` event handler will enable the application to import files that are dropped into the Create File zone, and the `dragover` event handler will signal a pending copy operation to the app. The app will respond to the signal by adding a copy decal to the file icon(s) being dragged into the Create File zone.

Add the code in the following listing right after the line `previewBtn.addEvent-Listener('click', previewFile, false)`.

Listing 3.17 app.js—Allowing users to import files by dropping them in the application

Designate the drop zone for files as the element with the ID filedrop.

```
var fileDropZone = document.getElementById('filedrop');

var importByDrop = function(e) {

    e.stopPropagation();
    e.preventDefault();

    var files = e.dataTransfer.files;

    if(files.length > 0) {
        importFiles(files);
    }
};
```

When files are dropped into the browser window, the default browser behavior is to load the files and navigate away from the app, so you need to cancel this default behavior. First, invoke stopPropagation to prevent the drop event from bubbling up to any ancestor elements of fileDropZone. Second, invoke preventDefault to stop the browser from calling the default event handler attached to fileDropZone.

If the user is dragging files, these will reside in the dataTransfer object. To load them into the app, pass them to the importFiles function (defined in listing 3.15).

```
var importDragOver = function(e) {
    e.preventDefault();
    e.dataTransfer.effectAllowed = 'copy';  ◄─┐

    e.dataTransfer.dropEffect = 'copy';
    return false;
};
```

> **Because you want the imported file(s) to be copied when they're dropped into the zone, set the dragover event properties, effectAllowed and dropEffect, to copy. When the user drags the file over the drop zone, the file image(s) will change to indicate a pending copy operation.**

```
fileDropZone.addEventListener('drop', importByDrop, false);
fileDropZone.addEventListener('dragover', importDragOver, false);
```

TRY IT OUT!

With this code added to your app, try it out by dragging an HTML file from your computer into the designated drop zone. If a file with the same name doesn't exist, it should be successfully imported into the filesystem, just as if you had manually selected the file using the regular file <input> dialog box. You can even drag multiple files into the application at a time. Next, you'll wrap things up by enabling users to export files by dragging them out of the application.

3.4.2   *Dragging files out of an application for export*

Some of the groundwork for your export drag-and-drop functionality has already been set. In listing 3.10 in the displayBrowserFileList function, you added code that created a new list item for each of the files in the filesystem. If you look at this code, you'll notice that the <li> element you constructed has an attribute, draggable, set to true:

```
...
files.forEach(function(file, i) {
    var li = '<li id="li_'+i+'" draggable="true">'+file.name
        + '<div><button id="view_'+i+'">View</button>'
        + '<button class="green" id="edit_'+i+'">Edit</button>'
        + '<button class="red" id="del_'+i+'">Delete</button>'
        + '</div></li>';
    ...
```

In addition, you'll see that a listener was added to the dragstart event of this item:

```
...
var doDrag = function(e) { dragFile(file, e); }
...
listItem.addEventListener('dragstart', doDrag, false);...
```

Believe it or not, all you need to do to implement the export functionality is to define the dragFile function. One last time, add the code in the next listing to app.js, right after the line fileDropZone.addEventListener('dragover', importDragOver, false).

Listing 3.18   app.js—Allowing users to export files by dragging them out of the app

```
var dragFile = function(file, e) {
    e.dataTransfer.effectAllowed = 'copy';
    e.dataTransfer.dropEffect = 'copy';
```

```
e.dataTransfer.setData('DownloadURL', 'application/octet-
    stream:'+file.name+':'+file.toURL());
};
```

When the user starts dragging a draggable item in the app, the setData method of the dataTransfer object can be used to define what data should be dropped.

If you were hoping for more code than that to implement the export functionality, you're probably disappointed—that really is all you need. The `toURL` method that was used previously in the `viewFile` method is put to use again, this time to construct a downloadable object (`DownloadURL`) that's saved to the user's computer. Be sure to give it a try; drag one of the files out of your application and drop it on your computer's desktop.

At long last the application is complete. At this point you should have a fully functional web-based HTML editor that allows you to import and export files using drag and drop.

3.5 Summary

Not long ago the idea that you could build a full client-side WYSIWYG HTML editor application featuring the ability to create, edit, save, and drag/drop files was nothing more than a daydream for web application developers. In HTML5 this is all now a reality, and as browser support steadily improves, we're getting closer to a situation where users will come to expect features like these to be a part of every web application. Progressive functionality like this will ensure that web applications can continue to evolve and become more innovative, while maintaining the web's tradition of openness and preference for standards-driven development.

Although we've been looking at HTML5 features for supporting rich UI applications, HTML5 can also support the development of social and collaborative applications. In the next chapter, you'll look at creating chat message and project planner applications. These apps will teach you about the many new messaging features in HTML5, including cross-domain messaging, WebSockets, and server-sent events (SSE).

Chapter 4 at a glance

Topic	Description, methods, and so on	Page
Server-sent events	Creating events in the browser from the server:	
	■ Creating an `EventSource()`	111
	■ Listening to server events with `addEventListener()`	111
WebSockets	Two-way, event-driven communication:	
	■ Writing applications using `WebSockets`	116
	■ Messaging on the client side	125
Cross-document messaging	Communication between scripts in different windows:	
	■ Sending messages with `postMessage()`	126
	■ Receiving messages with `onmessage()`	126

Core API

Look for this icon ➡ throughout the chapter to quickly locate the topics outlined in this table.

Messaging: communicating to and from scripts in HTML5 4

This chapter covers

- Server-sent events and event-driven communications from the server
- WebSockets for bidirectional, event-driven communication
- Client-side messaging between pages from different domains

In the last decade, the web has moved from communication based on uploading static content, similar to the traditional print publishing model, to a real-time communication system where tweets and friendings are instantly announced to hundreds of followers. We've all become so used to dynamically updating web pages that we don't realize most of this is built as a series of hacks on top of HTML4 and HTTP 1.0/1.1. HTML5 cleans up these hacks by providing well-defined APIs for messaging—between the browser and web servers and between different iframes or other objects loaded in the browser.

Because messaging is a complex subject, this will be a complex chapter. You're going to do a lot and learn a lot. Specifically, you're going to

- Learn how to use server-sent events (SSE). This new client-server API allows communication from the server without a specific client request.
- Learn how to use WebSockets.
- Dabble in one of the new event-driven, server-side technologies: Node.js.
- Learn about cross-document messaging, an API for communication between pages and scripts already loaded in the browser.

Why build this chapter's chat and planning board applications?
- You'll build a chat application based on a traditional LAMP/WIMP (Linux, Apache, MySQL, PHP/Windows, IIS, MySQL, PHP) server stack to learn about SSE.
- You'll build a collaborative agile planning board with WebSockets and Node.js.

After you build those two applications, we'll show you how to integrate them on the client using cross-document messaging.

If you need background on the principles of computer networking, take a side trip through appendix D. It'll help you understand the performance trade-offs to using the new HTML5 client-server APIs, as well as define terms like *protocol, network stack, latency, throughput, polling,* and *event-driven.* The appendix will also give you the background to understand why and when to use the new approaches we introduce in this chapter, such as server-sent events, which we cover in the next section.

4.1   *Server-sent events (SSE)*

Server-sent events (SSE) allow the web server to create an event in the browser. The event can contain raw data or it can be a notification or a ping. The API for SSE in the browser is the event listener in JavaScript, created using the same `addEventListener()` method you'd use for any other event listener. The only difference is that instead of adding a listener to the `document` object or an element, you add it to an instance of the new `WebSocket` object. Why is this any better than requesting new data with AJAX? SSE offers two main advantages:

- The server drives communication.
- There's less overhead of repeatedly creating a connection and adding headers.

In this section you'll learn how to use SSE as you build a simple chat application. As the section winds down, you'll also learn when it's good to use SSE and when another tool might be better.

4.1.1   *A simple SSE chat application*

Server-sent events are delivered to the browser in the form of a special file the browser requests by creating an `EventSource` object. Instead of a regular HTML file or image, the browser requests an event stream. Normally, the server attempts to deliver any file as fast as possible, but with the event stream the file is purposely delivered slowly. The browser stays connected to the server for as long as the file takes to be delivered, and the server can add data to the file at any time. This approach is identical to that used by the forever frame technique (defined in appendix D) except that instead of developers having to decide for themselves how to format the response, the format is laid down in the HTML5 standard. In return for following SSE conventions, you use the familiar addEventListener() approach you'd use for any other events.

Server-sent events	9	6	N/A	11	5

As we discuss how to build an SSE chat application, we'll focus on the front-end code, because we're not trying to teach PHP or MySQL. That said, the easiest way forward is to download the server files, listed in the "Chat application prerequisites" sidebar.

Chat application prerequisites

You'll need the following programs to make the application in this section work:

- *A web server that can host PHP*—We used Apache (http://apache.org/) for the example, but IIS on Windows also should work.
- *PHP*—Download from http://php.net/ with PDO support.
- *MySQL*—Download from http://dev.mysql.com/.
- *jQuery*—Download from http://jquery.com/ (included in code download).

The other files you need are available in the code download section of our book's website. If you don't want to do the setup yourself, you can also get all the needed components as part of most inexpensive web-hosting packages.

Figure 4.1 shows a screenshot of the finished application.

As you can see, the user types a message into the text input and hits Enter or the Chat button, and his words of wisdom are immediately distributed to everyone else online. The chat shown in figure 4.1 is, of course, entirely manufactured. Rest assured; the authors are not that corny in real life.

As you might guess from the name, server-*sent* events, the server sends events to the browser; it can't receive information via SSE. Communication from the browser back to the server, new chat messages entered by the

Figure 4.1 The simple chat application in action

Figure 4.2   The conceptual flow of chat messages in this section's application. Messages will be sent back to the server using standard AJAX techniques, but chat messages will be received from the server through server-sent events.

user, will use traditional AJAX methods. Figure 4.2 illustrates the flow of chat messages in the application.

The file structure you'll create, and which is provided in the companion source code for this book, is illustrated in figure 4.3.

For everything to work, these files will need to be located in a directory where your web server can find them. For Apache, this will likely be under /var/www/html, and for IIS, this will be C:\Inetpub\WWWRoot; check the details in the documentation for your OS and web server. Usually these folders have restricted access, so either create and edit the files in your home directory and copy them across or run your editor with appropriate permissions. Through the following steps we'll refer to this directory as the *working directory*.

We'll walk you through the build in eight steps:

- Step 1: Create a database in which to store chat messages.
- Step 2: Create a chat form.
- Step 3: Create a login form.
- Step 4: Implement a login process.
- Step 5: Send new chat messages to the server with AJAX.
- Step 6: Store new chat messages in the database.
- Step 7: Build an SSE stream at the server.
- Step 8: Connect to an SSE stream in the browser.

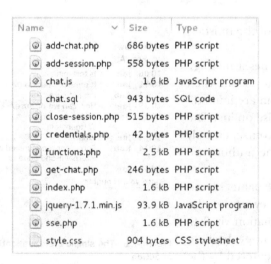

Name	Size	Type
add-chat.php	686 bytes	PHP script
add-session.php	558 bytes	PHP script
chat.js	1.6 kB	JavaScript program
chat.sql	943 bytes	SQL code
close-session.php	515 bytes	PHP script
credentials.php	42 bytes	PHP script
functions.php	2.5 kB	PHP script
get-chat.php	246 bytes	PHP script
index.php	1.6 kB	PHP script
jquery-1.7.1.min.js	93.9 kB	JavaScript program
sse.php	1.6 kB	PHP script
style.css	904 bytes	CSS stylesheet

Figure 4.3   The file layout for the chat application

SSE on older browsers

Server-sent events are a rationalized version of the forever-frame hack discussed in appendix D. The required server-side code is similar, so the most obvious approach for fallback in older browsers is to use the forever frame if SSE isn't available. An alternative is to use one of the prebuilt libraries, which implement a fallback transparently. One such library is Remy Sharp's EventSource.js polyfill: https://github.com/remy/polyfills/blob/master/EventSource.js.

STEP 1: CREATE A DATABASE IN WHICH TO STORE CHAT MESSAGES

Use your MySQL administration tool to create a database called ssechat (see appendix C). Included in the code download is a chat.sql file, which, when run, will create two tables in the database called sessions, to record who is logged in, and log, to record a log of the chat messages. Get the file credentials.php from the source code download and edit it to contain your database connection details. The example expects $user, $pass, and $db to define strings for the username, password, and connection string, respectively. The $db variable will look something like "mysql:host=local-host;dbname=ssechat".

STEP 2: CREATE A CHAT FORM

Create the index.php page and the markup that users will see. The markup will contain two forms that will be visible or not, depending on the status of the user. In this step you'll create the list of chat messages and a form for adding new ones; in the next step you'll create a form for logging in. The following listing shows the PHP source for the form shown in figure 4.1. It's a simple HTML template that makes a couple of function calls to render the main content, and it contains a form to allow new chat messages to be added.

Listing 4.1 index.php body content

```html
<body>
    <strong>Online now:</strong>
    <ul class="chatusers">
        <?php
        print_user_list($dbh);
        ?>
    </ul>
    <div class="chatwindow">
    <ul class="chatlog">
        <?php
        print_chat_log($dbh);
        ?>
    </ul>
    </div>
    <form id="chat" class="chatform" method="post"
        action="add-chat.php">
        <label for="message">Share your thoughts:</label>
        <input name="message" id="message" maxlength="512" autofocus>
```

The print_user_list function outputs an unordered list (the HTML element) of currently logged-on users.

The print_chat_log function outputs an unordered list of chat messages.

The chatform has an action defined that allows it to work, in a limited sense, without JavaScript enabled, but JavaScript will be used to override the default action in listing 4.6.

```
            <input type="submit" value="Chat">
        </form>
    </body>
</body>
```

You'll also need to set up basic links in the <head> section of index.php. The required code is shown in the next listing.

Listing 4.2 index.php head

```php
<?php
session_start();                              ◄──  This enables the standard
include_once "credentials.php";                    PHP session tracking.
include_once "functions.php";                 ◄──┐ Common variables and functions
try {                                            └ are included from separate files.
    $dbh = new PDO($db, $user, $pass);        ◄──┐
} catch (PDOException $e) {                        You'll be using PHP Data
    print "Error!: " . $e->getMessage(). "<br/>";  Objects (PDO) to connect
    die();                                         to the database.
}
?><!DOCTYPE html>
<html>                                                     Make the PHP
<head>                                                     session ID
    <meta charset="utf-8">                                 easily available
    <title>SSE Chat</title>                                to JavaScript
    <link href="style.css" rel="stylesheet">               (saves reading
    <script src="jquery-1.7.1.min.js"></script>            the cookie).
    <script>var uid='<?php print session_id(); ?>';</script>  ◄──┘
    <script src="chat.js"></script>           ◄──┐
</head>                                            chat.js is the file where you'll later
                                                   implement the client-side code for SSE.
```

STEP 3: CREATE A LOGIN FORM

In order to track which user is which, you need to have them log in, which means recording their chat handle along with their PHP session ID. As mentioned in step 2, rather than create a separate page for this, you're going to add another form into the index.php file, then use conditional statements to turn the visibility of the form on and off. You're not going to do anything fancy—the index.php page with the login form enabled is shown in figure 4.4.

Enter your handle:

        Join

Figure 4.4 A simple login page for the chat application

As we just discussed, you don't need to create a separate PHP file for displaying the previous form—instead, you'll add conditional functionality to your existing index.php page. The following listing contains the code that determines whether to show the login form or the chat form. It should go immediately after the <body> tag in listing 4.1.

Listing 4.3 Check to see if the user is logged on

```php
<?php
try {
    $checkOnline = $dbh->prepare(
        'SELECT * FROM sessions WHERE session_id = :sid');
    $checkOnline->execute(array(':sid' => session_id()));
    $rows = $checkOnline->fetchAll();
} catch (PDOException $e) {
    print "Error!: " . $e->getMessage(). "<br/>";
    die();
}
if (count($rows) > 0) {
?>
```

The rest of the code from listing 4.1, starting at <strong>, will continue here.

Look up all the sessions in the database with a session_id equal to the current session_id().

If one is found, assume the user is logged in. (This is intended to be the simplest code that will work—it's not best practice, secure PHP.)

Now that you've added a conditional statement before the code for the chat form, you have to close the first block of the condition, then add the code for the login form inside an else block after the chat page code. The code for the login form is shown in the next listing. It should be placed immediately before the closing </body> tag in index.php.

Listing 4.4 Display a login form

```php
<?php
} else {
?>
<form id="login" class="chatlogin"
  method="post" action="add-session.php">
    <label for="handle">Enter your handle:</label>
    <input name="handle" id="handle" maxlength="127" autofocus>
    <input type="submit" value="Join">
</form>
<?php
}
?>
```

This else statement corresponds to the if at the end of listing 4.3.

The add-session.php file will deal with inserting the user into the database.

TRY IT OUT

You should now be able to see the login form by browsing to the index.php file on your local server. It won't do anything yet, because you haven't created a PHP file to process the logins. In order to get users logged in, you'll need a working add-session.php file.

STEP 4: IMPLEMENT A LOGIN PROCESS

The add-session.php file is shown next. Put this file in the same directory as index.php, as per the file layout in figure 4.3.

Listing 4.5 The add-session.php file

```php
<?php
session_start();
include_once "credentials.php";
try {
    $dbh = new PDO($db, $user, $pass);
    $preparedStatement = $dbh->prepare(
```

```
          'INSERT INTO `sessions`(`session_id`, `handle`, `connected`)
          VALUES (:sid,:handle,NOW())');
      $preparedStatement->execute(
          array(':sid' => session_id(), ':handle' => $_POST["handle"] ));
      $rows = $preparedStatement->fetchAll();
      $dbh = null;
  } catch (PDOException $e) {
      print "Error!: " . $e->getMessage(). "<br/>";
      die();
  }
  header("Location: index.php");
  ?>
```

> `$preparedStatement->execute(` — You're not doing anything more complex than recording the submitted handle in the database with the session_id().

> `header("Location: index.php");` — Redirect to index.php when finished.

Now that you have the user's basic details sorted out, it's time to implement the application functionality.

STEP 5: SEND NEW CHAT MESSAGES TO THE SERVER WITH AJAX

You accomplish the transport of data back to the server with traditional AJAX techniques. The next listing shows the code for processing the chat form submit—nothing surprising for experienced front-end developers. Create a file chat.js in your working directory to contain all of your JavaScript code; as per figure 4.3 you can create it in the same directory as index.php and put the code from the following listing in it.

Listing 4.6   Add a chat message (client code)

```
$(document).ready(
    function() {
        var chatlog = $('.chatlog');
        if (chatlog.length > 0) {
            var chatformCallback = function() {
                chatform.find('input')[0].value = '';
            }
            chatform.bind('submit', function() {
                var ajax_params = {
                    url: 'add-chat.php',
                    type: 'POST',
                    data: chatform.serialize(),
                    success: chatformCallback,
                    error: function () {
                        window.alert('An error occurred');
                    }
                };
                $.ajax(ajax_params);
                return false;
            })
```

> `function() {` — You'll close the function and the condition in listing 4.9.

> `var chatformCallback = function() {` — A simple function to clear the chat input after the message has been successfully sent to the server.

> `url: 'add-chat.php',` — The add-chat.php takes the message and adds it to the database, along with some information from the session; check the download files for more details.

> `return false;` — Because the form is submitted by AJAX, you don't want the page to reload.

STEP 6: STORE NEW CHAT MESSAGES IN THE DATABASE

On the server you'll need a script to insert the chat messages in the database as they're created. The next listing shows the source code for add-chat.php, which grabs the message from a POST request and stores it with the appropriate details.

Listing 4.7 Add a chat message (server code)

```php
<?php
session_start();
include_once "credentials.php";
$dbh = new PDO($db, $user, $pass);
$preparedStatement = $dbh->prepare('
    INSERT INTO `log`(`session_id`,`handle`, `message`, `timestamp`)
    VALUES (
      :sid,
      (SELECT `handle` FROM `sessions` WHERE `session_id` = :sid),
      :message,NOW()
    )');
$preparedStatement->execute(
    array(':sid' => session_id(),
          ':message' => $_POST["message"] ));
$rows = $preparedStatement->fetchAll();
$dbh = null;
session_write_close();
header("HTTP/1.1 200 OK");
echo "OK";
ob_flush();
flush();
die();
?>
```

The database details are stored in a separate file.

The message table is simple: an ID, a user handle, and a time (the user handle is being stored for convenience).

All database access in this example is using PHP's PDO database library—this should be part of your standard PHP install.

You've created a simple interface and a way to add new chat messages—now at last you're ready to start using SSE. What you need next is a way to get the chat messages of other users to appear in your browser as they're entered by your fellow chatters. This is the sort of task SSE is designed for.

STEP 7: BUILD AN SSE STREAM AT THE SERVER

The following snippet shows an excerpt from an SSE event stream like the one you're about to create. It's all plain text and should be served with the MIME type text/event-stream (typically, because you're generating the event stream dynamically, you'll set the MIME type in your server-side code). A sample of the event stream you'll be generating is shown here:

On the following line, the data keyword gives the text to be associated with the event.

```
event: useradded
data: Rob

event: message
data: <time datetime="2011-10-24 10:13:17">10:13</time>
 <b>Joe</b> <span>How can we be sure?</span>

event: message
data: <time datetime="2011-10-24 10:13:40">10:13</time>
 <b>Rob</b> <span>Well, according to Wittgenstein...</span>
```

An event is defined by the keyword event, followed by a colon, followed by the name of the event.

Any string can be used to define the event name, but note that the events captured by any script in the browser will have the same name as the events being emitted.

The data can also be any string; the script in the browser is responsible for interpreting it correctly.

The event stream itself is similar to the forever-frame approach (see appendix D). A connection is opened and kept open, and the chat.js script periodically adds content to it. Each time new content arrives at the browser, it's converted into the simple event-driven JavaScript programming model with which we're all familiar.

The code on the server is straightforward. Create a file sse.php to generate the event stream in the same directory as index.php and add the same `session_start()`, `include_once`, and PDO creation code that starts off index.php. You don't need to add a `!DOCTYPE` declaration because you're not generating an HTML page. Then add code to loop, constantly looking for new messages. If you already have a forever-frame script, it's likely you can easily adapt it. The code for sse.php is shown in the following listing.

Listing 4.8   sse.php key code loop

```php
<?php
session_start();
include_once "credentials.php";
include_once "functions.php";
try {
    $dbh = new PDO($db, $user, $pass);
} catch (PDOException $e) {
    print "Error!: " . $e->getMessage(). "<br/>";
    die();
}
header('Content-Type: text/event-stream');
header('Cache-Control: no-cache');
$uid = $_REQUEST["uid"];
$lastUpdate = time();
$startedAt = time();
session_write_close();
var $lastupdate = now();
while (is_logged_on($dbh, $uid)) {
    $getChat = $dbh->prepare('SELECT `timestamp`,`handle`, `message`
    FROM `log`
    WHERE `timestamp` >= :lastupdate
    ORDER BY `timestamp`');
    $getChat->execute(
     array(':lastupdate' => strftime("%Y-%m-%d %H:%M:%S", $lastUpdate))
    );
    $rows = $getChat->fetchAll();
    foreach($rows as $row) {
        echo "event: message\n";
        echo "data: <time datetime=\"".$row['timestamp']."\">";
        echo strftime("%H:%M",strtotime($row['timestamp']));
        echo "</time> <b>".$row['handle']."</b> <span>";
        echo $row['message']."</span>\n\n";
        ob_flush();
        flush();
    }
    $lastUpdate = time();
    sleep(2);
}
?>
```

A quirk of PHP is that the session is single-threaded; if you leave it open in this script, it'll block any other pages using it.

Set the correct content-type.

Ensure the stream isn't cached.

Loop here until the user logs out. Nearly all web server configurations limit execution time to between 30 and 90 seconds to allow the script to time out, but the browser will automatically reconnect.

In a real application, you'd factor this inline SQL into a function. This example tries to keep all the logic visible.

In a real application you'd invoke some rendering logic here that's shared among your application files.

Fetch all chat messages added to the database since the last update; to keep things simple you'll worry about only the message event for now.

Send the data as HTML. You could also send it as a JSON-encoded object.

Stores the last time you updated, and sleeps for two seconds. This is necessary in this example because the MySQL timestamp column is only accurate to the closest second. Implementing a millisecond-accurate time field in MySQL is possible but has been avoided here to keep the code simple.

Like the forever frame, you gain a low overhead of passing data from the server to the client. Once the connection is open, the only data that needs to be transferred is that which is pertinent to the application. No headers need to be sent with each update.

STEP 8: CONNECT TO AN SSE STREAM IN THE BROWSER

Core API

Core API

To retrieve chat messages, you'll connect your index.php page to the event stream using an EventSource object. The next listing shows the relevant JavaScript. You should add it to the chat.js you created in step 5. In this listing the EventSource is established and event listeners are added. The annotations explain the key points.

Listing 4.9 Client code for connecting to an event stream

An EventSource is declared by linking to the script on the server that provides the event stream; the uid is a value passed via the host page to link users to their PHP session on the server side.

```
var evtSource = new EventSource("sse.php?uid=" + uid);

evtSource.addEventListener("message", function(e) {
    var el = document.createElement("li");
    el.innerHTML = e.data;
    chatlog.appendChild(el);
})
evtSource.addEventListener("useradded", function(e) {
    var el = document.createElement("li");
    el.innerHTML = e.data;
    chatusers.appendChild(el);
})
}
}
)
```

Event listeners can be added to the EventSource using normal DOM methods.

This closes the function and conditional opened in listing 4.6.

What the events will be called is determined in the server script; "message" and "useradded" aren't regular DOM events but the ones defined in the server-side code (see listing 4.8).

TRY IT OUT!

Everything is now in place for you to try the application. If you haven't already, copy all the files to a location where your web server can access them (as discussed earlier in this chapter, this is likely to be either /var/www/html or C:\Inetpub\WWWRoot) and have a go. You can use a couple of different browsers to simulate multiple users and try talking to yourself.

Controlling the default server timeout

There's one thing to bear in mind if you're using PHP on Apache, as in this example: The default script timeout is 30 seconds. This means that after 30 seconds the script on the server will be terminated and the connection will be dropped.

This isn't a problem on the client side, because it should automatically reconnect to the event source. By default, a reconnection will be attempted every 3 seconds, but it's also possible to control this from the event stream by emitting a retry directive:

```
retry: 10000
```

The number is a time in milliseconds. This should force the browser to wait 10 seconds before attempting a reconnect. Controlling the retry time would be useful if you knew the server was going to be unavailable or under high load for a short time.

4.1.2 When to use SSE

Before we move on to WebSockets, let's step back to consider why it was worth bothering with SSE. After all, server-sent events do have some obvious disadvantages:

- You can only communicate from the server to the client.
- SSE offers little advantage over long-polling or forever frame.

If your application implemented one of the older hacks, it would probably not be worth updating just to take advantage of an event-driven interface consistent with other HTML5 APIs. SSE won't dramatically lower the communication overhead compared to these hacks. If you're starting from scratch, SSE does have advantages over WebSockets (which we'll talk about in the next section):

- It's an extremely simple wire protocol.
- It's easy to implement on cheap hosting.

If you're working on a hobby project, SSE will probably be a good fit for you. But if you're working on high-load, web-scale startups where you're constantly tweaking the infrastructure, you'll want to look closely at WebSockets, the pièce de résistance of the HTML5 communication protocols.

In the next section you'll use Node.js web server (also commonly referred to as just plain *Node*) to write an application using WebSockets. Node is well suited to SSE and WebSockets because it's designed from the ground up to do event-driven communication (frequent, small, but irregular message sending; see appendix D). If you're used to web servers like Apache or IIS, it works differently than you might expect. It's therefore worth spending time becoming familiar with the basics.

4.2 Using WebSockets to build a real-time messaging web app

WebSockets allow bare-bones networking between clients and servers with far less overhead than the previously more common approach of tunneling other protocols through HTTP. With WebSockets it's possible to package your data using the appropriate protocol, XMPP (Extensible Messaging and Presence Protocol) for chat, for example, while also benefiting from the strengths of HTTP.

The WebSockets Protocol, which describes what browser vendors and servers must implement behind the scenes, is used at the network layer to establish and maintain socket connections and pass data through them. The WebSockets API describes the interface that needs to be available in the DOM so that WebSockets can be used from JavaScript. Appendix D more fully describes the protocol and API, so if you'd like more information before you build the next piece of this chapter's sample application—an agile planning board—detour to section D.6, "Understanding the WebSockets Protocol," now.

When you return, we'll give you an overview of the application you're going to build and help you get your prerequisites in order, have you create and test a WebSocket with Node.js, and build the planner application.

4.2.1 Application overview and prerequisites

In section 4.1 you built a simple chat system based on SSE. In this section you'll use WebSockets and Node.js to build an agile planning board which is intended to be a simple way to group tasks according to their status so that progress on the overall project can be discerned at a glance. Tasks, originally represented by sticky notes on a notice board (figure 4.5), are slotted into three or more simple categories such as to do, in progress, and done.

Agile methodologies are a particularly attractive target for tools based on messaging because agile is intended to be collaborative rather than dictatorial. So it's expected

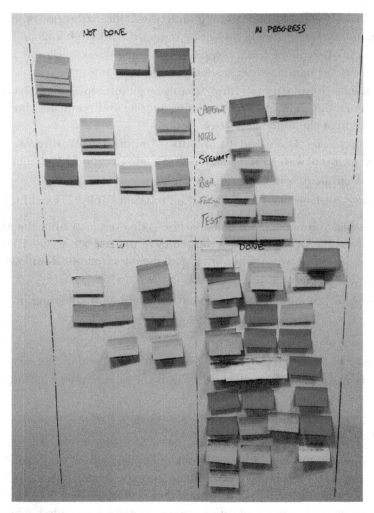

Figure 4.5   A real-life agile planning board at the TotalMobile offices in Belfast. The sticky notes describe tasks to be done, and the four quadrants are labeled, from top-left clockwise, NOT DONE, IN PROGRESS, DONE, and REVIEW. In this section you'll develop an electronic version of this board.

that you might have a bunch of people online trying to update the same plan at the same time.

BEFORE YOU PROCEED: PREREQUISITES

Before you begin this portion of the application, you'll need certain prerequisites to make the application in this section work. Specifically, you'll need the following:

- *The chat app*—See section 4.1.
- *Node.js*—Download from http://nodejs.org/; see appendix E for install instructions.
- You'll also need to install four Node modules (see appendix E for details of how to install):
  - *Director*—Download from https://github.com/flatiron/director or install with NPM; for handling routing (assigning requested URLs to handlers).
  - *Session.js*—Download from https://github.com/Marak/session.js or install with NPM; for handling user sessions.
  - *Mustache*—Download from http://mustache.github.com/ or install with NPM; for generating HTML from combining objects and templates, both within Node and in client-side JavaScript.
  - *WebSocket-Node*—Download from https://github.com/Worlize/WebSocket-Node or install with NPM; for extending Node to support WebSockets.
- *jQuery*—Download from http://jquery.com/.
- *EventEmitter.js*—Download from https://github.com/Wolfy87/EventEmitter.

The rest of the files you need are available in the code download from the Manning .com website; we won't list them here because they're not relevant to the WebSockets logic. You'll need to either create your own or grab the ones from the download.

AN OVERVIEW OF THE BUILDING PROCESS

After you load your prerequisites and test your installation, the building process will flow like this:

1 Create a template page.
2 Build planner logic that can be used both in the client and on the server.
3 Create browser event listeners to deal with incoming WebSocket events and update the plan.
4 Create server logic to listen to incoming messages, update the plan, and send updates to other clients.

The finished application (figure 4.6) won't look quite like the real-life example, but it will feature of the main components. To simulate the experience of a bunch of people all standing around a real notice board, sipping their coffee, and arguing about where to put particular tasks, the chat application from section 4.1 is provided in an iframe. All participants will still have to provide their own coffee.

The final file layout you'll create during the build is shown in figure 4.7.

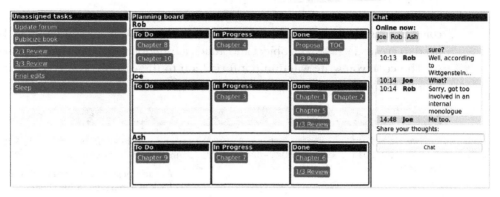

Figure 4.6 The finished planning application

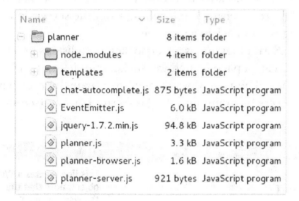

Figure 4.7 Planner application file layout

With prerequisites installed, but before you build the planner application, let's make sure that WebSockets are working for you. In the next section you'll write a quick test page to confirm that WebSockets are working correctly in Node and in the browser, before it all is obscured by your application logic.

4.2.2 Creating a WebSocket with Node.js

Rather than deal with all the low-level, bit-by-bit data manipulation required by the WebSockets Protocol, you'll be using the WebSocket-Node module. It allows you to concentrate on the APIs involved rather than the mundane details of packing bits together in the correct format—details described for you in appendix C. In this section you'll create two files:

- A JavaScript file to be run with Node.js
- An HTML page, which will be sent to the browser

WebSocket API 3 6 10 11 5

The onmessage event is used in every other messaging API in HTML5, so it should come as no surprise to you that it gets used in WebSockets, too. For WebSockets you need to create a WebSocket object and attach a function to the message event listener.

The code you write will dump information to the console as it receives it; sample console output is shown in the following listing.

Listing 4.10   Server output for a simple WebSocket test

```
Sun Nov 27 2011 23:59:13 GMT-0800 (PST) Server is listening on port 8080
Sun Nov 27 2011 23:59:24 GMT-0800 (PST) Connection accepted.
Received Message: My Message           ◁─┐  As each message is received, it's reflected
                                            back in a message to the client.
```

Figure 4.8 shows the corresponding output in the browser developer console. The browser requests the page; then it upgrades the connection to a WebSocket. It sends the message "My Message" before receiving the response from the server; in this case the same "My Message" string is sent back as a message.

 Core API

The next listing shows JavaScript that opens a WebSocket, then listens for messages from the server. You should create a page named websocket-sample.html and include this listing in a <script> block. The page doesn't need to do anything or have any content; you'll determine success by examining the JavaScript console (see step C in the listing).

Listing 4.11   A simple JavaScript WebSockets client

The familiar onmessage event →

```
var ws = new WebSocket('ws://localhost:8080');   ◁─┐  This line creates a WebSocket
ws.onmessage = function(e) {                          object; note that the URL uses
    console.log(e.data);      ◁─┐  Log the data to the  the ws:// protocol.
};                                console so you can see it.
ws.onopen = function() {    ◁─
    ws.send('My Message');
};
```

The onopen event fires when the socket created in the first step is successfully opened by a browser—this function then sends a message to the server.

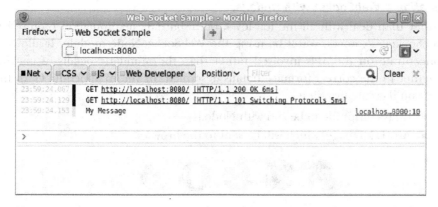

Figure 4.8   The simple WebSocket client running in the browser

On the server, the WebSocket-Node library is used to extend the base HTTP server. Appendix E provides the steps you need to take to install this module in Node; if you're following along step-by-step, please take that detour now.

With the module installed, you're ready to continue. Our next listing shows a Node.js app that will accept a WebSocket request and echo back any message sent to it. Save it as websocket-sample.js in the same directory as the file from listing 4.11.

Listing 4.12 A simple Node.js WebSockets server

```
var http = require("http");
var fs = require('fs');
var WebSocketServer = require('websocket').server;

function handler (req, res) {
    fs.readFile(__dirname + '/websocket-sample.html',
    function (err, data) {
        if (err) {
            res.writeHead(500);
            return res.end('Error loading websocket-sample.html');
        }
        res.writeHead(200);
        res.end(data);
    });
}

var app = http.createServer(handler);

app.listen(8080, function() {
    console.log((new Date()) + " Server is listening on port 8080");
});

wsServer = new WebSocketServer({
    httpServer: app
});

wsServer.on('request', function(request) {
    var connection = request.accept(null, request.origin);
    console.log((new Date()) + " Connection accepted.");
    connection.on('message', function(message) {
        console.log("Received Message: " + message.utf8Data);
        connection.sendUTF(message.utf8Data);
    });
});
```

This handler function will be run in response to any HTTP request.

Create a basic HTTP server object.

Start the server listening on port 8080.

The WebSocket-Node module is designed to extend an existing HTTP server; the HTTP server object is passed to the WebSocket server object as a parameter.

When a client connects to the WebSocket, add a handler for received messages.

This handler function will be run in response to any WebSocket request.

The handler will echo any message received back to the socket it was received from.

TRY IT OUT

Run listing 4.12 with Node (enter node websocket-sample.js on the command line). Now open your browser and connect to http://localhost:8080/ and check the console for the output.

4.2.3 *Building the planner application*

Now that you've confirmed that WebSockets are functioning both in Node and in your browser, and you know how to implement the WebSocket API in the client and how to set up Node.js to service those WebSockets, you're ready to build a real application that takes advantage of all of these features.

The steps you'll follow to build the planner application are these:

- Step 1: Create a template page.
- Step 2: Build multipurpose business logic in JavaScript to create and update plans.
- Step 3: Handle updates in the browser.
- Step 4: Handle updates on the server.

STEP 1: CREATE A TEMPLATE PAGE

The markup for the application page, index.html as normal, is shown in the following listing, though most of the interesting things in this application will be in the linked JavaScript files.

Listing 4.13   The planner index.html file

```
<body>
    <strong>Online now:</strong>
    <ul class="chatusers">
        <?php
        print_user_list($dbh);
        ?>
    </ul>
    <div class="chatwindow">
    <ul class="chatlog">
        <?php
        print_chat_log($dbh);
        ?>
    </ul>
    </div><!DOCTYPE html>
<html>
<head>
    <meta charset="utf-8">
    <title>Planner</title>
    <link rel="stylesheet" href="style.css">
    <script src="jquery-1.7.2.min.js"></script>
    <script src="EventEmitter.js"></script>
    <script src="planner.js"></script>
</head>
<body>
    <div id="plan">
        <div class="taskqueue">
            <strong>Unassigned tasks</strong>
        </div>
        <div class="grid">
            <strong>Planning board</strong>
            <div class="user">
                <div class="who">
                </div>
                <div>
                    <div class="todo">
```

This section will contain a list of tasks that are currently unassigned.

This section will have one or more resources; each has a section for to-do, in-progress, and completed tasks.

```
                    <strong>To Do</strong>
                </div>
                <div class="inprogress">
                    <strong>In Progress</strong>
                </div>
                <div class="done">
                    <strong>Done</strong>
                </div>
            </div>
        </div>
    </div>
    <div class="external">                                    ◄────┐
        <strong>Chat</strong>
        <iframe src="http://localhost/sse-chat/index.php">
        </iframe>                                                   The final section
    </div>                                                          embeds the chat
    </div>                                                          application from
</body>                                                             section 4.1.2.
</html>

    <form id="chat" class="chatform" method="post"
        action="add-chat.php">                                ◄───┘
        <label for="message">Share your thoughts:</label>
        <input name="message" id="message" maxlength="512" autofocus>
        <input type="submit" value="Chat">
    </form>
</body>
```

You now have the basic page structure out of the way, so let's delve into the JavaScript APIs that will make it all work.

STEP 2: BUILD MULTIPURPOSE BUSINESS LOGIC IN JAVASCRIPT TO CREATE AND UPDATE PLANS

A key advantage of having the server use the same programming language as the client is that they can share code. Instead of implementing the same functionality once in the server-side language and then again in JavaScript, implement it only one time. Figure 4.9 shows how this works.

Figure 4.10 shows the architecture of the application on the server and in two identical connected clients. As you can see, the structure on both client and server is similar. As each user makes changes, the same methods get fired on their local copy of the planner object as will be fired on the server planner object and on the planner objects used by other clients as the messages are passed between them using WebSockets.

Your model (the object containing the plan) will make use of the events framework, EventEmitter.js, as mentioned in the prerequisites. This is a browser-compatible version of the events module that comes as standard with Node. As methods are called on the model object, events will be fired. You'll then attach listeners to those events; when the model is run in the browser, those events will update the UI and send the changes back to the server. When the model is run on the server, those events will update all the other connected clients. The following listing shows the basic outline of the object you'll be using to store the plan, including some types and some utility functions. Add it to a file called planner.js. In the next listing you'll add some functionality.

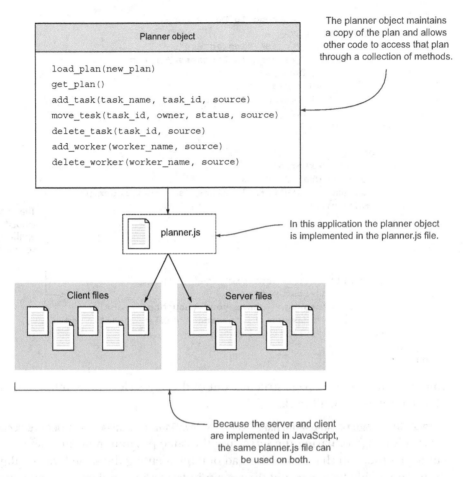

Figure 4.9 By using the same model (the plan held by the planner object) in the browser and on the server, the business logic (the methods in the planner object) can be the same in both places.

Listing 4.14 Creating the plan object and utility functions in planner.js

```
var Planner = function(ee) {                        ◁—— The planner expects an EventEmitter object
    var plan = {};                                        to be passed in when it's created.
    plan.tasks = [];
    plan.workers = [];
    plan.statuses = ['todo','inprogress','done'];   ◁—— This first section sets
    var Task = function(task_name, task_id) {       ◁——    up a few private
        var that = {};                                     variables.
        that.name = task_name;
        if (typeof task_id === 'undefined') {
            that.id = guidGenerator();                     A utility function to
        } else {                                           create a new task.
            that.id = task_id;
        }
```

```
        that.owner = '';
        that.status = '';                            A couple of utility
    }                                                functions for picking
    function get_task(task_id) {          ◁───┘     out tasks from the plan.
        return plan.tasks[get_task_index(task_id)];
    }
    function get_task_index(task_id) {
        for (var i = 0; i < plan.tasks.length; i++) {
            if (plan.tasks[i].id == task_id) { return i; }
        }
        return -1;
    }                                         A utility function to return a pseudo-GUID
    function guidGenerator(){        ◁───┤   (Globally Unique Identifier), so that every object
        var S4 = function() {                created in the plan can have a unique ID.
          return (
            ((1+Math.random())
              *0x10000)|0).toString(16).substring(1);
        };
        return (S4()+S4()+"-"+S4()+"-"+S4()+"-"+S4()+"-"+S4()+S4()+S4());
    }
    var that = { }                                You'll populate this object in
    return that;    ◁───┐                         listing 4.16; it will contain all the
}                       │   As mentioned in the previous    public properties and methods.
                            step, the that object is returned.
```

Using the EventEmitter library allows the event code to be identical on both server and client. The model, your plan object, emits events as the methods on it are called. On the client side, you'll listen to these events and update the display appropriately.

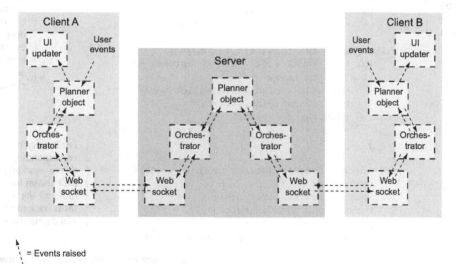

↖
 \ = Events raised
  \

Figure 4.10 Planner application architecture following through from User events in Client A: Events are generated by the client and update the local plan; an orchestrator monitors the plan and sends those updates through a WebSocket to the server. An orchestrator on the server updates the server planner object; then those updates are sent out via other WebSockets to the other connected clients, culminating in the UI of the other clients being updated.

The model itself will be updated from two sources:

- User input
- Messages from the server

The next listing is the part of planner.js that creates the plan object (that), which will be returned when the planner is initialized; it should replace var that = { } in listing 4.14.

Listing 4.15   More planner.js

```
var that = {
    load_plan: function(new_plan) {
        plan = JSON.parse(new_plan);
        ee.emit('loadPlan',plan);
    },
    get_plan: function() {
        return JSON.stringify(plan);
    },
    add_task: function(task_name, task_id, source) {
        var task = Task(task_name, task_id);
        plan.tasks.push(task);
        ee.emit('addTask',task, source);
        return task.id;
    },
    move_task: function(task_id, owner, status, source) {
        var task = get_task(task_id);
        task.owner = owner;
        task.status = status;
        ee.emit('moveTask', task, source);
    },
    delete_task: function(task_id, source) {
        var task_index = get_task_index(task_id);
        if (task_index >= 0) {
            var head = plan.tasks.splice(task_index,1);
            head.concat(plan.tasks);
            plan.tasks = head;
            ee.emit('deleteTask', task_id, source);
        }
    },
    add_worker: function(worker_name, source) {
        var worker = {};
        worker.name = worker_name;
        worker.id = guidGenerator();
        plan.workers.push(worker);
        ee.emit('addWorker', worker, source);
    },
    eachListener: ee.eachListener,
    addListener: ee.addListener,
    on: ee.on,
    once: ee.once,
    removeListener: ee.removeListener,
    removeAllListeners: ee.removeAllListeners,
    listeners: ee.listeners,
```

In a real application you'd add validation logic here to check to see if the JSON string constitutes a valid plan.

The task is created with the utility function and then pushed into the task's array on the plan.

Once the that object is returned by planner constructor (listing 4.14), it will access private functions of planner (i.e., get_task()) via JavaScript's closure feature.

A corresponding method to allow the plan's current state to be saved outside the object.

An event is emitted containing the new task.

Each method will follow a similar pattern. Let's look at the add_task method in detail. Note that the task_id parameter is optional—it's not needed when the task is created, but it will be needed when this event is replicated back on the server and in other clients.

For brevity, the corresponding delete_worker() method isn't shown here; it will move all the worker's tasks back to the queue and delete the worker.

The EventEmitter methods are now monkey-patched onto the return object.

You'll be able to use the on method to add event listeners to the plan object.

```
        emit: ee.emit,
        setMaxListeners: ee.setMaxListeners
    };
```

The UI is mostly drag and drop. We covered this HTML5 API in great detail in chapter 3, so there's no need to go over it all again. Similarly, updating the display uses the standard jQuery DOM manipulation methods you're already familiar with. More interesting to us right now is what happens when the plan object is updated by these UI actions and events that arrive via a WebSocket. In the next step, you'll look at the code that handles this; in the following step, you'll look at the server-side code to handle the updates.

STEP 3: HANDLE UPDATES IN THE BROWSER

Now create the client orchestrator code; for this create a new file called planner-browser.js in your working directory. The next listing shows the event listeners on the WebSocket that will update the model and the event listeners on the planner object that trigger messages to be sent through the WebSocket.

Core API

The WebSocket listeners are added by setting `ws.onmessage`. And listeners on the planner object are added with `plan.on()`.

Listing 4.16 The planner-browser.js (partial) browser code

```
function init() {
    var ee = new EventEmitter();
    var planner = new Planner(ee);
    var render;
    if (typeof  MozWebSocket !== 'undefined') {
        WebSocket = MozWebSocket;
    }
    var ws = new WebSocket('ws://localhost:8080');
    ws.onmessage = function(msg_json) {
        var msg = JSON.parse(msg_json);
        switch (msg.type) {
            case 'loadPlan':
                planner.load_plan(msg.args.plan);
                render = new Renderer(planner);
                break;
            case 'addTask':
                planner.add_task(msg.args.task_name,
                                 msg.args.task_id,
                                 'socket');
                break;
            case 'moveTask':
                planner.move_task(msg.args.task_id,
                                  msg.args.task_owner,
                                  msg.args.task_status,
                                  'socket');
                break;
            case 'deleteTask':
                planner.delete_task(msg.args.task_id,
                                    'socket');
```

Because this code creates the planner object, it also has to create the EventEmitter.

Create a new planner object using the EventEmitter.

In Firefox the WebSocket object is called MozWebSocket and will be until the spec is finalized. For practical use, MozWebSocket is identical to WebSocket, so map one to the other.

Add a listener to the WebSocket.

Assume that anything received on the WebSocket is a JSON-encoded object.

The type property of the decoded message object will be used to determine the correct action.

When the client first connects, expect the server to deliver a JSON-encoded planner object with the latest version of the plan.

The rest of the potential messages are mapped onto their equivalent planner actions.

```
                        break;
                }
        };
        ws.onerror = function(e) {        ←——  Log any errors to
                console.log(e.reason);          the console to aid
        }                                       any debugging.
        planner.on('addTask', function(task, source) {   ←——
                if (source !== 'socket') {
                        var msg = {};
                        msg.type = 'addTask';
                        msg.args = { 'task_name': task.name, 'task_id': task.id };
                        ws.send(JSON.stringify(msg));
                }
        });
        planner.on('moveTask', function(task, source) {
                if (source !== 'socket') {
                        var msg = {};
                        msg.type = 'moveTask';
                        msg.args = { 'task_id': task.id, 'owner': task.owner,
                                'status': task.status };
                        ws.send(JSON.stringify(msg))
                }
        });
        planner.on('deleteTask', function(task_id, source) {
                if (source !== 'socket') {
                        var msg = {};
                        msg.type = 'deleteTask';
                        msg.args = { 'task_id': task_id };
                        ws.send(JSON.stringify(msg))
                }
        });
}
```

Because adding a task will trigger an addTask event, there's no need to do anything if the original source of the event was this code.

The on method on the planner object attaches an event listener. When events are raised by the in-browser planner object, they are detected and sent to the server.

STEP 4: HANDLE UPDATES ON THE SERVER

Similarly on the server, the model will be updated by incoming messages from various clients. Create a file called planner-server.js in your working directory for this code, or grab the version from the code download. In this file you'll need to set up listeners on the model to send those same updates to any other connected client. The key part of the code for responding to a moveTask message is shown in the following listing. Check the planner-server.js file in the code download for the rest of the code.

Listing 4.17   planner-server.js server code

```
planner.on('moveTask', function(task, source) {
        var msg = {};
        msg.type = 'moveTask';
        msg.args = { 'task_id': task.id, 'owner': task.owner,
                        'status': task.status };
        var jMsg = JSON.stringify(msg);
        for (var i=0; i<clients.length; i++) {
                if (source !== clients[i].client_id) {
```

There's no need to send the message to the client that originated it.

This part of the code is the same as the equivalent in listing 4.16. In a more complex application, you may want to extract it to a separate shared module.

The clients variable is an array of objects representing connected clients. Each time a connection is created, an entry is added to the array.

```
        clients[i].ws.send(jMsg)
    }
  }
});
```

←── **The WebSocket is also
stored in the clients array.**

Security and validation

In a real application, the server has additional responsibilities in terms of validating data and persistence. A general tenet of server-side development is to never trust data you've received over the wire. In order to concentrate on using WebSockets, those features have been left out of the sample application in this section.

If you've followed along and either downloaded or re-created the UI logic, you should now have a working planning-board application. In this model of web application development, the server becomes another client. The bulk of the code involved is identical to what's running in all the users' browsers. You should also have the chat application from section 4.1 sitting in an iframe alongside it, but so far they're independent applications on different domains. We assume you have the chat application on port 80 from a standard web server, and the planning board is running on port 8080 from Node. Normally, the browser wouldn't allow scripts on either page to exchange data with each other. In the next section, you'll learn about some HTML5 APIs that enable client-side communication between scripts from different domains.

4.3 Messaging on the client side

Client-side messaging refers to the communication between windows and scripts that are loaded in the browser. These could be browser windows, iframes, framesets, or worker threads; the HTML5 specification refers to these with the umbrella term *script contexts.*

Before HTML5, communication between different script contexts has been done by direct DOM manipulation. If you want to build web pages out of loosely coupled components, this isn't a good approach for two reasons:

- Changes to the structure of one component could easily break all the components that try to communicate with it.
- Each component needs access to the full DOM of the hosting page and vice versa. You can't share only a limited set of information. Often it's easier to communicate via the server. In the new world of disconnected web applications, that's sometimes no longer an option.

Cross-document versus cross-domain

You'll often hear cross-document messaging referred to as cross-domain messaging. It's not a requirement to have the two documents served from different domains. Messaging will work just as well if the two pages are on the same domain. But that option doesn't represent new functionality in HTML, rather a different way of doing something we've been doing for years. As a result, people tend to focus on the cross-domain aspect.

In this section you'll have a brief introduction to HTML5's cross-document messaging API, and then you'll look at how to use it to connect the applications from sections 4.1 and 4.2.

4.3.1   *Communicating across domains with postMessage*

Web browsers usually restrict communication between windows according to the Same Origin Policy: Scripts on pages loaded from one domain can't access content in windows loaded from another domain. This is a sound security approach. Without it, a website could create an iframe, load your Facebook page into it, and steal your personal details or post on your wall. But you'll find plenty of situations where you'll want to embed content from other sites in web pages; for example, Google ads and analytics, Facebook Like buttons, and Twitter feed widgets. You can implement all these examples by loading JavaScript from other sites using `<script>` elements. When scripts are included this way, they have as much access to your content as scripts on your own domain; they bypass the Same Origin Policy.

Cross-document messaging   1   3   8   9.5   4

Until HTML5, the options for any foreign domain content embedded in your pages were these:

- No access to any of your content
- Complete access to all of your content

It would be nice to have a middle ground between these extremes. Although there may be some sources you don't trust at all, it's likely you have plenty you trust a little bit. HTML5 satisfies this demand for flexibility with cross-document messaging. The cross-document messaging API allows a controlled messaging channel to be created between two pages by using the `postMessage` method and the `onmessage` event.

Core API   The `postMessage` method should be passed two parameters:

- The message itself
- The domain of the page being targeted:

```
windowRef.postMessage('The message', 'http://domain2.com');
```

The domain parameter is important because it ensures that if a different page is loaded into the iframe, either by the user clicking a link or through some other activity, the message won't be passed. It's possible to pass a wildcard, `'*'`, as the second parameter and avoid all the security, but be careful because you could end up sending your user's information to a malicious website.

Core API   When a window receives a message, the aptly named `message` event is fired. As usual, with DOM events this handler can either be attached declaratively using an `onmessage` attribute on the body element or with `addEventListener`:

```
window.addEventListener('message', receiver, false);
```

The `receiver` function will accept the event as a parameter. The message passed will be in the `data` property of the event. In the next section, you'll implement `receiver` functions in the context of the planner and chat apps you built in previous sections.

4.3.2 Joining the applications with cross-document messaging

At this point, you have two applications, from different servers, coexisting in the same web page. In this section, you'll use the cross-domain messaging API to allow the data in the planner object to be used to feed an auto-complete feature in the chat window. This will offer user names and task titles in a drop-down list to speed up typing while retaining accuracy, as shown in figure 4.11.

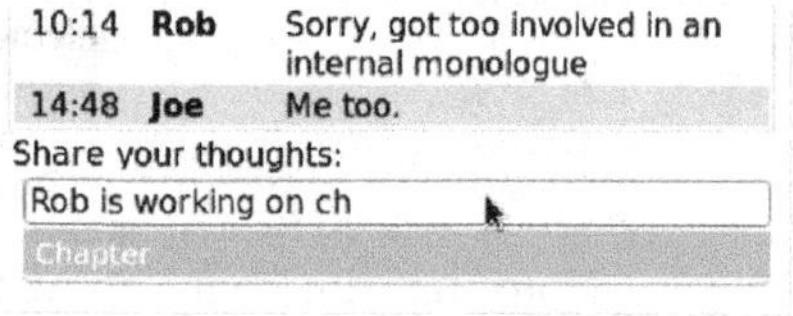

10:14 **Rob**	Sorry, got too involved in an internal monologue	
14:48 **Joe**	Me too.	

Share your thoughts:

Rob is working on ch

Chapter

Figure 4.11 As the user types into the chat, the letters will be compared to words in the plan and matches will be shown in a drop-down list, where they can be selected using the down arrow.

Auto-complete prerequisite

This section relies on having a JavaScript auto-completer script. In order to concentrate on the HTML5 features, this section won't cover the details; a suitable script is included in the code download. Add the file to the working directory of the chat application.

To implement auto-complete, you need to set up message handlers on both the planner and the chat applications. The chat application will wait for the user to start typing and then send the letters of each word as they are typed to the parent window. The parent window will receive the message, compare the typed letters to the labels existing within the plan object, and send a message back with a list of matching words. The code for the chat application part of this is shown in the following listing; add it to the chat.js file in the SSE chat application.

Listing 4.18 Auto-complete interface for the chat application

Called from an onKeyPress listener on the chat text input.

```
function getWords(letters) {
    var msg = {};
    msg.type = 'getWordList';
    msg.params = {};
    msg.params.letters = letter;
    parent.postMessage(JSON.stringify(msg), 'http://localhost');
}
```

Create an object to contain the message; the variety of message types sent by the chat app is what defines the services provided by the parent window and is what defines the interface expected in the parent window. In more complex applications, you might want to create a function to define the interface explicitly.

Encode the object to a string and send it in the message to the parent window.

The standard onmessage listener.

```
window.addEventListener('message', receiver, false);
function receiver(e) {
```

The messages
accepted
here define
the interface
for the
calling page.

```
if (e.origin == 'http://localhost:8080') {
    var msg = JSON.parse(e.data);
    switch (msg.type) {
        case 'wordList':
            showAutocompleter(msg.params.words);
            break;
    }
}
```

In the sample, there's
only one domain you
expect to receive
messages from, but
more complex
checking could be
inserted here to allow
dynamic registration
of components.

For brevity, the code to create an
element containing the list of words isn't shown
here, but it's much the same as the hundreds of
auto-complete scripts available on the web.
Download the sample code for further details.

Note that the chat application code is entirely generic—it doesn't matter what application has embedded it as long as it can return a list of words when sent a message in the correct form. The corresponding code in the planner application is necessarily specific to the planner. The following listing shows a new method for the planner object; add it to the planner.js file.

Listing 4.19   Word-completion service in the planner application

```
get_words: function(letters) {
    var words = [];
    for (var i=0; i<plan.tasks.length; i++) {
        var tokens = plan.tasks[i].name.split(' ');
        for (var j=0; j<tokens.length; j++) {
            if (tokens[j].length > 3 &&
                tokens[j].indexOf(letters) > -1) {
                words.push(tokens[j]);
            }
        }
    }
    return words;
}
```

This method goes inside the
planner object from listing 4.16.

Go through each
task in the plan. . .

. . .and each
word in the
task name.

Add them to the list if
they are at least two
letters long and contain
the requested letters.

This is the list of words that will end
up getting passed to listing 4.18.

The planner.get_words method needs to be hooked up to the window's onmessage event. The next listing shows the code for this, still in planner.js.

Listing 4.20   Listening to the onmessage event in the planner application

```
window.addEventListener('message', receiver, false);
function receiver(e) {
    if (e.origin == 'http://localhost') {
        var msg = JSON.parse(e.data);
        switch (msg.type) {
            case 'getWordList':
                var words = planner.get_words(msg.params.letters);
                var el = document
                    .getElementsByTagName('iframe')[0]
                    .contentWindow;
                var response = {};
                response.type = 'wordList';
                response.params = {};
                response.params.words = words;
```

Check that the message
came from the page you
expected it to come from.

Create an object to contain the
message, as in listing 4.20. For more
complex applications, you might want
to create a function to define this.

```
el.postMessage(JSON.stringify(response),
    'http://localhost:8080');
break;
        }
    }
}
```

Encode the object to a string and send it in the message to the iframe.

This value needs to match the return words; line in listing 4.I9.

With all this code in place, your work is complete. You should now be able to re-create the drop-down, shown again here for your convenience in figure 4.12.

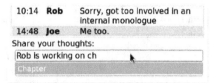

Figure 4.12 Planner-chat auto-complete one more time

Cross-document versus channel messaging

HTML5 has a more general-purpose alternative to cross-document messaging known as channel messaging. It allows you to create as many message ports as you want, not only between windows but also between any sorts of JavaScript object. Channel messaging wasn't necessary to complete the application in this chapter, but if you think you'll find it useful in your own applications, we've included a short introduction in appendix F.

4.4 Summary

In this chapter, you've learned about the new messaging APIs in HTML5, between pages in different windows on the client, with cross-document messaging, and between client and server, with server-sent events and WebSockets. You've also gained a practical understanding of how to use one of the new wave of web servers optimized for event-driven communication, Node.js. With all this new knowledge you're well equipped to build the next generation of web applications, based on lightweight, event-driven data communication between client and server, and you'll be able to join several such applications together in client browsers in a lightly coupled way thanks to cross-document messaging.

In the next chapter, you'll move on to consider an application environment where saving every byte makes a real difference: mobile web applications. HTML5 offers new capabilities that allow your application to keep working when no network is available.

Chapter 5 at a glance

Topic	Description, methods, and so on	Page
Web storage and management of simple key/value pair data on client-side local storage	Methods: • `getItem()` • `localStorage` • `removeItem()` • `clear()`	140 140 141 142
Indexed database	Complex, indexed client-side database functionality Database/object store methods: • `open()` • `createObjectStore()` • `createIndex()` • `loadTasks` • `objectStore()` • `deleteDatabase()` Cursor method • `continue`	 145 145 146 150 152 155 150
Application cache	Enable web applications to be used when client is offline Method: • `swapCache()`	 160

Look for this icon ⟶ Core API throughout the chapter to quickly locate the topics outlined in this table.

Mobile applications: client storage and offline execution

This chapter covers

- Storing data on the client side with the Web Storage API
- Managing a full client-side IndexedDB database
- Enabling applications to work offline with the Application Cache API

HTML5 is finally providing the web with a solution to the problem of working offline. Although a plethora of solutions for saving web pages for later use in an offline environment already exist, until now there's been no solution for using web applications in such a manner. By allowing web applications to store data locally on the client, HTML5 now enables web applications to work without a constant connection to a central server.

When might this be useful? Think of a sales representative in the field being able to use his firm's customer relationship management application on the go, even in areas with poor network coverage, such as a remote location or an underground train. With the new capabilities provided by HTML5, that rep can still use the application in such areas, viewing data that has already been downloaded to the device, and even being able to enter new data, which is stored temporarily on the device and synchronized back to the central server when the network is available again. Also, think of an HTML5 game like the ones you will build in chapters 6 and 7. Rather than storing game saves and state data on a server, you can increase performance and reduce latency and load by saving the data locally. One feature in particular—the application cache manifest—gives you the ability to create a game that can be run completely offline.

In this chapter, we're going to show you how to put these features and concepts into practice by building a simple mobile web application called My Tasks. This application, which will be fully functional when the user is offline, will create, update, and delete tasks that are stored locally in the browser. In addition, My Tasks will allow the user to change settings for the application's display.

> **Why build the sample My Tasks application?**
> While working through this chapter's sample application, you'll learn how to
>
> - Store data on the client side using the Web Storage API
> - Store data on the client side using the IndexedDB database
> - Use the application cache manifest file to build web applications that will function while offline

Let's get started by taking a closer look at the sample application.

5.1 *My Tasks: application overview, prerequisites, and first steps*

My Tasks is a simple task management application for mobile devices. All data will be stored on the client side, and the application will be fully functional offline. In building it, you'll take advantage of the following HTML5 features:

- *Storage*—Allows the app to save small amounts of data to the user's local storage. My Tasks will use this feature to store user settings like name and preferred color scheme.
- *Indexed database (aka IndexedDB)*—Enables the application to create a database of key/value records. My Tasks will use IndexedDB to store task data, allowing users to easily view, add, update, and delete task items. The application will use the now-defunct Web SQL to provide a fallback for devices that don't yet support IndexedDB.
- *Application cache manifest*—Enables the application to be used offline. The cache manifest ensures that the user's browser keeps a copy of needed files for offline use. Upon reconnection to the web, the browser can look for updates and allow the user to reload the application and apply the updates.

As you can see in figure 5.1, the application is split into three distinct views—Task List, Add Task, and Settings.

Figure 5.1 The three main views of the My Tasks application: Task List, Add Task, and Settings. To select a view, the application includes a navigation bar near the top.

Task List displays a list of existing tasks, each with a check box to mark the task as completed and a Delete button to remove it. Task List also features a search box, which allows you to filter the task list by description. Add Task contains a form to add a new task to the database. Settings contains a form to customize the application and to reset all locally stored data (deleting all Storage data and IndexedDB/Web SQL data). The navigation bar at the top of the screen lets you easily switch among the three views.

All three views are contained in a single HTML page, and you will use `location`.`hash` to switch among them, ensuring the application is highly responsive and fast.

We'll walk you through seven major steps to build the application:

- Step 1: Create the basic structure of the application: the HTML page with the application's three views and the JavaScript code to navigate among them.
- Step 2: Implement the data management of the Settings view using the Web Storage API.
- Step 3: Connect to the database and create a storage area for tasks.
- Step 4: Enable data entry and search of the Task List view using the IndexedDB API.
- Step 5: Allow users to add, update, and delete tasks.
- Step 6: Create a cache manifest file to allow the application to work offline.
- Step 7: Implement automatic updating of the application.

NOTE   The application should be run from a web server rather than the local filesystem. Otherwise, you won't be able to use it on a mobile device and offline support won't work. Also note that the application has been tested on iOS, Android, and BlackBerry Torch mobile devices, as well as on Opera Mobile. It's also fully functional in the Chrome, Firefox, Safari, and Opera desktop browsers.

If you're looking for a quick and easy way to set up a web server for this chapter's application, we suggest you try Python's built-in server, http.server. You can get this server module by downloading and installing the latest version of the Python programming language from http://python.org/download/. Once you have it installed, you can start the server by changing your current directory to the directory of your web app and then invoking the web server with the following command:

```
python -m http.server
```

Python's web server will start running on port 8000. If you don't like the default 8000 port, you can specify another port by adding the desired port number at the end of the python command:

```
python -m http.server 8080
```

In this section, you'll define the application's HTML structure, use CSS to define visibility for each view, and write the JavaScript to implement navigation between the views. For the development of the My Tasks basic structure, the process consists of four steps:

- Step 1: Define the top-level HTML structure.
- Step 2: Write HTML code for the navigation bar.
- Step 3: Create views with `<section>` elements.
- Step 4a: Enable navigation between views by using CSS to define section visibility rules.
- Step 4b: Enable navigation between views by using JavaScript to initiate view changes.

Prerequisites

Before you create the application, you need to handle a few prerequisites:

- Create a new directory on your web server. When the chapter tells you to create or edit a file, save it to this directory.
- You won't be creating the CSS style sheet. Instead copy the CSS style sheet for chapter 5 from the code package at the book's website: www.manning.com/crowther2; then save the style sheet to the directory mentioned in the first prerequisite.

Note that all files for this chapter and the book are available at the Manning website: www.manning.com/crowther2.

Enough chatter about what you're going to build, let's get building!

5.1.1   *Defining the HTML document structure*

In this section, the index.html file will define a very basic <head> and <body> framework for the application. The index.html file will contain a title and font for the application, as well as a <script> element to tell the application where the JavaScript file is located. Near the end of index.html, a <body> element will be added to hold the HTML markup coming in subsequent sections.

STEP 1: DEFINE THE TOP-LEVEL HTML STRUCTURE

Create a file named index.html and include the contents of the following listing. This code defines the basic layout of the page and loads external CSS and JavaScript files.

> **Listing 5.1   index.html—Application HTML structure**

```
<!DOCTYPE html>
<html lang="en" class="blue">     ◄─── A class attribute on the root element defines the color
<head>                                   scheme. Later in the chapter, the application will use this
                                         attribute to allow the user to change the color scheme.
    <meta charset="utf-8">
    <meta name="viewport" content="width=device-width,
        initial-scale=1.0, maximum-scale=1.0, user-scalable=0">     Load a
    <title>My Tasks</title>                                        custom font
    <link rel="stylesheet"                                         using the
        href="http://fonts.googleapis.com/css?family=Carter+One">  ◄─ Google Font
    <link rel="stylesheet" href="style.css">                       API.
    <script src="app.js"></script>
</head>
<body class="list">     ◄─── A class attribute on the <body> element will direct the browser, via
</body>                      a CSS rule, to display one of three views: Task List, Add Task, or
</html>                      Settings. The class attribute also directs the browser, via another CSS
                             rule, to highlight the corresponding button on the navigation bar.
```

STEP 2: WRITE HTML CODE FOR THE NAVIGATION BAR

This code comprises a <nav> element with three list items, one for each view in the application: Task List, Add Task, and Settings. Add the navigation bar's HTML code in the next listing within the <body> of your HTML document.

> **Listing 5.2   index.html—Adding a navigation bar**

Create a list with three links, each pointing to a hash reference for the view in question.

```
<header>
    <h1><span id="user_name">My</span> Tasks</h1>     ◄───────────
    <nav>
        <ul>
            <li><a href="#list" class="list">Task List</a></li>
            <li><a href="#add" class="add">Add Task</a></li>
            <li><a href="#settings" class="settings">Settings</a></li>
        </ul>
    </nav>                          In the Settings view, the user has the option to replace the "My"
</header>                           with any other string of characters. The markup surrounding
                                    "My" will make finding and changing the title easy.
```

STEP 3: CREATE VIEWS WITH `<SECTION>` ELEMENTS

The final part of the HTML page uses `<section>` elements to define the application's three views. The first view, Task List, contains a search form and a results list, which will be generated by a JavaScript function. The next view, Add Task, contains a form that allows the user to create a new task and due date. The last view, Settings, contains a form to set the name and color scheme preference for the application. A class attribute bound to each `<section>` element will allow the forthcoming CSS and JavaScript code to control the view's visibility. Insert the code in the following listing directly after the code from listing 5.2.

Listing 5.3   index.html—Main application views

```html
<section class="list">
    <form name="search">
        <input type="search" name="query" placeholder="Search tasks...">
    </form>
    <ul id="task_list"></ul>
</section>
<section class="add">
    <form name="add">
        <label>
            Task Description
            <textarea name="desc"></textarea>
        </label>
        <label>
            Due Date (MM/DD/YYYY)
            <input type="date" name="due_date">
        </label>
        <input type="submit" value="Add Task">
    </form>
</section>
<section class="settings">
    <form name="settings">
        <label>
            Your Name
            <input type="text" name="name">
        </label>
        <label>
            Color Scheme
            <select name="color_scheme">
                <option>Blue</option>
                <option>Red</option>
                <option>Green</option>
            </select>
        </label>
        <input type="submit" value="Save Settings">
        <input type="reset" value="Reset All Data">
    </form>
</section>
```

This form allows the user to search the Task List by task description.

Place the results of the search in an empty unordered list with the ID "task_list."

Put a form in the Add Task section that allows users to add a new task to the list. The form contains a task description `<textarea>` and a due date `<input>`.

In the Settings section, create a settings form that allows users to set their name and choose a color scheme for the application (red, blue, or green).

Use an `<input>` element to implement a button that resets user settings and removes all tasks.

5.1.2   Controlling visibility of views using CSS

Now that you have the three views implemented in one HTML file, you need the ability to switch among the different views. You will do this by turning off the visibility of the previous view and turning on the visibility of the next view. (You won't need to make these changes to the CSS file, because you should have already copied the Manning-supplied CSS file to your server's directory. See "Prerequisites.")

STEP 4A: ENABLE NAVIGATION BETWEEN VIEWS BY USING CSS TO DEFINE <SECTION> VISIBILITY RULES
In order to have only one view visible at a time, the application's CSS file defines rules to control the visibility of each view's <section> element:

```
section {
    display: none;
}
```

The first rule declares that a section element should be invisible wherever a section element is defined.

In order to make a specific view visible, the application defines some counteracting rules:

```
body.list section.list,
body.add section.add,
body.settings section.settings {
    display: block;
}
```

These rules declare that a <section> element should be visible when a <body> element and its embedded <section> element have a class attribute in common (either list, add, or settings). In this situation, the <section> element would also match the first rule, but the more specific rule will override the first rule.

To see how this works, consider what happens when the user wants to switch views. When the user taps the Add Task button on the navigation bar, the application changes the <body>'s class attribute to add. Because the <body>'s class attribute now matches the <section> with a class attribute of add, the section.add element becomes visible, and all other <section>s are rendered invisible.

The CSS rules only get you part of the way toward implementing the navigation of the views. Although the CSS rules declare the conditions for switching views, the rules can't initiate the view switching. As mentioned earlier, a user's tap of a button on the navigation bar initiates the view switch by changing the class attribute of the <body> element. The next section describes how to implement this attribute change and link it to the view buttons.

5.1.3   Implementing navigation with JavaScript

In this section, you'll use JavaScript to modify the class attribute of the <body> element. Each time the class value is changed to a different value, one or more CSS rules will be activated to change the application's view. The user will initiate these changes by tapping one of three buttons: Add Task, Settings, or Task List. Each button is implemented as a link with an anchor name of #add, #settings, or #list. So when a link is selected, it will change the location.hash property to one of the three anchor names. The browser will detect the change in location.hash and then invoke an event handler defined by the application. The event handler will respond by using the value of the location.hash property to set the value of the <body> element's class attribute. If the attribute value is different from the previous one, the application will switch to the new view.

STEP 4B: ENABLE NAVIGATION BETWEEN VIEWS USING JAVASCRIPT TO INITIATE VIEW CHANGES

Let's start off by defining methods to switch between views in the application. The code in the next listing creates a new object constructor, Tasks, containing two functions, nudge and jump. When the page has loaded, a new Tasks object is created, which forms the basis for your application. Take the code in the following listing and insert it into a new file, app.js. Store this file in the same directory as index.html.

Listing 5.4   app.js—Foundation JavaScript code for the application

```
(function() {
    var Tasks = function() {                    The nudge function hides the browser toolbar on
        var nudge = function() {                iOS devices to gain extra space for the application.
            setTimeout(function(){ window.scrollTo(0,0); }, 1000);
        }
        var jump = function() {                              The jump function takes
            switch(location.hash) {                          the value of location.hash
                case '#add':                                 and uses it to define the
                    document.body.className = 'add';         current view. Notice how
                    break;                                   the Tasks constructor calls
                case '#settings':                            jump after its definition.
                    document.body.className = 'settings';    Because the user may have
                    break;                                   bookmarked a view other
                default:                                     than the application's
                    document.body.className = 'list';        home view of Task List, the
            }                                                Tasks constructor uses
            nudge();                                         jump to check the value
        }                                                    of location.hash for a
        jump();                                              non-default view.
        window.addEventListener('hashchange', jump, false);
        window.addEventListener('orientationchange', nudge, false);
    }
    window.addEventListener('load', function() {
        new Tasks();
    }, false);
})();
```

When a user wants to change the view, they click a button on the navigation bar. This action changes the value of location.hash and raises a hashchange event. You want to call jump when a hashchange is detected.

After the page loads, create a new instance of the Tasks object to start the application.

On mobile devices, when the screen orientation changes, call the nudge function to hide the browser toolbar, if possible.

TRY IT OUT

If you run the application in any HTML5-compatible web browser, you should be able to navigate between the different views of the application and see the current view highlighted in the navigation bar. This is illustrated in figure 5.2.

If you are trying to run this app on your desktop browser with the Python web server, start the My Tasks app by entering localhost:8000 into your browser's address

Task List	Add Task	Settings
Task List	Add Task	**Settings**
Task List	**Add Task**	Settings

Figure 5.2 The application highlights the current view by displaying a navigation button with a darker background and blue text.

box. (If you configured the web server with a different port number, use that number instead of 8000.)

With the basics out of the way, let's move on to implementing the Settings view using the Web Storage API in HTML5.

5.2 Managing data with the Web Storage API

Among other features, the Settings view allows users to choose a name and color scheme for the application. Traditionally, web applications would have implemented this either by storing the user's settings in a remote database on the server side or by storing the preferences in a cookie, which often gets deleted when the user clears their browsing history.

Web Storage API	4.0	3.5	8.0	10.5	4.0

Fortunately, we have better options with HTML5: the Web Storage specification. It defines two `window` attributes for storing data locally on the client: `localStorage` and `sessionStorage`. The `localStorage` attribute allows you to store data that will persist on the client machine between sessions. The data can be overwritten or erased only by the application itself or by the user performing a manual clear down of the local storage area. The API of the `sessionStorage` attribute is identical to that of the `localStorage` attribute, but `sessionStorage` won't persist data between browser sessions, so if the user closes the browser, the data is immediately erased.

> **TIP** You can try `sessionStorage` in this section by replacing any reference to `localStorage` with `sessionStorage` in the listing to come.

In this section, you'll learn
- How to read data from `localStorage`
- How to write data to `localStorage`
- How to delete some or all data from `localStorage`

To implement the management of the application's settings using the Web Storage API and to integrate the setting functions with the UI, you'll need to follow these four steps:

- Step 1: Read application settings from `localStorage`.
- Step 2: Save application settings to `localStorage`.
- Step 3: Clear all settings and data from `localStorage`.
- Step 4: Connect the UI to `localStorage` functions.

NOTE You need to complete all the steps before you can run and test the code in this section.

5.2.1   Reading data from localStorage

When the application starts, it will need to read the user's name and chosen color scheme from some client-based data store, then apply them to the UI. You'll use `localStorage` as a repository for this information and store each piece of data as a key/value pair. Retrieving items from `localStorage` is done by calling its Storage API method `getItem` with the value's key.

STEP 1: READING APPLICATION SETTINGS FROM LOCALSTORAGE

Core API

For the purpose of retrieving application settings from `localStorage`, the application will need a `loadSettings` function. This function reads the user's name and color scheme from `localStorage` using the Web Storage API method `getItem` and then adjusts the navigation bar's header to include the user's name, and changes the document element's `class` attribute to assign the selected color scheme.

Open the app.js file you created earlier in the chapter, and add the code from the next listing to the `Tasks` constructor function (just below the line where you attach a handler to the `orientationchange` event).

> **Listing 5.5   app.js—Reading data from `localStorage`**

```
var localStorageAvailable = ('localStorage' in window);

var loadSettings = function() {
    if(localStorageAvailable) {
        var name = localStorage.getItem('name'),
            colorScheme = localStorage.getItem('colorScheme'),
            nameDisplay = document.getElementById('user_name'),
            nameField = document.forms.settings.name,
            doc = document.documentElement,
            colorSchemeField = document.forms.settings.color_scheme;
        if(name) {
            nameDisplay.innerHTML = name+"'s";
            nameField.value = name;
        } else {
            nameDisplay.innerHTML = 'My';
            nameField.value = '';
        }
        if(colorScheme) {
            doc.className = colorScheme.toLowerCase();
            colorSchemeField.value = colorScheme;
        } else {
            doc.className = 'blue';
            colorSchemeField.value = 'Blue';
```

Use the Storage API method getItem to retrieve data from localStorage. If the data does not exist, getItem will return a null value instead.

Before you start to access localStorage, query the window object for a localStorage attribute. The variable localStorageAvailable will be true if the browser supports the localStorage attribute.

```
        }
    }
}
```

At this point you're probably wondering how your application is going to read data from localStorage when you haven't actually saved anything in the first place. Fear not! You're going to solve that problem next by creating a function that will save the user's selected settings to localStorage.

5.2.2 Saving data to localStorage

Saving the user's settings is relatively easy. Save data in localStorage by using its Web Storage API method setItem, passing two arguments: a key and value.

STEP 2: SAVE NAME AND COLOR SCHEME TO LOCALSTORAGE

In order to save the user's name and chosen color scheme, you'll implement a new function, saveSettings. It will store the user's preferences and change the location .hash to #list, the Task List view. Add the code from the next listing directly after the loadSettings function from the previous listing.

> **Listing 5.6 app.js—Saving data to localStorage**

```
var saveSettings = function(e) {
    e.preventDefault();
    if(localStorageAvailable) {
        var name = document.forms.settings.name.value;
        if(name.length > 0) {
            var colorScheme = document.forms.settings.color_scheme.value;

            localStorage.setItem('name', name);
            localStorage.setItem('colorScheme', colorScheme);
            loadSettings();
            alert('Settings saved successfully', 'Settings saved');
            location.hash = '#list';
        } else {
            alert('Please enter your name', 'Settings error');
        }
    } else {
        alert('Browser does not support localStorage', 'Settings error');
    }
}
```

Use the setItem method to store data in localStorage. If an item with this name already exists, it will be overwritten without warning.

When the data has been stored, call loadSettings to update the application with the new settings.

Setting location.hash to #list will trigger a redirect to the Task List view.

You've now seen how to read and write data using the Web Storage API. Next, we'll show you how to remove data.

5.2.3 Deleting data from localStorage

In the Settings view of My Tasks, the user has an option to remove all items and settings from the application. So, you'll need to consider the two data-removal methods in the Storage API. The first, removeItem, is useful when you need to delete a single item from localStorage. The method requires one argument, the key to identify and remove the value from localStorage. Because the application needs to reset all settings and data in the application, you won't use removeItem. Instead, you'll want the second method, clear, which removes all items from localStorage.

STEP 3: CLEAR ALL SETTINGS AND DATA FROM LOCALSTORAGE

You'll need a function, resetSettings, to erase all the settings data in the application. Before resetSettings erases the data, you should ask the user to confirm this action. After erasing the data, load the default user settings into the application and change the location.hash to #list, the Task List view.

Add the following code immediately after the code from the previous listing.

> **Listing 5.7   app.js—Clearing data from** localStorage

```
var resetSettings = function(e) {
    e.preventDefault();
    if(confirm('This will erase all data. Are you sure?', 'Reset data')) {
        if(localStorageAvailable) {
            localStorage.clear();
        }
        loadSettings();
        alert('Application data has been reset', 'Reset successful');
        location.hash = '#list';
    }
}
```

When the data has been removed, call loadSettings to restore application defaults.

Before clear down of localStorage, the application will prompt the user to confirm deletion of user settings.

Change location.hash to trigger a redirect to the Task List view.

At this point, all of the functions for interacting with localStorage have been created, and all that's left is to connect the UI to these functions.

STEP 4: CONNECT THE UI TO THE LOCALSTORAGE FUNCTIONS

The final piece of the puzzle for our sample application is to add event handlers to the Settings view so that data is saved and reset when the buttons are pressed. Aside from connecting the storage methods to the buttons, you'll need to call loadSettings so that data is read from localStorage each time the application page loads. The code you need to add (again, add it below the code from the previous listing) is in the following listing.

> **Listing 5.8   app.js—Connecting the UI to the** localStorage **functions**

```
loadSettings();
document.forms.settings.addEventListener('submit', saveSettings, false);
document.forms.settings.addEventListener('reset', resetSettings, false);
```

Attach event handlers to the submit and reset events of the Settings form.

TRY IT OUT!

If you now launch the application in a compatible browser, you should be able to navigate to the Settings view and change the name and color scheme from the default settings. Figure 5.3 shows this happening on a BlackBerry Torch 9860 smartphone.

If you were to press the Reset All Data button, the application would return to its default color and name.

Because you're using localStorage, these name and color settings will persist between browser sessions (unless the user specifically clears down their localStorage

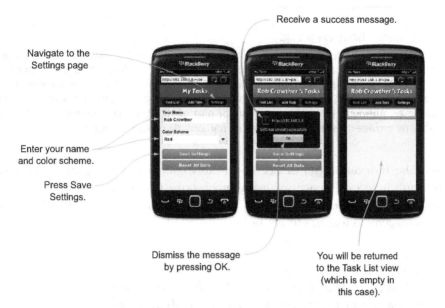

Receive a success message.

Navigate to the Settings page

Enter your name and color scheme.

Press Save Settings.

Dismiss the message by pressing OK.

You will be returned to the Task List view (which is empty in this case).

Figure 5.3 The user fills out the Settings form and presses the Save Settings button. When the data has been saved to localStorage, the settings are reloaded, and a message is displayed to the user. When the user dismisses this message, they are taken back to the Task List view (which is empty for now).

area via the browser preferences screen). Try refreshing the page, restarting your browser, and even restarting your computer; the data should persist. Pretty neat.

In the next section, we'll show you how to take things even further with client-side data storage using the IndexedDB API. We'll do so by having you add real meat to your sample application by implementing the ability to add, edit, delete, view, and search tasks.

5.3 Managing data using IndexedDB

IndexedDB provides an API for a transactional database that is stored on the client side. The Web Storage API stores and retrieves values using keys; IndexedDB supports more advanced functionality, including in-order retrieval of keys, support for duplicate values, and efficient value searching using indexes.

| IndexedDB | 11.0 | 4.0 | 10.0 | N/A | N/A |

In the cases where the application detects no browser support for IndexedDB, you'll use Web SQL as a fallback.

FYI: More about Web SQL

IndexedDB was added to HTML5 quite late in the specification process. As a result, browser support for it has been much slower than with other parts of the specification. Prior to IndexedDB, HTML5 included a client-side database specification known as Web SQL, which defined an API for a full relational database that would live in the browser. Although Web SQL is no longer part of HTML5, many browser vendors had already provided decent support for it, particularly mobile browsers.

Using the IndexedDB API can be notoriously complex at first glance, particularly if you don't have experience writing asynchronous JavaScript code that uses callback functions. But this section will slowly guide you in the use of IndexedDB as you add task management features to My Tasks.

In this section, you'll learn

- How to create and connect to an IndexedDB database
- How to load existing data from an IndexedDB database
- How to perform queries on an IndexedDB database using IndexedDB's key ranges
- How to store new data in an IndexedDB database
- How to delete single data items from an IndexedDB database
- How to clear an entire data store from an IndexedDB database

As you learn how to use the database services of IndexedDB and Web SQL, you'll also implement the UI for the Add Task and Task List views. Overall, building out the UI and application features happens in eight steps:

- Step 1: Detect IndexedDB or Web SQL.
- Step 2: Connect to the database and create an object store.
- Step 3: Develop the UI for the Task List view.
- Step 4: Implement a search engine for the database and display search results.
- Step 5: Implement the search interface for the Task List view.
- Step 6: Add new tasks from the Add Task view to the database.
- Step 7: Update and delete tasks from the Task List view.
- Step 8: Drop the database to clear all tasks.

5.3.1   *Detecting database support on a browser*

Before you can create a database, you need to detect what database system is running within a browser. Currently two systems can be found: IndexedDB and Web SQL. Detection of the database system is done by assigning a variable to a logical expression of alternating or operators (||) and vendor-prefixed IndexDB object identifiers. Because IndexedDB isn't a standard feature, you must use the vendor prefixes to access the database system object on the various browsers.

If a database object is found, the application saves the found database object to a variable for later use; otherwise, the application assigns a `false` value to the variable. You also need to find and save the database key range. We'll discuss the key range later in the section.

STEP 1: DETECT INDEXEDDB OR WEB SQL
Now, to add feature detection to the sample application, add the code from the following listing to the app.js file. This code should be added immediately after the code you inserted in the previous section.

Listing 5.9   app.js—Feature detection for database-related objects

```
var indexedDB = window.indexedDB || window.webkitIndexedDB
        || window.mozIndexedDB || window.msIndexedDB || false,

IDBKeyRange = window.IDBKeyRange || window.webkitIDBKeyRange
        || window.mozIDBKeyRange || window.msIDBKeyRange || false,

    webSQLSupport = ('openDatabase' in window);
```

Web SQL object is not implemented as a member of window. To detect if the browser supports Web SQL, check for the existence of openDatabase as a member of window.

5.3.2   Creating or connecting to an IndexedDB database, creating an object store and index

 To create or connect to an IndexedDB database, the application needs to invoke the IndexedDB method open. If no database exists when the open method is called, a new database will be created, and a connection object will be created. Once indexedDB.open successfully creates a connection, the onsuccess and/or upgradeNeeded event handler will be called, and the connection object will be accessible through the event object passed to the event handler.[1] With this connection object, the application can create an object store or index for the application.

Before looking at how an application would create object stores and indexes, let's discuss how data is stored in an IndexedDB database. All data in an IndexedDB database is stored inside an object store. Each database can contain many object stores, which can be roughly thought of as equivalent to tables in a relational database management system (RDBMS). In turn, each object store comprises a collection of zero or more objects, the equivalent of rows in a RDBMS. Figure 5.4 illustrates the structure of an IndexedDB database.

Now that you have a better idea of how objects are stored in the IndexedDB database, let's get back to creating object stores and indexes.

 Object stores can only be created while the application is handling an upgradNeeded event. This event can occur in two situations: when a new database is created and when a database's version number is increased. Once the application has entered the upgradeNeeded event handler, the object store is created by calling the

---

[1] If a new database is created, events upgradeNeeded and onsuccess will be fired, but upgradeNeeded will be handled before onsuccess.

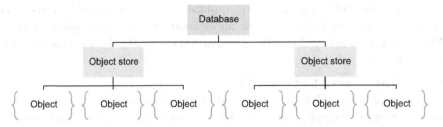

Figure 5.4   Hierarchical structure of an IndexedDB database. Each database can have many object stores, which themselves can contain many objects. The object is the structure for a data record, equivalent to a row in a relational database.

`createObjectStore` method with two arguments: a name and keypath for the new object store. The keypath defines what property within each object will serve as the key for retrieving the object from its store.

Once the object store is created, you can create one or more indexes for it. Creating an index allows the application to retrieve an object with a key different than the one defined in the object store. To create a new index, use the object store's method `createIndex` and pass it three arguments: the name of the new index, the name of the object property that will serve as the key, and an `options` object.

The `options` object has two properties that serve as flag parameters. The first flag, `unique`, allows the application to specify whether or not a key can be shared. The second flag, `multiEntry`, allows the application to specify how to handle array-based keys: Either enter an object under several different keys listed in an array, or enter an object using the entire array as a key. You won't need to use the second flag in the My Tasks application (for more detail about `multiEntry`, see appendix B or www.w3.org/TR/IndexedDB/#dfn-multientry).

Let's look at the database-creation process and apply it to our application.

STEP 2: CONNECT TO THE DATABASE AND CREATE AN OBJECT STORE

You will need to create an object store, "tasks", for all the tasks the user will want to keep track of. Remember to first create the database connection, because you'll need this to create the object store and the index. You'll use the index to access the object store by the task's description. This will be useful when you implement the application's search engine that allows the user to filter their task list by a task's description.

You'll also add a call to the `loadTasks` function here. It's not related to object store or index creation, but it will be useful later when the application is in the startup phase and needs to load the existing `task` objects into the Task List view. You'll implement `loadTasks` later in this section.

The following listing might seem like a lot of code, but it's doing quite a bit for us: opening a database connection, creating an object store, and providing a Web SQL fallback for browsers that don't support IndexedDB. Add the code from this listing to app.js, just below the code you added from listing 5.9.

Listing 5.10 app.js—Connecting to and configuring the database

```
var db;                                    ← Use db to store the
                                              database connection.
var openDB = function() {
    if(indexedDB) {
        var request = indexedDB.open('tasks', 1),  ←
            upgradeNeeded = ('onupgradeneeded' in request);
        request.onsuccess = function(e) {
            db = e.target.result;
            if(!upgradeNeeded && db.version != '1') {    ←
                var setVersionRequest = db.setVersion('1');
                setVersionRequest.onsuccess = function(e) {
                    var objectStore = db.createObjectStore('tasks', {
                        keyPath: 'id'
                    });
                    objectStore.createIndex('desc', 'descUpper', {   ←
                        unique: false
                    });
                    loadTasks();
                }
            } else {
                loadTasks();
            }
        }
        if(upgradeNeeded) {
            request.onupgradeneeded = function(e) {    ←
                db = e.target.result;
                var objectStore = db.createObjectStore('tasks', {
                    keyPath: 'id'
                });
                objectStore.createIndex('desc', 'descUpper', {
                    unique: false
                });
            }
        }
    } else if(webSQLSupport) {
        db = openDatabase('tasks','1.0','Tasks database',(5*1024*1024));  ←
        db.transaction(function(tx) {
            var sql = 'CREATE TABLE IF NOT EXISTS tasks ('+
                      'id INTEGER PRIMARY KEY ASC,'+
                      'desc TEXT,'+
                      'due DATETIME,'+
                      'complete BOOLEAN'+
                      ')';
            tx.executeSql(sql, [], loadTasks);    ←
        });
    }
}
openDB();
```

Use db to store the database connection.

The open method is asynchronous; while the request is in progress, open immediately returns an IDBRequest. If no database exists, create one, and then create a connection to the database.

If upgradeNeeded is a member of the request object, then the browser supports upgradeNeeded event.

If the event upgradeNeeded doesn't exist, then the browser supports the deprecated setVersion method.

If db.version is not equal to 1, then no object store exists and it must be created. Object stores can only be created during a version-change transaction. So, increase the version number of the current database by calling db.setVersion with a version argument set to 'I'.

Use createIndex to create another index for the objectStore. This index will be used later to implement the application's search feature.

This event handler will be called when the database is created for the first time.

Allocate 5 MB (5 * 1024 * 1024) for the tasks database.

Use the executeSql method of the transaction object, tx, to create a tasks table if it doesn't already exist. A [ ] means no optional argument array being passed. loadTasks is the callback function.

Now that you can open a connection to the database and create an object store, let's look at how users will interact with the tasks database by developing the UI for the

Task List view. Building this interface will generate a list of user features to guide your later development of database management functions.

5.3.3   Developing a dynamic list with HTML and JavaScript

Your Task List view will require a list of to-do items that can change as the user adds and deletes tasks. Building a web page with a varying list requires the use of JavaScript to generate new HTML markup for each list item and its UI controls. In addition, you'll need to insert those new list items by making modifications to the DOM. If a user needs to delete an item, the application will regenerate the entire list rather than try to remove an individual list item from the DOM. Although this isn't the most efficient way to handle list management, it's fast to implement and allows you to get on to more interesting tasks like learning about the HTML5 IndexedDB API!

STEP 3: DEVELOP THE UI FOR THE TASK LIST VIEW

The Task List view is a dynamic part of the application's webpage that updates itself in response to user actions. Here's a list of those actions and how to implement them:

- *Adding a task to the list*—The application needs to define a function, showTask, to generate the HTML markup for each added task and then insert the markup into the view's DOM.
- *Checking off and deleting tasks*—You'll also use showTask to add check boxes and Delete buttons to each added task. showTask will also define and bind an event handler for each check box and delete button.

Figure 5.5 illustrates how the buttons and check boxes will appear.

The code in listing 5.11 implements the showTask and createEmptyItem functions. CreateEmptyItem is a helper function to handle the boundary conditions where the user has no task items to display in the to-do list. This can occur in two situations:

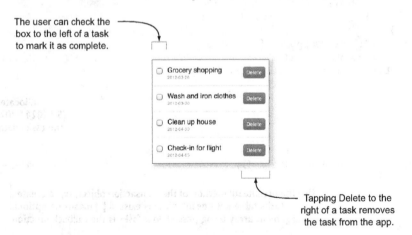

The user can check the box to the left of a task to mark it as complete.

Tapping Delete to the right of a task removes the task from the app.

Figure 5.5   Each task item has two components that allow the user to update the task list. Checking the box on the left-hand side will mark the task as complete, whereas pressing the red Delete button on the right-hand side will remove the task.

when no task items exist in the database and when a search of the task list yields no matches. In order to handle these cases, createEmptyItem will create an "empty item," actually a message that says either "No tasks to display. Add one?" or "No tasks match your query."

Add the following code to your application, just after the code from the previous listing.

Listing 5.11 app.js—Generating the markup for task items

```
var createEmptyItem = function(query, taskList) {          If a query doesn't
    var emptyItem = document.createElement('li');          exist, the search will
    if(query.length > 0) {                             ◁─┘ return zero results.
        emptyItem.innerHTML = '<div class="item_title">'+
            'No tasks match your query <strong>'+query+'</strong>.'+
            '</div>';
    } else {
        emptyItem.innerHTML = '<div class="item_title">'+
            'No tasks to display. <a href="#add">Add one</a>?'+
            '</div>';
    }
    taskList.appendChild(emptyItem);                       The showTask function creates
}                                                          and displays a task list item
                                                           containing a title, due date,
var showTask = function(task, list) {                 ◁─┘ check box, and Delete button.
    var newItem = document.createElement('li'),
        checked = (task.complete == 1) ? ' checked="checked"' : '';

    newItem.innerHTML =
        '<div class="item_complete">'+
            '<input type="checkbox" name="item_complete" '+
                'id="chk_'+task.id+'"'+checked+'>'+
        '</div>'+
        '<div class="item_delete">'+
            '<a href="#" id="del_'+task.id+'">Delete</a>'+
        '</div>'+
        '<div class="item_title">'+task.desc+'</div>'+
        '<div class="item_due">'+task.due+'</div>';
    list.appendChild(newItem);

    var markAsComplete = function(e) {                ◁──    The markAsComplete event
        e.preventDefault();                                 handler is executed when
        var updatedTask = {                                 the user marks or unmarks
            id: task.id,                                     the check box.
            desc: task.desc,
            descUpper: task.desc.toUpperCase(),
            due: task.due,
            complete: e.target.checked
        };
        updateTask(updatedTask);                            The remove event handler
    }                                                       is executed when the user
                                                            clicks the Delete button for
    var remove = function(e) {                        ◁─┘  a task item.
        e.preventDefault();
        if(confirm('Deleting task. Are you sure?', 'Delete')) {
```

```
                      deleteTask(task.id);
            }
        }
        document.getElementById('chk_'+task.id).onchange =
            markAsComplete;
        document.getElementById('del_'+task.id).onclick = remove;
    }
```

> This code attaches event handlers to the task item's check box and remove button.

5.3.4 Searching an IndexedDB database

Core API

Now that the UI for the Task List view is complete, you need to search the IndexedDB database to extract a list of task objects for display in the Task View list. To do this, IndexedDB requires the creation of a transaction to define an array of object stores to scan and the type of transaction to execute. The transaction type defines how the database will be accessed. IndexedDB provides two options: read-only and read-write. In the case of implementing a search for the My Tasks application, the transaction would need to be defined with tasks as the object store to search and a transaction type of 'readonly'. The application could use the read/write option, but the search performance would be slower.

Once the transaction is defined, you then need to extract the index from the object store. The index will enable the application to filter the object store based on some property of the object. In your application, the index's key is based on the task's description property. Using this index and a string describing some portion of the task description, you'll create a database cursor using the IndexedDB API method openCursor. The application will then use this cursor's continue method to iterate over the database and find all of the tasks containing a portion of the task description.

Core API

Using cursors to iterate through database records

Cursor is a generic term describing a control structure in a database that allows you to iterate through the records stored in it. Cursors typically enable you to filter out records based on certain characteristics and to define the order in which the result set is returned. Using the cursor's continue method, you can then sequentially move through the record set returned by the cursor, retrieving the data for use in your applications. Cursors in IndexedDB allow you to traverse a result set that's defined by a key range, moving in a direction of either an increasing or decreasing order of keys.

STEP 4: IMPLEMENT A SEARCH ENGINE FOR THE DATABASE AND DISPLAY SEARCH RESULTS
In the application, the loadTasks function is responsible for retrieving and displaying tasks from the IndexedDB or Web SQL database. loadTasks will either retrieve a filtered set of tasks or all tasks and then pass them to the showTask function, which will render them onto the Task List view. Add the code from the next listing immediately after the code from the previous listing.

Listing 5.12   app.js—Searching the database and displaying the resulting tasks

```
var loadTasks = function(q) {
    var taskList = document.getElementById('task_list'),
        query = q || '';
    taskList.innerHTML = '';

    if(indexedDB) {
        var tx = db.transaction(['tasks'], 'readonly'),
            objectStore = tx.objectStore('tasks'), cursor, i = 0;
        if(query.length > 0) {
            var index = objectStore.index('desc'),
                upperQ = query.toUpperCase(),
                keyRange = IDBKeyRange.bound(upperQ, upperQ+'z');
            cursor = index.openCursor(keyRange);
        } else {
            cursor = objectStore.openCursor();
        }

        cursor.onsuccess = function(e) {
            var result = e.target.result;
            if(result == null) return;
            i++;
            showTask(result.value, taskList);
            result['continue']();
        }

        tx.oncomplete = function(e) {
            if(i == 0) { createEmptyItem(query, taskList); }
        }
    } else if(webSQLSupport) {
        db.transaction(function(tx) {
            var sql, args = [];
            if(query.length > 0) {
                sql = 'SELECT * FROM tasks WHERE desc LIKE ?';
                args[0] = query+'%';
            } else {
                sql = 'SELECT * FROM tasks';
            }
            var iterateRows = function(tx, results) {
                var i = 0, len = results.rows.length;
                for(;i<len;i++) {
                    showTask(results.rows.item(i), taskList);
                }
                if(len === 0) { createEmptyItem(query, taskList); }
            }
            tx.executeSql(sql, args, iterateRows);
        });
    }
}
```

Build a key range on the uppercase version of the task description. The 'z' appended to the second argument allows the application to search for a task description beginning with the search term (otherwise, it would only return exact matches).

e.target references the cursor, so get the result set from the cursor.

Count the number of tasks passed to showTask. The resulting value will be used by the transaction event handler, tx.onComplete, to determine if an empty task list should be rendered.

Use result['continue'] to find the next matching task in the index or next task in the object store (if not searching). Using result.continue, rather than result['continue'], might result in a conflict with the JavaScript reserved word continue.

If IndexedDB isn't supported and Web SQL is, build a query that will retrieve the tasks from the database.

NOTE You may have noticed that the loadTasks function accepts an optional argument, q. The application will only pass a query to loadTasks when it wants to filter the results by what the user has entered in the search box.

STEP 5: IMPLEMENT THE SEARCH INTERFACE FOR THE TASK VIEW LIST

To implement the search interface for the application, add the following code immediately after the code from the previous listing.

Listing 5.13 app.js—Searching for tasks

```
var searchTasks = function(e) {
    e.preventDefault();
    var query = document.forms.search.query.value;
    if(query.length > 0) {
        loadTasks(query);
    } else {
        loadTasks();
    }
}

document.forms.search.addEventListener('submit', searchTasks, false);
```

If a query was typed in, pass the query as an argument to the loadTasks function.

When the user submits the search form, call the searchTasks function.

TRY IT OUT

If you reload the application in your browser, you should see a friendly message telling you that you have no tasks to display, as shown in figure 5.6.

As you can see from figure 5.6, displaying a list of tasks isn't very useful if you have no way of adding tasks to the database. Let's solve that problem right now.

5.3.5 *Adding data to a database using IndexedDB or Web SQL*

Core API

Adding data to an IndexedDB database requires the creation of a transaction to define an array of object stores you'll be using to store the data and the type of transaction needed, in this case 'readwrite'. Once you have the transaction created, you then call its method objectStore, with the name of the object store you want to add a data item to. The method will respond to this call by returning the object store. From here, adding the data item to the store is easy. Call the object

Figure 5.6 In the left screenshot, the application finds no tasks in the database. Therefore, it displays a message and links the question "Add one?" to the Add Task form. In the right screenshot, if you try to search for a task, you'll see that no tasks match your query, no matter what you enter.

store's method add, and pass the new data item to its only argument. The method will immediately return a request object. If you'd like the application to respond to the object store's successful addition of the data item, then define an event handler for the transaction's oncomplete event.

Now, let's see how this addition procedure can be applied to the application.

STEP 6: ADD NEW TASKS FROM THE ADD TASK VIEW TO THE DATABASE

This code creates a new function called insertTask that manages the process of inserting the task into the database and updating the display of the Task List view. InsertTask first constructs a new task object from the Add Task form; second, it adds the task to the IndexedDB database (or Web SQL if the browser doesn't support IndexedDB). Finally, it triggers the callback function, updateView, when the task has been successfully added to the database. Add the code from the following listing after the code from the previous listing.

Listing 5.14 app.js—Adding new tasks

```
var insertTask = function(e) {
    e.preventDefault();
    var desc = document.forms.add.desc.value,
        dueDate = document.forms.add.due_date.value;
    if(desc.length > 0 && dueDate.length > 0) {
        var task = {
            id: new Date().getTime(),
            desc: desc,
            descUpper: desc.toUpperCase(),
            due: dueDate,
            complete: false
        }
        if(indexedDB) {
            var tx = db.transaction(['tasks'], 'readwrite');
            var objectStore = tx.objectStore('tasks');
            var request = objectStore.add(task);
            tx.oncomplete = updateView;
        } else if(webSQLSupport) {
            db.transaction(function(tx) {
                var sql = 'INSERT INTO tasks(desc, due, complete) '+
                    'VALUES(?, ?, ?)',
                    args = [task.desc, task.due, task.complete];
                tx.executeSql(sql, args, updateView);
            });
        }
    } else {
        alert('Please fill out all fields', 'Add task error');
    }
}
function updateView(){
    loadTasks();
    alert('Task added successfully', 'Task added');
    document.forms.add.desc.value = '';
    document.forms.add.due_date.value = '';
```

Construct a task object to store in the database. The key is the id property, which is the current time, and you also store the uppercase version of the description in order to implement case-insensitive indexing.

When a task has been successfully added, call the event handler updateView. The definition for updateView appears immediately after insertTask.

Add the task to the object store using the IndexedDB method add.

For the Web SQL fallback, use an INSERT statement to add the task.

updateView loads tasks from the database, clears input fields in the Add Task form, and redirects the user to the Task List view.

```
                    location.hash = '#list';
                 }
document.forms.add.addEventListener('submit', insertTask, false);              ◄──
```

> **Add the event handler insertTask to the Add Task form's submit button.**

TRY IT OUT

At this point, you should be able to add tasks to the database using the Add Task form. When the task has been saved, you are taken back to the Task List view, which should display the task you just created. Feel free to try it now—add some tasks. Also, be sure to try out the Search form, because this should now be fully functional. The application is starting to take shape, but you still have a small number of features to add before it's complete. Next, you'll write code to allow users to update and delete existing tasks.

5.3.6   *Updating and deleting data from an IndexedDB database*

The IndexedDB database has a relatively simple procedure for changing existing data objects in the object store. First, the application needs to define the database transaction about to occur, and then the application uses the transaction to write a data object to the specified object store.

In order to define the database transaction for updating an object store, the application would call the IndexedDB method transaction to define the type and scope of the transaction. Because updating a database requires writing to the object store, the type is specified as 'readwrite'. The second parameter, the scope of the transaction, specifies the various object stores the application will be writing to.

With the transaction defined, the application can now get the object store it needs to update. Calling the transaction's method, objectStore, with a parameter specifying the name of the object store will return the object store. At this point, the application can update the object store by invoking its put method, with the changed data object as its parameter.

Deleting task items follows a similar procedure. But once the application has the object store, it will invoke the object store's delete method, with the data object's key as a parameter. Delete will use the key to find and delete the data object within the object store.

Let's apply these update and delete operations to the application.

STEP 7: UPDATE AND DELETE TASKS FROM THE TASK LIST VIEW

You've already done some of the work required for updating and deleting a task. If you look at the Task List view in the application, you'll notice that each task has a check box and a Delete button. The check box has an updateTask embedded into the markAsComplete event handler, and the Delete button has a deleteTask embedded into the remove event handler.

All that's left to do is to insert the procedures for updating and deleting the object store into their respective updateTask and deleteTask function definitions. Because not all browsers support IndexedDB, you'll also insert a Web SQL fallback. Add the code from this listing right beneath the code from the previous listing..

Listing 5.15 app.js—Updating and deleting tasks

```
var updateTask = function(task) {
    if(indexedDB) {
        var tx = db.transaction(['tasks'], 'readwrite');
        var objectStore = tx.objectStore('tasks');
        var request = objectStore.put(task);                      ◄─
    } else if(webSQLSupport) {
        var complete = (task.complete) ? 1 : 0;
        db.transaction(function(tx) {
            var sql = 'UPDATE tasks SET complete = ? WHERE id = ?',
                args = [complete, task.id];
            tx.executeSql(sql, args);
        });
    }
}

var deleteTask = function(id) {
    if(indexedDB) {
        var tx = db.transaction(['tasks'], 'readwrite');
        var objectStore = tx.objectStore('tasks');
        var request = objectStore['delete'](id);                  ◄─
        tx.oncomplete = loadTasks;                                ◄─┐
    } else if(webSQLSupport) {
        db.transaction(function(tx) {
            var sql = 'DELETE FROM tasks WHERE id = ?',
                args = [id];
            tx.executeSql(sql, args, loadTasks);
        });
    }
}
```

> Use the put method, passing the task object as an argument, to update the task in the database. The task object must have the correct key value, or the database may create a new object in the store rather than update the existing one.

> Use the delete method to remove a task. Some browsers will choke if you use dot-notation here, because delete is a reserved word in JavaScript. So to be safe, use the square bracket notation.

> When the delete operation has successfully completed, load the Task List view to show the updated items.

TRY IT OUT

You should now be able to mark the completed check box and delete items in the Task List view. But one final function remains to complete the application: the drop-Database function. This will delete the entire tasks database (or truncate the tasks table if using the Web SQL fallback).

5.3.7 Dropping a database using IndexedDB

 Core API

Dropping a database in IndexedDB is easy and involves just one method: the delete-Database method of the IndexedDB object. Call deleteDatabase while passing the name of the target object store, and then the entire database will be removed.

STEP 8: DROP THE DATABASE TO CLEAR ALL TASKS

To enable a user to clear all tasks from the application, you need to do two things:

1. Create a new function, dropDatabase, that will remove the tasks database, and therefore all task items, from the application.

2. Call dropDatabase from the resetSettings function you created earlier in the localStorage section of this chapter. Adding this call now completes reset-Settings's function, which is to reset a user's personal settings and erase all of a user's tasks.

For browsers that don't support IndexedDB, you'll need to provide a Web SQL fallback as well. In this case, you won't drop the database; you'll just delete the tasks table from the Web SQL database.

To define the `dropDatabase` function, add the code from the next listing directly below the code from the previous listing in your app.js file.

Listing 5.16   app.js—Dropping the database

```
var dropDatabase = function() {
    if(indexedDB) {
        var delDBRequest = indexedDB.deleteDatabase('tasks');
        delDBRequest.onsuccess = window.location.reload();
    } else if(webSQLSupport) {
        db.transaction(function(tx) {
            var sql = 'DELETE FROM tasks';
            tx.executeSql(sql, [], loadTasks);
        });
    }
}
```

Use the **deleteDatabase** method to drop the tasks database.

Reload the page to initiate a load event. This will trigger the load event handler to create a fresh copy of the database.

In your Web SQL fallback, clear down the tasks table rather than drop the entire database.

With the `dropDatabase` function defined, you can now call it from the `resetSettings` function you created in section 5.2.3. In this function, locate the line `location.hash = '#list';` and add the following line just beneath it:

```
dropDatabase();
```

TRY IT OUT

That's it! The sample application should now be fully functional. Try it out on a device or browser that supports IndexedDB or Web SQL. (iOS, Android, BlackBerry Torch, Opera Mobile, Chrome, Firefox, Safari, and Opera all work.) If both IndexedDB and Web SQL are available in the browser, the application will favor the former. In the next and final section of this chapter, you'll learn how to ensure an application will work offline using an application cache manifest file. You should then have an application that stores all of its data on the client and is usable both online and offline.

5.4   Creating a web application that works offline: using the application cache manifest

Until recently, web applications have been used primarily in connected environments, on desktop or laptop computers, where the majority of the time an internet connection is available. But as rich web applications become more prominent as realistic alternatives to their desktop counterparts, and as mobile applications continue to gather momentum, the need grows for web applications to work in scenarios where connectivity is not available.

Application cache manifest   4.0   3.5   10.0   10.6   4.0

To address these demands, HTML5 provides a file called the application cache manifest. This file, in its most basic form, specifies a list of web resources needed by a web application. Browsers that support the manifest feature will use the list to provide a web application with access to a local cache of these web resources. As a result, the web application can run offline.

For resources only available from the network, the cache manifest can specify fallback client-side URIs for offline activity. For instance, if an application relies on a JavaScript file to save data to a server, then the cache manifest would specify a client-side URI pointing to a JavaScript file that uses local requests for client-side storage.

> **NOTE** If you've been working through this chapter's example without a web server, it's worth pointing out that you won't be able to use the application cache manifest unless your application resides on an actual web server (rather than just sitting in a local directory). You'll also need to do a small bit of configuration to get cache manifests to work, which we'll cover later in the section.

The cache manifest can also specify URIs that must be fetched from the network. They will never be downloaded from the application cache, even if the application is offline.

In this section, you'll learn
- How to configure a web server for an application cache manifest MIME type
- How to create a cache manifest file
- How to detect changes in the manifest file

Now that you have a basic understanding of the application cache manifest, let's implement offline functionality for My Tasks. This process will be broken down into three steps:

- Step 1: Configure the web server to serve application cache manifest files for My Tasks.
- Step 2: Create an application cache manifest file for My Tasks.
- Step 3: Detect changes in the My Tasks application cache manifest file.

5.4.1 Configuring a web server for an application cache manifest's MIME type

In order for a manifest file to be correctly loaded, your web server needs to serve a manifest file using the correct MIME type. The manifest MIME type is not typically set by default in a web server's configuration, so you'll need to add the MIME type, `text/cache-manifest`, to your web server's configuration.

STEP 1: CONFIGURE THE WEB SERVER TO SERVE APPLICATION MANIFEST FILES FOR MY TASKS
If you're using the Apache web server, you can typically add MIME types by either modifying the httpd.conf configuration file or by serving an .htaccess file in the root of your

web application. If you're using Python's built-in web server, then create an .htaccess file in the root directory of your web application, and then add the MIME type to the .htaccess file. In either case, to serve the correct MIME type for files with the extension .appcache, you need to add the following line to the end of the configuration or .htaccess file:

```
addType text/cache-manifest .appcache
```

> **NOTE** A cache manifest file can have any file extension, but the file must be served with the MIME type `text/cache-manifest`.

If you're using the nginx web server, you add MIME types by adding an entry to the mime.types file in the nginx conf directory. This file typically has the following format:

```
types {
    text/html               html htm shtml;
    text/css                css;
    text/xml                xml;
    ...
}
```

To enable the cache manifest MIME type, add an entry to this file as follows:

```
    text/cache-manifest         appcache;
```

After editing the configuration file, restart your web server, and your cache manifest file should be served correctly from now on. If you're using another web server, please consult your web server's documentation for further information on how to add MIME types.

With the web server configured correctly, you're now ready to create a cache manifest file, which we'll cover next.

5.4.2 Creating a cache manifest file

The manifest file is a basic text file that contains a title header, CACHE MANIFEST, and up to three subsections with the headings CACHE, NETWORK, and FALLBACK. For explanatory purposes only, here's a sample cache manifest file:

```
CACHE MANIFEST
# Rev 3

CACHE:
index.html
pics/logo.png
stylesheet.css

FALLBACK:
*.html          /offline.html

NETWORK:
http://api.stockwebsite.com
```

The CACHE section represents the default section for entries. URIs listed under this header will be cached after they're downloaded for the first time.

> **NOTE** You can also forgo specifying a CACHE header and simply place the URIs to be cached immediately under the title header, CACHE MANIFEST.

The FALLBACK section is optional and specifies one or more pairs of URIs to use when a resource is offline. The first URI in a pair is the online resource; the second is the local fallback resource. Wildcards can be used.

> **NOTE** Both URIs must have a relative path name. Also, the URIs here, as well as in other sections of the cache manifest, must have the same scheme, host, and port as the manifest.

The NETWORK section serves as the application's whitelist for online access. All URIs listed under this header must bypass the cache and access an online source. Wildcards can be used.

You can also specify comments in the application cache manifest. They consist of any number of tabs or spaces followed by a single # and then followed by a string of characters. Comments must exist on a line separate from other section headers and URIs.

Now, equipped with knowledge of the basic structure and syntax of an application cache manifest, let's put that knowledge to work by creating one for My Tasks.

STEP 2: CREATE THE APPLICATION CACHE MANIFEST FILE FOR MY TASKS

Your cache manifest will have a CACHE section and a NETWORK section. The CACHE section will list the index.html, style.css, and app.js files as cacheable resources. The NETWORK section will contain only an asterisk, the wildcard character. Create a new file named tasks.appcache in the root directory of your web application, then add the contents of the following listing to tasks.appcache.

> **NOTE** After entering this code listing, don't try to run the application. It will work, but you'll have to do extra work in the final section of this chapter, "Automating application updates," to get it working correctly.

Listing 5.17   tasks.appcache—Defining resources that are available offline

This denotes the start of the cache manifest file.

```
CACHE MANIFEST
# Rev 1
CACHE:
index.html
style.css
app.js

NETWORK:
*
```

Use a comment in your manifest to define the current revision number of the web application. This allows you to easily monitor and log application revisions, even if no changes are being made to the manifest file itself. Later, we'll show how to use these revision numbers to trigger application updates.

The wildcard under **NETWORK** specifies that the online whitelist is open; any other URIs not listed under **CACHE MANIFEST, CACHE** must be retrieved from the network.

In order for your application to read this file, you need to modify your HTML document with the manifest's filename. Open index.html and replace the current opening `<html>` element definition with the following:

```
<html lang="en" class="blue" manifest="tasks.appcache">
```

We're almost there. In the final step, you will give My Tasks the ability to detect changes in the manifest file. My Tasks will use this ability to determine when to download a newer version of My Tasks.

5.4.3 Automating application updates

When you created the cache manifest file, you used a comment with a revision number to update the manifest, to document changes in the manifest or in one or more of the web resources listed in the manifest. This practice has a function beyond documentation; it can also be used to detect and trigger application updates.

If any change is made to the text in the manifest, the application will download the new manifest and all files listed in the CACHE MANIFEST or CACHE section. When this is done, a new cache is created and an updateready event is fired. To update the application, you have to attach an event handler to updateready. The handler will swap the old cache for the new one, then ask the user for permission to update the application. If the user grants permission, the event handler will force an application reload. The reload ensures that resources from the new cache are loaded into the application. If the user declines the update, the application will use the new cache the next time the user loads the application.

Now, let's add this update feature to My Tasks.

STEP 3: DETECT CHANGES IN THE MY TASKS APPLICATION CACHE MANIFEST FILE

Core API

As mentioned before, you'll use the updateready event to detect changes in the application manifest. So, all you need to do is define and attach an event handler to the application cache's updateready event. The event handler will call the application cache's swapCache method and ask the user for permission to reload the application using the new version of the cache. If the user confirms, the event handler will call window.location.reload to reload the application using the new cache version.

Add the code from the following listing to app.js, just after the dropDatabase function you created in listing 5.16.

Listing 5.18 app.js—Automatic update detection and loading

```
if('applicationCache' in window) {                              Detect if the user's browser
    var appCache = window.applicationCache;                     supports the Application Cache API.
    appCache.addEventListener('updateready', function() {
        appCache.swapCache();
        if(confirm('App update is available. Update now?')) {
            window.location.reload();
        }
    }, false);                  Ask the user if they want to update the application now. If they
}                              click Yes, the page will reload using the new cache; otherwise,
                               the new cache will be used the next time they load the page.
```

When updateready fires, the browser will have already redownloaded the resources listed in the manifest and created a new cache. The event handler for updateready will call swapCache to replace the old cache with the new cache.

Figure 5.7   My Tasks application running offline. You'll notice the airplane icon in the top left indicating that the phone has no network access. You may also notice that the jazzy font we used in the heading is no longer showing; this font was loaded from the Google Font API, which isn't available when you're offline.

TRY IT OUT

That's all there is to it! If you've followed these steps correctly, you should now be able to use your application offline. If you put this application on a server with a registered domain name, you could test this application on your mobile device's browser. Just visit the site in order to load the application for the first time. Now, turn on Airplane Mode on your device, which should kill all network connectivity. Refresh the page in your device's web browser, and you should still be able to use the application in full. The result can be seen in the screenshots in figure 5.7.

If you are trying to run this app on your desktop browser with the Python web server, start the My Tasks app by entering localhost:8000 into your browser's address box. (If you configured the web server with a different port number, use that number instead.)

To simulate an offline condition for the My Tasks app running in your desktop browser, kill the Python web server process, then refresh the page in your web browser. You should still be able to use the application in full.

NOTE   If you tried to run this application with the cache manifest before entering the code from this final listing, then you must first flush your browser's cache before loading the application from the server.

To test the application's ability to load a newer version, update the revision number in the tasks.appcache file and save it. Next, reload the application. You should see the

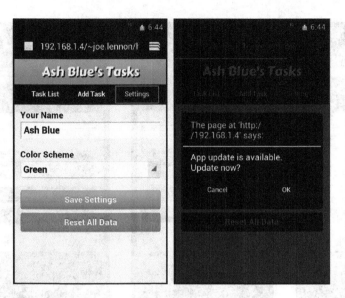

Figure 5.8   When the manifest file has been updated and a new application cache has been created, the updateready event is fired. The application attaches a handler to this event that swaps the old cache for the new cache, then asks the user if they want to update the application (this simply reloads the page, which loads the latest application version from the new cache).

confirmation dialog asking you if you want to update. This is illustrated in the Android device screenshot in figure 5.8.

5.5   Summary

As you've learned in this chapter, HTML5 makes it possible to create offline database applications using client-side code. This allows you to build faster, more responsive applications that store data on the device itself and work regardless of the browser's state of internet connectivity. These abilities expand the range of web applications and make the web a more viable platform for cross-platform mobile application development.

In the next chapter, you'll learn about the 2D canvas API in HTML5 and how it allows you to build animations and games using native JavaScript APIs. The chapter will introduce you to Canvas's support for drawing graphic elements using gradients, paths, and arcs. You'll also learn how to use the API to create smooth, high-frame-rate animations. In addition, the chapter will show the API in action while building an entire game.

Interactive graphics, media, and gaming

Interactive media APIs such as Canvas, SVG, Video, and WebGL are making graphics creation, media players, and games available without plugins. You've probably used these technologies with YouTube's HTML5 video player and/or Google Maps WebGL version. Some companies such as Ludei (CocoonJS) and Goo Technologies (Goo Engine) are investing in such tech for game engines. Once you've completed this section, you'll be fully equipped to start rolling your own interactive applications without plugins.

How do HTML5's interactive media APIs stand up to RIA (Rich Internet Application) plugins such as Flash, Unity, and Silverlight? These systems are much more mature, but they're limited in mobile distribution by requiring a native app or some form of conversion. You can write a game in HTML5, for example, and it magically becomes accessible in-browser on mobile and desktop. (Please note that this is ideal and not quite how it works yet.) There are many limitations on mobile for HTML5 APIs and you should check caniuse.com for more details. Some people argue that RIAs provide advanced encryption security over web apps and they're right. On the other hand, demand is rapidly increasing for non-plugin-based solutions.

How important are the interactive media APIs? To front-end and some mobile developers they're becoming vital tools. Many companies are hiring specifically for HTML5 specialists in Canvas. One of us worked at a shop where they moved most of their Flash work to Canvas development. In fact they're still hiring more Canvas developers because they can't supply all of the requests they get from clients. What we're trying to say is, these skills will make you more in demand and increase your long-term value.

Chapter 6 at a glance

Topic	Description, methods, and so on	Page
API overview	Fundamentals for drawing with the Canvas API	
	▪ Canvas context and origins	166
	▪ getContext()	169
Drawing assets	Creating static Canvas objects with visual output	
	▪ App's general structure	170
	▪ requestAnimationFrame()	173
	▪ ctx.drawImage()	174
	▪ ctx.fillRect()	175
	▪ ctx.createLinearGradient()	177
	▪ ctx.arc() for circles	178
	▪ Paths via moveTo() and lineTo()	179
	▪ ctx.arcTo() for round corners	179
Animate/overlap	Making assets interactive and detecting overlap	
	▪ Moving your visual assets	182
	▪ Overlap detection	183
	▪ Keyboard and mouse input	185
	▪ Touch input	187
Game mechanics	Game features such as counters and screens	
	▪ Score and level output	190
	▪ Progressive level enhancement	191
	▪ Welcome and Game Over screens	193
	▪ HTML5 game libraries	195

Look for this icon ^{Core API} ➡ throughout the chapter to quickly locate the topics outlined in this table.

2D Canvas: low-level, 2D graphics rendering

6

This chapter covers

- Canvas basics
- Shape, path, and text creation
- Creating animation
- Overlap detection
- HTML5 Canvas games from scratch

For many years, developers used Adobe's Flash to create highly interactive web applications. Sadly, Flash wasn't ready when the mobile market explosion for smartphones occurred. Those dark days without an alternative have ended because of HTML5's Canvas API. It allows you to create 2D shapes in a single DOM element without a plug-in. An application written with Canvas is distributable to multiple platforms and through frameworks like PhoneGap.com. Although simple to use, Canvas lets you do complex work, like emulating medical training procedures, creating interactive lobbying presentations, and even building education applications.

> ### Can I use Canvas for drawing graphs and infographics?
> One common misconception about Canvas is that it's good for creating graphs and infographics. Although you could use it to visualize simple information, the Canvas API is better for complex animations and interactivity. If you want simple visuals or animation, check out SVG in chapter 7. It's for creating logos, graphs, and infographics, and it comes with many built-in features Canvas lacks, such as animation, resizability, and CSS support.

In this chapter, you'll explore the Canvas API by implementing a simple engine pattern to maintain and draw graphics. After that, you'll create and animate unique shapes. When you've finished, you'll be able to apply both of those exercises to creating full-length animations, interactive data, or drawing applications. Here, though, you'll use the principles for the true reason of all technology: creating games!

> ### What makes this tutorial special
> We know you can find tutorials similar to Canvas Ricochet online, but our lesson is far more in-depth. Here are a few of the topics covered in this chapter that go beyond what you find in free tutorials:
>
> - Advanced Canvas API usage (gradients, paths, arcs, and more)
> - Progressive level enhancement with scorekeeping
> - Implementing a Canvas design pattern into a fully functional application

You'll create a simple ball-and-paddle–based game called Canvas Ricochet, which includes animated elements, collision detection, and keyboard/mouse/touch controls. After you assemble those components, you'll take everything a step further and create a fully polished product, which includes a score counter, progressively increasing difficulty, and an opening/closing screen. Adding polish greatly helps to monetize a game's worth, resulting in a better return on investment.

After completing this chapter on 2D Canvas, you'll have learned all the necessary tools to build your own Canvas applications from scratch. First up is the Canvas context.

6.1   Canvas basics

No matter what type of Canvas application you build, your first two steps will involve the Canvas context: setting it and generating it. Without a context, you won't be able to draw anything. Then, you'll need to verify that the current browser can actually support Canvas.

6.1.1   Setting the Canvas context

Core API Before working with Canvas, you must choose a set of drawing tools from the API via JavaScript (also known as setting the *context*). As with most HTML5, you must use

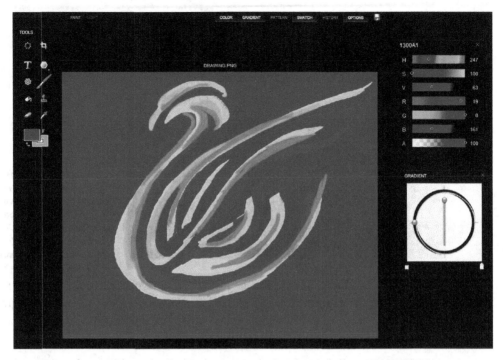

Figure 6.1   Sketchpad (http://mudcu.be/sketchpad/) is a robust drawing application that features gradients, textures, swatches, shape creation, and more. You'll be using a lot of these drawing features during your game's creation process.

JavaScript to program with the API. The most commonly used context draws a 2D plane where everything is flat. Figure 6.1 features a robust drawing application known as Sketchpad, which utilizes Canvas's built-in drawing tools. We'll have you set the context for this chapter's game right after we explain more about what it does.

An alternative to the 2D context is a set of 3D drawing tools. Although 3D context allows for advanced applications, not all browsers support it. With 3D graphics and JavaScript, you can create interactive 3D applications such as the music video shown in figure 6.2 (more about 3D when we get to WebGL in chapter 9).

Canvas: a product of Apple's iOS
Canvas isn't the W3C's brainchild for HTML5. It originally came in 2004 as part of the Mac OS X WebKit by Apple. Two years later, Gecko and Opera browsers adopted it. Popularity since then has significantly grown, and Canvas is now an official HTML5 API.

Because 2D is great for programming simple games, we'll teach you how to use Canvas as we guide you through building Canvas Ricochet with the 2D Canvas context, JavaScript, and HTML. As you'll soon see, a majority of the creation process involves

Figure 6.2   "3 Dreams of Black" is an interactive music video created exclusively for Google Chrome. You can experience Chris Milk's masterpiece at http://ro.me and download the source code!

accessing a set of drawing tools via JavaScript, so you can send an object to the `CanvasRenderingContext2D` interface object. Although `CanvasRenderingContext2D` interface object sounds long and fancy, it really means accessing Canvas to draw. Each newly drawn piece sits on top of any previous drawings.

> **PREREQUISITE**   Before you begin, download the book's complementary files from http://www.manning.com/crowther2/. Also, test-drive the game at http://html5inaction.com/app/ch6/ to see all of its cool features in action.

Each drawing you create is layered on a simple graph system inside the <canvas> tag, as shown in figure 6.3. At first glance, the graph appears to be a normal Cartesian

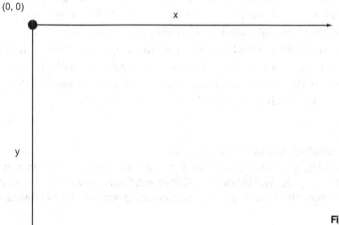

Figure 6.3   The invisible Cartesian graph where Canvas drawings are created. Notice that the x and y coordinates begin in the top left and the y-axis increments downward.

graph. Upon further investigation, you'll notice that the starting point is located in the top-left corner. Another difference is that the y-axis increases while moving downward, instead of incrementing upward.

6.1.2 Generating a Canvas context

Although you *get the context* with JavaScript, you have to pull it out of the <canvas> element's DOM data.

PREPARING THE CANVAS FOR YOUR GAME

Start by opening a text editor to create a document called index.html. Inside your document place a <canvas> tag in the <body> with id, width, and height attributes, as shown in listing 6.1. Failure to declare this size information via HTML, CSS, or JavaScript will result in Canvas receiving a default width and height from the browser. Note that you can place whatever you want inside the <canvas> tag, because its contents are thrown out when rendered. Create an empty game.js file and include it right next to index.html.

Listing 6.1 index.html—Default Canvas HTML

```html
<!DOCTYPE html>

<html>
<head>
    <title>Canvas Ricochet</title>
</head>
<body style="text-align: center">
    <canvas id="canvas" width="408" height="250">
        Your browser shall not pass! Download Google Chrome to view this.
    </canvas>

    <script type="text/javascript" src="game.js"></script>
</body>

</html>
```

When the browser successfully loads the Canvas element, it replaces all content inside.

Create this file now, because you'll be placing all your game logic in it later.

VERIFYING BROWSER SUPPORT

 Core API

Refreshing your browser will remove the nested text inside your <canvas> element. When a Canvas element is successfully rendered, all the content inside is removed, which makes it a great place to include content or messages for browsers that can't support it.

You can access the Canvas API's context from <canvas> and store it in a variable. Code used to render your Canvas would look something like the following two lines; you'll implement it in the next section.

```javascript
var canvas = document.getElementById('canvas');
var context = canvas.getContext('2d');
```

Canvas's context element is useful for defining 2D drawing and you can use it for feature detection. Simply encapsulate the context variable in an if statement, and it will check to make sure the Canvas variable has a `getContext` method. Here's what basic feature detection looks like with Canvas.

```
var canvas = document.getElementById('canvas');

if (canvas.getContext && canvas.getContext('2d'))
    var ctx = canvas.getContext('2d');
```

This checks both `getContext` and `getContext('2d')` because some mobile browsers return `true` for the `getContext` test but `false` for the `getContext('2d')` test.

| Canvas API | 4 | 3.5 | 9 | 10.5 | 4 |

NOTE IE7 and IE8 will crash when using Canvas API commands unless you use explorercanvas (http://code.google.com/p/explorercanvas/wiki/Instructions). To use it, click the download tab, unzip the files, put excanvas.js in your root directory, and add a script element loading excanvas.js inside a conditional comment targeting IE. IE9 gives great support, and IE10's support is looking quite solid. Our disclaimer for explorercanvas is that with it you can do simple animations, but more advanced support (such as that needed for the Canvas Ricochet game tutorial) might not work.

Now that you have your index.html file set up and you understand exactly what the Canvas context is, it's time to create your first game, Canvas Ricochet.

6.2   Creating a Canvas game

Your first Canvas game, shown in figure 6.4, will make use of overlap detection, animation, keyboard/mouse/touch controls, and some polish.

Although overlap detection and advanced animation might sound scary, no prior knowledge is necessary, and we'll walk you through each step of the way.

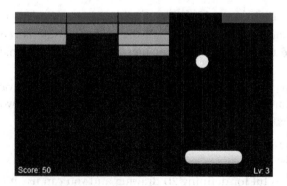

Figure 6.4   Canvas Ricochet's objective is to bounce a ball via a paddle to break bricks. When the ball goes out of bounds, the game shuts down. You can play the game now at http://html5inaction.com/app/ch6/ and download all the files needed to complete your own Canvas Ricochet game from www.manning.com/crowther2/.

In this section, you'll learn

- How to use the Canvas API to dynamically draw squares and circles, then shade them with specific coloring techniques (solid colors and gradients)
- How to use basic visual programming concepts that can be applied to other languages
- How to draw an image via the Canvas API

In this section, you'll create the main game engine and the game's visual assets in 7 steps:

- Step 1: Create the main engine components.
- Step 2: Create HTML5-optimized animation.
- Step 3: Display a background image.
- Step 4: Calculate the width and height of rectangular bricks.
- Step 5: Color the bricks.
- Step 6: Create the game ball.
- Step 7: Create the paddle.

6.2.1 Creating the main engine components

You're going to place *all* proceeding JavaScript listings you write into a single self-executing function. Why would we have you do this? Because it allows you to keep variable names from appearing in the global scope and prevents conflicts with code from other files.

Optional HTML5 Canvas companions

Before you proceed, we strongly recommend that you download and print nihilogic's HTML5 Canvas Cheat Sheet for reference: http://blog.nihilogic.dk/2009/02/html5-canvas-cheat-sheet.html. Another great companion is WHATWG's (Web Hypertext Application Technology Working Group) Canvas element document at http://www.whatwg.org/specs/web-apps/current-work/multipage/the-canvas-element.html. It provides detailed documentation about the Canvas element's inner workings, meant more for browser vendors but very useful for the curious developer.

STEP 1: CREATE THE MAIN ENGINE COMPONENTS

Core API Fill game.js with the code in listing 6.2. The listing has you create a Canvas engine object. Instead of declaring variables and functions, the object uses methods (the equivalent of functions) and properties (act like variables). For example, you can access the number of bricks on a page by declaring var bricks = {count: 20, row: 3, col: 2 }; and then calling bricks.count to get the current value. For more information on working with JavaScript objects, please see https://developer.mozilla.org/en-US/docs/JavaScript/Guide/Working_with_Objects.

Listing 6.2   game.js—Default JavaScript

```
(function () {
    var ctx = null;
    var Game = {
        canvas: document.getElementById('canvas'),

        setup: function() {
            if (this.canvas.getContext) {
                ctx = this.canvas.getContext('2d');

                this.width = this.canvas.width;
                this.height = this.canvas.height;

                this.init();
                Ctrl.init();
            }
        },

        animate: function() {},

        init: function() {
            Background.init();
            Ball.init();
            Paddle.init();
            Bricks.init();

            this.animate();
        },

        draw: function() {
            ctx.clearRect(0, 0, this.width, this.height);

            Background.draw();
            Bricks.draw();
            Paddle.draw();
            Ball.draw();
        }
    };

    var Background = {
        init: function() {},
        draw: function() {}
    };

    var Bricks = {
        init: function() {},
        draw: function() {}
    };

    var Ball = {
        init: function() {},
        draw: function() {}
    };

    var Paddle = {
        init: function() {},
        draw: function() {}
```

Place all proceeding JavaScript code listings inside this self-executing function. It prevents your variables from leaking into the global scope.

An empty variable that your 2D context will be dumped into.

Cache width and height from the Canvas element.

init() houses all of your object instantiations.

draw() handles all the logic to update and draw your objects.

This clears the Canvas drawing board, so previously drawn shapes are removed each time it's updated.

Proceeding objects will contain all of the game's visual assets. As of now, they're placeholders to prevent your game from crashing when it runs.

```
    };
    var Ctrl = {
        init: function() {}
    };
    window.onload = function() {
        Game.setup();
    };
}());
```

> **window.onload will delay your code from running until everything else has completely loaded.**

You'll notice that you've wrapped your `Game.setup()` code in `window.onload`. It makes the browser wait to fire setup until index.html has completely loaded. Running Canvas code too soon could result in crashing if essential assets (such as libraries) haven't loaded yet.

STEP 2: CREATE HTML5-OPTIMIZED ANIMATION

Before you start drawing, you'll need to set up animation. But there's a catch: Canvas relies on JavaScript timers because animation isn't built in. To create animation you must use a timer to constantly draw shapes. Normally you'd use JavaScript's `setInterval()`, but that won't provide users with an optimal experience. `setInterval()` is designed for running equations or carrying out DOM manipulation, not processor-intensive animation loops.

In response, browser vendors created a JavaScript function, `requestAnimationFrame()`, that interprets the number of frames to display for a user's computer (https://developer.mozilla.org/en/DOM/window.requestAnimationFrame). The bad news is that `requestAnimationFrame()` isn't supported by all major browsers. The good news is that Paul Irish created a polyfill that lets you use it anyway (http://mng.bz/h9v9).

Controlling fluctuating frames

`requestAnimationFrame()` is inconsistent in how many frames it shows per second. It dynamically adjusts to what a computer can handle with a goal of 60 fps, so it might return anywhere from 1 to 60 fps. If it's returning less than 60 fps, it can cause movement logic such as x += 1 to tear, become choppy, or randomly speed up and slow down because of frame rates fluctuating. If you need your code to run at a consistent speed, you have two options.

Option 1 is to put logic updates into `setInterval()` and drawing logic into `requestAnimationFrame()`. The second and best option is to create a delta and multiply all of your movement values by it (example x += 1 * delta); that way, animation is always consistent (more info on rolling your own delta is available at http://creativejs.com/resources/requestanimationframe/).

Core API

Integrate animations into your engine with the following listing by adding `window.requestAnimFrame` directly above your `Game` object. Then add to your existing `Game` object with a new method that uses `requestAnimFrame()`.

Listing 6.3   game.js—Animating Canvas Ricochet

```
window.requestAnimFrame = (function() {
    return  window.requestAnimationFrame         ||
    window.webkitRequestAnimationFrame           ||
    window.mozRequestAnimationFrame              ||
    window.oRequestAnimationFrame                ||
    window.msRequestAnimationFrame               ||
    function(callback) {
        window.setTimeout(callback, 1000 / 60);
    };
})();

var Game = {
    animate: function() {
        Game.play = requestAnimFrame(Game.animate);
        Game.draw();
    }
};
```

Animate constantly refers back to itself when called.

Because animate() is a self-referring function that fires outside the Game object, you must refer to Game instead of referring to "this."

Make sure all of your properties/methods end with a comma unless they are the last method. In that case, there should be no comma at the end.

NOTE You should be aware of two important points related to listing 6.3. First, if a code example repeats an object property/method declaration, then you need to replace the existing code. For example, new methods inside var Game = should be added onto your existing Game object. Worried about modifying objects while you follow along? We'll let you know whenever you need to modify or replace objects. Second, instead of using a clear rectangle to wipe a Canvas clean during animation, some developers set a new width to clear the Canvas drawing area. Although changing the width sounds more clever than creating clear rectangles, it causes instability in browsers. We recommend using clear rectangles to erase all previously drawn frames instead of fiddling with the width constantly.

STEP 3: DISPLAY A BACKGROUND IMAGE

 Core API

Replace your background object code with the following code so it displays an image. You must get background.jpg from Manning's source files and place it in your root directory for the listing to work.

Listing 6.4   game.js—Default JavaScript

```
var Background = {
    init: function() {
        this.ready = false;
        this.img = new Image();
        this.img.src = 'background.jpg';

        this.img.onload = function() {
            Background.ready = true;
        };
    },

    draw: function() {
        if (this.ready) {
```

Canvas requires an Image object to draw the background. Image.src uses the filename of the background image you retrieved from Manning's website.

```
        ctx.drawImage(this.img, 0, 0);
      }
    }
  }
};
```

Now that you've set up the main engine components, the next step is to create the game's visual assets. If you have no experience creating visual assets with a language like C++, you might find some of the following listings difficult. Once you've completed the listings, you'll understand basic concepts that you can use for 2D programming in multiple languages.

6.2.2 *Creating dynamic rectangles*

 Bricks are the easiest shape to create because they're rectangles. Rectangles in Canvas are clear, filled, or outlined and accept four parameters, as shown in figure 6.5. The first two parameters determine the spawning position (x and y on a graph). Although the current viewing space shows only positive x and y coordinates, you can also spawn shapes at negative values. The next two parameters specify the width and height in pixels.

STEP 4: CALCULATE THE WIDTH OF AND HEIGHT OF RECTANGULAR BRICKS

To get the width for each brick, you'll need to do some calculations. Five bricks need to be placed on a row with 2px gaps between each brick (4 gaps x 2px = 8px). These bricks need to fit inside the <canvas> width of 408px that was placed in your HTML markup earlier. Removing the gaps from the total width (408px – 8px), five bricks need to fit inside 400px. Each brick therefore needs to be 80px (400px / 5 bricks = 80px). Following all our math for the bricks can be frustrating; we've included a visual diagram (figure 6.6) to help you out.

You could place bricks by rewriting a basic shape command over and over and over. Instead, create a two-dimensional array as shown in the following listing to hold each brick's row and column. To lay down the bricks, loop through the array data and place each according to its row and column. Modify the Bricks object with the code in listing 6.5.

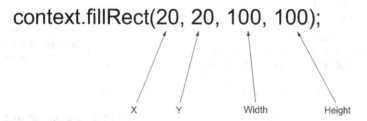

Figure 6.5 Creating a rectangle requires four different parameters. The current figure would create a 100 x 100 pixel square at the 20-pixel x and y position. Currently, rectangles are the only universally supported basic shape component in Canvas. To create items that are more complex, you'll need to use paths or images.

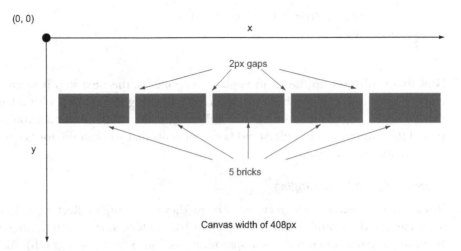

(0, 0)

x

2px gaps

y

5 bricks

Canvas width of 408px

Figure 6.6   **Include four gaps at 2px each. You'll need to subtract 8px from the `<canvas>` width, leaving 400px. Distribute the remaining width to each brick, leaving 80px for each (400px / 5 bricks = 80px).**

Listing 6.5   game.js—Brick array creation

```
var Bricks = {
    gap: 2,
    col: 5,
    w: 80,
    h: 15,

    init: function() {
        this.row = 3;
        this.total = 0;

        this.count = [this.row];
        for (var i = this.row; i--;) {          Array of bricks based
            this.count[i] = [this.col];         on your brick.row
        }                                       and brick.col data.
    },

    draw: function() {
        var i, j;                                       Stored bricks are drawn
                                                        here unless they're set
        for (i = this.row; i--;) {                      to false, which means
            for (j = this.col; j--;) {                  they're destroyed.
                if (this.count[i][j] !== false) {
                    ctx.fillStyle = this.gradient(i);
                    ctx.fillRect(this.x(j), this.y(i), this.w, this.h);
                }
            }                                   When you create color code in the
        }                                       next listing, this will automatically
    },                                          color your brick with a pretty
    x: function(row) {                          gradient based on its row.
        return (row * this.w) + (row * this.gap);
    },
```

```
    y: function(col) {
        return (col * this.h) + (col * this.gap);
    }
};
```

No box model?

If you've worked with CSS, you're probably familiar with the box model, which determines layout and positioning of HTML elements. Canvas doesn't use it, meaning shapes won't grow and shrink to the proportion of their container; instead, they overflow without stopping. A line of text that's too long, for example, won't automatically wrap to fit the <canvas> tag's width and height. Also, Canvas doesn't use CSS; you must manually program all visual output in JavaScript.

STEP 5: COLOR THE BRICKS

 Core API

Your bricks are set up, but you need to skin them so they're visible. You'll create a cached linear gradient (colors that change between two defined points on a Cartesian graph) with the following listing by coloring each brick based on its row via a switch statement. Add your new gradient and makeGradient methods to the existing Bricks object.

Listing 6.6 game.js—Coloring bricks

```
var Bricks = {
    gradient: function(row) {
        switch(row) {
            case 0:
                return this.gradientPurple ?
                    this.gradientPurple :
                    this.gradientPurple =
                        this.makeGradient(row, '#bd06f9', '#9604c7');
            case 1:
                return this.gradientRed ?
                    this.gradientRed :
                    this.gradientRed =
                        this.makeGradient(row, '#F9064A', '#c7043b');
            case 2:
                return this.gradientGreen ?
                    this.gradientGreen :
                    this.gradientGreen =
                        this.makeGradient(row, '#05fa15', '#04c711');
            default:
                return this.gradientOrange ?
                    this.gradientOrange :
                    this.gradientOrange =
                        this.makeGradient(row, '#faa105', '#c77f04');
        }
    },
    makeGradient: function(row, color1, color2) {
        var y = this.y(row);
        var grad = ctx.createLinearGradient(0, y, 0, y + this.h);
```

Row 1, purple.

If a cached gradient exists, use it; if not, create a new gradient. Makes use of a ternary operator instead of an if statement.

Row 2, red.

Row 3, green.

Row 4 or greater, orange.

Creates a new linear gradient at a specific location.

```
        grad.addColorStop(0, color1);          | Makes the gradient start at
        grad.addColorStop(1, color2);          | color1 and end at color2.

        return grad;
    }
};
```

Your bricks are ready to go; now let's work on the ball.

6.2.3 *Creating arcs and circles*

You'll create the ball using arc(x, y, radius, startAngle, endAngle), as illustrated in figure 6.7, which is what you use to create circular shapes. Unlike the rectangles you drew, which started from the top left, arc()'s starting point is in the center. You'll give the arc() a radius in pixels, then a startAngle and endAngle, which creates the circle. StartAngle is usually 0pi, whereas the endAngle is 2pi because it's the circumference of a circle (using only 1pi will create half a circle).

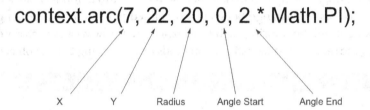

Figure 6.7 An arc with these parameters creates a shape at 7, 22 (x, y) on a graph. Because the angle starts from 0 and goes to 2pi, it creates a full circle. If you were to make the end angle 1pi, it would produce half a circle.

STEP 6: CREATE THE BALL

Now, with your new knowledge of arcs, you can create the ball using the next listing. Modify the existing Ball object with the following code.

Listing 6.7 game.js—Ball creation

```
var Ball = {
    r: 10,                    | Ball's radius, which can increase or
                              | decrease its size if you adjust this number.
    init: function() {
        this.x = 120;         | init() contains only values that need to be reset if the game
        this.y = 120;         | is currently running (more on that later). Values like radius
        this.sx = 2;          | (r) are kept separate because they don't need to change.
        this.sy = -2;
    },                        | this.sx increments the speed on the
                              | x-axis, whereas this.sy increments
    draw: function() {        | the speed on the y-axis. These
        this.edges();         | properties will be integrated later
        this.collide();       | when you add movement.
        this.move();

        ctx.beginPath();
        ctx.arc(this.x, this.y, this.r, 0, 2 * Math.PI);
```

```
        ctx.closePath();
        ctx.fillStyle = '#eee';
        ctx.fill();
    },

    edges: function() {},
    collide: function() {},
    move: function() {}
};
```

| Placeholder methods for configuring your ball's movement logic later.

Next up, you'll work on the paddle.

6.2.4 *Using paths to create complex shapes*

 Creating the game's paddle requires a Canvas path composed of multiple arcs and lines. This single step of creating a paddle is pretty complex, so we've broken it down into another step-wise process, all of which will happen within a single listing:

1 Start drawing a path with `ctx.beginPath()`.
2 Use `ctx.moveTo(x, y)` to move the path without drawing on the Canvas (optional).
3 Draw lines as needed with `ctx.lineTo(x, y)`.
4 Close the currently drawn path via `ctx.closePath()` to prevent abnormal drawing behavior.
5 Use steps 2 and 3 as often as you want.
6 Set the color of the line with `ctx.strokeStyle` or `ctx.fillStyle`; the game uses the browser's default color if you don't manually set it.
7 Fill in the path by using `ctx.stroke()`.

 In addition to the `lineTo` command, you'll use `arcTo(x1, y1, x2, y2, radius)` to create curves for your paddle.

> **NOTE** `arcTo()` is slightly unstable in Opera v12.01. It won't break your game, but it will cause the paddle you're creating to look like surreal art. IE9 requires you to declare an extra `lineTo()` between the `arcTo()`s; otherwise, the paddle will look like a bunch of randomly placed curves. Normally you can use `arcTo()` without `lineTo()`s between them, and the arcs will form a full shape without crashing.

STEP 7: CREATE THE PADDLE
To complete all of these tasks and create a paddle, follow the next listing, which combines four arcs into a pill shape and colors that shape with a gradient. Add the following methods and properties to your existing `Paddle` object.

Listing 6.8 game.js—Paddle creation

```
var Paddle = {
    w: 90,
    h: 20,
    r: 9,
```

```
init: function() {
    this.x = 100;
    this.y = 210;
    this.speed = 4;
},
```

| Useful for determining your ball's speed, which you'll configure in a later listing.

```
draw: function() {
    this.move();

    ctx.beginPath();
    ctx.moveTo(this.x, this.y);
    ctx.arcTo(this.x + this.w, this.y,
        this.x + this.w, this.y + this.r, this.r);
    ctx.lineTo(this.x + this.w, this.y + this.h - this.r);
    ctx.arcTo(this.x + this.w, this.y + this.h,
        this.x + this.w - this.r, this.y + this.h, this.r);
    ctx.lineTo(this.x + this.r, this.y + this.h);
    ctx.arcTo(this.x, this.y + this.h,
        this.x, this.y + this.h - this.r, this.r);
    ctx.lineTo(this.x, this.y + this.r);
    ctx.arcTo(this.x, this.y, this.x + this.r, this.y, this.r);
    ctx.closePath();

    ctx.fillStyle = this.gradient();
    ctx.fill();
},

move: function() {},

gradient: function() {
    if (this.gradientCache) {
        return this.gradientCache;
    }

    this.gradientCache = ctx.createLinearGradient(this.x, this.y,
        this.x, this.y + 20);
    this.gradientCache.addColorStop(0, '#eee');
    this.gradientCache.addColorStop(1, '#999');

    return this.gradientCache;
    }
};
```

| Set paddle's spawn origin by moving it before drawing arcs.

| Closing paths can prevent buggy behavior such as graphic tears and vanishing objects.

| Used at a later time to configure movement.

PROGRESS CHECK!

With all the static assets in place, double-check that your game looks like what you see in figure 6.8. If it doesn't, make sure your browser is up to date. If that fails, make sure that your Game object is set up correctly; then proceed to tackle each object that isn't outputting correctly.

So far, you've created all the core graphic assets of Canvas Ricochet. Because nothing moves, the game is as useless as a rod without a reel. In the next section, we'll teach you how to bring your game's static design to life!

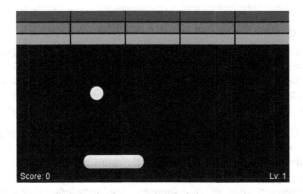

Figure 6.8 Using previous code snippets, you created a ball, paddle, and bricks with gradients. After refreshing your browser, the current result should look like this.

6.3   Breathing life into Canvas elements

Your game looks cool right now, but it doesn't do anything. Using several different techniques, we'll show you how to animate game elements, detect collisions, and move the paddle with a keyboard/mouse/touch.

> ### In this section, you'll learn
> - How to dynamically move objects around the screen
> - How to create responses between overlapping objects
> - How to prevent moving objects from leaving the `<canvas>` boundaries
> - How to remove basic objects (bricks) from the game
> - How to create keyboard, mouse, and touch controls from scratch
> - How to trigger a Game Over

This section's work will happen in two groups of steps.

Group 1—Making the application interactive.	Group 2—Capturing user input.
- Step 1: Move the paddle horizontally. - Step 2: Make the ball move. - Step 3: Enable edge detection for the paddle and ball. - Step 4: Enable collision detection. - Step 5: Remove hit bricks.	- Step 1: Create a keyboard listener. - Step 2: Add mouse control. - Step 3: Add touch support. - Step 4: Add control info via HTML.

Let's get started.

6.3.1   Animating game elements

Diving into the first set of tasks, let's make the paddle move horizontally. After that, you'll make the ball move diagonally.

Canvas data processing

When creating Canvas drawings through JavaScript, the browser re-creates all graphical assets from scratch because it uses bitmap technology. Bitmap graphics are created by storing graphical data in an organized array. When the data is processed by a computer, Canvas spits out pixels to create an image. This means that Canvas has a memory span shorter than that of a goldfish, so it redraws everything constantly.

If you're wondering why Canvas infinitely re-creates its images, you aren't alone. Many people have asked why Apple used a bitmap-based system when a solution exists that doesn't require everything to be constantly redrawn (Scalable Vector Graphics, or SVG). Canvas, though, is currently stomping SVG in popularity. One could explain Canvas's triumph through the lack of awareness and knowledge developers have of SVG.

STEP 1: MOVE THE PADDLE HORIZONTALLY

To make the paddle move, adjust the x-axis each time it's drawn. Making x positive will draw the paddle forward (pushed to the right), a negative value will pull it back (pushed to the left). Earlier you created a `Paddle.speed` property with a value of 4 in your `init()`. Just fill the empty `Paddle.move()` method with the following snippet, and your paddle will move:

```
var Paddle = {
    move: function() {
        this.x += this.speed;
    }
};
```

Now, refresh your page. Oh no! The paddle swims off into oblivion because it lacks a movement limiter. The only way to keep your paddle from vanishing is to integrate overlap detection, which you'll deal with in the next section. First though, you need to get the ball moving.

STEP 2: MAKE THE BALL MOVE

Making the ball move is almost identical to moving the paddle. Use the `Ball.sx` and `Ball.sy` properties you declared earlier to modify the ball's x and y coordinates. Replace `Ball.move()` with the following snippet:

```
var Ball = {
    move: function() {
        this.x += this.sx;
        this.y += this.sy;
    }
};
```

If you'd like to try refreshing, you'll notice that the ball and paddle fly off the screen and disappear. Although their disappearance may leave you depressed and lonely, never fear! You'll soon retrieve them by integrating overlap detection.

6.3.2   *Detecting overlap*

In simple 2D games, you create collisions by testing for object overlap. These checks occur each time the interval refreshes and draws an updated set of objects. If an object is overlapping another, some logic that causes a response is activated. For instance, if a ball and paddle overlap, then one object should repel the other.

What about real game physics?

Sad to say, we're teaching you only how to detect overlapping shapes, which isn't real physics integration. Physics in programming is a complicated subject that we could easily fill a hundred books with and still have more to write about. If you're interested in learning how to make games more lifelike, please see Glenn Fiedler's robust article on game physics at http://gafferongames.com/game-physics/.

You'll start building collisions detection into Canvas Ricochet by keeping objects contained inside the play area. After taming objects, you'll focus on using the paddle to bounce the ball at the bricks. Once the ball is bouncing back, you'll configure ball-to-brick overlap logic. When that's done, you'll create rules to determine when the game shuts down. Let's get started.

STEP 3: ENABLE EDGE DETECTION FOR THE PADDLE AND BALL

Core API

To prevent your ball and paddle from flying offscreen, check them against the `<canvas>` DOM element's width and height stored in `Game.width` and `Game.height`.

Go to your `Paddle.move()` method and replace its contents with the following snippet, which checks to see if the paddle has a positive x coordinate and is within the play area's width. If it is, then `Paddle.x` updates as normal; otherwise, it stops halfway into the right edge.

```
var Paddle = {
    move: function() {
        if (this.x > -(this.w / 2) &&
            this.x < Game.width - (this.w / 2))
            this.x += this.speed;
    }
};
```

To stop the ball from dropping out of gameplay, reverse the direction if the ball is overlapping the `<canvas>`'s edge. In addition to reversing the ball, you must place it inside the play area; otherwise, it will stick to edges at higher movement speeds. Use the code in the next listing to make the ball repel off the gameplay area's sides by replacing `edges()` in your `Ball` object.

Listing 6.9   game.js—Ball edge detection

```
var Ball = {
    edges: function() {
        if (this.y < 1) {
```
Top edge of your
game's container.

Hides the ball and triggers a Game Over with some methods and objects created in a later section.

```
            this.y = 1;
            this.sy = -this.sy;                              Bottom
        } else if (this.y > Game.height) {        ←┘        edge.
            this.sy = this.sx = 0;
            this.y = this.x = 1000;
            Screen.gameover();
            canvas.addEventListener('click', Game.restartGame, false);
            return;
        }
                                              Left
                                              edge.
        if (this.x < 1) {              ←┘
            this.x = 1;
            this.sx = -this.sx;                             Right
        } else if (this.x > Game.width) {        ←┘        edge.
            this.x = Game.width - 1;
            this.sx = -this.sx;
        }
    }
};
```

STEP 4: ENABLE COLLISION DETECTION

With the ball ricocheting, you'll need to use the paddle to deflect it toward the bricks. Because the ball changes direction on impact and the paddle stays stationary, you'll put your deflection logic inside a `Ball.collide()` method, as in the following snippet. When the ball's x and y coordinates overlap the paddle, you'll make the ball bounce in the opposite direction by reversing the y-axis direction. Replace the `Ball` object's `collide()` with the following listing.

Listing 6.10   game.js—Ball touching paddle

```
var Ball = {
    collide: function() {
        if (this.x >= Paddle.x &&                     Modifies the x coordinate for the
            this.x <= (Paddle.x + Paddle.w) &&        ball when it bounces back, based
            this.y >= Paddle.y &&                         on where it hits the paddle.
            this.y <= (Paddle.y + Paddle.h)) {
            this.sx = 7 * ((this.x - (Paddle.x + Paddle.w / 2)) / Paddle.w);   ←┘
            this.sy = -this.sy;
        }
    }
};
```

STEP 5: REMOVE HIT BRICKS

When the ball hits a brick, that brick needs to disappear. Replace `Brick.draw()` with the code in the next listing, which tests if the ball is overlapping when a brick is drawn. If so, it reverses the ball's y-axis and sets the brick's array data to `false` to remove it from gameplay. Use the following listing to add a new `Bricks.collide()` method.

Listing 6.11   game.js—Removing bricks

```
var Bricks = {
    draw: function() {
        var i, j;
```

```
        for (i = this.row; i--;) {
            for (j = this.col; j--;) {
                if (this.count[i][j] !== false) {
                    if (Ball.x >= this.x(j) &&             Collision test to see
                        Ball.x <= (this.x(j) + this.w) &&  if a ball overlaps
                        Ball.y >= this.y(i) &&             the currently
                        Ball.y <= (this.y(i) + this.h)) {  drawn brick.
                        this.collide(i, j);
                        continue;
                    }

                    ctx.fillStyle = this.gradient(i);
                    ctx.fillRect(this.x(j), this.y(i), this.w, this.h);
                }
            }
        }

        if (this.total === (this.row * this.col)) {
            Game.levelUp();
        }
    },
    collide: function(i, j) {
        this.count[i][j] = false;     If the ball really is overlapping a brick, set it to
        Ball.sy = -Ball.sy;           false and reverse the ball's y-axis direction.
    }
};
```

Now that the paddle can deflect the ball back toward the bricks, players have the ability to defend themselves. Well, not exactly. You still haven't given players the ability to control the paddle. Whipping up a little bit of window event magic, we'll give you some simple code recipes to create keyboard, mouse, and touch functionality—the second group of tasks in this section.

6.3.3 Creating keyboard, mouse, and touch controls

To create an interactive game experience, keyboard, mouse, and/or touch input is required. Although you could build controller detection into your Game object, we'll have you build it into a separate Ctrl object to prevent cluttering your objects. Here are the steps you'll follow in this group of tasks:

- Group 2—Capture user input.
  - Step 1: Create a keyboard listener.
  - Step 2: Add mouse control.
  - Step 3: Add touch support.
  - Step 4: Add control info via HTML.

First, you'll create keyboard listeners for left- and right-arrow keys. Second, you'll create a mouse listener that monitors cursor movement and places the paddle there. Third, you'll add touch functionality for devices that support the W3C's Touch Events draft (http://www.w3.org/TR/2011/CR-touch-events-20111215/). When you've finished with the controls, we'll give you a few tips on best practices for input techniques that improve user experience.

STEP 1: CREATE A KEYBOARD LISTENER

Core API

To detect keyboard events, you'll need to modify the existing `Ctrl` object with methods to monitor up and down key presses shown in the next listing. Think of these as switches for activating left or right paddle movement. Note that the listing's `Ctrl.init()` is called from `Game.setup()` to fire input monitoring.

Listing 6.12   game.js—Keyboard listeners

```
var Ctrl = {
    init: function() {
        window.addEventListener('keydown', this.keyDown, true);
        window.addEventListener('keyup', this.keyUp, true);
    },

    keyDown: function(event) {
        switch(event.keyCode) {
            case 39:
                Ctrl.left = true;
                break;
            case 37:
                Ctrl.right = true;
                break;
            default:
                break;
        }
    },

    keyUp: function(event) {
        switch(event.keyCode) {
            case 39:
                Ctrl.left = false;
                break;
            case 37:
                Ctrl.right = false;
                break;
            default:
                break;
        }
    }
};
```

39 will monitor a player's left-arrow key.

37 will monitor a player's right-arrow key.

keyUp will reset Ctrl's keyboard monitoring when a key is released.

If you want to try it, refresh the page; you'll see that the paddle won't acknowledge input commands. With `Ctrl.left` and `Ctrl.right` properties storing keyboard input, your `Paddle.move()` needs to references those properties with the following snippet:

```
var Paddle = {
    move: function() {
        if (Ctrl.left && (this.x < Game.width - (this.w / 2))) {
            this.x += this.speed;
        } else if (Ctrl.right && this.x > -this.w / 2) {
            this.x += -this.speed;
        }
    }
};
```

More key codes!

If you'd like to know more about the state of keyboard detection and get a complete list of key codes, please see Jan Wolter's article "JavaScript Madness: Keyboard Events" (http://unixpapa.com/js/key.html).

STEP 2: ADD MOUSE CONTROL

Monitoring for mouse movement is similar to keyboard monitoring, except you need to take into account the Canvas's position on the page and cross-reference it with the mouse. To get the current mouse location, update `Ctrl.init()` and add a new `move-Paddle()` method with the following listing.

Listing 6.13　game.js—Mouse controls

```
var Ctrl = {
    init: function() {
        window.addEventListener('keydown', this.keyDown, true);
        window.addEventListener('keyup', this.keyUp, true);
        window.addEventListener('mousemove', this. movePaddle, true);
    },
    movePaddle: function(event) {
        var mouseX = event.pageX;
        var canvasX = Game.canvas.offsetLeft;

        var paddleMid = Paddle.w / 2;

        if (mouseX > canvasX && mouseX < canvasX + Game.width) {
            var newX = mouseX - canvasX;
            newX -= paddleMid;

            Paddle.x = newX;
        }
    }
};
```

> **X location of the mouse.** (mouseX = event.pageX)

> **Measurement from the left side of the browser window to the Canvas element in pixels.** (canvasX = Game.canvas.offsetLeft)

> **Offsets the paddle's new location so it lines up in the middle of the mouse.** (newX -= paddleMid)

> **Hijacks the existing Paddle object and replaces the x coordinate.** (Paddle.x = newX)

STEP 3: ADD TOUCH SUPPORT

 Core API

Adding touch support to your game requires only six additional lines of code. What's even better is that you don't have to modify your existing objects. Just drop the code from the next listing into the `Ctrl` object and Boom!, touch support is added.

Listing 6.14　game.js—Touch controls

```
var Ctrl = {
    init: function() {
        window.addEventListener('keydown', this.keyDown, true);
        window.addEventListener('keyup', this.keyUp, true);
        window.addEventListener('mousemove', this.movePaddle, true);

        Game.canvas.addEventListener('touchstart', this.movePaddle, false);
        Game.canvas.addEventListener('touchmove', this.movePaddle, false);
```

```
        Game.canvas.addEventListener('touchmove', this.stopTouchScroll,
            false);
    },
```

| ``` stopTouchScroll: function(event) {   event.preventDefault(); } ``` | **Touch scrolling causes issues with Canvas Ricochet, so you have to disable touchmove's default functionality.** |

```
};
```

> **NOTE** If a device doesn't support the touch events you created, don't worry; unsupported events will be ignored and the game will run normally. You can try any mobile device, but we can't guarantee it will work.

6.3.4 *Control input considerations*

In the past couple of years JavaScript keyboard support for applications and websites has grown by leaps and bounds. YouTube, Gmail, and other popular applications use keyboard shortcuts to increase user productivity. Although allowing users to speed up interaction is great, it can quickly unravel into a usability nightmare.

You need to be careful when declaring keyboard keys in JavaScript. You could override default browser shortcuts, remove OS functionality (copy, paste, and so on), and even accidentally close the browser. The best way to avoid angering players is to stick to arrow and letter keys. Specialty keys such as the spacebar can be used, but overriding Shift, the Mac/Windows key, and/or Caps Lock could have unforeseen repercussions. If you must use a keyboard combination or specialty key, ask yourself, "Will these controls be problematic for my users?"

Application users don't want to spend their first 10 minutes randomly smashing keys and clicking everywhere. Put your game's controls in an easy-to-find location and use concise wording. For instance, placing the controls directly under a game is a great way to help users.

STEP 4: ADD CONTROL INFO VIA HTML

To add a control description to Canvas Ricochet, add a simple `<p>` tag directly below `<canvas>`. It should say, "LEFT and RIGHT arrow keys or MOUSE to move." If you really want, you could create a graphical illustration that's easier to see, but for now you'll just use text for simplicity.

```
<canvas id="canvas" width="408" height="250">
    Your browser shall not pass! Download Google Chrome to view this.
</canvas>

<p>LEFT and RIGHT arrow keys or MOUSE to move</p>

<script type="text/javascript" src="game.js"></script>
```

Congratulations! You've just completed an HTML5 game from beginning to end. You can now play a complete level of Canvas Ricochet without interruption. We know it's been a difficult journey to get this far, but why not take your game farther? With just a little more work, you can add progressive level enhancement and screens to make your game shine.

6.4 *Polishing Canvas games*

Your game is technically complete, but it lacks the polish necessary to attract players. Addictive elements such as scoreboards, increased difficulty levels, and an enjoyable user experience are essential. They help to increase game revenue, maximize the number of users, and, most important, keep people playing.

In this section you'll learn
- How to implement and maintain a player's score
- How to integrate social score-sharing
- How to avoid security issues in your apps
- How to integrate a leveling system
- How to create an introduction and Game Over screen
- How to choose a Canvas game engine

We're going to skyrocket the usefulness of your Canvas Ricochet game by showing you how to polish it to perfection in only four steps.

- Step 1: Create a score and level counter.
- Step 2: Store high scores online (optional).
- Step 3: Create a Welcome screen.
- Step 4: Create a Game Over screen.

After you add a point system and optional Facebook scoreboard for users, you'll create a dynamic leveling system with a few code modifications, so users play harder and faster as their skills improve. Then, you'll place the cherry on top of Canvas Ricochet with opening and closing screens. Lastly, we'll cover the current Canvas gaming engines to help with writing your next game.

First up is tracking score and levels.

6.4.1 *Tracking score and levels*

When we were about 10 years old (okay, maybe some of us were older!), we played Breakout all the time. One of us played on the now-ancient Atari gaming system; another played at Pizza Hut every Friday. We'd play over and over to keep raising our scores. Back then, you could only compete with a local community; now, with social media, it's quite easy to put your game's scoreboard online so people can compete on a global scale. But before your users can post their high scores online, you'll need to tweak your game to record brick breaks.

STEP 1: CREATE A SCORE AND LEVEL COUNTER

Your heads-up display (HUD) requires that you create text with the Canvas API. Just like CSS you have access to text align, vertical align (called text baseline), and @font-face fonts. Be warned: You don't have access to any letter-spacing properties, so your text might end up looking a bit cramped.

> **WARNING** Use vector fonts instead of bitmap for your Canvas applications. According to the W3C Canvas Working Draft, "transformations would likely make the font look very ugly." What that means is that if you use a bitmap-based font, your text will corrode in a macabre fashion when rotated.

Core API The simplest way to create counters is to add a new Hud object below your Game object and then run it through Game.init() and Game.draw(), which is what the next listing does. Also note that including HUD's startup logic in init will automatically reset it when you integrate Game Over functionality later.

Listing 6.15   game.js—Score and level output

```
var Hud = {
    init: function() {
        this.lv = 1;
        this.score = 0;
    },

    draw: function() {
        ctx.font = '12px helvetica, arial';        Specify text's
        ctx.fillStyle = 'white';                   display properties.    Create
        ctx.textAlign = 'left';                                           score
        ctx.fillText('Score: ' + this.score, 5, Game.height - 5);   <─    text.
        ctx.textAlign = 'right';
        ctx.fillText('Lv: ' + this.lv, Game.width - 5, Game.height - 5);   <─┐
    }
};                                                                Create level text.

var Game = {
    init: function() {
        Background.init();
        Hud.init();
        Bricks.init();
        Ball.init();
        Paddle.init();

        this.animate();
    },
    draw: function() {
        ctx.clearRect(0, 0, this.width, this.height);

        Background.draw();
        Bricks.draw();
        Paddle.draw();
        Hud.draw();
        Ball.draw();
    }
};
```

You need to increment the score counter every time a brick is hit. To do so, add logic to increment Hud.score by modifying Bricks.collide() with the following listing. Note that you already added the code to fire the level up earlier in a Brick.draw() listing, so you don't need to worry about that.

Listing 6.16 game.js—Adjusting brick destruction

```
var Bricks = {
    collide: function(i, j) {
        Hud.score += 1;
        this.total += 1;
        this.count[i][j] = false;
        Ball.sy = -Ball.sy;
    }
};
```

Increments your score counter after a brick is destroyed.

Increments brick count so the game can figure out when all the bricks are gone.

 Core API

Next, increment the ball's speed in Ball.init() and multiply the number of bricks in Bricks.init() with a level multiplier. A *level multiplier* is a technique that scales certain properties based on a player's current level. Using the level multiplier in the following listing, you can change object properties when a level up occurs.

Listing 6.17 game.js—Ball and brick upgrades

```
var Ball = {
    init: function() {
        this.x = 120;
        this.y = 120;
        this.sx = 1 + (0.4 * Hud.lv);
        this.sy = -1.5 - (0.4 * Hud.lv);
    }
};

var Bricks = {
    init: function() {
        this.row = 2 + Hud.lv;
        this.total = 0;

        this.count = [this.row];
        for (var i = this.row; i--;) {
            this.count[i] = [this.col];
        }
    }
};
```

Makes ball's speed relative to the current level.

Number of brick rows now relative to current level.

When a level up occurs, everything except the Hud needs to be updated with a new method called Game.levelUp(). Problem is, allowing players to level up past 5 will cause your game's bricks to take over the screen. To prevent brick overflow, you need to add a Game.levelLimit() method and modify the Bricks.init() logic to use it. Once you've inserted the code from the next listing, Canvas Ricochet can be played with multiple levels.

Listing 6.18   game.js—Game upgrades

```
var Game = {
    levelUp: function() {                        Level-up logic fired every
        Hud.lv += 1;                             time the level increases.
        Bricks.init();
        Ball.init();
        Paddle.init();
    },

    levelLimit: function(lv) {          Limits bricks growth
        return lv > 5 ? 5 : lv;          to five rows.
    }
};

var Bricks = {
    init: function() {
        this.row = 2 + Game.levelLimit(Hud.lv);     Only line changed in this
        this.total = 0;                              method so you prevent
                                                     bricks from overflowing
        this.count = [this.row];                     on the screen.
        for (var i = this.row; i--;) {
            this.count[i] = [this.col];
        }
    }
};
```

STEP 2: STORE HIGH SCORES ONLINE (OPTIONAL)

With a live score counter, you can easily let users post their high scores. The easiest way to do this is visit http://clay.io and check out their leaderboard documentation.

Security, because cheaters are gonna cheat

Because your game is running in JavaScript, it's quite easy for hackers to manipulate high scores, lives, and other information. Many consider JavaScript's security limitations a huge problem for scoreboards and making income from in-game content.

If you absolutely need some security, a few options are available.

The most straightforward is to have a server handle all of the play data and run checks before storing anything. The downside is it requires users to have an account to cross-reference play data with heavy-duty servers.

A less-used option is to hide a security code in your JavaScript files that AJAX uses as a handshake with the database to see if the current game is valid. Or you can use a design pattern that emulates private properties/variables in JavaScript. Although these two methods will work, they'll only temporarily prevent users from hacking your game.

If you're thinking that you'll have to develop your game in Flash or Java because of security issues, then please realize that these systems also have security flaws.

Anyway, it's about how you program for security instead of the programming language used to achieve it.

6.4.2 Adding opening and closing screens

When a user loads up your game, they must play immediately or lose. In order to let the user begin the game, create a Welcome screen (figure 6.9) that starts on click via an event listener.

Figure 6.9 A simple Welcome screen that initiates gameplay through a click listener. All text and coloring are created through Canvas.

STEP 3: CREATE A WELCOME SCREEN

The first step to making a Welcome screen is adding a new object called `Screen` (in the following listing) right below your `Game` object. The screen needs a background with a width and height large enough to cover everything. It should say "CANVAS RICOCHET" and "Click To Start."

Listing 6.19 game.js—Creating the Welcome screen and listener

```
var Screen = {
    welcome: function() {
        this.text = 'CANVAS RICOCHET';        Creation of screen's
        this.textSub = 'Click To Start';      base values.
        this.textColor = 'white';
                                              Setup screen after
        this.create();                        initial properties
    },                                        have been set.

                                   create() only outputs the set parameters so the
    create: function() {           screen's text can be adjusted as necessary.
        ctx.fillStyle = 'black';
        ctx.fillRect(0, 0, Game.width, Game.height);       Background.

        ctx.fillStyle = this.textColor;
        ctx.textAlign = 'center';
        ctx.font = '40px helvetica, arial';
        ctx.fillText(this.text, Game.width / 2, Game.height / 2);       Main text.

        ctx.fillStyle = '#999999';
        ctx.font = '20px helvetica, arial';
        ctx.fillText(this.textSub, Game.width / 2, Game.height / 2 + 30);
    }
};                                                                     Subtext.
```

Your Welcome screen needs a click event listener added into a new method called `Game.setup()`. Also, `Game.init()` needs to be modified so it fires from the new screen listener. In addition, with the next listing, you'll make the listener reusable by adding its logic into a new `Game.runGame()` method.

Listing 6.20 game.js—Creating the Welcome screen and new event listener

```
var Game = {
    init: function() {
        Background.init();
        Hud.init();
```

```
        Bricks.init();
        Ball.init();
        Paddle.init();
    },

    setup: function() {
        if (this.canvas.getContext){
            ctx = this.canvas.getContext('2d');

            this.width = this.canvas.width;
            this.height = this.canvas.height;

            Screen.welcome();
            this.canvas.addEventListener('click', this.runGame, false);
            Ctrl.init();
        }
    },

    runGame: function() {
        Game.canvas.removeEventListener('click', Game.runGame, false);
        Game.init();

        Game.animate();
    }
};
```

Adds the new event listener.

Removes event listener after firing.

The next screen you'll set up, the Game Over screen, is shown in figure 6.10.

STEP 4: CREATE A GAME OVER SCREEN

With a Welcome screen in place, users can seamlessly play until their ball disappears. When the ball is gone, you'll throw up a Game Over screen by adding a `Screen.gameover()` method with the following snippet. You don't need to call `Screen.gameover()` in your code, because it was placed in `Ball.draw()`.

```
var Screen = {
    gameover: function() {
        this.text = 'Game Over';
        this.textSub = 'Click To Retry';
        this.textColor = 'red';

        this.create();
    }
};
```

Figure 6.10   Game Over screen with a second chance at life. Letting users easily try again allows them to continue playing without a page refresh.

You also need to add code for another listener placed earlier called `Game.restart-Game()`. On a click event, that listener fires to the following snippet to reset the game to its initial setup state. You'll need to add `Game.restartGame()` as a new method to Game for it to work:

```
var Game = {
    restartGame: function() {
        Game.canvas.removeEventListener('click', Game.restartGame, false);
        Game.init();
    }
};
```

And that's it! With that last snippet, your Canvas Ricochet application is complete. Try it out, and then share it to amaze your family and friends.

6.4.3 *Getting help from code libraries*

 Core API

By completing Canvas Ricochet, you're now capable of coding games from scratch in Canvas. It did take a while to code everything. To help save time and money on projects, you might want to use a JavaScript library. For example, Impact.js would let you write Canvas Ricochet in 100 lines or less (but then you wouldn't have learned how to use Canvas, either). You also need to consider that engines *aren't* optimized for your code and will often decrease a game's speed performance. Currently most developers prefer ImpactJS, but there are other options you can find out more about at http://html5gameengine.com/.

IMPACTJS

ImpactJS, or the Impact JavaScript Engine, is one of the fastest and most-effective HTML5 libraries. It has documentation that's rapidly growing and video tutorials to get you moving. The only catch is that it costs $99 per license, which is kind of steep if you just want to test it. Figure 6.11 shows a complex game created with this library.

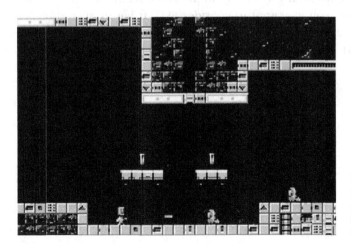

Figure 6.11 Code libraries like ImpactJS allow you to create complex games in significantly less time than coding a game from scratch.

Want to convert HTML5 games into mobile apps?

HTML5 apps should be written once and work on all devices, but it's no secret that mobile devices aren't there yet. If you want to turn your HTML5 games into mobile applications for Android, iOS, and other systems, check out appMobi.com and Phone-Gap.com. They offer powerful conversion tools that give you access to all major mobile devices. We'd love to walk you through creating a mobile app from Canvas Ricochet, but it's complicated enough that entire books are available on the subject.

6.5   Summary

Canvas isn't limited to a small box for video games; it's useful for a multitude of purposes and works well for websites. Thinking out of the box, you can create interactive backgrounds, image-editing tools, and more. For instance, you could make a footer in which users play a game of Canvas Ricochet, destroying footer elements once they've initiated the game.

Although you did play with many Canvas features, we've barely delved into its capabilities. For instance, you could animate a small film, which will become more possible as Canvas's GUI tools become available. In the meantime, you can make pages react to mouse position location or activate animation sequences based on mouse clicks or hover.

2D Canvas games can be fun to make, but they aren't exactly generating record sales. In addition, most HTML5 Canvas game startups haven't been successful. If in-browser application developers wants to compete with native desktop applications (games and anything else), better libraries and processing power are necessary. On the other hand, Canvas-based 2D applications can be cheap to produce and widely accessible. The only problem with these applications is that they don't scale well to various screen sizes without additional programming, although Canvas's 3D context from WebGL gives it the ability to do so. If you want a simple and effective way to scale 2D graphics for any device's size, you may want to consider SVG. It has an incredibly large set of features and puts Canvas to shame for graphic creation. And we're going to explore it in more detail next.

Chapter 7 at a glance

Topic	Description, methods, and so on	Page
Setting up SVG	Overview of basic setup for using SVG	
	■ Vector vs. bitmap	200
	■ `<svg>` configuration	204
	■ CSS for SVG and DOM	205
SVG tags	How to create shapes with the XML syntax	
	■ Basic shapes	206
	■ Gradients and `<g>`	207
	■ `<text>` and animation	208
	■ XLink	208
	■ Paths for advanced shapes	209
	■ `viewBox`	211
JavaScript usage	Advanced usage with JavaScript and SVG	
	■ XML namespacing	212
	■ SVG libraries	213
	■ Simple design pattern	216
	■ Dynamically generating a large SVG group	227
	■ Generating SVG paths via software	228
	■ CSS for SVG animation	229
	■ `getBBox()`	231
Canvas vs. SVG	Using SVG vs. Canvas for projects	
	■ Community	232
	■ Code comparison	233
	■ DOM	233

Look for this icon ➡️ (Core API) throughout the chapter to quickly locate the topics outlined in this table.

SVG: responsive in-browser graphics

7

This chapter covers

- Comparing bitmap and vector graphics
- Creating SVG from scratch
- Harnessing SVG for liquid layout graphics
- Using JavaScript with SVG
- Using SVG versus Canvas

Scalable Vector Graphics (SVG), an XML language for creating vector graphics, has been around since 2001. Its draft isn't part of HTML5, but the HTML5 specification gives you the ability to use SVG directly in your HTML markup. When you harness SVG's power, simple shapes, gradients, and complex illustrations will automatically adjust to your website and application's layout. What could be better than images that automatically resize without degrading? How about creating images inside HTML5 documents without graphical editing programs like Photoshop or Illustrator? That's the power of SVG.

As the chapter unfolds, you'll glide through a refresher on bitmaps and vectors to understand how SVG works. Then, you'll start constructing the chapter's teaching application, SVG Aliens, by developing SVG assets for constructing UFOs, ships, and shields with simple XML tags. With all the necessary components set up, you'll

Why build SVG Aliens?

In our SVG tutorial, SVG Aliens, you'll find lots of great content you won't find elsewhere, such as:

- A reusable SVG JavaScript design pattern
- How to control a dynamically resizable SVG element via attributes and CSS
- Optimized SVG animation with CSS for imported graphics
- How to manage large-scale SVG groups

focus on integrating JavaScript to bring your creations to life and allow players to interact with the game's assets. You'll polish your application by adding screen transitions, a score counter, and progressively enhanced difficulty. Finally, you'll decide whether Canvas or SVG would be best for your next project with a summary review of Canvas and SVG features.

After completing this chapter on SVG, you'll be ready to build your own SVG applications, use SVG inside HTML documents, and take advantage of SVG's CSS support. To get started, let's review the pros and cons of vectors.

7.1   *How bitmap and vector graphics compare*

Core API

Resizable files such as SVG use *vectors* (mathematical equations that create shapes) instead of *bitmaps* (arrays of image data), letting you change the height and width of an image without degrading its quality. Although vector graphics may seem like a replacement for all graphics, they bring with them several issues. If you're familiar with the differences between bitmaps and vectors, this section might be a review for you; if you'd like, glance at table 7.1 for a quick summary, or skip to section 7.2 and start building the game.

Table 7.1   Major differences between bitmap and vector (SVG). Note that neither has a clear advantage.

Topic	Bitmap	Vector (SVG)
Files	.gif, .jpg, .png	.svg, .ai, .eps
Created with	Pixels	Math equations
Created in programs like	Photoshop, Gimp	Illustrator, Inkscape
When you enlarge images	Image deterioration	No issues
Mainly used for	Websites, photography	Icons, logos
File size	Large	Small
3D usage	Textures	Objects (shapes)

As the dominant form of computer graphics on the web, bitmap has been ruling with .gif, .jpg, and .png formats. Opening a bitmap in a text editor reveals data for every

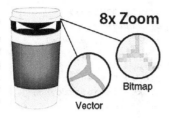

Figure 7.1 Effects of zooming into a vector versus a bitmap image. Our evil coffee cup demonstrates that vector is the clear winner. But great zoomability comes with great issues when you're creating complex graphics.

pixel in an image. Because a fixed number of pixels are individually declared, bitmaps suffer from image deterioration when you increase the size. When it comes to resizing, SVG has a clear advantage because it doesn't pixelate images when you enlarge them (see figure 7.1).

Another advantage is that you can write SVG directly into an HTML document without a file reference. It also requires less code to create graphics, resulting in faster page loads.

You've probably worked with an .ai, .eps, or .svg vector file for a website's logo. Vector images are composed of mathematical equations with plotted points, Bezier curves, and shapes. Because of their mathematical nature, these images don't suffer from resizing limitations, also shown in figure 7.1.

WILSON, THE RESIZABLE SMILEY

To help you see how a vector graphic works, we've created a simple smiley face known as Wilson with SVG's XML tags, as shown in figure 7.2.

Figure 7.2 Wilson is capable of changing to any size at will, and you can edit him in a graphical editing program like Illustrator. No JavaScript is required to create him, only SVG tags and a little bit of CSS.

Look at our first listing, where you can see that Wilson is composed entirely of XML data. Drop the code for Wilson into a file called wilson.svg and open it in any modern browser to see its smooth edges and amazing ability to resize.

Listing 7.1 wilson.svg—SVG code sample

Circles are the equivalent of Canvas's arc() draw method.

```
<?xml version="1.0" encoding="UTF-8"?>
<!DOCTYPE svg PUBLIC "-//W3C//DTD SVG 1.1//EN" "http://www.w3.org/Graphics/
    SVG/1.1/DTD/svg11.dtd">

<svg version="1.1" xmlns="http://www.w3.org/2000/svg" x="0px" y="0px"
    viewBox="0 0 140 140" xml:space="preserve">

    <circle cx="70" cy="70" r="70" style="fill:#ff0"/>
```

SVG tags usually contain XML data, version number, a viewBox, and more.

```
<path d="M38,57 A7,7 0 0,1 52,57 z" style="fill:#777;"/>
<path d="M88,57 A7,7 0 0,1 102,57 z" style="fill:#777;"/>
<path d="M40,90 A30,30 0 0,0 100,90 z" style="stroke:#000;
    fill:#fff;"/>
<path d="M30,40 L30,70 L60,70 L60,40 L30,40 z
    M60,60 L80,60 M80,40 L80,70 L110,70 L110,40 L80,40 z"
    style="stroke:#000; stroke-width:3; stroke-linejoin:round;
    fill:none;"/>
</svg>
```

**Path tags
work similarly
to Canvas's
paths, except
you declare
everything in
one line.**

Creating Wilson's .svg file requires an XML declaration with specific attributes on an
`<svg>` tag. If you open Wilson's file in a browser and resize the window, you'll notice
that it conforms to the new size. Wilson's face could move if you used a simple `<animate>`
tag, and it could respond to mouse clicks with a little bit of JavaScript.

Basic SVG support   4   3   9   9   3.2

All modern browsers can open SVG files, which is why using SVG in your HTML documents works well for drawing shapes and scaling graphics. But support waivers if you
try to perform complicated animations or use features implemented only in a specific
browser. This makes sense, because the W3C Recommendation for SVG is a gigantic
document (http://www.w3.org/TR/SVG); you can't expect browser vendors to integrate everything. No need to worry; the features you'll use in the proceeding code will
be consistent across modern browsers unless otherwise noted.

Vectors aren't a perfect image format, but they have a clear advantage over bitmaps for simple graphics and illustrations. By running Wilson's code example, you've
seen how seamlessly SVG can resize graphics in a liquid website layout.

Now, let's take your new SVG knowledge and use it to create graphic assets for this
chapter's game, SVG Aliens.

7.2 Starting SVG Aliens with XML

Before building your SVG game (see figure 7.3), play it at the *HTML5 in Action* website
(http://html5inaction.com/app/ch7). After a few test runs, head over to http://
manning.com/crowther2/ and download the source code. Inside a zip file, you'll
find ufo.svg, mothership.svg, and cursor.png, all of which go into your application's
root directory.

In the previous chapter, you built Canvas Ricochet, a game using a ball and paddle
to destroy bricks. SVG Aliens uses similar mechanics but adds a few layers of complexity. Your paddle will become a ship that moves left or right. Lasers will replace a
bouncing ball, destroying both friend and foe. Instead of bricks, aliens progressively
scurry toward the ship to destroy it. With increased complexity comes more difficulty,
so we'll show you how to add a life counter and shields to help ships survive incoming
laser fire.

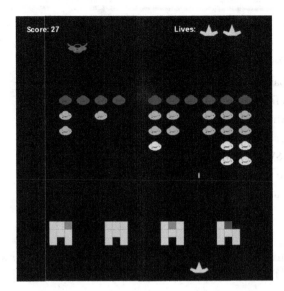

Figure 7.3 Get ready to defend Earth from the coming apocalypse in SVG Aliens. Play the game at http://html5inaction.com/app/ch7 before you build it from scratch. Download the source code from http://www.manning.com/crowther2/. The game's artwork is by Rachel Blue, http://www.linkedin.com/pub/rachel-blue/23/702/99b.

In this section, you'll learn the following reusable SVG techniques:

- How to integrate SVG's XML language into an HTML document
- How to create text and simple shapes
- How to make simple illustrations with paths
- How to use XLink to inject .svg files into a page
- How to animate elements with properties
- How to tweak SVG shapes with CSS
- How to work with the `viewBox` property for liquid layouts

Note that SVG requires the use of a modern browser. Chrome seems to have the smoothest SVG performance, but you can use any browser except for Opera, which lacks the bounding box support you need to complete this chapter's application. Please note that SVG is a massive specification and no browser supports it 100%.

| **Inline SVG in HTML5** | 7 | 4 | 9 | 11.6 | 5.1 |

In this section, you'll start building SVG Aliens by setting up an SVG XML tag in an HTML document, along with CSS and a JavaScript file. You'll also make a flexible viewing window similar to Wilson's by configuring the `viewBox` property on an `<svg>` tag. Let's get started with the basic game setup.

7.2.1 Setting up SVG inside HTML

As you move through the rest of this section, you'll follow seven steps that will yield the basic framework for a resizable, browser-based game:

- Step 1: Set up SVG tag basics.
- Step 2: Create your CSS file.
- Step 3: Add shapes for the Game Start screen.
- Step 4: Add text to the screen and animate it.
- Step 5: Import existing SVG files via XLink.
- Step 6: Create the Game Over screen.
- Step 7: Configure the game's flexible viewBox.

Let's get started.

STEP 1: SET UP SVG TAG BASICS

Open a simple text editor to create three files called index.html, style.css, and game.js, and save them all to the same folder. In this section, we'll start populating the first two files.

Core API

Create a file called index.html in the root and paste listing 7.2 into it. Inside the pasted code you now have an <svg> tag that accepts parameters for width, height, and an additional declaration for its viewing window called viewBox. We're going to hold off configuring your viewBox, because you need some CSS for it to work.

Listing 7.2　index.html—Default html

```html
<!DOCTYPE html>
<html>
<head>
    <title>SVG Aliens</title>
    <meta charset="UTF-8">
    <link rel="stylesheet" type="text/css" href="style.css" />
</head>

<body>

    <div id="container">

        <svg
            id="svg"
            version="1.1"
            xmlns="http://www.w3.org/2000/svg"
            xmlns:xlink="http://www.w3.org/1999/xlink">
        </svg>

        <div id="instructions">
            <p>Arrow keys or mouse to move. Space or click to shoot.</p>
        </div>

    </div>

    <script type="text/javascript" src="game.js"></script>
```

Your application's colors and basic layout are determined by a CSS file. → (points to `<link rel="stylesheet" ...>`)

Wrapping your SVG tag with a container allows more placement control. → (points to `<div id="container">`)

XML naming scheme. Using <svg> requires an xmlns (XML naming scheme) so your browser knows how to process the XML data. → (points to `xmlns="http://www.w3.org/2000/svg"`)

XML naming scheme for XLink (XML Linking Language). → (points to `xmlns:xlink="http://www.w3.org/1999/xlink"`)

It's considered a best practice to display game controls in an easy-to-see location. → (points to `<div id="instructions">`)

game.js will be responsible for your game's functionality. → (points to `<script ... src="game.js">`)

```
</body>
</html>
```

STEP 2: CREATE YOUR CSS FILE

Core API

Create a style.css file with the following listing and place it in your root next to index.html. Its contents will configure your game's color and layout. You must have cursor.png in your root folder from Manning's website for the following listing to work.

Listing 7.3 style.css—Primary CSS

```
body { margin: 0; background: black; color: #999;
    -webkit-user-select: none; -moz-user-select: none;
    -ms-user-select: none; user-select: none; }
```
> The CSS property user-select prevents users from accidentally highlighting text or images.

```
#container { margin: auto auto; text-align: center }
#instructions { position: absolute; display: block; bottom: 1%; width:
    100%; height: 10% }
#instructions p { font-size: 1em; margin: 0 0 5px; padding: 0 }

svg {
    overflow: hidden;
    display: block;
    height: 90%;
    position: absolute;
    top: 0%;
    width: 100%;
    min-height: 500px;
    min-width: 500px;
    font: bold 14px arial;
    cursor: url('cursor.png'), default;
    cursor: none;
    fill: #ddd;
}
```
> Width needs to be set at 100%, and make sure to set a minimum width and height so your viewing window doesn't get too small.

> 'cursor.png' replaces a user's mouse with a blank 1px image for all browsers except IE. Setting cursor: none will hide the cursor from IE. Usually, a mouse cursor vanishes via the Pointer Lock API, but it isn't supported across enough browsers.

> The fill property is how SVG determines color. Fills are the equivalent of CSS's color and background combined into one property because they literally "fill" objects.

```
#screenWelcome text { font-size: 20px; }
#screenWelcome #title1 { font: bold 130px arial }
#screenWelcome #title2 { font: bold 73px arial; fill: #0af }
text#more { font: 28px 'Courier New', Courier, monospace }

#goTitle { font: bold 45px arial; fill: #c00 }
#retry { font: 20px 'Courier New', Courier, monospace }
.quote { font: bold 12px arial; fill: #000 }

.life, .player, .shield, .ship { fill: #0af }
.ufo .a { fill: #8C19FF }
.ufo .b { fill: #1EE861 }
.ufo .c { fill: #FFE14D }
```
> You can overwrite the color of an imported SVG file by setting a fill via CSS. More on that in a later section.

```
.closed .anim1, .open .anim2 { display: none }
.open .anim1, .closed .anim2 { display: inherit }
```

TRY IT OUT

Refresh your browser to reveal a black screen with one line of text. Don't be alarmed that your mouse has disappeared. We had you replace the default mouse cursor with a blank image called cursor.png from the assets you downloaded earlier (placed in your root folder).

HTML5 Pointer Lock API and CSS coloring alternative

Normally when you want to collect movement data and hide the cursor, you lock the mouse in a specific position. Although browsers don't allow you to toggle OS movement controls for security reasons, there's an HTML5 API called Pointer Lock that allows you to collect mouse data with movement locked. See http://www.w3.org/TR/pointerlock/ for more information from the latest W3C draft.

An alternative to declaring CSS fills would be adding the property `fill="#453"` directly to XML tags. Professional frontend developers consider inline styles bad practice with applications, because repeating properties on HTML elements can quickly make files an unmaintainable mess.

7.2.2 Programming simple shapes and text

Those who actively use CSS3 are probably guessing that CSS or JavaScript determines SVG Alien's animation, gradients, and other complex features. Thankfully, SVG has an `<animate>` tag and built-in gradient support. With these features in mind, let's create your Game Start and Game Over screens.

STEP 3: ADD SHAPES FOR THE GAME START SCREEN

The start screen in figure 7.4 requires a game title, information about the point system, and a message that clicking activates game play. We'll create this start screen first.

CREATING SIMPLE SHAPES

To create a square, use the rectangle tag `<rect x y width height>`. You can create circles with `<circle cx cy r>`, ellipses with `<ellipse cx cy rx ry>`, lines with `<line x1 x2 y1 y2>`, polylines with `<polyline points>`, and polygons with `<polygon points>`. These shapes usually take x and y coordinates, whereas others require multiple points

Figure 7.4   SVG Alien's Welcome screen teaches players about its point system and allows them a chance to initiate gameplay.

plotted out on a Cartesian graph. Each shape accepts attributes for fill, stroke colors/ width, and even gradients. Table 7.2 offers an overview on how to use these tags.

Table 7.2   Shapes you can create with SVG and corresponding examples

Shape	Formatting example
Rectangle	`<rect x="5" y="20" width="80" height="20" fill="#c00" />`
Circle	`<circle cx="130" cy="43" r="20" fill="black" stroke="#aaa" stroke-width="5" />`
Ellipse	`<ellipse cx="45" cy="130" rx="40" ry="20" fill="#00f" />`
Line	`<line x1="110" x2="160" y1="110" y2="150" fill="#000" />`
Polyline	`<polyline points="5 200 20 220 30 230 40 210 50 240 60 200 80 210 90 190 60 300 5 200" fill="transparent" stroke="orange" stroke-width="5" />`
Polygon	`<polygon points="110 200 110 240 130 280 150 240 150 200" stroke="#0f0" fill="#000" stroke-width="5" />`

Core API

You can combine XML tags from table 7.2 into a group as follows: `<g>content</g>`. Think of groups as `<div>`s for storing complex shape creations. You can easily target groups with JavaScript and CSS selectors instead of individually selecting every element inside. Create your first group and a gradient by integrating the following listing inside your `<svg>` tag.

Listing 7.4   index.html—Background setup

```
<svg id="svg" version="1.1" xmlns="http://www.w3.org/2000/svg"
    xmlns:xlink="http://www.w3.org/1999/xlink" clip-path="url(#clip)">

    <defs>                                        <-- Stores special SVG rendering instructions.

        <radialGradient id="background" cx="0.5" cy="0.3" r="0.7">

            <stop offset="0%" stop-color="#333" />          Literal declaration of the
            <stop offset="70%" stop-color="#000" />         gradient's stop colors

        </radialGradient>

        <clipPath id="clip">
            <rect x="0" y="0" width="100%" height="100%" />
        </clipPath>

    </defs>

    <rect x="0" y="0" width="500" height="500"
        fill="url(#background)" />    <--

    <g id="screenWelcome"></g>

    <g id="screenGameover"></g>

</svg>
```

`<svg clip-path>` clips the SVG container with the referenced id #clip.

Your radial gradient acts like a fillable gradient for SVG tags. It goes from its center (cx=0.5) to one-third (cy=0.3) of the way down its container. Size of the radial gradient is set to 70% (r=0.7) of the shape it resides in.

clipPath declares a clipping path (similar to Illustrator's pathfinder). Setting a simple `<clipPath>` at 100% width and height will hide any overflowing elements.

This rectangle is the same width and height as your application's viewing window. A radial gradient definition is applied to your rectangle with fill="url(#background)".

When you refresh your screen, you should see a black background with a subtle circular gradient. Don't be alarmed that your gradient is off-center (you'll fix that when the viewBox is set up). If you cannot see the background gradient on your monitor, adjust `<stop offset="0%" stop-color="#333" />` to a brighter color such as #555.

STEP 4: ADD TEXT TO THE SCREEN AND ANIMATE IT

Core API

With a background set up, it's time for typography. Each `<text>` tag accepts x and y coordinates for placement. You might have noticed that "Click To Play" slowly faded in when you demonstrated the complete SVG Aliens game. You perform fades by inserting an `<animate>` tag inside text tags. You create animation by targeting the CSS (attributeType), declaring a specific style attribute (attributeName), start (from) and end (to) values, and the duration (dur) in seconds. Nest an `<animate>` tag inside most SVG elements, and you'll be able to create animation without the need for JavaScript or CSS3. Create your text with animation by including the following snippet inside `<g id="screenWelcome"></g>`:

```
<g id="screenWelcome">

    <text id="title1" x="110" y="137">SVG</text>
    <text id="title2" x="115" y="200">ALIENS</text>

    <text id="more" x="130" y="400">
        <animate attributeType="CSS" attributeName="opacity" from="0"
            to="1" dur="5s" />
        Click To Play
    </text>

</g>
```

> **What else can you animate?**
> In addition to CSS, you can animate transforms and movement directions and more. Visit http://www.w3.org/TR/SVG11/animate.html to delve into the nitty-gritty details. Be warned, the document contains more than 14,000 words and seems to favor browser vendors over developers in its terminology and examples.

7.2.3   *Using XLink and advanced shapes*

With basic shapes, text, and gradients set up, we'll make use of more advanced SVG tags to create graphics. First, we'll start by showing you a shortcut method to pull graphics in through XLink. After that, you can create graphics from scratch using a `<path>`.

Core API

XLink, a W3C specification, stands for XML Linking Language. We're primarily using it to import SVG files, but it serves other purposes, such as creating links inside SVG through the `<a>` element.

> **Want more information on XLink?**
> Would you like to learn more about XLink? Check out Jakob Jenkov's tutorial, "SVG: a Element" at http://tutorials.jenkov.com/svg/a-element.html.

Although you could draw your UFOs from scratch in SVG, you'll find it easier to use <image> with XLink to import an .svg file. You can quickly resize imported .svg files and create them with popular vector-editing programs such as Adobe Illustrator or Inkscape. The only trick is that creating files in a visual editor requires you to save as .svg in the Save As menu.

> **WARNING** Before proceeding, make sure the mothership.svg and ufo.svg assets you retrieved from Manning's website are in your root folder. Without these files, nothing will appear where XLink images should be.

STEP 5: IMPORT EXISTING SVG FILES VIA XLINK

Create a player's ship using a <path> tag, by inserting the following code snippet into <g id="screenWelcome">. Notice that your path's d attribute contains a series of points to create your ship's shape. Insert your new XLink images and path by appending the following listing inside <g id="screenWelcome"></g>.

Listing 7.5   index.html—Using XLink

```
<image x="200" y="230" width="25" height="19" xlink:href="ufo.svg" />    ◄─┐
<text x="233" y="247">= 1pt</text>
                                                              xlink:href allows you to include
                                                                 SVG files in your HTML.
<text x="145" y="328">+1</text>
<path class="ship" d="M 175 312 m 0 15 l 9 5 h 17 l 9 -5 l -2 -5 l -10
    3 l -6 -15 l -6 15 l -10 -3 l -2 5" />                     ◄─┐
<text x="217" y="328">life = 100pts</text>

<image x="185" y="270" width="40" height="20" xlink:href="mothership.svg" />
<text x="233" y="287">= 30pts</text>
```

> Declares a drawing path with a d attribute. Notice that paths don't have x and y
> attributes; instead they use M followed by an x and y declaration to set the
> initial position. m, l, and h move the drawing points.

USING PATHS FOR ADVANCED SHAPES

 Core API

You probably noticed that the previous listing's <path> used a series of letters and numbers to indicate particular directions. For an explanation of the different movement commands, see table 7.3.

Table 7.3   Capital letters indicate measurements relative to the SVG element; lowercase letters indicate measurements relative to previous x and y coordinates.

Path drawing commands	Explanation
M or m	Move path to specific x and y point without drawing
H or h	Draw path horizontally to x
V or v	Draw path vertically to y
L or l	Draw path to a specific x and y point

Using a capital letter to declare a location, such as V, indicates the measurement is relative to the <svg> tag's position in your HTML document. Using a lowercase letter, such as v, indicates it's relative to any previously declared x and y coordinates.

CODE AND PROGRESS CHECK

You've integrated several different code snippets throughout this chapter. Double-check index.html against the following listing to verify that you've properly set up your SVG code.

Listing 7.6   index.html—Welcome screen

```
<g id="screenWelcome">
    <text id="title1" x="110" y="137">SVG</text>
    <text id="title2" x="115" y="200">ALIENS</text>

    <image x="200" y="230" width="25" height="19" xlink:href="ufo.svg" />

    <text x="233" y="247">= 1pt</text>

    <image x="185" y="270" width="40" height="20"
        xlink:href="mothership.svg" />
    <text x="233" y="287">= 30pts</text>

    <text x="145" y="328">+1</text>
    <path class="ship" d="M 175 312 m 0 15 l 9 5 h 17 l 9 -5 l -2 -5
        l -10 3 l -6 -15 l -6 15 l -10 -3 l -2 5" />
    <text x="217" y="328">life = 100pts</text>

    <text id="more" x="130" y="400">
        <animate attributeType="CSS" attributeName="opacity" from="0"
            to="1" dur="5s" />
        Click To Play
    </text>
</g>
```

After a browser refresh, your screen should look identical to the Welcome screen shown in figure 7.5.

Figure 7.5   The Welcome screen should look like this one after you refresh your browser.

Figure 7.6 Nothing makes people rage quite like getting powned by an SVG alien. Game Over screens are a great way to encourage players to develop addictive behaviors (such as playing repeatedly).

Make sure to set `display` to `none` for your Welcome screen by inserting the following code snippet at the bottom of style.css. Hiding your Welcome screen makes creating the Game Over screen, explained in the next step, much easier.

```
#screenWelcome { display: none }
```

STEP 6: CREATE THE GAME OVER SCREEN

Ideal Game Over screens entertain and encourage players to try again. Using the same tools from the Welcome screen, you can quickly assemble what you need to create the Game Over screen shown in figure 7.6.

Use the following listing to replace `<g id="screenGameover"></g>` right after `<g id="screenWelcome"></g>`. It uses all the same tags and attributes used to create your Welcome screen. Therefore, its code content should be straightforward.

Listing 7.7 index.html—Game Over screen

```
<g id="screenGameover">
    <text id="goTitle" x="110" y="199">GAME OVER</text>
    <text id="retry" x="165" y="224">Click To Retry</text>

    <image x="145" y="289" width="60" height="40" xlink:href="ufo.svg" />

    <rect x="230" y="249" width="134" height="50" />
    <path d="M 231 274 l -20 20 L 231 289 L 231 284" />
    <text class="quote" x="240" y="269">Ready to be powned</text>
    <text class="quote" x="240" y="286">again human?</text>
</g>
```

STEP 7: CONFIGURE THE GAME'S FLEXIBLE VIEWBOX

Core API

Let's configure your `viewBox` by altering `<svg>` to conform to a user's window size, without affecting the game's Cartesian graph. Set `viewBox` with four different attributes

for min-x, min-y, width, and height (`<svg viewBox="min-x min-y width height">`).
You don't need a minimum x and y because you want to center the game, so feed it
0 values for both. Then set the width and height to 500, which is the size of your
SVG application.

Your modified `<svg>` tag should look like the following snippet:

```
<svg id="svg" viewBox="0 0 500 500" version="1.1"
xmlns="http://www.w3.org/2000/svg"
xmlns:xlink="http://www.w3.org/1999/xlink" clip-path="url(#clip)">
```

Confirm that your game's flexible layout is working with a browser refresh; then replace
`#screenWelcome { display: none }` with `#screenGameover { display: none }` in your
style.css. You should now see the Welcome screen when you refresh your browser.

```
#screenWelcome { display: none }
#screenGameover { display: none }
```

Understanding how `<svg>`'s `viewBox` parameter works is difficult if you're new to the
concept of vector-based viewports. If you're confused about how all the resizing works,
we recommend tinkering with the `viewBox` parameter before proceeding.

Wow, you created two game screens that dynamically resize with HTML, XML, and
CSS. Although it would be ideal to finish the game with these languages, it's not possible. We'll have to rely on JavaScript to create game logic, collisions, and artificial intel-
ligence (AI).

7.3 *Adding JavaScript for interactivity*

When you consider how easy it is to create vector assets with SVG, you might expect it
to have revolutionary JavaScript integration. Sadly, it doesn't. In fact, it can be clunky
to access and modify SVG because it relies heavily on the DOM. It would be nice to
stick with SVG tag attributes, but using the language at its full potential requires
JavaScript (just like HTML5 APIs).

In this section, you'll learn
- How to create an SVG JavaScript engine
- How to create a simple SVG design pattern
- How to dynamically generate elements
- How to properly get XML data through JavaScript with a naming scheme
- How to use CSS to simplify complicated path animations

 Core API   Matters become further complicated because JavaScript needs extra configuration at
times to play nicely with XML. Because of these limitations, a clever design pattern is
required to program your game. Never fear. We've a couple of JavaScript solutions
that will ride in to save the day.

XML namespace issues

Before proceeding, we need to warn you about namespaces and JavaScript. Namespaces are keys that define what kind of information you're asking the browser to interpret (in this case XML or HTML data). When interacting with XML, you must declare a namespace or the browser won't know you've changed namespaces. Some of the symptoms of incorrect namespace usage include incorrectly returned data, new DOM elements inserting into the wrong location, and instability in general. To prevent namespace issues, make use of methods ending in `NS` such as `get-AttributeNS(NS,element)`. For a complete list of namespace methods, visit Mozilla's documentation on JavaScript DOM elements at https://developer.mozilla.org/en-US/docs/DOM/element#Methods.

Major JavaScript libraries such as jQuery and MooTools are ignorant of namespaces in most situations, meaning they won't mix well with manipulating SVG elements.

 Core API

Until recently, you had to work with VML (Vector Markup Language), Flash, or another program to use vector graphics on the web. Because IE8 and below don't support SVG, in production applications you may want to use a JavaScript vector graphics library that generates code that can be rendered by both older and newer browsers. Currently, the most popular of these libraries is RaphaelJS, which was used to create the tiger in figure 7.7.

RaphaelJS uses SVG and its predecessor Vector Markup Language (VML) to create vector graphics. It also has great plug-ins that calculate complex math for pie charts and other data visualizations. RaphaelJS's competitor is svgweb, which uses Flash to render SVG elements. If you don't need to support older browsers, d3.js (http://d3js.org) is a good library to consider.

Because we aren't concerned with old versions of IE, you'll be using JavaScript without a fallback library to write your game. We'll walk you through the creation of a basic SVG design pattern, plus teach you to create reusable a reusable asset with JavaScript objects. Then you'll develop shields to protect players from enemy fire. As a

Figure 7.7 RaphaelJS is capable of creating astounding graphics in all modern-day browsers.

final step, you'll set up the UFO flock, which is a bit complex because it requires you to create 50-plus objects.

To make a complex task somewhat easier, we've broken the work down into three groups of steps.

Group 1: Engine and basic object setup	Group 2: Complex objects and overlap	Group 3: The UFO flock
▪ Step 1: Set up basic game utilities, metadata, and XML naming schemes. ▪ Step 2: Integrate screen transitions. ▪ Step 3: Create the big UFO. ▪ Step 4: Create the player's ship. ▪ Step 5: Make the player respond to keyboard input. ▪ Step 6: Capture keyboard and mouse controls.	▪ Step 1: Create shields for defense. ▪ Step 2: Construct lasers. ▪ Step 3: Integrate laser collision detection. ▪ Step 4: Create the heads-up display.	▪ Step 1: Set up the UFO flock. ▪ Step 2: Generate paths for the UFOs. ▪ Step 3: Animate the UFOs. ▪ Step 4: Make the UFOs randomly shoot.

First up, the core programming of the game's engine.

7.3.1   *Game engine essentials and using screens*

Because building SVG Aliens involves complex logic, an effective design pattern is required for organizing your code. At the core you're going to need an object called Game that acts as an engine to manage initializing, updating objects, screen transitions, Game Overs, removing objects, and more.

STEP 1: SET UP BASIC GAME UTILITIES, METADATA, AND XML NAMING SCHEMES

From here on out, place all of your code inside a self-executing function to prevent JavaScript variables from leaking into the global scope. The following provides everything your game engine needs to set up the game's basic utilities, metadata (such as width and height), XML naming schemes, and anything extra that doesn't belong in your other objects. Place all of the following code into game.js.

Listing 7.8   game.js—Game engine base

```
(function() {
    var Game = {
        svg: document.getElementById('svg'),
        welcome: document.getElementById('screenWelcome'),      Store your screens to
        restart: document.getElementById('screenGameover'),     easily access them later.

        support: document.implementation.hasFeature(            Using this
            "http://www.w3.org/TR/SVG11/feature#Shape", "1.1"),  property, you
                                                                can easily detect
        width: 500,                                             SVG support.
        height: 500,

        ns: 'http://www.w3.org/2000/svg',      Name schemes are
        xlink: 'http://www.w3.org/1999/xlink', sometimes necessary for
                                               JavaScript to properly
                                               access XML data.
```

```
            run: function() {
                this.svg.addEventListener('click', this.runGame, false);
            },
            init: function() {              All of your object setup
                Hud.init();                 methods are run here.
                Shield.init();
                Ufo.init();
                Ship.init();
                UfoBig.init();

                if (!this.play) {                                          Creates
                    this.play = window.setInterval(Game.update, 20);       animation
                }                                                          for the SVG
            },                                                             elements.

            update: function() {            update() method handles x/y
                Ship.update();              attributes, collision data,
                UfoBig.update();            and advanced game logic.
                Laser.update();
            }
        };

        var Ctrl = {
            init: function() {}             Placeholder controller object to
        };                                  prevent listing 7.9 from crashing.

        window.onload = function() {
            Game.run();
        };
}());
```

Your engine starts out with run() to test for SVG support, then moves on to setting up all of the game's objects. The update() method is responsible for removing and/or changing game assets. You'll notice that a few of the init() items aren't in the update() because they require a separate timer to fire.

> **WARNING** Although it might seem like a good idea to use the animation timer requestAnimationFrame here—as you did in the Canvas game in chapter 6—don't. Clearing an animation timer is difficult, programming in polyfills for intervals and/or timeouts is very buggy, and some browsers don't like SVG coupled with timer-based animation. Until support improves, you're better off using setTimeout() and setInterval() unless you're working with a Canvas application.

STEP 2: INTEGRATE SCREEN TRANSITIONS
In order to make use of the Welcome and Game Over screens you created earlier, you'll need the code in the following listing to add a few more methods for deleting SVG elements and mouse-click monitoring.

Listing 7.9 game.js—Screen transitions

```
var Game = {                                          Starts the game after
    runGame: function() {                             the user clicks Start.
        Game.svg.removeEventListener('click', Game.runGame, false);
        Game.svg.removeChild(Game.welcome);
```

```
        Ctrl.init();
        Game.init();
    },
    restartGame: function() {
        Game.svg.removeEventListener('click', Game.restartGame, false);
        Game.restart.setAttribute('style', 'display: none');

        Game.init();
    },
    endGame: function() {
        window.clearInterval(UfoBig.timer);
        window.clearInterval(Ufo.timer);

        this.elRemove('.shield .player .life .laser
            #flock #ufoShip #textScore #textLives');

        this.restart.setAttribute('style', 'display: inline');
        this.svg.addEventListener('click', this.restartGame, false);
    },

    elRemove: function(name) {
        var items = name.split(' '), type, string, el;
        for (var i = items.length; i--;) {
            type = items[i].charAt(0);
            string = items[i].slice(1);

            el = (type === '.') ?
                document.getElementsByClassName(string) :
                document.getElementById(string);

            if (type === '.') {
                while(el[0])
                    el[0].parentNode.removeChild(el[0]);
            } else {
                if (typeof el === 'object' && el !== null)
                    this.svg.removeChild(el);
            }
        }
    }
};
```

Resets all game data; should occur after clicking a Game Over screen.

Logic for handling a Game Over. It clears out all active elements and waits for a user to restart the game.

To remove all the leftover DOM elements at the end of a game, you add a cleanup helping method. It'll remove multiple elements with one call.

Everything is set up to maintain your game's objects. Now let's create them. You'll start with the simplest objects and work your way toward more complex ones in the next section.

7.3.2 Design patterns, dynamic object creation, and input

 Core API

Every game object created will follow a design pattern with specific methods. You'll place all nonchanging properties for an object at the top before any methods. Some of these properties will include path data, width, height, speeds, and so on. All objects require an init() method that handles all necessary setup for x/y coordinates and timers and resets properties. init(), which should also call to an object's build() method if necessary, will create any DOM-related data. Use update() to execute any logic that needs to fire inside a timer. The last method you'll need to use is collide(), which handles collision logic. To review how your objects are structured, see table 7.4.

Table 7.4 An explanation of major methods used in the SVG Aliens design pattern

Method	Explanation
Constant properties	All unchanging properties are set up before any methods.
init()	Place all setup logic in this method, except DOM element creation.
build()	Anything related to creating DOM elements.
update()	Logic that fires every time a timer is updated.
collide()	Logic that resolves a collision caused by hitting a laser.

Now that you know how to organize your objects, let's start programming one of the larger UFOs.

Step 3: Create the big UFO

Big UFOs (see figure 7.8) spawn out of view in the top left after a set amount of time. You'll want to create them at an x coordinate equal to negative their width so they're hidden initially from view. For instance, if a ship is 45px wide, spawn it at x = -45px. Killing a big UFO will reward players with a nice sum of 30 points because of their rarity.

Figure 7.8 A big UFO that randomly appears. Players may shoot it down for bonus points.

Using the previously discussed design pattern, create a big UFO object by pasting the code from the following listing into the self-executing function after the Game object declaration.

Listing 7.10 game.js—Big UFO (mothership)

```
var UfoBig = {
    width: 45,
    height: 20,
    x: -46,
    y: 50,
    speed: 1,

    delay: 30000,
    init: function() {
        this.timer = window.setInterval(this.build, this.delay);
    },

    build: function() {
        var el = document.createElementNS(Game.ns, 'image');

        el.setAttribute('id', 'ufoShip');
        el.setAttribute('class', 'ufoShip active');
        el.setAttribute('x', UfoBig.x);
```

- A negative x value makes the ship fly in from offscreen.
- 1 is a fairly slow speed but okay for the ship.
- Your timer will build a new ship once every 30 seconds.
- You have to make use of SVG's naming scheme (Game.ns) to create an element.

```
        el.setAttribute('y', UfoBig.y);
        el.setAttribute('width', UfoBig.width);
        el.setAttribute('height', UfoBig.height);
        el.setAttributeNS(Game.xlink, 'xlink:href', ' mothership.svg');    ◄─┐
                                                                              │
        Game.svg.appendChild(el);                      XLink must be set with a │
    },                                                 separate NS from Game.xlink. │

    update: function() {                          ◄─┐
        var el = document.getElementById('ufoShip');  │
        if (el) {                                      Moves the ship
            var x = parseInt(el.getAttribute('x'), 10); from left to
                                                        right and then
            if (x > Game.width) {                       removes it.
                Game.svg.removeChild(el);
            } else {
                el.setAttribute('x', x + this.speed);
            }
        }
    },

    collide: function(el) {          ◄─┐  When destroyed,
        Hud.updateScore(30);              the red ship will
        Game.svg.removeChild(el);         grant 30 points.
    }
};
```

Your big UFO ship object wasn't too difficult to create. Let's tackle the player's ship next, because it follows similar mechanics but adds an input monitor and SVG path.

STEP 4: CREATE THE PLAYER'S SHIP

Because you created a path for a player's green ship with the Welcome screen, you can reuse that code. Path d attributes have x and y coordinates built in, so you'll need to separate the x/y coordinates and path data into two separate parameters. By doing so, you can dynamically generate an x/y position for the ship's graphic. Create the player's ship with the following listing.

> **Listing 7.11   game.js—Player ship setup**

```
var Ship = {                                  Path contains only the shape data
    width: 35,                                of the ship; x and y information
    height: 12,                               will be generated later.
    speed: 3,
    path: 'm 0 15 l 9 5 h 17 l 9 -5 l -2 -5 l -10 3 l -6 -15 l -6 15 l
        -10 -3 l -2 5',                                              ◄─┘

    init: function() {
        this.x = 220;             Sets the default spawning       You need to make
        this.y = 460;             location at game startup.        the build method
                                                                   take parameters so
        this.build(this.x, this.y, 'player active');               it's reusable later
    },                                                             to draw lives in the
                                                                   heads-up display.
    build: function(x, y , shipClass) {       ◄─────────────────┘
        var el = document.createElementNS(Game.ns,'path');
```

```
var pathNew = 'M' + x + ' ' + (y + 8) + this.path;     ◄─┐ Sets x and y to
                                                           │ generate the
el.setAttribute('class', shipClass);                       │ ship's path at a
el.setAttribute('d', pathNew);                             │ specific position.
Game.svg.appendChild(el);

this.player = document.getElementsByClassName('player');
    }
};
```

STEP 5: MAKE THE PLAYER RESPOND TO KEYBOARD INPUT

In addition to the previous listing, you'll need an update() method to add values for monitoring keyboard input. Using a mouse will also be available, but it's stored inside a Ctrl object that you'll create. First, finish your Ship object with the code in the next listing.

Listing 7.12   game.js—Player ship interactivity

```
var Ship = {                                          ┌─ Move left if keyboard input is
    update: function() {                              │  detected and not against a wall.
        if (Ctrl.left && this.x >= 0) {       ◄──────┘
            this.x -= this.speed;
        } else if (Ctrl.right && this.x <= (Game.width - this.width)) {
            this.x += this.speed;
        }

        var pathNew = 'M' + this.x + ' ' + (this.y + 8) + this.path;
        if (this.player[0]) this.player[0].setAttribute('d', pathNew);
    },
                                          ┌─ Logic for when the player's
    collide: function() {          ◄──────┘  ship gets hit by a bullet.
        Hud.lives -= 1;
        Game.svg.removeChild(this.player[0]);        ┌─ Removes a life visually
        Game.svg.removeChild(this.lives[Hud.lives]); │  and decrements
                                                     │  a counter.
        if (Hud.lives > 0) {                    ◄─┐
            window.setTimeout(function() {        │ Whether to
                Ship.build(Ship.x, Ship.y, 'player active'); │ generate a new
            }, 1000);                             │ ship or shut
        } else {                                  │ down the game.
            return Game.endGame();
        }
    }
};
```

Move right if keyboard input is detected and not against a wall.

Updates a player with the latest x and y coordinates.

Note that you can test your new blue ship by commenting out uncreated objects in Game to suppress errors. Be careful to check your browser's console log to make sure no errors accidentally fire. If you choose to tinker with your game, make sure to repair it to look like our previous listings before proceeding. You may need to suppress any errors from missing objects to make the following snippets work too.

STEP 6: CAPTURE KEYBOARD AND MOUSE CONTROLS

Many tutorials depend on jQuery or another library to create keyboard bindings. Most keyboard keys are consistent enough between browsers these days that you don't need a library. You can safely implement arrow keys, a spacebar, letters, mouse movement, and a mouse click at the least, which is what you'll do in the next listing by replacing your existing `Ctrl` object.

Listing 7.13   game.js—Keyboard/mouse setup

```
var Ctrl = {                                                    Binds all mouse and keyboard
    init: function() {                                          events to their proper methods.
        window.addEventListener('keydown', this.keyDown, true);
        window.addEventListener('keyup', this.keyUp, true);
        window.addEventListener('mousemove', this.mouse, true);
        window.addEventListener('click', this.click, true);
    },

    keyDown: function(event) {                                  Passes an event on
        switch(event.keyCode) {                                 keydown to move or shoot.
            case 32:
                var laser = document.getElementsByClassName('negative');
                var player = document.getElementsByClassName('player');
                if (! laser.length && player.length)
                    Laser.build(Ship.x + (Ship.width / 2) - Laser.width,
                        Ship.y - Laser.height, true);
                break;
            case 39: Ctrl.right = true; break;                  Right-arrow
            case 37: Ctrl.left = true;  break;                  key.
            default: break;
        }                                                       Left-arrow
    },                                                          key.

    keyUp: function(event) {                                    Stops movement
        switch(event.keyCode) {                                 or shooting input
            case 39: Ctrl.right = false; break;                 on keyup.
            case 37: Ctrl.left = false; break;
            default: break;
        }
    },

    mouse: function(event) {
        var mouseX = event.pageX;                               Makes sure your
        var xNew = mouseX - Ship.xPrev + Ship.x;                player's ship stays
                                                                inside the game's
        if (xNew > 0 && xNew < Game.width - Ship.width)         boundaries.
            Ship.x = xNew;

        Ship.xPrev = mouseX;                                    For firing lasers, a click() method is
    },                                                          used. It only fires if a laser isn't present
                                                                and a player's ship is still alive.
    click: function(event) {
        var laser = document.getElementsByClassName('negative');

        var player = document.getElementsByClassName('player');

        if (event.button === 0 &&
            player.length &&
            !laser.length)
```

Spacebar key. [annotation for `case 32`]

Only player's lasers are marked as negative. These are retrieved to verify that no laser is already firing. [annotation for click function]

```
Laser.build(Ship.x + (Ship.width / 2) - Laser.width,
    Ship.y - Laser.height, true);
}
};
```

Fires laser from center of the ship.

After suppressing any errors, you should be able to move your players around via keyboard and mouse. Make sure if you fiddle with any code to reset it to the previous listings, as mentioned before.

Now that the player's ship is set up and your input bindings are complete, it's time to work through the steps in group 2, in which you'll start programming objects that are a bit complex. These objects will require more logic, because they're more dependent on data in their surrounding environment.

7.3.3 Creating and organizing complex shapes

In group 2 you'll create a couple of objects that require abstract logic for movement and placement.

- Group 2: Complex objects and overlap
  - Step 1: Create shields for defense.
  - Step 2: Construct lasers.
  - Step 3: Integrate laser collision detection.
  - Step 4: Create the heads-up display.

You'll start by creating blue shields that protect a player's ships from incoming fire. After that, you'll create laser rounds, which need to handle the game's collision logic. Lastly, you'll set up the HUD, which presents a player's remaining lives and accumulated points. Here we go.

STEP 1: CREATE SHIELDS FOR DEFENSE

The shield in figure 7.9 is more complex than anything you've created because it comprises several pieces. Every shield piece must have hit points (hp) and an opacity value attached to it. Hit points are a measurement of how many times something can take damage.

You'll create four shields, each with eight different pieces. Assemble them with the following listing.

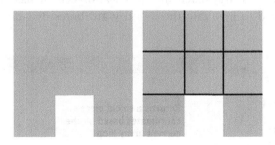

Figure 7.9   Shields comprise eight different pieces (right image) that take three shots each before disappearing.

Listing 7.14   game.js—Shield setup

```
var Shield = {
    x: 64,
    y: 390,
    hp: 3,
    size: 15,                               ◄──  Number of pixels
                                                 per shield piece.
    init: function() {
        for (var block = 4; block--;) {     ◄──  Loops through and
            for (var piece = 8; piece--;) {       creates all four shields
                this.build(block, piece);         with eight pieces.
            }
        }
    },
                                                 Structured to build
                                                 individual shield
                                                 pieces based on their
                                                 location in an array.
    build: function(loc, piece) {           ◄──
        var x = this.x + (loc * this.x) + (loc * (this.size * 3));

        var el = document.createElementNS(Game.ns, 'rect');
        el.setAttribute('x', this.locX(piece, x));
        el.setAttribute('y', this.locY(piece));
        el.setAttribute('class', 'shield active');
        el.setAttribute('hp', this.hp);
        el.setAttribute('width', this.size);
        el.setAttribute('height', this.size);
        Game.svg.appendChild(el);
    },

    collide: function(el) {
        var hp = parseInt(el.getAttribute('hp'), 10) - 1;

        switch(hp) {                                    A shield's opacity drops
            case 1: var opacity = 0.33; break;          each time it takes a hit.
            case 2: var opacity = 0.66; break;          When opacity reaches
            default: return Game.svg.removeChild(el);   zero, it's removed from
        }                                               the game.

        el.setAttribute('hp', hp);
        el.setAttribute('fill-opacity', opacity);
    }
};
```

Your shield-building process requires a 2D array. It'll have four shields with eight pieces inside each. This data is then translated into physical objects by passing it to build(). Notice that you'll need to generate the x and y attributes dynamically, as shown in the following listing.

Listing 7.15   game.js—Shield helpers

```
var Shield = {
    locX: function(piece, x) {                  Returns a shield piece's
        switch(piece) {                   ◄──   coordinates based on the
            case 0: return x;                   current array loop.
            case 1: return x;
            case 2: return x;
```

```
                case 3: return x + this.size;
                case 4: return x + this.size;
                case 5: return x + (this.size * 2);
                case 6: return x + (this.size * 2);
                case 7: return x + (this.size * 2);
            }
        },

    locY: function(piece) {
        switch(piece) {
            case 0: return this.y;
            case 1: return this.y + this.size;
            case 2: return this.y + (this.size * 2);
            case 3: return this.y;
            case 4: return this.y + this.size;
            case 5: return this.y;
            case 6: return this.y + this.size;
            case 7: return this.y + (this.size * 2);
        }
    }
};
```

STEP 2: CONSTRUCT LASERS

Now create a universal laser that can hit any element tagged with class="active". UFOs and players will use the exact same laser object when they shoot. Create a new Laser object with the following code.

Listing 7.16 game.js—Building lasers

```
var Laser = {
    speed: 8,
    width: 2,
    height: 10,

    build: function(x, y, negative) {
        var el = document.createElementNS(Game.ns, 'rect');

        if (negative) {                                          ◁── If negative is set to true,
            el.setAttribute('class', 'laser negative');              the laser travels in the
        } else {                                                     opposite direction.
            el.setAttribute('class', 'laser');                       Mainly used for the
        }                                                            player's lasers.

        el.setAttribute('x', x);
        el.setAttribute('y', y);
        el.setAttribute('width', this.width);
        el.setAttribute('height', this.height);
        Game.svg.appendChild(el);                                ◁── Uses the passed
    },                                                               laser class to see if
                                                                     the current laser
    direction: function(y, laserClass) {                         ◁── moves up or down.
        var speed = laserClass === 'laser negative' ?
            -this.speed : this.speed;
        return y += speed;
    },
```

```
    collide: function(laser) {
        if (laser !== undefined) Game.svg.removeChild(laser);
    }
};
```

> When hit, a laser dissolves, as long as it's present.

STEP 3: INTEGRATE LASER COLLISION DETECTION

Collision detection in SVG Aliens requires a couple of simple steps:

1 Collect all of the active lasers and store their DOM data.

2 Compare their retrieved information against currently active SVG elements. If a collision is true, then fire that object's hit method.

Use the following listing to configure your Laser.update(), because it allows you to integrate collision detection. It's a bit difficult to follow because of all the DOM access, but please bear with us for this listing.

Listing 7.17   game.js—Moving lasers

```
var Laser = {
    update: function() {
        var lasers = document.getElementsByClassName('laser');

        if (lasers.length) {
            var active = document.getElementsByClassName('active');

            var laserX, laserY, cur, num, activeClass,
                activeX, activeY, activeW, activeH;

            for (cur = lasers.length; cur--;) {
                laserX = parseInt(lasers[cur].getAttribute('x'), 10)
                laserY = parseInt(lasers[cur].getAttribute('y'), 10);

                if (laserY < 0 || laserY > Game.height) {
                    this.collide(lasers[cur]);
                    continue;
                } else {
                    laserY = this.direction(laserY,
                        lasers[cur].getAttribute('class'));
                    lasers[cur].setAttribute('y', laserY);
                }

                for (num = active.length; num--;) {
                    if (active[num] === undefined) return;

                    activeX = parseInt(active[num].getAttribute('x'), 10)
                        || Ship.x;
                    activeY = parseInt(active[num].getAttribute('y'), 10)
                        || Ship.y;
                    activeW = parseInt(active[num].getAttribute('width'),
                        10) || Ship.width;
                    activeH = parseInt(active[num].getAttribute('height'),
                        10) || Ship.height;

                    if (laserX + this.width >= activeX &&
                        laserX <= (activeX + activeW) &&
                        laserY + this.height >= activeY &&
                        laserY <= (activeY + activeH)) {
```

Annotations:
- Collect all active lasers.
- Retrieve laser's x and y from the DOM. You'll need it for comparison against active objects.
- Double-check that the laser hasn't gone out of bounds.
- Compare each laser against all active elements for overlap.
- Collision check for overlapping squares.

```
                          this.collide(lasers[cur]);

Regular UFO               activeClass = active[num].getAttribute('class');
minion hit.               if (activeClass === 'ufo active') {
                              Ufo.collide(active[num]);
                          } else if (activeClass === 'shield active') {      Shield
                              Shield.collide(active[num]);                    hit.
The big UFO               } else if (activeClass === 'ufoShip active') {
ship has                      UfoBig.collide(active[num]);
been hit.                 } else if (Ship.player[0]) {
                              Ship.collide();                                  Player
                          }                                                   ship hit.
                      }
                  }
              }
          }
      }
};
```

TRY IT OUT

Suppress any errors you might have, and you can see your collision detection in action by shooting shields via clicking. As before, make sure to set any code you might have fiddled with back to look like previous listings.

STEP 4: CREATE THE HEADS-UP DISPLAY

Users need to know their life count and current score. You can easily present this information by creating a few SVG elements (as you'll see in the next listing). Once you've created it, you'll need extra logic to maintain the presented game data.

Listing 7.18   game.js—HUD building

```
var Hud = {
    livesX: 360,
    livesY: 10,                    Information on where
    livesGap: 10,                  to place life counter.
    init: function() {
        this.score = 0;
        this.bonus = 0;            All of these properties       Logic to visually create
        this.lives = 3;           need to be reset when          a life counter with
        this.level = 1;           your HUD is built.             preexisting player
                                                                 ship's build method.
        var x;
        for (var life = 0; life < Hud.lives; life++) {
            x = this.livesX + (Ship.width * life) + (this.livesGap * life);
            Ship.build(x, this.livesY, 'life');
        }

        this.build('Lives:', 310, 30, 'textLives');
        this.build('Score: 0', 20, 30, 'textScore');
                                                                 Builds an SVG
        Ship.lives = document.getElementsByClassName('life');   text element
    },                                                          associated
                                                                 with the HUD.
    build: function(text, x, y, classText) {
        var el = document.createElementNS(Game.ns, 'text');
        el.setAttribute('x', x);
```

```
            el.setAttribute('y', y);
            el.setAttribute('id', classText);
            el.appendChild(document.createTextNode(text));
            Game.svg.appendChild(el);
        }
    };
```

Your HUD creates all of its necessary text elements when you set it up. To create the life counter, it uses your existing method for building a player's ship. Next, let's outfit your HUD with the ability to update its information, using the following listing.

Listing 7.19 game.js—HUD updating

```
var Hud = {
    updateScore: function(pts) {
        this.score += pts;                        Increments the
        this.bonus += pts;                        existing score.

        var el = document.getElementById('textScore');
        el.replaceChild(document.createTextNode('Score: ' + this.score),
            el.firstChild);

        if (this.bonus < 100 || this.lives === 3) return;    Stops executing logic
                                                             if the player can't
        var x = this.livesX + (Ship.width * this.lives) +   receive a bonus life;
            (this.livesGap * this.lives);                    otherwise, it adds a
        Ship.build(x, this.livesY, 'life');                  new life.
        this.lives += 1;
        this.bonus = 0;
    },

    levelUp: function() {                         Logic to increment
        Ufo.counter += 1;                         the level's difficulty
        var invTotal = Ufo.col * Ufo.row;         by speeding up UFOs.

        if (Ufo.counter === invTotal) {
            this.level += 1;
            Ufo.counter = 0;

            window.clearInterval(Ufo.timer);
            Game.svg.removeChild(Ufo.flock);

            setTimeout(function() {
                Ufo.init();
            }, 300);

        } else if (Ufo.counter === Math.round(invTotal / 2)) {    Always clear
            Ufo.delay -= 250;                                     an interval
            window.clearInterval(Ufo.timer);                      before trying
            Ufo.timer = window.setInterval(Ufo.update, Ufo.delay);  to set it.
        } else if (Ufo.counter === (Ufo.col * Ufo.row) - 3) {
            Ufo.delay -= 300;
            window.clearInterval(Ufo.timer);
            Ufo.timer = window.setInterval(Ufo.update, Ufo.delay);
        }
    }
};
```

Updates the score counter visually by re-creating the display text.

Figure 7.10 UFOs are not only cute; they're also an evil dominant force in numbers.

As your HUD updates a player's score, it increments and checks to see if they've earned an extra life. At each update, the score text is completely replaced in the DOM, whereas an extra life tacks on a new life image. Each time a UFO dies, `Hud.update.level()` fires to see if you need to adjust the UFO's speed. If you need to make a UFO speed adjustment, its timer must be stopped, then started again with a fresh timer.

7.3.4 *Maintaining a complex SVG group*

With the work in group 3, which creates your UFO flock, you need to account for 55 UFOs (see figure 7.10) that dynamically move around the screen. Although it's possible to build each one manually, that's pointless when you can program a method to do it for you. Instead, you'll use our code to generate your UFOs.

Here for your reference are the steps for this section.

- Group 3: The UFO flock
  - Step 1: Set up the UFO flock.
  - Step 2: Generate paths for the UFOs.
  - Step 3: Animate the UFOs.
  - Step 4: Make the UFOs randomly shoot.

STEP 1: SET UP THE UFO FLOCK

Core API

Logic for creating your UFO's placement and AI requires a lot of math. We won't pretend it's easy, but working through the following listings will help you to understand very basic AI programming in games. The next listing determines the number of UFOs to create, groups those UFOs, and sets up to animate them.

Listing 7.20   game.js—UFO flock setup

```
var Ufo = {
    width: 25,
    height: 19,
    x: 64,
    y: 90,
    gap: 10,
    row: 5,                      Determines the number
    col: 11,                     of UFOs to generate.

    init: function() {
        this.speed = 10;
        this.counter = 0;

        this.build();

        this.delay = 800 - (20 * Hud.level);
```

```
        if (this.timer)
            window.clearInterval(Ufo.timer);

        this.timer = window.setInterval(this.update, this.delay);
    },
    build: function() {
        var group = document.createElementNS(Game.ns, 'g');
        group.setAttribute('class', 'open');
        group.setAttribute('id', 'flock');

        var col, el, imageA, imageB;
        for (var row = this.row; row--;) {
            for (col = this.col; col--;) {
                el = document.createElementNS(Game.ns, 'svg');
                el.setAttribute('x', this.locX(col));
                el.setAttribute('y', this.locY(row));
                el.setAttribute('class', 'ufo active');
                el.setAttribute('row', row);
                el.setAttribute('col', col);
                el.setAttribute('width', this.width);
                el.setAttribute('height', this.height);
                el.setAttribute('viewBox', '0 0 25 19');

                imageA = document.createElementNS(Game.ns, 'path');
                imageB = document.createElementNS(Game.ns, 'path');
                imageA.setAttribute('d', this.pathA);
                imageB.setAttribute('d', this.pathB);
                imageA.setAttribute('class','anim1 ' + this.type(row));
                imageB.setAttribute('class','anim2 ' + this.type(row));
                el.appendChild(imageA);
                el.appendChild(imageB);

                group.appendChild(el);
            }
        }

        Game.svg.appendChild(group);
        this.flock = document.getElementById('flock');
    }
};
```

Stores all your UFO creations inside a group. You'll find it much easier to target them as a whole this way.

For animating between the two UFO turning paths, you'll need to add an "open" CSS class. More on that later in this tutorial.

Creates an offset for the UFO's SVG image; that way, it lines up properly with its width and height boxes.

Two different paths are used for each UFO's animation. You can alternate between these by using class "open" and "closed."

STEP 2: GENERATE PATHS FOR THE UFOs

Core API

To generate the massive paths required for different UFOs, you can use Adobe Illustrator or Inkscape (http://inkscape.org/). Either program can save vector creations in SVG format. Once it's saved as SVG, pop open your creation in a text editor, and you'll get all the path information you need to create an illustration. (You can use the ufo SVG file from the book's website for this task.)

Using CSS to make SVG easier

Similar to the concept of placing content inside <div>s in HTML, your UFOs are in an SVG group. Working with groups allows you to target all of the elements inside through CSS inheritance to tweak color, display, and more. In short, groups give you

(continued)

more control and require less maintenance and markup. The following snippet shows CSS rules you've already added to style.css, so you don't need to add them. The `.open` and `.closed` selectors will toggle between the two paths for each UFO. The following snippet will also paint UFOs with different colors depending on a class of `.a`, `.b`, or `.c`.

```
.closed .anim1, .open .anim2 { display: none }
.open .anim1, .closed .anim2 { display: inherit }
.ufo .a { fill: #8C19FF }
.ufo .b { fill: #1EE861 }
.ufo .c { fill: #FFE14D }
```

We've prebuilt the paths for you in the next listing so you don't have to go through all the work required to create them.

Listing 7.21 game.js—UFO paths

Paths like these can be generated from Inkscape and/or Illustrator by saving and opening SVG files in a text editor.

```
var Ufo = {
    pathA: 'M6.5,8.8c1.1,1.6,3.2,2.5,6.2,2.5c3.3,0,4.9-1.4,5.6-2.6c0.9-
    1.5,0.9-3.4,0.5-4.4c0,0,0,0,0,0 c0,0-1.9-3.4-6.5-3.4c-4.3,0-5.9,2.8-
    6.1,3.2l0,0C5.7,5.3,5.5,7.2,6.5,8.8z M19.2,4.4c0.4,1.2,0.4,2.9-0.4,4.6
    c-0.6,1.3-2.5,3.6-6.1,3.6c-4.1,0-5.9-2.2-6.7-
    3.5C5.4,8,5.3,6.9,5.5,5.8C5.4,5.9,5.2,6,4.9,6C4.5,6,4.2,5.8,4.2,5.6 c0-
    0.2,0.3-0.3,0.7-0.3c0.3,0,0.6,0.1,0.6,0.3c0.1-0.5,0.2-0.9,0.4-
    1.3C2.4,5.6,0,7.4,0,10.1c0,4.2,5.5,7.6,12.4,7.6 c6.8,0,12.4-3.4,12.4-
    7.6C24.7,7.4,22.7,5.7,19.2,4.4z M6.9,13.9c-0.8,0-1.5-0.4-1.5-0.9c0-
    0.5,0.7-0.9,1.5-0.9 c0.8,0,1.5,0.4,1.5,0.9C8.4,13.5,7.7,13.9,6.9,13.9z
    M21.2,10.7c-0.7,0-1.3-0.3-1.3-0.7c0-0.4,0.6-0.7,1.3-0.7s1.3,0.3,1.3,0.7
    C22.4,10.4,21.9,10.7,21.2,10.7z',
    pathB: 'M6.5,8.8c1.1,1.6,3.2,2.5,6.3,2.5c3.4,0,4.9-1.4,5.7-2.6c0.9-
    1.5,0.9-3.4,0.5-4.4c0,0,0,0,0,0 c0,0-1.9-3.4-6.5-
    3.4C8.1,1,6.5,3.7,6.3,4.1l0,0C5.8,5.3,5.5,7.2,6.5,8.8z
    M19.3,4.4c0.4,1.2,0.4,2.9-0.4,4.6 c-0.6,1.3-2.5,3.6-6.1,3.6c-4.1,0-5.9-
    2.2-6.8-
    3.5C5,7.5,5.4,4.5,6,5.9,4.3C2.4,5.6,0,7.4,0,10.1c0,4.2,5.6,7.6,12.4,7.6
    c6.9,0,12.4-3.4,12.4-7.6C24.8,7.4,22.8,5.7,19.3,4.4z M3.5,9.2c-0.6,0-
    1.1-0.3-1.1-0.6C2.4,8.2,2.9,8,3.5,8
    c0.6,0,1.1,0.3,1.1,0.6C4.6,8.9,4.2,9.2,3.5,9.2z M16.5,14.6c-0.9,0-1.7-
    0.4-1.7-0.9c0-0.5,0.8-0.9,1.7-0.9s1.7,0.4,1.7,0.9
    C18.2,14.2,17.5,14.6,16.5,14.6z M20.2,5.6c-0.4,0-0.6-0.1-0.6-0.3c0-
    0.2,0.3-0.3,0.6-0.3c0.4,0,0.6,0.1,0.6,0.3 C20.8,5.5,20.5,5.6,20.2,5.6z'
};
```

STEP 3: ANIMATE THE UFOS

 Core API

To create simple animation we're hiding and displaying one of two illustrations for each UFO. SVG can create animation on its own, but using a CSS method is cleaner and less processor-intensive when applicable. To finish your animation and helper methods for `build()`, integrate the following listing into your UFO object.

Listing 7.22   game.js—UFO animation and helpers

```
var Ufo = {
    animate: function() {
        if (this.flock.getAttribute('class') === 'open') {      ◄─┐  A CSS trick to
            this.flock.setAttribute('class','closed');             │  alternate UFO
        } else {                                                   │  graphics between
            this.flock.setAttribute('class','open');               │  two different images.
        }
    },

    type: function(row) {                           ◄─┐  Returns a class for
        switch(row) {                                  │  coloring based on
            case 0: return 'a';                        │  the UFO's row.
            case 1: return 'b';
            case 2: return 'b';
            case 3: return 'c';
            case 4: return 'c';
        }
    },

    locX: function(col) {
        return this.x + (col * this.width) + (col * this.gap);
    },

    locY: function(row) {
        return this.y + (row * this.height) + (row * this.gap);
    },

    collide: function(el) {
        Hud.updateScore(1);
        Hud.levelUp();
        el.parentNode.removeChild(el);
    }
};
```

Help! What to do if your SVG file paths are broken

If you notice that SVG path information from a vector-editing tool is offset or broken, you can probably fix it. In some cases, moving the graphics to the center or top-left corner of your SVG file's canvas fixes the issue. Another method is to remove any whitespace surrounding your graphics (crop it). If all else fails, you can usually get away with manually adding an offset by configuring SVG's viewBox property (as we did for your UFOs).

CREATING DYNAMIC MOVEMENT

Every time the flock moves, it needs to test against the game's width and height because SVG's collision detection isn't stable in all browsers at the time of writing. When SVG's collision detection is more usable, you'll be able to use getInter-sectionList, getEnclosureList, checkIntersection, and checkEnclosure (more info at the official W3C docs www.w3.org/TR/SVG/struct.html#__svg__SVGSVGElement __getIntersectionList).

Core API

You need to calculate an imaginary box around all the existing UFOs (called a *bounding box*). Instead of trying to manually calculate a bounding box, you're going to call getBBox() on the SVG flock element <g id="flock">. It will do all the heavy lifting of calculating a box around the UFOs and return it to you as an object similar to { x: 20, y: 20, width: 325, height: 120 }.

To summarize, the logic flows like this:

1. Get the bounding box of the UFO flock.
2. Check if they've hit a wall (if so increment their positions differently).
3. Increment each x/y as appropriate and check if the player lost.
4. Toggle animations.
5. Potentially shoot.

Now, create your update() method to move UFOs in the flock with this code.

Listing 7.23   game.js—UFO movement AI

```
var Ufo = {
    update: function() {
        var invs = document.getElementsByClassName('ufo');

        if (invs.length === 0) return;

        var flockData = Ufo.flock.getBBox(),
        flockWidth = Math.round(flockData.width),
        flockHeight = Math.round(flockData.height),
        flockX = Math.round(flockData.x),
        flockY = Math.round(flockData.y),
        moveX = 0,
        moveY = 0;

        if (flockWidth + flockX + Ufo.speed >= Game.width ||
            flockX + Ufo.speed <= 0) {
            moveY = Math.abs(Ufo.speed);
            Ufo.speed = Ufo.speed * -1;
        } else {
            moveX = Ufo.speed;
        }
        var newX, newY;
        for (var i = invs.length; i--;) {
            newX = parseInt(invs[i].getAttribute('x'), 10) + moveX;
            newY = parseInt(invs[i].getAttribute('y'), 10) + moveY;

            invs[i].setAttribute('x', newX);
            invs[i].setAttribute('y', newY);
        }

        if (flockY + flockHeight >= Shield.y) {
            return Game.endGame();
        }

        Ufo.animate();
        Ufo.shoot(invs, flockY + flockHeight - Ufo.height);
    }
};
```

Immediately returns if no UFOs exist.

Calling getBBox() on an SVG elements returns a representation of it as a rectangle and as an object, for example: { x, y, width, height }.

Decides where to move next, based on the current flock position.

Loops through and updates the positions of all the UFOs.

Causes a Game Over if UFOs have pushed too far.

You'll set up UFO shooting in the next listing.

Switches out the UFO graphic to emulate rotating.

NOTE Until Opera comes up with a fix, using `getBBox()` on an SVG element in Opera won't work as expected.

STEP 4: MAKE THE UFOS RANDOMLY SHOOT

Each time your `update()` method is called, a shot might be fired based on a random number check. If a UFO does shoot, you're going to use a piece of the bounding box you generated in the previous listing to fire from one of the bottom-row UFOs. You could make the firing more dynamic, such as only from the bottom row of each column, but that takes a lot more logic, and this way you can use the SVG bounding box data again to speed things up. Integrate the following listing to make your UFOs fire lasers.

Listing 7.24   game.js—UFO shooting AI

```
var Ufo = {
    shoot: function(invs, lastRowY) {
        if (Math.floor(Math.random() * 5) !== 1) return;    ◁── A random number test that checks to see if the UFOs can fire.

        var stack = [], currentY;
        for (var i = invs.length; i--;) {                    ◁── Gets all the UFOs from the bottommost row and stores them in an array.
            currentY = parseInt(invs[i].getAttribute('y'), 10);
            if (currentY >= lastRowY)
                stack.push(invs[i]);
        }

        var invRandom = Math.floor(Math.random() * stack.length);   ──▷ Choose a random UFO from the bottom and shoot with it.
        Laser.build(parseInt(stack[invRandom].getAttribute('x'), 10) +
            (this.width / 2), lastRowY + this.height + 10, false);   ──▷
    }
};
```

Choose a random UFO from the bottom and shoot with it.

TRY IT OUT!

You've completed your UFO flock, thereby successfully creating SVG Aliens. When you run the game, it should look similar to figure 7.11. Because you've worked a bit with SVG and understand its basic concepts, we'll compare and contrast it against Canvas (from chapter 6) in the next section.

7.3.5   SVG vs. Canvas

Currently, the optimal way to generate in-browser graphics is through Canvas or SVG. Because you know that Canvas is bitmap-based, you're probably inclined to choose SVG, considering its graphic flexibility. But you might not be aware of a few issues.

WHERE'S THE COMMUNITY?

Core API Anybody with intermediate JavaScript skills can quickly digest Canvas's documentation. If the official documentation is too complex, you'll find entire websites available with educational materials. Contrast that with SVG's documentation, which is *massive*, difficult to comprehend, and aims to tackle a much larger scope. A lot of SVG's documentation can be difficult to follow, and we had to look for articles that translated what we read into easy explanations. Searching online for SVG tutorials led to more woe, because few experts are writing on the subject.

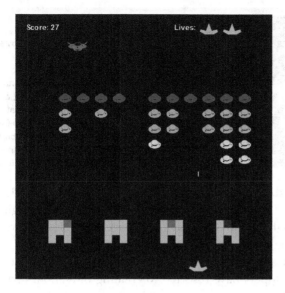

Figure 7.11 Congratulations. You've created a complete game of SVG Aliens. Alternatively, you've also created an endless loop of UFOs, dooming an addicted player to a life of gaming.

Entire libraries for Canvas seem to materialize overnight. Its community is growing surprisingly fast and could easily become a major competitor to Flash in the next few years. Sadly, SVG doesn't have this kind of community involvement yet.

WHAT ABOUT JAVASCRIPT INTEGRATION?

 When it comes to creating complex applications, Canvas handles JavaScript integration much better than SVG, because Canvas doesn't interact with the DOM. For instance, if you want to update SVG elements, they'll need to be loaded into the DOM, processed, and then injected into the page. Although programmers may find some advantages to using the DOM, it also adds a thick layer of extra coding many won't enjoy. Look at the next listing, where you can see how much code it takes to update a square with Canvas versus SVG.

Listing 7.25 example.js—Canvas and SVG JS code samples, respectively

```
x += 1;
y += 1;
context.fillRect(x, y, 100, 100);

rect = document.getElementById('rect');
x = parseInt(rect.getAttribute('x'));
y = parseInt(rect.getAttribute('y'));
rect.setAttribute('x', x + 1);
rect.setAttribute('y', y + 1);
```

Canvas requires only three lines of code to animate a simple rectangle.

SVG requires significantly more programming to move a rectangle in JavaScript, although it would be simpler to use <animate> tags.

Accessing DOM data makes SVG slower than Canvas when using JavaScript.

PROS AND CONS OF SVG IN THE DOM

 SVG's ability to use inline XML elements with HTML markup is its greatest strength, even if it makes the language difficult with JavaScript. Using XML allows developers to create animated graphics without relying on another language. In addition, these shapes are DOM elements, meaning they can be selected and modified during runtime, event

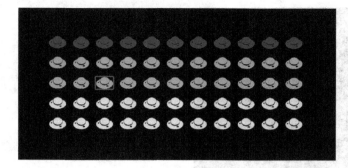

Figure 7.12   SVG allows you to interact with elements in real time. Because of this, you can use Firebug for debugging and coding help. Looking at the screenshot of the UFO flock, you can see that Firebug is highlighting the UFO in the third row and third column.

listeners can be easily attached, and CSS can be applied. Canvas doesn't reside in the DOM, so it doesn't have any of the cool out-of-the-box features that SVG gets. Figure 7.12 shows you how Firebug can highlight an SVG image on a page. Try doing this with Canvas elements, and you'll only be able to see the container's `<canvas>` tag.

One of the most frustrating problems with Canvas is the poor quality of text rendering. It's so bad many developers have resorted to creating old-school text glyphs (prerendered images of text) and writing custom scripts to parse them with Canvas. SVG's text is crystal clear, making it the obvious choice for text-heavy applications.

The current state of SVG

SVG 1.1 has its flaws, but the group that created it is working on SVG 2 to fix those. For mobile devices, SVG Tiny 1.2 is in production. Although you won't yet find good support for SVG on mobile devices, it's coming along. For official updates on the state of SVG, see the W3C page at http://www.w3.org/Graphics/SVG/.

When you want to create a circle in Canvas, you need to create a path and add a series of declarations. SVG gives you the ability to declare a `<circle>` and other complex shapes with a single HTML element instead of creating them in JavaScript with multiple points. This makes for quick and simple creation of complex shapes.

Because Canvas is self-contained inside JavaScript, we think there's little hope it could one day be accessible to screen readers. On the other hand, SVG uses real page elements (such as `<text>`), which means a screen reader "could" potentially interpret the information.

Where are all the SVG games?

You won't find many results from a Google search on "SVG games" as compared to the results for "Canvas games." People in the development community aren't catching on to SVG, in particular for game-based applications. Games require lots of rendering power and the ability to generate many assets such as particles, enemies, and scenery on the fly. Because SVG is inside the DOM, large amounts of assets may cause slow performance. In addition, the large amount of Canvas propaganda isn't helping (in particular for its 3D counterpart, WebGL).

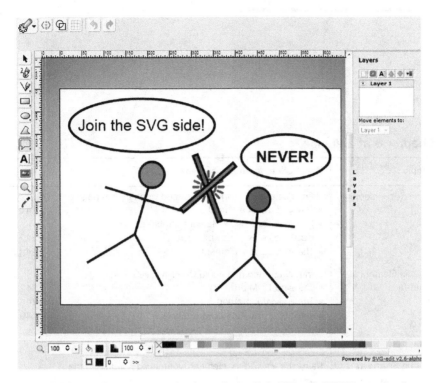

Figure 7.13 We drew you this epic piece of artwork in SVG-edit (MIT Licensed and source code at http://code.google.com/p/svg-edit/). Look closely and you can observe the epic struggle between SVG and Canvas.

WHICH SHOULD YOU USE?

In our opinion, generating simple graphics and animation is for SVG. If you want to create an application heavy on raster graphics and processing, use Canvas.

7.4 Summary

SVG isn't limited to games; developers use it for graphic-editing programs, animation tools, charts, and even HTML5 video. It also allows for resizing backgrounds, screen-conforming artwork, and interactive logo designs that don't pixelate when enlarged. SVG awareness is growing, and frontend developers are using it primarily to create flexible website graphics, like the one you see in figure 7.13.

Although SVG is an ambitious language, because of its DOM integration and massive scope developers aren't yet pursuing it. If SVG is to compete with Canvas, it needs to come up with an API that's more JavaScript friendly. But by exploring it now, you've put yourself ahead of the curve; you'll be ready to leap forward when SVG 2.0 hits the market.

A vital part of interactive applications is sound effects and video integration for complex animations. In the next chapter, we'll be covering HTML5's audio and video APIs so you can integrate them into your applications.

Chapter 8 at a glance

Topic	Description, methods, and so on	Page
`<video>` element	Using declarative markup to embed video in web pages:	
	■ The `<video>` element	241
	■ Common `<video>` element attributes: `src`, `controls`, `width`, `height`	242
	■ The `<source>` element	248
Media Element Interface	Controlling video and audio through JavaScript:	
	■ The `src` DOM attribute	242
	■ The `play()` method	244
	■ The `currentSrc` DOM attribute	249
	■ `currentTime`, `duration`, and `playbackRate` DOM attributes	255
Using `<canvas>` with `<video>`	Using the `<video>` element as an image source in the `<canvas>` element:	
	■ `<video>` as a parameter to `context.drawImage()`	259
	■ `context.globalAlpha`	260
	■ `context.globalCompositeOperation`	258
	■ Using `context.getImageData()` and `context.putImageData()` to process the video	261

Look for this icon Core API ➡ throughout the chapter to quickly locate the topics outlined in this table.

Video and audio: playing media in the browser

This chapter covers

- Navigating the cross-browser and cross-device issues inherent in video
- Converting between different audio and video formats
- Controlling video playback
- Performing video post-processing in the browser using the `<canvas>` element
- Integrating video playback with other content

Clearly, the web is about more than text, but until HTML5 came along we had no built-in way to play audio and video in the HTML standard. Instead, browsers had to depend on third-party applications known as plug-ins.

Not so today. The web is increasingly being used as a replacement for traditional broadcast media. Services like Netflix, YouTube, Spotify, last.fm, and Google Music seek to replace your DVD and CD collections with online players. With HTML5, video and audio become first-class citizens of web content. Rather than handing responsibility for playing media to a third-party application, it's played within the browser, allowing you to control and manipulate media from within your web application.

In this chapter you'll learn to use HTML5's Media Element Interface while building a video telestrator jukebox. A telestrator, made famous by U.S. football coach and announcer John Madden, allows the user to draw directly onto a playing video; the term comes from television sports broadcasting (television + illustrate = telestrate).

Why build the video telestrator jukebox?
These are the benefits:

- You'll learn to use the `<video>` element to add a video to a web page.
- You'll see how to control video playback with JavaScript using Media Element Interface.
- You'll discover how to support different browsers with different file formats using the `<source>` element.

As you move through the chapter, you'll do the following:

- Build the basic jukebox framework
- Add videos to the web page with HTML5
- Use the HTMLMediaElement interface to load and play videos based on user selection
- Attach event handlers to provide user feedback, enable UI options, and start playback
- Use the `<source>` element to provide multiple videos in different formats to support all browsers
- Control video from JavaScript with the HTMLMediaElement interface
- Combine playing video with other web content

We'll show you the application and help you get your prerequisites in order, and then we'll get you started building the basic video player.

8.1 Playing video with HTML5

Placing a video in HTML5 markup is simple, and no more complex for any given browser than placing an image. In this section you'll take full advantage of the built-in browser support to build the simplest possible video jukebox.

We'll show you what the finished product will look like and help you get your prerequisites aligned. Next, you'll lay the application's basic framework and then use the `<video>` element to add videos to the web page.

8.1.1 Application preview and prerequisites

The sample player you'll be building in this chapter is shown in figure 8.1.

Figure 8.1 The finished telestrator jukebox application, showing a video, some artistic telestration, a playlist of videos to choose from, and, underneath the video, a toolbar for controlling the playback

The figure shows the four main components of the player:

- The video itself, showing American football action
- Some artistic telestration saying "HTML5 in Action"
- A playlist of videos to choose from on the right side
- A toolbar to control the playback below the video

WHICH BROWSER TO USE?
For this section please use Chrome, Safari, or Internet Explorer. For the time being you'll have to avoid Firefox and Opera because of the cross-browser video file format issues. We'll discuss these issues, and perform a few tricks to make everything work in Firefox and Opera, in section 8.1.3.

`<video>`/`<audio>` elements	3	3.5	9	10.5	4.0

PREREQUISITES
Before you begin, download the set of sample videos from this book's website and the latest version of jQuery from http://jquery.com/. Put the videos in a directory of the same name in your working directory, and place jQuery in the working directory itself.

You'll also need the requestAnimationFrame polyfill from https://gist.github.com/ 1579671 for the later sections. The code at that URL will go in the script section when you start animating in section 8.4.1.

With those preliminaries out of the way, you're ready to build the framework.

8.1.2   Building the basic jukebox framework

Listing 8.1 shows the framework around which you'll be building the application. It creates a simple layout and has placeholders for the video player and the playlist, the major components you'll be adding in the later sections.

Create a new HTML page in your working directory called index.html, with the following listing as its contents.

Listing 8.1   index.html—Basic jukebox layout

```
<!DOCTYPE html>
<html>
<head>
    <meta charset="utf-8">
    <title>Video Telestrator Jukebox</title>
    <script src="jquery-1.8.2.min.js"></script>           ◁── Latest version of jQuery.
    <script src="raf-polyfill.js"></script>               ◁── requestAnimationFrame polyfill from https://gist.github.com/1579671.
    <style>                                                ◁── Basic CSS to lay everything out.
        body {
            font-family:  sans-serif;
            border: 0;
            margin: 0;
            padding: 0;
        }
        header {
            text-align: center;
        }
        #player {
            display: table;
            width: 100%;
            padding: 4px;
        }
        #player > div, #player > nav {
            display: table-cell;
            vertical-align: top;
        }

        #player canvas {
            display: block;
        }
        #player menu, #player label {
            display: inline-block;
            padding: 0;
        }
        input[type=number] {
            width: 36px;
        }
    </style>
```

```
    </head>
    <body>
        <header>
            <h1>HTML5 Video Telestrator Jukebox</h1>
        </header>
        <section id="player">
            <div>
                <!-- The video will appear here-->
            </div>
            <nav>
                <h2>Playlist</h2>
                <ul>
                    <!-- The video playlist will appear here-->
                </ul>
            </nav>
        </section>
    </body>
</html>
```

You'll add a <video> element here in section 8.1.3.

You'll add a playlist here in section 8.2.

Now, with the foundation laid, let's get to the fun parts of the application by adding a video to the page.

8.1.3 Using the video element to add videos to web pages

The goal in designing HTML5's <video> element was to make the embedding of video within a web page as straightforward as embedding an image. Although you'll encounter additional complexities due to video file formats being more feature-rich than image formats, the design goal has been attained. Figure 8.2 shows the <video> element applied in Google Chrome.

Core API

The next listing shows all of the code required to display the video in figure 8.2. As you can see, it's not complicated. Insert this code in place of the first comment in listing 8.1, and refresh the page to reproduce figure 8.2.

Figure 8.2 Basic HTML5 video player in Chrome

Listing 8.2   index.html—Embed a video

Show the standard play/pause/ fast forward controls to the user.

The src attribute specifies the video to display, like the <img> element.

The width and height don't have to match the video—the browser will scale everything to fit, as with images.

```
<video src="videos/VID_20120122_133036.mp4"
       controls
       width="720" height="480">
    Your browser does not support the video element, please
    try <a href="videos/VID_20120122_133036.mp4">downloading
    the video instead</a>
</video>
```

Browsers that don't support the <video> element will display the fallback content.

 Core API

You used four attributes, `src`, `controls`, `width`, and `height`, in the code in listing 8.2. Table 8.1 summarizes those attributes; for a full list of attributes see appendix B.

Table 8.1   Media element attributes

Attribute	Description
src	The video to play.
controls	A Boolean attribute. If you add it, the browser will provide a standard set of controls for play/pause/seek/volume, and so on. If you leave the attribute out, your code has to control the player (see section 8.3.2).
width	The width of the media (video only).
height	The height of the media (video only).

For your application, displaying a single video isn't enough. You need more videos and the ability to switch between them and control their playback in response to user commands. To do this you'll need to learn about the HTMLMediaElement interface—a collection of attributes and functions for both <video> and <audio> elements, which can be used to start playing the media, pause the media, and change the volume, among other things. We'll tackle that in the next section.

Where's the audio?

Perhaps you've already noticed, but in this chapter you'll be considering and using the <video> element rather than the <audio> element. This isn't because the <audio> element is less important (it isn't) or because it's more complex (it's not) but because this is a book. Although a book may not be an ideal medium for presenting moving pictures, it's an even worse one for invisible sound. But both elements share a single API, the HTMLMediaElement interface, and it's this API that's the focus of this chapter. The only differences between the <audio> and <video> elements are related to visual properties. The <video> element allows you to specify a width and a height for the media, the <audio> element does not.

Figure 8.3   A video playing in IE9 selected from the playlist. The videos have been taken directly off of author Rob Crowther's mobile phone, default names included.

8.2   *Controlling videos with the HTMLMediaElement interface*

Now that you have a video playing, let's start implementing the jukebox feature by allowing users to select from a list of videos, which will appear alongside the <video> element (figure 8.3).

Over the next two sections you'll work through five steps, writing code that allows you to do the following:

- Step 1: Load a list of videos.
- Step 2: Start a video when selected.
- Step 3: Change between videos.
- Step 4: Use event handlers to handle the changing of video in greater detail.
- Step 5: Provide multiple video formats to support all browsers.

As we mentioned, in this section you'll be making use of the HTMLMediaElement interface from JavaScript; as usual with HTML5, the markup only gets you so far. Most of the interesting stuff is done with JavaScript!

STEP 1: LOAD A LIST OF VIDEOS

First, let's hardcode a list of videos into the playlist and hook up everything so that when a user clicks a video it starts playing. Listing 8.3 shows the markup for the playlist; insert it in place of the second comment placeholder in listing 8.1. In a real application you'd almost certainly be generating this list dynamically, but we're going to avoid requiring backend code in this chapter.

Listing 8.3   index.html—Markup for the video playlist

```
<h2>Playlist</h2>
<ul class="playlist">
    <li>VID_20120122_133036.mp4</li>
    <li>VID_20120122_132933.mp4</li>
    <li>VID_20120122_132348.mp4</li>
    <li>VID_20120122_132307.mp4</li>
    <li>VID_20120122_132223.mp4</li>
    <li>VID_20120122_132134.mp4</li>
</ul>
```

◄———— Slot this code in the placeholder section in listing 8.1.

◄———— The videos listed are available in the book's code download.

STEP 2: START A VIDEO WHEN SELECTED

In order to start a video when the user clicks one of the list items, you'll need to know one property and one method of the HTMLMediaElement interface, both of which are summarized in table 8.2.

Table 8.2   HTMLMediaElement interface

Attribute/method	Description
.src	Read/write, reflects the value of the src attribute; use it to select a new video.
.play()	Start playing the current media.

STEP 3: CHANGE BETWEEN VIDEOS

 Core API

You'll also need the change_video function, shown in the next listing. As you can see, it uses both the src property and the play() method to change the video being played. Include the listing in a script block at the end of your code's head section.

Listing 8.4   index.html—Handling the user clicking the playlist

The function that handles the click events on the playlist. ┌─►

```
function change_video(event) {

    var v = $(event.target).text().trim();   ◄——

    var p = $('#player video:first-of-type')[0];   ◄——

    p.src = 'videos/' + v;   ◄——

    p.play();   ◄——

}

$(document).ready(

    function() {

        $('.playlist').bind('click', change_video);   ◄——

    }

)
```

The video name is the text content of the clicked-on item; if you want a more user-friendly interface, you could put in a more readable text label and have the filename on a data-* attribute.

Get a reference to the <video> element.

Set the src value to the new filename.

Start playing the file.

Bind the handler to the click event of the playlist.

STEP 4: USE EVENT HANDLERS TO HANDLE THE CHANGING OF VIDEO IN GREATER DETAIL

In the previous code, the `src` of the `<video>` element is set, and the `play()` method is called immediately. This works well because all of the videos are relatively small and everything is being loaded off the local disk. If you had a much larger video, it's likely that not enough of it will have loaded to start playback if the `play()` method is called immediately, leading to an error. A more reliable approach would be to wait until the video is loaded before starting to play. The HTMLMediaElement interface includes a number of events that fire as the media is loading. The events fired during the loading of a media file are listed in table 8.3 (all of them will fire during the loading of the media).

Table 8.3   Media element events

Event	Occurs when
`loadedmetadata`	The browser has determined the duration and dimensions of the media resource and the text tracks are ready.
`loadeddata`	The browser can render the media data at the current playback position for the first time.
`canplay`	The browser can resume playback of the media but estimates that if playback were to be started, the media couldn't be rendered at the current playback rate up to its end, without having to stop for further buffering of content.
`canplaythrough`	The browser estimates that if playback were to be started, the media could be rendered at the current playback rate all the way to its end, without having to stop for further buffering.

If you were loading a large media file across the network, then you'd have time to display a notification to the user as each of these events occurred. In this section you'll bind event listeners to each of these events and start the playback on `canplaythrough`. But first, let's look at the network-related information available through the HTMLMediaElement interface.

DETERMINING THE STATE OF MEDIA RESOURCES WITH .NETWORKSTATE AND .READYSTATE

The HTMLMediaElement interface includes two useful properties that allow you to determine the state that the media resource is in: `.networkState` and `.readyState`. In a real application you could use the information provided by these properties to give visual feedback about the state of the loading media resource; for example, a progress bar or a loading spinner. Table 8.4 lists the values each property can assume. The `.networkState` is similar to the `.readyState` property on the request object in an `XMLHTTPRequest` and the media `.readyState` corresponds closely to the events listed in table 8.3.

Table 8.4   HTMLMediaElement interface properties and values

Property/values	Description
`.networkState`	Returns the current network state of the element; the value returned is one of the four shown next.
`NETWORK_EMPTY`	Numeric value: 0 (no data yet).

Table 8.4 HTMLMediaElement interface properties and values (*continued*)

Property/values	Description
NETWORK_IDLE	Numeric value: 1 (the network is temporarily idle).
NETWORK_LOADING	Numeric value: 2 (the network is currently active).
NETWORK_NO_SOURCE	Numeric value: 3 (no source has been set on the media element).
.readyState	Returns a value that expresses the current state of the element, with respect to rendering the current playback position.
HAVE_NOTHING	Numeric value: 0 (no data has yet been loaded).
HAVE_METADATA	Numeric value: 1 (enough data has loaded to provide media metadata).
HAVE_CURRENT_DATA	Numeric value: 2 (enough data is available to play the current frame, but not enough for continuous streaming).
HAVE_FUTURE_DATA	Numeric value: 3 (enough data is available to play several frames into the future).
HAVE_ENOUGH_DATA	Numeric value: 4 (enough data is available and continuing to become available that the media can be streamed).

PLAYING VIDEO ON THE CANPLAYTHROUGH EVENT

The next listing shows a simple example of how to use the HTMLMediaEvent interface events and investigate the networkState and readyState. Insert this code in place of the $(document).ready part of listing 8.4.

Listing 8.5 index.html—Capturing HTMLMediaElement interface events

```
function play_video(event) {
    event.target.play();
}
function log_state(event) {
    console.log(event.type);
    console.log('networkState: ' + event.target.networkState);
    console.log('readyState: ' + event.target.readyState);
}
$(document).ready(
    function() {
        $('.playlist').bind('click', change_video);
        var v = $('#player video:first-of-type')[0];
        v.addEventListener('loadedmetadata', log_state);
        v.addEventListener('loadeddata', log_state);
        v.addEventListener('canplay', log_state);
        v.addEventListener('canplaythrough', log_state);
        v.addEventListener('canplaythrough', play_video);
    }
)
```

You'll use this function to start playing the video as soon as it hits the canplaythrough event; this replaces p.play() in listing 8.4. (This is functionally equivalent to adding the autoplay attribute.)

This generic function will log some information about each event as it fires.

Bind all four events to the log_state function.

TRY IT OUT

Apart from the video playing automatically, the previous listing shouldn't work any differently from listing 8.4, which allowed you to switch between videos. But if you open up your browser's console, you should see output similar to that shown in the following listing (exact values may vary from browser to browser).

Listing 8.6   Console output from listing 8.5

```
loadedmetadata
networkState: 1
readyState: 4
loadeddata
networkState: 1
readyState: 4
canplay
networkState: 1
readyState: 4
canplaythrough
networkState: 1
readyState: 4
```

Remember that `networkState: 1` is `NETWORK_IDLE` and `readyState: 4` is `HAVE_ENOUGH _DATA`. With all of the videos on local disk you shouldn't expect too much else, although you may see a `networkState` of 2 on IE. If you have some larger videos online, you should see some different values in each event.

PROGRESS CHECK!

If you've been following along in Chrome, Safari, or IE9 as we recommended at the start of this chapter, you should now have a simple interface, which allows you to click a list of videos and see them play. Figure 8.4 shows what you should be seeing; compare your code to the file index-2.html in the chapter's code download if you're having any problems.

Figure 8.4   What your app should look like in the browser at this point

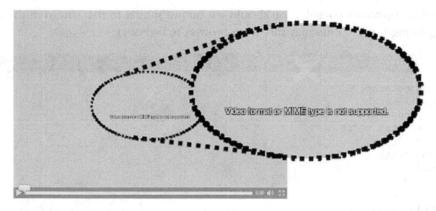

Figure 8.5   An MP4 video in Firefox, where video format or MIME type isn't supported

USING FIREFOX OR OPERA?

If you've tried out the page in Firefox or Opera, you've probably seen a gray screen similar to the one in figure 8.5, which says "Video format or MIME type is not supported."

The issue illustrated in figure 8.5 is that neither Firefox nor Opera supports the MP4 video format even though they support the `<video>` element itself.[1] But the `<video>` and `<audio>` elements provide a workaround for this issue: It's possible to specify multiple media files by using the `<source>` element.

8.3   Specifying multiple formats with the `<source>` element

Each `<video>` element can have multiple `<source>` elements as children. Each `<source>` specifies a video, and the browser tries each one in turn and uses the first video format it can support. Figure 8.6 shows the same video player in Firefox we showed you earlier after `<source>` elements have been added, instead of using the src attribute.

STEP 5: PROVIDE MULTIPLE VIDEO FORMATS TO SUPPORT ALL BROWSERS

Core API   **Now** let's implement. The next listing shows the new markup for the `<video>` element, using child `<source>` elements. Insert the code in place of the existing `<video>` element in your working file.

Listing 8.7   index.html—Adding the `<source>` element

```
<video controls
  width="720" height="480">                                    The original
    <source src="videos/VID_20120122_133036.mp4"              .mp4 video.
            type="video/mp4">                ◄─┘
    <source src="videos/VID_20120122_133036.webm"             A version of the video
            type="video/webm">               ◄─┤              in .webm format.
    Your browser does not support for video element, please
    try <a href="videos/VID_20120122_133036.mp4">downloading
    the video instead</a>
</video>
```

---

[1] Recent versions of Firefox will play MP4 videos on Windows using the support available in the OS.

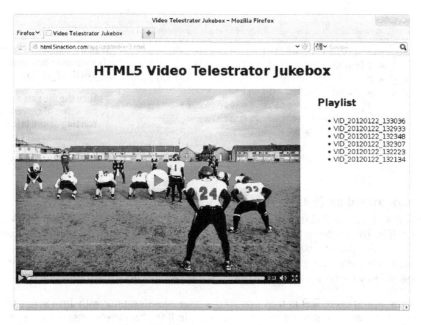

Figure 8.6 `<video>` element in Firefox with multiple sources

CODE CHECK!

This is a good time to stop and check your progress in the browser. You can find the code to this point in the build in the code download, in a file named index-3.html. Compare your index.html code with that code if you have any problems.

8.3.1 *Discovering which video is playing with .currentSrc*

With the new code, Firefox will now load the video it's able to play. This does introduce a problem for your jukebox feature. Before, you were able to set the `.src` property to change the video, but now you need to set the `.src` differently depending on what video file the browser selected to play. Unfortunately, you can't replace all of the child `<source>` elements with a new set; to change the playing video you have to set the `.src` property.

Core API
To solve this problem you need to know about another property of the HTMLMedia-Element interface: `.currentSrc`. This property tells you the filename of the currently selected media.

Because all of your video files are consistently named, you can remove the file extension for all of the `<li>` elements in the playlist (do this now). Instead of getting the complete filename from the `<li>` elements, the `change_video` method can copy the file extension from the `.currentSrc` property and use that to compose the filename of the selected video. The following listing shows the updated `change_video` function, which used this approach; use it to replace the existing one in your file.

Listing 8.8   index.html—Using `currentSrc` to determine the video type

```
function change_video(event) {
    var v = $(event.target).text().trim();
    var p = $('#player video:first-of-type')[0];
    var ext = p.currentSrc.slice(
            p.currentSrc.lastIndexOf('.'),
            p.currentSrc.length);
    p.src = 'videos/' + v + ext;
}
```

The playlist should now contain only extension-less entries like **VID_20120122_132933**.

Slice the file extension from the value of currentSrc starting at the last period.

Combine the file extension with the name to set the new source.

A workaround for IE9's currentSrc bug

The code in listing 8.8 is straightforward, but you may find that it doesn't work properly in IE9. The problem is a bug in IE9: Once a <source> element is added, it immediately takes priority over the `src` attribute and the `currentSrc` property of the <video> element. This means that if you run the app in IE9, then instead of selecting a new video when you click the playlist, you'll see the first video repeated.

Another limitation of IE9 is that updating <source> elements with JavaScript has no effect. If you want to update the playing video in IE9 when you've used <source> elements, then the only workable solution is to replace the entire <video> element. The following snippet shows just such an approach:

```
function change_video(event) {
    var v = $(event.target).text().trim();
    var vp = $('#player video:first-of-type');
    var p = vp[0];
    var ext = p.currentSrc.slice(
            p.currentSrc.lastIndexOf('.'),
            p.currentSrc.length);
    var nv = $('<video controls src="videos/' + v + ext + '" ' +
    'width="720" height="480">' +
    'Your browser does not support the video element, please ' +
    'try <a href="videos/' + v + ext+ '">downloading ' +
    'the video instead</a></video>');
    vp.parent().append(nv);
    vp.remove();
    nv[0].play();
}.
```

For this workaround you'll need a reference to both the actual <video> element and the jQuery object.

Add the new <video> element alongside the current one.

Remove the current <video> element, leaving only the new one.

Instead of updating currentSrc, create a new <video> element with the correct src attribute.

Fortunately this bug is fixed in IE10. Because of this, and to avoid the code complexity getting in the way of learning about the APIs, not to mention that this approach will create new issues in other browsers (which will require further workarounds), the rest of the code in this chapter will ignore this issue. If you're using IE9, then please check the code download files for versions that have been fixed to work in IE9 (they have IE9 in the filename).

You now have a working video jukebox, but you probably still have questions:

- What are these different video formats such as .mp4 and .webm?
- How many different formats do I need to provide to support all browsers?
- If I don't have a particular video in a certain format, how can I convert between them?

We'll discuss changing video formats in the next section. Before we do, we want to answer the first two questions by looking at which browsers support which video and audio formats; table 8.5 summarizes this information.

Table 8.5   Browser video and audio format support

Video formats/ codecs						For broad desktop support, you should provide at least two versions of your media.
MPEG-4/H.264	3	~	9	~	3.2	For video, your best bet is to provide MPEG-4/H.264 and WebM/VP8, at minimum, to cover all current browsers.
Ogg/Theora	3	3.6	~	10.5	*	
WebM/VP8	6	4	*	10.6	*	

* IE and Safari will play additional formats if users install the codec within Windows Media Player or QuickTime, respectively. Currently there's no compatible Ogg/Theora codec for Windows.

Audio formats/ codecs						
MP3	3	~	9	~	3.2	For audio, we recommend that you provide MP3 and Ogg, at minimum, to cover all current browsers.
AAC	3	~	9	~	3.2	
Ogg	3	3.6	~	10.5	*	
WAV	3	3.6	~	10.5	3.2	

* Safari will play additional formats if users install the codec within QuickTime.

As you can see, no single format is universally adopted across all browsers. For broad desktop support, you need to provide at least two versions of your media: for video at least WebM/VP8 and MPEG-4/H.264, for audio MP3 and OGG.

Media format support is something of a contentious issue in the HTML5 world. The sidebar "Why doesn't HTML5 mandate a format that all browsers support?" explains why.

Why doesn't HTML5 mandate a format that all browsers support?

Initially, the HTML5 specification mandated the Ogg/Theora video format. This seemed like a good choice because it's an open source format and the codec is royalty free. But Apple and Microsoft refused to implement Ogg/Theora, preferring instead the MP4/h.264 combination. MPEG LA, LLC, administers MP4/h.264 and

(continued)

sells licenses for encoders and decoders on behalf of companies that hold patents covering the h.264 codec. (Apple and Microsoft are two such companies.)

Supporters of h.264 argue that Ogg/Theora is technically lower quality, has no hardware support (important on battery-powered devices with low-end CPUs), and is more at risk from patent trolls because the obvious way to make money out of infringers is to sue them, whereas submarine patents affecting h.264 can be monetized through MPEG LA.

Supporters of Ogg/Theora argue that the openness of the web requires an open video format. Mozilla couldn't distribute its source code if it contained an h.264 decoder because then everyone who downloaded the code would require a license from MPEG LA. Google avoided this issue by splitting its browser into free parts (the open source Chromium project) and closed parts.

Because the vendors were divided on which format to make standard, and because one of the goals of HTML5 is to document the reality of the implementation, the requirement for supporting any particular codec was removed from the specification. This isn't without precedent in the HTML world—the <img> element doesn't specify which image formats should be supported. We can see some light at the end of the tunnel: Google subsequently released the WebM format as open source with an open license. As the owner of the number-one video site on the web, YouTube, and a provider of the Android mobile OS, it's well-positioned to overcome h.264's commercial advantages.

8.3.2   Converting between media formats

For practical purposes, what you need to know is how to convert a video in one of the supported formats to a different format. A tool called a *transcoder* can convert between different container formats and encodings. There are several online and downloadable tools that convert individual media files; several are listed in the links and resources in appendix J. But for batch processing large numbers of files you'll need to use a command-line tool. Appendix H explains how to use `ffmpeg` to transcode the video files used in this chapter.

You're at the point where you can play a video in every browser that supports the `<video>` element, thanks to the `<source>` element. You also know which video formats you need to provide to support which browsers. Now it's time to create the telestrator feature, which will let you draw directly onto the playing video.

8.4   Combining user input with video to build a telestrator

As we mentioned earlier, the telestrator allows the user to draw directly on a playing video to illustrate the action to the television audience. To create this feature in your application, you'll need a way to combine the video with other image data. For this you'll use the `<canvas>` element. You should be familiar with Canvas from chapter 6.

In that chapter you learned about the drawing capabilities of Canvas to create an interactive game. In this chapter you'll concentrate on the general-purpose, image data-manipulation features to combine images and other content with a video feed.

In this section, you'll learn

- How to use the `<canvas>` element to play a video
- How to create controls for video playback (because the `<canvas>` element renders the video image data, not the `<video>` element)
- How to combine the video on the canvas with other content, such as images
- How to perform basic image-processing using the `<canvas>` element
- How to capture the user's drawings (telestrations) and add them to the video during playback

---

Your work on the telestrator will happen in three groups of steps:

Group 1: Playing video through a `<canvas>` element	Group 2: Manipulating video as it's playing	Group 3: Building the telestrator feature
• Step 1: Add the `<canvas>` element. • Step 2: Grab and display image data. • Step 3: Add markup for and implement video player controls.	• Step 1: Add a frame image to the video. • Step 2: Adjust how the frame and video combine on the canvas. • Step 3: Adjust the opacity of the video. • Step 4: Grayscale the video being played back.	• Step 1: Capture mouse movement. • Step 2: Display the captured path over the video. • Step 3: Add a "clear" button so users can remove telestrations and start again.

Let's start with how to play video through the `<canvas>` element.

8.4.1 Playing video through the `<canvas>` element

The first requirement is to be able to modify the video as it's being played back. You could do this by layering elements on the page and hiding and showing things at the required time. If you were stuck using plug-ins to render the video, that would be your only option for modifying the video from HTML. But the `<video>` element makes its data available as images. You can access each frame of the video as it's ready and treat it as image data. It's then quite straightforward to use the `<canvas>` element to grab that image data and display it.

STEP 1: ADD THE `<CANVAS>` ELEMENT

The following listing shows the basic setup required in the markup. The `<style>` element should be placed in the head section of the document, or you can add the rule to your existing `<style>` element. The div replaces the existing one, where your `<video>` element is located.

Listing 8.9   index.html—Adding a `<canvas>` element to display video

```
<style>
    #player video:first-of-type {
        display: none;
    }
</style>

<div>
    <canvas width="720" height="480"></canvas>
    <video controls
           width="720" height="480">
        <source src="videos/VID_20120122_133036.mp4"
                type="video/mp4">
        <source src="videos/VID_20120122_133036.webm"
                type="video/webm">
        Your browser does not support for the video element, please
        try <a href="videos/VID_20120122_133036.mp4">downloading
        the video instead</a>
    </video>
</div>
```

CSS is used to hide the `<video>` element.

Add a `<canvas>` element with the same dimensions as the video.

The `<video>` element remains as it was, although now that it's invisible, the controls parameter and fallback content aren't strictly necessary.

STEP 2: GRAB AND DISPLAY IMAGE DATA

Now you need to listen for the play event on the `<video>` element and use that as a trigger to start grabbing video frames and rendering on the canvas. The `$(docu-ment).ready` in the next listing should replace the existing function you added previously in listing 8.8.

Listing 8.10   index.html—Adjusting the `draw()` function to use the `<canvas>` element

```
$(document).ready(
    function() {
        $('.playlist').bind('click', change_video);
        var v = $('#player video:first-of-type')[0];
        var canvas = $('#player canvas:first-of-type')[0];
        var context = canvas.getContext('2d');
        function draw() {
            if(v.paused || v.ended) return false;
            context.drawImage(v,0,0,720,480);
            requestAnimationFrame(draw);
        }
        v.addEventListener('play', draw);
    }
)
```

This part of the code remains the same as before.

If the video has stopped playing, don't do any additional work.

The draw() function will draw the video frames one by one on the canvas; a closure is used to cache references to the video and the canvas context.

A recursive call is made to the draw() function using the requestAnimationFrame polyfill (see listing 8.I).

Listen for the play event on the `<video>` element to kick off the draw function.

Now you're able to play back the video through the `<canvas>` element, but you'll notice that something is missing. The controls you got for free as part of the `<video>` element are no longer accessible now that the video is being played through `<canvas>`. The next section deals with creating your own controls.

Figure 8.7 Custom playback buttons in Opera

8.4.2 Creating custom video playback controls

In this section you'll create a simple menu of buttons to control video playback. Figure 8.7 shows the final effect. Obviously, we're not aiming to win any points for design here; it's the functionality we're interested in.

STEP 3: ADD MARKUP FOR AND IMPLEMENT VIDEO PLAYER CONTROLS

The simple markup for the controls we're adding—return to start, slow down playback, pause, play, and speed up playback—is shown here; add this code directly after the <canvas> element.

Listing 8.11   index.html—Creating video player controls

```
<menu>
    <button>|&lt;</button>          ← Return to start.
    <button>&lt;&lt;</button>        ← Slow down playback.
    <button>||</button>             ← Pause.
    <button> &gt; </button>         ← Play.
    <button>&gt;&gt;</button>        ← Speed up playback.
</menu>
```

 Core API To make the buttons functional, you'll have to learn about a few more properties and methods on the HTMLMediaElement interface. A summary of these methods is shown in table 8.6.

Table 8.6   More HTMLMediaElement interface methods

Attribute/method	Description
.currentTime	Read/write the current position (in seconds) of the playback
.duration	The length of the media in seconds

Table 8.6   More HTMLMediaElement interface methods *(continued)*

Attribute/method	Description
.defaultPlaybackRate	The speed, expressed as a multiple of the standard playback speed of the media
.playbackRate	The rate at which the media is currently playing back as a positive multiple of the standard playback speed of the media (less than 1 is slower; greater than 1 is faster)
.pause()	Pauses the currently playing media

With these properties and methods you have enough information to implement the five buttons. In the $(document).ready function you added in listing 8.10, you'll need to bind a handler to the menu, like the one shown next. It can be added anywhere in that function as long as it's after the declaration for the v variable. If you're not sure, add it at the end.

Listing 8.12   index.html—Handler function for the control menu

```
$('menu').bind('click', function(event) {
    var action = $(event.target).text().trim();      ◁── For simplicity, you can use the
    switch (action) {                                       text content of the buttons to
        case '|<':                                          determine which one was clicked.
            v.currentTime = 0;            ◁──┤  To go back to the start of the
            break;                              video, set the currentTime to 0.
        case '<<':
            v.playbackRate = v.playbackRate * 0.5;  ◁─┐
            break;                                      │
        case '||':                                      │  Repeatedly hitting
            v.pause();                                  │  the fast or slow
            break;                                      │  buttons will multiply
        case '>':                                       │  the playback rate,
            v.playbackRate = 1.0;            ◁──────────┤  but hitting play will
            v.play();                                   │  reset it to 1.
            break;                                      │
        case '>>':                                      │
            v.playbackRate = v.playbackRate * 2.0;  ◁─┘
            break;
    }
    return false;
})
```

pause() and play() do exactly what it says on the tin.

CODE CHECK!

You've now restored basic functionality to your video player. The working code to this point in the chapter is in the file index-5.html in the code download, so you can compare what you've written. For extra credit, consider how you might use .currentTime and .duration in concert with a <meter> element (see section 2.3.3) to reproduce the seek bar. Otherwise, move on to the next section, where you'll explore the effects you can achieve now that playback is occurring through a <canvas> element.

Figure 8.8 Grayscale video playback through `canvas` **combined with an image at 90 percent opacity**

8.4.3 *Manipulating video as it's playing*

The point of playing the video through the `<canvas>` element wasn't to merely replicate the behavior you get for free with the `<video>` element but to process the video output. In this section you'll learn basic techniques for processing the video, ending up with something that looks like figure 8.8. You'll use these same techniques in later sections to build the telestrator.

Figure 8.8 also shows the result of the next group of four steps you'll walk through:

- Group 2: Manipulating video as it's playing
  - Step 1: Add a frame image to the video.
  - Step 2: Adjust how the frame and video combine on the canvas.
  - Step 3: Adjust the opacity of the video.
  - Step 4: Grayscale the video being played back.

STEP 1: ADD A FRAME IMAGE TO THE VIDEO

You learned about drawing images on canvas in chapter 6; the basic approach is the same for this step. First, you need an image on the page. It can go anywhere inside the `<#player>` element (hide it with CSS `display: none`):

```
<img src="images/frame.svg">
```

To give users the ability to turn the frame on and off, you'll need a button in the menu from listing 8.11:

```
<button>Framed</button>
```

Because it's on the menu, you can take advantage of the existing click-handling code for that—the additional cases for the switch statement are shown in the following listing—and add them to the handler from listing 8.11.

Listing 8.13   index.html—Handler for the Frame button

```
case 'Framed':
    framed = false;
    $(event.target).text('Frame');          You'll set up the
    break;                                   framed variable
case 'Frame':                                in listing 8.14.
    framed = true;
    $(event.target).text('Framed');
    break;
```

With this next listing, you need to adjust the draw() function to draw the frame.

Listing 8.14   index.html—Adjust the draw() function to show the frame

```
var framed = true;                              This is the framed variable you
var frame = $('#player img:first-of-type')[0];  were promised in listing 8.13.
//...                                            For brevity, all the other declarations
function draw() {                                have been left out; leave them as
    if(v.paused || v.ended) return false;       they are in your code.
    context.drawImage(v,0,0,720,480);
    if (framed) {                               Draw the frame only if
        context.drawImage(frame,0,0,720,480);   the user has requested it.
    }
    requestAnimationFrame(draw);
    return true;                                The drawImage function is as you
}                                               remember it; note that the frame gets
                                                drawn after (on top of) the video.
```

And that's it! You should now be able to get a frame to appear over the video playback at the click of a button. In the next step you'll learn how to adjust how the two images, the frame and video, are composed (combined) together on the Canvas.

STEP 2: ADJUST HOW THE FRAME AND VIDEO COMBINE ON THE CANVAS

 By default, things you draw on the Canvas layer on top of each other; each new drawing replaces the pixels below it. But it's possible to make this layering work differently with the .globalCompositeOperation property of the context.

Figure 8.9 provides an example of each composition mode available to you.

To allow you to experiment, we've created a <select> element with all of the possible modes in listing 8.15. The composition operations split the world into two segments:

- Destination, what's already drawn
- Source, the new stuff you're trying to draw

Add the code from the following listing (place it after the <menu> element you added in listing 8.11).

Listing 8.15   index.html—`<select>` element for composition mode

```
<label>
    Composition:
    <select>
        <option>copy</option>
        <option>destination-atop</option>
        <option>destination-in</option>
        <option>destination-out</option>
        <option>destination-over</option>
        <option>source-atop</option>
        <option>source-in</option>
        <option>source-out</option>
        <option selected>source-over</option>
        <option>lighter</option>
        <option>xor</option>
    </select>
</label>
```

Display the source, where source and destination overlap.

Display the source in the transparent parts of the destination.

Add the source only where it overlaps destination, but put the destination on top.

Set the overlap of destination and source to transparent; elsewhere display the destination.

Where the two overlap, display the destination; elsewhere display the source.

Add the source where it overlaps the destination, with the source on top; elsewhere, the destination is transparent.

Display the source where it overlaps the destination; show the destination elsewhere.

Set the destination to transparent. Set the overlap of source and destination to transparent; elsewhere display the source.

The default; draw the new stuff over the old.

Add the source and destination colors together.

Parts are transparent where both overlap; elsewhere display destination or source.

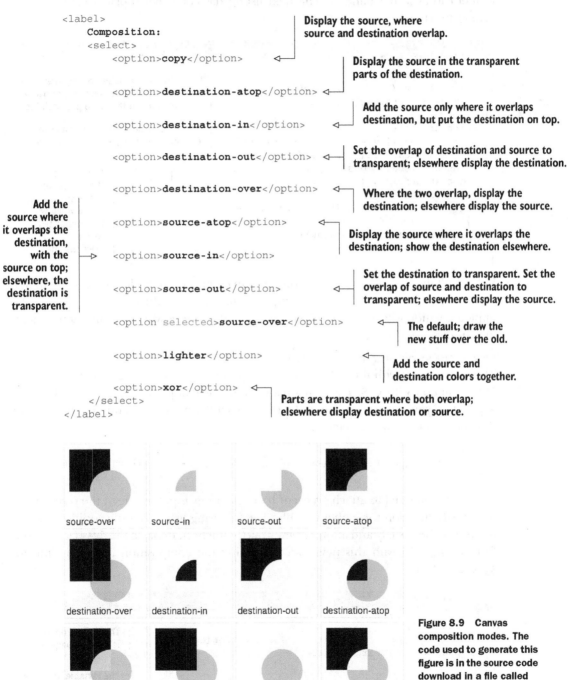

source-over   source-in   source-out   source-atop

destination-over destination-in destination-out destination-atop

lighter   darker   copy   xor

Figure 8.9   Canvas composition modes. The code used to generate this figure is in the source code download in a file called canvas-composition-modes.html.

Now, so that your application can respond to changes, you need to bind the `<select>` element to an event handler. The next listing has code that replaces your existing `draw()` function.

Listing 8.16 index.html—Change the composition mode in the `draw()` function

```
var c_mode = 'source-over';
$('select').bind('change', function(event) {
    c_mode = event.target.value;
})
function draw() {
    if(v.paused || v.ended) return false;
    context.clearRect(0,0,720,480);
    context.globalCompositeOperation = c_mode;
    context.drawImage(v,0,0,720,480);
    if (framed) {
        context.drawImage(frame,0,0,720,480);
    }
    requestAnimationFrame(draw);
    return true;
}
```

Create a variable to keep track of the state as before; saves expensive DOM lookups in the video playback loop.

You've used the JavaScript names in the select options, so this bit is easy.

Set the mode.

If you don't clear the canvas, each successive frame of the video will be composited with the previous one.

Video isn't the ideal format to experiment with composition modes because it's always a fully opaque image, and in this example it's taking up all the pixels. But this simple implementation will allow you to experiment and consider where you might use them in your own projects.

STEP 3: ADJUST THE OPACITY OF THE VIDEO

 Core API

The opacity is set with the `.globalAlpha` property. It should be a value between 0 and 1; in common with CSS, 1 is fully opaque and 0 is completely transparent. In your application you can add an item to let the user set the value with a number input; add this code after the `<menu>` element:

```
<label>
    Opacity:<input type="number" step="0.1" min="0" max="1" value="1.0">
</label>
```

As before, you need to attach an event handler to this input and feed the results into the `draw()` function through a variable. The following listing has the additional code to capture the opacity and another new `draw()` function. Replace the `draw()` function from listing 8.15 with this new code (retaining the composition mode binding to `$('select')`):

Listing 8.17 index.html—Change the opacity in the `draw()` function

```
var c_opac = 1;
$('input[type=number]').bind('input', function(event) {
    c_opac = event.target.value;
})
function draw() {
    if(v.paused || v.ended) return false;
    context.clearRect(0,0,720,480);
```

The default opacity is 1 (fully opaque).

Set the variable when the user changes the value.

```
context.globalCompositeOperation = c_mode;
context.globalAlpha = c_opac;
context.drawImage(v,0,0,720,480);
if (framed) {
    context.drawImage(frame,0,0,720,480);
}
requestAnimationFrame(draw);
return true;
}
```

> **Use the variable to set the opacity within the draw() function. You can use opacity to create interesting effects when used in combination with the composition mode.**

Step 4: Grayscale the video being played back

 The `<canvas>` element is also a general-purpose, image-processing tool, thanks to its `.getImageData` and `.putImageData` methods. These methods directly access the array of pixels making up the canvas. Once you have the pixels, you can implement standard image-processing algorithms in JavaScript. The next listing is a JavaScript implementation of an algorithm to turn an image gray. This code can be included anywhere inside your `<script>` element.

Listing 8.18   index.html—A function to make an image grayscale

```
function grayscale(pixels) {
    var d = pixels.data;
    for (var i=0; i<d.length; i+=4) {
      var r = d[i];
      var g = d[i+1];
      var b = d[i+2];
      var v = 0.2126*r + 0.7152*g + 0.0722*b;
      d[i] = d[i+1] = d[i+2] = v
    }
    return pixels;
};
```

NOTE   The grayscale function in listing 8.18 is adapted from the HTML Rocks article on image filters; see www.html5rocks.com/en/tutorials/canvas/imagefilters/ for more details.

With the complex math all safely hidden in a general-purpose function, all that remains is to apply it to the canvas. Listing 8.19 shows how you'd call the `grayscale()` function from within your `draw()` function. For this to work, you need to declare a variable `grayed` alongside the `framed` one you created in listing 8.14 and set it to an initial value of `false`.

Listing 8.19   index.html—Use the `grayscale()` function within `draw()`

```
context.drawImage(v,0,0,720,480);
if (grayed) {
    context.putImageData(
        grayscale(context.getImageData(0,0,720,480))
        ,0
        ,0
    );
}
```

> **You have to first draw the video as an image to the canvas before you can start processing it.**

> **Get the image data from the canvas and pass it through the grayscale function.**

> **Draw the results back on to the canvas starting at the top left (0,0).**

NOTE   The getImageData() method will trigger a security error if you access the example from a file:// URL. If you run into any problems, try accessing the file using a local web server. In Chrome there's also a bug that causes a security violation when getImageData() is called after an SVG image has been drawn on the canvas. Check https://code.google.com/p/chromium/issues/detail?id=68568 for updates.

You will also need a Grayed button inside the menu and a handler in the switch statement. This will work analogously to the Framed button you created in listing 8.13, so we won't repeat the code here.

CODE CHECK!

The file index-6.html in the book's code download is a working version of the code to this point (but see section 8.3.1 if you're using IE9).

NOTE   Image processing works pixel by pixel, which means it becomes increasingly more expensive the higher the quality of the video. Unless you're building an application to preview video processing results, your users will usually be grateful if you do expensive real-time processing on the server, instead of in their browser.

8.4.4   *Building the telestrator features*

Using the techniques from the previous section of rendering the video through a <canvas> element and overlaying graphics on that video, you can now add the telestration feature. The results, demonstrating the artistic abilities of the authors, are shown in figure 8.10.

Figure 8.10   After working through this final section, you'll be ready to telestrate!

It will take just three remaining steps to get you there:

- Group 3: Building the telestrator feature
  - Step 1: Capture mouse movement.
  - Step 2: Display the captured path over the video.
  - Step 3: Add a "clear" button so users can remove telestrations and start again.

STEP 1: CAPTURE MOUSE MOVEMENT

To capture mouse movement, you'll need to modify your `$(document).ready` function to include the following code. It doesn't matter where you add it; in the downloadable example it's between the initial declarations and the `draw()` function.

Listing 8.20　index.html—Capturing the mouse movement

This variable determines whether you're currently recording mouse movements.

```
var clickX = new Array();
var clickY = new Array();
var clickDrag = new Array();
var paint = false;

var canvas = $('#player canvas:first-of-type');
var pos = canvas.position();
canvas.bind('mousedown', function(event) {
    var mouseX = event.pageX - pos.left;
    var mouseY = event.pageY - pos.top;
    paint = true;
    addClick(mouseX, mouseY);
}).bind('mousemove', function(event) {
    if(paint){
        var mouseX = event.pageX - pos.left;
        var mouseY = event.pageY - pos.top;
        addClick(mouseX, mouseY, true);
    }
}).bind('mouseup', function(event) {
    paint = false;
}).bind('mouseleave', function(event) {
    paint = false;
});

function addClick(x, y, dragging) {
    clickX.push(x);
    clickY.push(y);
    clickDrag.push(dragging);
}
```

Set up global variables to record the movement of the mouse.

You are now using jQuery to attach event handlers to the canvas, so you will use the jQuery reference in code rather than the DOM reference as before. Remember to update the assignment which gets the context to use canvas[0] instead of canvas.

Cache the position of the <canvas> element on the page so you don't have to do expensive DOM queries.

As the user moves the mouse around, and if you're currently painting, add further positions.

When the user presses the mouse button, set the paint variable to true and record the initial position with the addClick function.

If the user releases the button or moves off the canvas, set the paint variable to false.

The addClick function populates the variables created in the first step in this listing.

NOTE To keep the `draw()` function simple, in this section we've removed the code and buttons for `Grayed` and `Framed`. Leaving them in your code won't harm anything, but bear this in mind as you follow the instructions to replace and include code in this section.

STEP 2: DISPLAY THE CAPTURED PATH OVER THE VIDEO

The next step is to display the path within the `draw()` function. The following listing has yet another new `draw()` function.

Listing 8.21   index.html—Modifying the `draw()` function to show the path

```
function draw() {

    if(v.paused || v.ended) return false;

    context.clearRect(0,0,720,480);
    context.globalCompositeOperation = c_mode;
    context.globalAlpha = c_opac;
    context.drawImage(v,0,0,720,480);
    context.strokeStyle = "#ffff00";
    context.lineJoin = "round";
    context.lineWidth = 8;
    for(var i=0; i < clickX.length; i++) {
        context.beginPath();
        if(clickDrag[i] && i){
            context.moveTo(clickX[i-1], clickY[i-1]);
        } else {
            context.moveTo(clickX[i]-1, clickY[i]);
        }
        context.lineTo(clickX[i], clickY[i]);
        context.closePath();
        context.stroke();
    }
    requestAnimationFrame(draw);
    return true;
}
```

Note that to keep things simple, if the video is paused, nothing will be drawn, even though new telestrations will continue to be recorded.

We will telestrate in a nice, visible yellow.

Loop through the coordinates stored in the path.

Special handling for the first coordinate because you can't access element <-1> of an array.

STEP 3: ADD A CLEAR BUTTON SO USERS CAN REMOVE TELESTRATIONS AND START AGAIN

As a final step you need to add a Clear button so users can remove their telestrations and start again. An easy place to put this is in the controls menu you already have, by adding another button:

```
<button>Clear</button>
```

The new case for your big `switch` statement is shown in the next listing.

Listing 8.22   index.html—Process the clear action

```
case 'Clear':
    clickX = new Array();
    clickY = new Array();
    clickDrag = new Array();
    paint = false;
    break;
```

Reset all the stored path data.

Stop capturing new drawing data.

With that you should have a fully functioning video jukebox telestrator and be well on your way to adding your own garish yellow annotations to the videos of your choice. Figure 8.11 shows the authors' feeble attempt at a John Madden impersonation along with the Clear button ready to consign that attempt to history.

CODE CHECK!

In the code download you'll find a working version of the code from this section in the file index-9.html. There's also an index-10.html file, which includes the code from

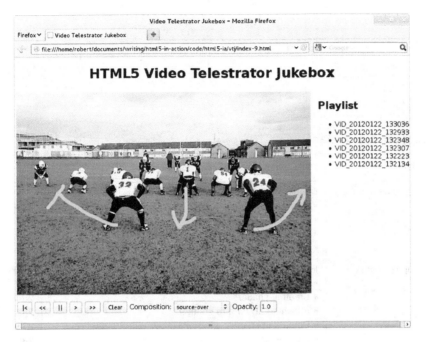

Figure 8.11 The finished application in Firefox

this section as well as the Grayed and Framed functionality from the previous section we took out to simplify the listings.

8.5 Summary

In this chapter you've learned how HTML5 makes it as straightforward a process to add video and audio to web pages as it is to add images. You've taken the news of browser incompatibilities in format support in stride and learned how to convert between video formats, and you've learned how to control media elements with JavaScript. The added bonus of having video within HTML5 is that you can use it as input for other content, in particular the <canvas> element. You've also learned how to combine video with images and, finally, how to combine it with live drawing. We hope that in addition to all the technical knowledge you've gained, you've also thought of ideas on how to incorporate media within your web applications, as well as playing media on your page.

In the next chapter, you'll continue to learn about exciting visual effects you can create with HTML5 as you learn about WebGL. The WebGL format allows you direct access to the computer's graphics hardware from JavaScript, raising the possibility of implementing real 3D games and data visualizations.

Chapter 9 at a glance

Topic	Description, methods, and so on	Page
Engine creation	Creating a WebGL engine from scratch	
	■ Time-saving scripts	274
	■ Basic engine pattern	277
	■ Default entity class	279
	■ Helper methods	280
Graphics cards	Interacting with a graphics card	
	■ OpenGL	282
	■ Creating shaders	284
	■ Attaching 3D data to entities	283
	■ Outputting shapes	288
	■ Matrices usage	288
WebGL app	Putting everything together to create an app	
	■ 2D triangle in 3D	296
	■ 3D basics	297
	■ Large complex polygons	300
	■ Cubes	305
	■ Particle generation	308

Look for this icon _{Core API} ➡ throughout the chapter to quickly locate the topics outlined in this table.

WebGL: 3D
application development

This chapter covers

- Developing a WebGL engine
- Communicating with a graphics card
- Creating 3D shapes

Web developers have been trying for years to overcome 3D limitations to create better interactive games, education tools, and infographics. In the past, plug-ins such as Unity, Flash, and Quicksilver created Google Maps and online 3D explorations programs. Plug-ins can be useful, but they leave you at the browser vendor's mercy for updates, usually lack hardware acceleration, and are often proprietary. To solve these issues, the Khronos Group created a Web Graphics Library (WebGL). WebGL, as mentioned in chapter 1, gives you the ability to create awesome 3D applications like X-Wing, shown in figure 9.1, without plug-ins. Several developers have even used WebGL to make drawing interfaces that create 2D images and rotate those creations in 3D.

> **WARNING!** You should be very familiar with Canvas and JavaScript object-oriented programming (OOP) before working through this chapter's sample application. If you aren't, please go through chapter 6 on 2D Canvas first, because the concepts we cover here build on chapter 6's application, mainly because WebGL builds on top of the Canvas API.

Figure 9.1   A simple WebGL application called X-Wing created by OutsideOfSociety. He worked on the popular WebGL project http://ro.me.

You could learn basic 3D programming elsewhere, but we've provided it all for you—all in one place—along with thorough explanations of 3D programming concepts, mathematics, diagrams, and more. We even teach you how to apply your new knowledge by walking you through the creation of a game: Geometry Destroyer!

Why build Geometry Destroyer?

Some online tutorials teach the basics of what you can do with WebGL. But this chapter's tutorial doesn't cover creating simple demos—you'll be creating a real application from the ground up. A few of the subjects you'll learn during the build include how to

- Create a reusable WebGL class
- Generate and maintain large numbers of WebGL entities
- Create different shape buffers with reusable code
- Work with assets in 2D and 3D space
- Handle 2D collision detection in 3D space with particle generation

In this chapter you'll first learn how to use WebGL to create an engine from scratch. Knowing how an engine works teaches you the fundamentals of managing 3D assets.

After you've built the engine's entity management to control visual objects, we'll walk you through making a request with WebGL, processing returned data, and displaying the resulting 3D shapes. For the last part of the lesson, we'll show you how to create your game's player and bullets with 2D shapes in 3D. We'll then expand on the

> ### Need a prebuilt WebGL engine?
>
> In a rush to get a WebGL application rolling? We recommend downloading Copper-Licht for 3D gaming at http://www.ambiera.com/copperlicht/download.html. After you've downloaded the package, you should take a look at the documentation and demos at www.ambiera.com/copperlicht/documentation/ to get started. For any other projects (interactive data representations, architecture, animated videos, maps, and the like), grab a copy of Mr. Doob's three.js from GitHub at https://github.com/mrdoob/three.js. You'll find examples, documents, and usage guides to get you started at http://mng.bz/1iDu.

2D drawing ideas to create 3D rotating polygons that explode into cubes and squares when destroyed.

After completing this chapter, you'll understand how WebGL creates and manages 3D data. In addition, you'll walk away with a reusable basic WebGL engine and a fun game! Let's start by rolling out the engine's entity-management components.

9.1   *Building a WebGL engine*

Even though using a prebuilt engine can save a lot of time, it may cause problems if it doesn't support the functionality you need. We recommend rolling your own engine for JavaScript applications *when time permits.* You'll not only learn how to be a better programmer, you'll also create reusable code for future projects.

> ### In this section, you'll learn the following reusable WebGL concepts:
> - How to structure an engine that creates visual output
> - How to create simple JavaScript inheritance with John Resig's script
> - Where to get and how to use assets that make writing WebGL faster
> - Methods for handling collisions, deletion, and other entity-management-related tasks

For example, the techniques you'll learn building Geometry Destroyer (figure 9.2) in this chapter will be transferable to other visual APIs such as Canvas and SVG.

WARNING: BUILDING AN ENGINE ISN'T EASY!   If you don't want to copy and paste tons of JavaScript code to create the 3D engine, we recommend that you simply read along in sections 9.1 and 9.2 and then download the engine from Manning's source code. You can use that source code as your starting point and then write the game with us in section 9.3. Feeling adventurous and want to put your coding chops to work? Great! We invite you to build the engine from scratch by following and using the code listings.

Figure 9.2   Get pumped to build your application by going to http://html5inaction.com/
app/ch9/ and playing Geometry Destroyer before you build it. Download the source code
from Manning's website at http://manning.com/crowther2/.

BROWSER NOTE: USE CHROME OR FIREFOX FOR THIS CHAPTER'S SAMPLE APPLICATION
Whether or not you're building the engine with us, we recommend that you use
Google Chrome or Firefox's latest version. Other browsers may not support advanced
3D features or the necessary graphics acceleration. Although browsers may "support"
WebGL, "support" doesn't mean that all features have been implemented.

WebGL for IE?
Want to enable WebGL in older versions of IE? Check out a plug-in called IEWebGL
(http://iewebgl.com). It provides support for IE 6, 7, 8, 9, and 10. Because it's a
downloaded executable, you can present it to users when they're using IE. Keep in
mind that it doesn't work with our demo, but it works great with libraries like Three.js
(see the site for a complete list).

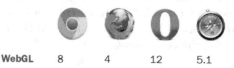

WebGL   8   4   12   5.1

We've broken the engine-building work into seven steps to help you follow along and see the big picture:

- Step 1: Review/create the JavaScript code base and index.html.
- Step 2: Create style.css.
- Step 3: Implement time-saving scripts.
- Step 4: Create base engine logic.
- Step 5: Manage entity storage.
- Step 6: Create shape entities with 3D data.
- Step 7: Add reusable methods that speed up programming and make files easier to maintain.

Let's get started.

9.1.1 Setting up the engine's layout

Creating a WebGL engine requires several different developer tools and a file structure like the one you see in figure 9.3.

For now you can create an empty copy of each folder and file with the proper hierarchy ahead of time, or you can follow along and create each file and folder as we mention them. The JavaScript folder (named js) will house everything for your engine. Inside the JavaScript folder, place a run.js file and an engine folder. We're keeping engine's contents separate from everything else to keep things neatly organized.

> **GRAPHICS CARD WARNING**   Please note that not all graphics cards will support WebGL. If you're running the latest version of Chrome or Firefox and can't run the 3D files for this chapter on your hardware, the only solution we can think of is to try another computer. We apologize if you can't run WebGL; the lack of graphics card support has been frustrating for many developers.

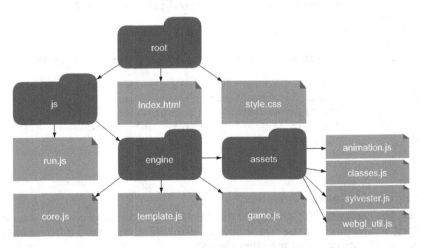

Figure 9.3   Your engine's file structure should be identical to this figure. We've organized it in a manner that's conducive to learning.

STEP 1: REVIEW/CREATE THE JAVASCRIPT CODE BASE AND INDEX.HTML

Create a file called index.html from the following listing, as a base for running all of your JavaScript code. You'll be including a <canvas> tag because WebGL runs on top of the Canvas API.

Listing 9.1 index.html—Creating the engine HTML

```html
<!DOCTYPE html>
<html>
<head>
    <title>Geometry Destroyer</title>
    <link rel="stylesheet" type="text/css" href="style.css" />
</head>

<body>
    <div id="container">
        <canvas id="canvas" width="800" height="600">
            Download Chrome to experience the demo!
        </canvas>

        <span id="score">Score: <span id="count">0</span></span>

        <p id="title" class="strong screen">Geometry Destroyer</p>
        <p id="start" class="screen">Push <span class="strong">X</span> to
    Start</p>

        <p id="end" class="screen hide">
            <span class="strong">Game Over</span>
        </p>

        <p id="ctrls">Move: Arrow Keys | Shoot: Hold X</p>
    </div>

    <script type="text/javascript" src="js/engine/assets/sylvester.js"></
        script>
    <script type="text/javascript" src="js/engine/assets/webgl_util.js"></
        script>
    <script type="text/javascript" src="js/engine/assets/animation.js"></
        script>
    <script type="text/javascript" src="js/engine/assets/classes.js"></
        script>
    <script type="text/javascript" src="js/engine/core.js"></script>
    <script type="text/javascript" src="js/engine/game.js"></script>
    <script type="text/javascript" src="js/engine/template.js"></script>
    <script type="text/javascript" src="js/run.js"></script>
</body>
</html>
```

Annotations:
- **Canvas is required to run WebGL. Make sure you include a canvas tag when running it.**
- **Score counter.**
- **Initial text presented to a player.**
- **Text presented at Game Over.**
- **Include all of your engine's JavaScript files here.**

Can I use 2D Canvas in WebGL?

Sadly, you can't use 2D Canvas and the WebGL API in the same context. The trick to getting around this is to use two <canvas> elements to create two different contexts and then sit one on top of the other via CSS.

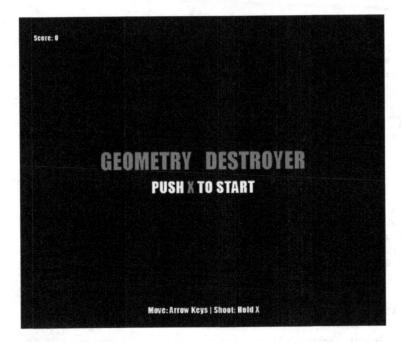

Figure 9.4 Result of running the index.html file with CSS and HTML only. In the final screen, the triangular player will appear between the words *Geometry* and *Destroyer*.

STEP 2: CREATE STYLE.CSS

Because creating text in WebGL isn't easy, you'll use text from HTML markup. We've included in the previous index.html listing an introduction and starting screen, but it needs some styling (see figure 9.4).

Place the next listing inside a new file called style.css. Put the file in the same folder that contains index.html.

Listing 9.2   style.css—Adding styling

```css
body {
    background: #111;
    color: #aaa;
    font-family: Impact, Helvetica, Arial;
    letter-spacing: 1px;
}

#container {
    width: 800px;
    margin: 40px auto;
    position: relative;
}

#canvas {
    border: 1px solid #333;
}
```

```
#score {
    position: absolute;
    top: 5px;
    left: 8px;
    margin: 0;
    font-size: 15px;
}

.strong {
    color: #a00;
}

.screen {
    font-size: 34px;
    text-transform: uppercase;
    text-align: center;
    text-align: center;
    position: absolute;
    width: 100%;
    left: 0;
}

#title {
    top: 214px;
    font-size: 50px;
    word-spacing: 20px;
}

#start {
    top: 300px;
}

#end {
    top: 220px;
    display: none;
    font-size: 50px;
}

#ctrls {
    text-align: center;
    font-size: 18px;
}
```

STEP 3: IMPLEMENT TIME-SAVING SCRIPTS

Core API

Next, create a folder called js to house all of your JavaScript files. Inside create a file called run.js that will house all of your run code. Next to run.js create a folder called engine. Inside of engine create another folder called assets. You'll fill up the assets folder with four scripts that will save you time.

Getting your engine up and running requires several different external files. You'll need the following:

- Paul Irish's requestAnimationFrame() inside animation.js
- A slightly modified version of John Resig's Class Extension script called classes.js
- A transformation matrix library called sylvester.js
- Helpers from webgl_util.js

We'll explain exactly what each component does and how it aids your engine's functionality as we proceed.

PAUL IRISH'S REQUESTANIMATIONFRAME

Our goal is to equip your engine with best animation practices similar to those we discussed in chapter 6 on 2D Canvas. When we say "best animation practices," we mean

- Using `requestAnimationFrame()` instead of `setInterval` for mobile compatibility, to prevent updates when in another tab, and to prevent frame rate tearing
- Testing for the `requestAnimationFrame()` in other browsers with Paul Irish's polyfill and guaranteeing support for older browsers like IE8

To start building your dependencies, or the files your engine is dependent on, navigate to the assets folder. Inside create a file called animation.js using Paul Irish's `requestAnimationFrame()` shown in the following listing (http://mng.bz/h9v9).

Listing 9.3   animation.js—Requesting animation and intervals

```
window.requestAnimFrame = (function() {
    return window.requestAnimationFrame      ||
        window.webkitRequestAnimationFrame   ||
        window.mozRequestAnimationFrame      ||
        window.oRequestAnimationFrame        ||
        window.msRequestAnimationFrame       ||
        function(callback) {
            window.setTimeout(callback, 1000 / 60);
        };
})();
```

JOHN RESIG'S SIMPLE JAVASCRIPT INHERITANCE

Because your engine requires you to create objects that can be modified, tweaked, and inherited on the fly, you need an extendable class. The problem is that classes usually require a robust library like prototype.js because JavaScript doesn't natively support them. To keep your engine's file size and dependencies limited, we're using a slightly modified version of John Resig's Simple JavaScript Inheritance script (http://ejohn.org/blog/simple-javascript-inheritance/). Insert a modified version of John Resig's script from the following listing into a file called classes.js in the assets folder.

Listing 9.4   classes.js—JavaScript inheritance

```
(function(){
    var initializing = false, fnTest = /xyz/.test(function(){xyz;}) ?
        /\b_super\b/ : /.*/;
    this.Class = function(){};

    Class.extend = function(prop) {
        var _super = this.prototype;

        initializing = true;
        var prototype = new this();
        initializing = false;
```

```
        for (var name in prop) {
            prototype[name] = typeof prop[name] == "function" &&
            typeof _super[name] == "function" && fnTest.test(prop[name]) ?
            (function(name, fn){
                return function() {
                    var tmp = this._super;

                    this._super = _super[name];

                    var ret = fn.apply(this, arguments);
                    this._super = tmp;

                    return ret;
                };
            })(name, prop[name]) :
            prop[name];
        }

        function Class() {}

        Class.prototype = prototype;
        Class.prototype.constructor = Class;
        Class.extend = arguments.callee;

        return Class;
    };
})();
```

> The only piece of code we changed from the original inheritance script was removing a call to init() here. Originally, the script would automatically call init() if it were present on an object.

> **WANT MORE JAVASCRIPT?**
>
> If you want to learn more about JavaScript's prototype-based inheritance, pick up a copy of John Resig and Bear Bibeault's *Secrets of the JavaScript Ninja* (Manning, 2012). It's loaded with great techniques to help you work with libraries, create cross-browser solutions, and maintain your code.

SYLVESTER.JS

To create 3D shape objects, you also need to send the graphics card some packaged matrix information, such as [0 1 3 0], but JavaScript doesn't have built-in tools for handling such information. You could write a matrix processing library for your engine from scratch, but it's quite a lot of work. Instead, you'll use sylvester.js to process everything. Get the latest version of the script from http://sylvester.jcoglan.com/, unzip it, and include the sylvester.js file in your assets folder.

WEBGL_UTIL.JS

The last asset you need is webgl_util.js, which contains lots of prewritten code to help with generating a perspective, processing matrixes, and more. We wish we could credit the author of this great script, but as Mozilla says, "Nobody seems entirely clear on where it came from." Grab the file at http://mng.bz/P7Vi and place it in assets.

> ## Wait—didn't you say "custom rolled engine"?
>
> Earlier we said that our WebGL tutorial centers on a built-from-scratch engine, which may lead you to ask, "Why are you making me use assets that aren't from scratch?" Truth is, we don't have time to custom roll everything; it would take at least 100 more pages to explain a complete engine step by step, so we thought that adding a few scripts to simplify everything was a good idea. We hope you agree!

9.1.2 Tools to create, alter, and delete objects

With your assets in place, let's get to work on the engine.

STEP 4: CREATE BASE ENGINE LOGIC

Core API

Use the following listing to create your first engine file, core.js, inside js/engine. With this listing, you are detecting WebGL support, setting up the base configuration for WebGL, creating a helper method to detect collisions, and creating placeholders for code in later listings.

Listing 9.5 core.js—Engine startup

```
var gd = gd || {};            ◄──┤  Inherits a previously existing gd variable or creates a
                                     new one. Great for accessing gd across multiple files.
gd.core = {
    canvas: document.getElementById("canvas"),

    size: function(width, height) {              ◄──┐  WebGL requires you to set an
        this.horizAspect = width / height;           │  aspect ratio; failure to do so
    },                                                │  will distort the correct aspect
                                                         ratio of your canvas.
    init: function(width, height, run) {
        this.size(width, height);

        if (!this.canvas.getContext) return alert('Please download ' +
            'a browser that supports Canvas like Google Chrome ' +
            'to proceed.');
        gd.gl = this.canvas.getContext("experimental-webgl");

        if (gd.gl === null || gd.gl === undefined)
            return alert('Uhhh, your browser doesn\'t support WebGL. ' +
                'Your options are build a large wooden badger ' +
                'or download Google Chrome.');

        gd.gl.clearColor(0.05, 0.05, 0.05, 1.0);    ◄──┤  Sets a clear color of slightly
        gd.gl.enable(gd.gl.DEPTH_TEST);                    off-black for WebGL.
        gd.gl.depthFunc(gd.gl.LEQUAL);
        gd.gl.clear(gd.gl.COLOR_BUFFER_BIT | gd.gl.DEPTH_BUFFER_BIT);

        this.shader.init();
        this.animate();                      ┌  Fires the run code
                                             │  argument after everything
        window.onload = run;        ◄──────  │  has been set up.
    },

    animate: function() {
        requestAnimFrame(gd.core.animate);
```

Manually check for WebGL support; some browsers return null and some undefined if getContext() fails.

These two lines of code set up depth perception.

```
        gd.core.draw();
    },
    shader: {
        init: function() {},
        get: function(id) {},
        store: function() {}
    },

    draw: function() {},

    overlap: function(
        x1, y1, width1, height1,
        x2, y2, width2, height2) {
        x1 = x1 - (width1 / 2);
        y1 = y1 - (height1 / 2);
        x2 = x2 - (width2 / 2);
        y2 = y2 - (height2 / 2);

        return x1 < x2 + width2 &&
            x1 + width1 > x2 &&
            y1 < y2 + width2 &&
            y1 + height1 > y2;
    }
};
```

Shaders will be covered later; this is a placeholder for now.

Drawing will be covered during graphic creation; this is currently a placeholder.

The gd.core.overlap() method is for detecting overlap between two squares.

WebGL objects are drawn from the center, and you need to calculate from the top left. You need to adjust the width and height calculations to account for that.

STEP 5: MANAGE ENTITY STORAGE

Now you need to manage entity storage and create a graveyard to handle cleaning out deleted entities. Add the following listing to complete core.js's entity management inside your existing gd.core object. These methods make maintaining entities significantly easier when you program the run.js file later.

Listing 9.6   core.js—Engine entity management

```
gd.core = {
    id: {
        count: 0,
        get: function() {
            return this.count++;
        }
    },

    storage: {
        all: [],
        a: [],
        b: []
    },

    graveyard: {
        storage: [],
        purge: function() {
            if (this.storage) {
                for (var obj = this.storage.length; obj--;) {
                    this.remove(this.storage[obj]);
                }
                this.graveyard = [];
```

Gives new entities a unique ID identifier. Speeds up searching for and deleting objects.

Storage container for holding all the objects you generate. The A and B containers are used to cut down on collision-detection comparisons by placing friendlies in A, enemies in B.

Used to destroy entities at the end of your update loop to prevent accidentally referencing a nonexistent entity.

```
            }
        },
        remove: function(object) {
            var obj;
            for (obj = gd.core.storage.all.length; obj--;) {
                if (gd.core.storage.all[obj].id === object.id) {
                    gd.core.storage.all.splice(obj, 1);
                    break;
                }
            }

            switch (object.type) {
                case 'a':
                    for (obj = gd.core.storage.a.length; obj--;) {
                        if (gd.core.storage.a[obj].id === object.id) {
                            gd.core.storage.a.splice(obj, 1);
                            break;
                        }
                    }
                    break;
                case 'b':
                    for (obj = gd.core.storage.b.length; obj--;) {
                        if (gd.core.storage.b[obj].id === object.id) {
                            gd.core.storage.b.splice(obj, 1);
                            break;
                        }
                    }
                    break;
                default:
                    break;
            }
            gd.gl.deleteBuffer(object.colorStorage);
            gd.gl.deleteBuffer(object.shapeStorage);
        }
    }
};
```

> JavaScript's garbage cleanup is subpar. You need to manually purge 3D data from entities to prevent your application from slowing down.

STEP 6: CREATE SHAPE ENTITIES WITH 3D DATA

 Core API

You need to set up an extendable class to create entities that contain 3D data. You'll use John Resig's Simple JavaScript Inheritance script that you added earlier in combination with a template object. Think of templates as molds for all of your game's reusable visual assets, such as players, enemies, and particles. Add the next listing in a file right next to core.js called template.js.

Listing 9.7 template.js—Entity default template

```
var gd = gd || {};

gd.template = {
    Entity: Class.extend({
        type: 0,

        x: 0,
        y: 0,
        z: 0,
```

> Set the collision detection to a string of "a" = friendly, "b" = enemy, and "0" = passive. Friends and enemies will collide, but passive entities won't during collision detection.

> Z-axis makes elements 3D; we'll cover this in more detail later.

We're using zoom to create an artificial camera in WebGL. Normally, a good chunk of extra programming is required, so it's kind of a hack to speed up programming.

```
zoom: -80,

position: function() {
    return [this.x, this.y, this.z + this.zoom];
},

width: 0,
height: 0,

update: function() {},

collide: function() {
    this.kill();
},

kill: function() {
    gd.core.graveyard.storage.push(this);
},

rotate: {
    angle: 0,
    axis: false
}
    })
};
```

Assembles and returns a position in a WebGL editable format.

update() is always called before an entity is drawn.

Collisions fire the kill method.

Send the entity to the graveyard for deletion before cp.core.draw() can run again.

Rotation will be used later to configure unique angles for entities.

STEP 7: ADD REUSABLE METHODS THAT SPEED UP PROGRAMMING AND MAKE FILES EASIER TO MAINTAIN

Core API

We know that the previous code doesn't directly create any 3D graphics, but it makes working with 3D much easier. Bear with us for one more code snippet, and we'll cover WebGL right after.

Let's create the last file, game.js, which will have several generic methods to speed up programming. These methods will slim down your run.js file and make it easier to maintain. Populate the game.js file in the engine directory with the following listing.

Listing 9.8   game.js—Entity helper methods

```
var gd = gd || {};

gd.game = {
    spawn: function(name, params) {
        var entity = new gd.template[name];

        entity.id = gd.core.id.get();

        gd.core.storage.all.push(entity);
        switch (entity.type) {
            case 'a':
                gd.core.storage.a.push(entity);
                break;
            case 'b':
                gd.core.storage.b.push(entity);
                break;
            default:
                break;
        }
```

gd.game.spawn() will generate any entity template when given a name with type String. It'll also pass any additional parameters to your init() method if you declared them.

Pushes the newly created entity into storage.

```
        if (arguments.length > 1 && entity.init) {
            var args = [].slice.call(arguments, 1);
            entity.init.apply(entity, args);
        } else if (entity.init) {
            entity.init();
        }
    },
    boundaries: function(obj, top, right, bottom, left, offset) {
        if (offset === undefined)
            offset = 0;

        if (obj.x < - this.size.width - offset) {
            return left.call(obj);
        } else if (obj.x > this.size.width + offset) {
            return right.call(obj);
        } else if (obj.y < - this.size.height - offset) {
            return bottom.call(obj);
        } else if (obj.y > this.size.height + offset) {
            return top.call(obj);
        }
    },
    rotate: function(obj) {
        var currentTime = Date.now();
        if (obj.lastUpdate < currentTime) {
            var delta = currentTime - obj.lastUpdate;

            obj.rotate.angle += (30 * delta) / obj.rotate.speed;
        }
        obj.lastUpdate = currentTime;
    },
    random: {
        polarity: function() {
            return Math.random() < 0.5 ? -1 : 1;
        },
        number: function(max, min) {
            return Math.floor(Math.random() * (max - min + 1) + min);
        }
    }
};
```

If you added additional arguments to init(), they'll be passed in via the currying technique of prefilling function arguments. John Resig blogs about curring in JavaScript.[1]

Allows you to easily set logic for leaving the game's play area. You'll need to manually set the game's width and height later because 3D environment units are subjective. Most 3D engines allow you to set measurements because none exist by default.

Rotation method will allow you to move an object around its center point (originally taken from Mozilla's WebGL tutorial).[2]

Random number generation helpers.

If everything was set up correctly, you can run index.html, and your browser's console will only inform you of no errors or that run.js doesn't exist. If you happened to create the run.js file earlier, it won't fire the error shown in figure 9.5.

Now that your engine's mechanics are set up, you need to complete it by sending your object's 3D data to a user's graphics card, then displaying the returned information.

---

[1] John Resig blog, "Partial Application in JavaScript," last updated February 2008, http://mng.bz/6SU0.

[2] "Animating objects with WebGL," Mozilla Developer Network, last updated Aug 7, 2012, http://mng.bz/O5Z2.

Figure 9.5   If you load up index.html and take a look at your console, it will display no errors or that run.js is missing. Know that if you've created a run.js file already, it won't fire the shown error.

9.2   Communicating with a graphics card

While a war rages on to establish online standards, so does another for computer graphics. OpenGL and Direct X are two heavily competing graphics API libraries for 3D applications. Although the two have many differences between them, you mainly need to know that OpenGL is open source and Direct X is proprietary. Because of OpenGL's open source nature, support for its internet baby, WebGL, has grown significantly.

> **NOTE**   We're deeply indebted to Mozilla's WebGL tutorials (https://developer .mozilla.org/en/WebGL) and Learning WebGL's lessons (http://learningwebgl .com) for the code you'll be using in this section. Thanks, Mozilla and WebGL!

Core API

OpenGL is a cross-platform library for Mac OS X, Unix/Linux, and Windows. It allows for graphics hardware control at a low level. WebGL is based on OpenGL ES (OpenGL for Embedded Systems), which is a subset of OpenGL for mobile devices. Although WebGL's ability to render 3D data via browser seems great, it's also violating the internet's security model of not letting web pages access hardware. The good news, though, is that browsers integrate extra security features to "hopefully" prevent someone from setting your graphics card on fire, stealing graphic memory, and/or launching DoS attacks (more details at http://www.contextis.com/resources/blog/webgl2/). We're going to be optimistic here and assume those things won't happen.

> **In this section, you'll learn how**
> - WebGL processes data inside a computer
> - To create shader data and store
> - To create and store shape data with buffers
> - To manipulate matrices to output assembled 3D data on a screen
> - To use a few scripts that make writing matrices easier

Let's start by looking at how WebGL renders data before you see it.

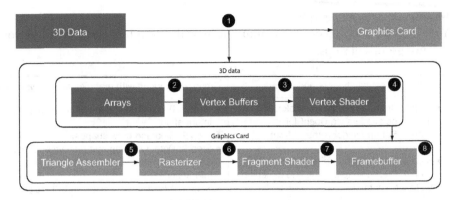

Figure 9.6 A clean version of the rendering pipeline. Although not a be-all-end-all explanation, it explains the basic steps WebGL goes through as it processes 3D data from start to finish.

9.2.1 Graphics cards: a quick primer

Consider the game you're creating: How will a user's browser process and display the 3D data for your objects? Take a look at figure 9.6.

What figure 9.6 shows you is that when sending over the 3D data ❶ for entities to a *graphics card*, the data starts as *arrays* ❷ (computer data) and gets processed by the GPU (graphics processing unit) into *vertex buffers* ❸ (more data). During this rendering stage, additional information is required to assemble your 3D shapes (such as buffer variables). After processing vertex buffers, the data runs through a *vertex shader* ❹ to generate screen positioning and color information. 3D data is then further processed by the GPU into triangle segments through the *triangle assembler* ❺ and then sent to a *rasterizer* ❻ that removes unnecessary visual data from shapes, generates pixel fragments, and smooth's out color surfaces. Shape data then flows through a *fragment shader* ❼, which outputs color and depth for each pixel. Lastly, everything is drawn onto a user's screen by a *framebuffer* ❽.

> **3D graphics and triangles? I don't get it.**
> When you're learning to create shapes with a 2D surface, you usually create a rectangle first. But it isn't the simplest of shapes, and you can't easily fit a bunch of tiny rectangles together to create a person's face or a ball. On the other hand, tiny triangles can fit together to easily create almost any shape imaginable. For a great overview of triangles in 3D programming, see Rene Froeleke's article "Introduction to 3D graphics" at http://mng.bz/STHc.

If you need more detailed information on how WebGL processes data, we recommend reading Opera's explanation at http://mng.bz/4Lao. Our version is quick and simple, because we don't want to put you to sleep.

MEANWHILE, BACK AT THE ENGINE

Your engine currently doesn't communicate with a graphics card. To do so, you'll follow two groups of steps:

Group 1—Creating shaders and buffers	Group 2—Working with matrices and drawing shapes
▪ Step 1: Create and configure color, vertex, and shape shaders via OpenGL ES. ▪ Step 2: Set up shader retrieval from the DOM. ▪ Step 3: Pull shader data from the DOM. ▪ Step 4: Create shape, color, and dimension buffers for entities.	▪ Step 1: Use matrices and buffers to visually output information. ▪ Step 2: Bind and draw shapes. ▪ Step 3: Detect overlap and remove entities. ▪ Step 4: Add matrix helpers to simplify matrix interaction. ▪ Step 5: Add Vlad Vukićević's WebGL helpers for rotation.

Once you've completed these tasks, you'll be ready to program the game.

9.2.2 Creating shaders for 3D data

Before you begin with the Group 1 set of tasks, pick up Jacob Seidelin's helpful WebGL Cheat Sheet at http://blog.nihilogic.dk/2009/10/webgl-cheat-sheet.html. It breaks down all of the methods for WebGL's context into categories such as shaders, buffers, and more, which will help as you move through these next few sections.

> **WHAT ARE SHADERS AGAIN?**
> We're throwing "shaders" around like it's a hip word. A long time ago it may have meant shading in shapes with color, but now it means much more than that. Today's shaders program the GPU for transformations, pixel shading, and special effects such as lighting.

STEP 1: CREATE AND CONFIGURE COLOR, VERTEX, AND SHAPE SHADERS VIA OPENGL ES

To start up your shaders, gd.core.shader.init() needs to call gd.core.shader.get() and gd.core.shader.store() to retrieve shading data. In addition, you'll need to write a little bit of code in a mystery language—OpenGL ES (see the sidebar on OpenGL ES for more information)—and place that code in your HTML document. Add the following listing inside index.html right before your JavaScript files. Note that if you put it anywhere other than right before your JavaScript files, your game will probably fail to load.

Listing 9.9   index.html—Color, vertex, and shape shaders

```
<script id="shader-vertex" type="x-shader/x-vertex">
    attribute vec3 aVertexPosition;          Configuration for position
    attribute vec4 aVertexColor;             and color in your shaders.

    uniform mat4 uMVMatrix;                   Uniform declares this is a constant variable,
    uniform mat4 uPMatrix;                    and mat4 references a 4-by-4 float matrix.
```

Varying declares color data will vary over the surface of a primitive shape.

```
     varying lowp vec4 vColor;

     void main(void) {
         gl_Position = uPMatrix * uMVMatrix * vec4(aVertexPosition, 1.0);
         vColor = aVertexColor;
     }
</script>

<script id="shader-fragment" type="x-shader/x-fragment">

     varying lowp vec4 vColor;

     void main(void) {
         gl_FragColor = vColor;
     }
</script>
```

Stores your data inside appropriate variables.

shader-vertex handles position and vertex info; shader-fragment handles color assignment.

OpenGL ES shading language cheat sheet

OpenGL ES is a subset of OpenGL aimed at embedded systems such as mobile phones, game consoles, and similar devices. The Khronos Group has compiled a PDF for WebGL that contains a cheat sheet on OpenGL ES Shading Language. It significantly helps with writing your own custom shader scripts. Pick up your copy at http://mng.bz/1TA3.

STEP 2: SET UP SHADER RETRIEVAL FROM THE DOM

With your shader scripts configured, you need to process them via JavaScript. Replace `gd.core.shader.init()` with the following listing in core.js.

Listing 9.10 core.js—Shader setup

```
gd.core = {
    shader: {
        init: function() {
            this.fragments = this.get('shader-fragment');
            this.vertex = this.get('shader-vertex');

            this.program = gd.gl.createProgram();

            gd.gl.attachShader(this.program, this.vertex);
            gd.gl.attachShader(this.program, this.fragments);
            gd.gl.linkProgram(this.program);

            if (!gd.gl.getProgramParameter(this.program, gd.gl.LINK_STATUS)) {
                return alert("Shaders have FAILED to load.");
            }

            gd.gl.useProgram(this.program);

            this.store();

            gd.gl.deleteShader(this.fragments);
            gd.gl.deleteShader(this.vertex);
            gd.gl.deleteProgram(this.program);
        }
    }
};
```

Creates a "program" for your shader (holds one fragment and vertex shader).

Failsafe in case shaders crash as they're loading.

Stores the shader data for later use.

Pulls shader programs from the DOM. Notice that shader-fragment and shader-vertex reference the two shader scripts you wrote.

Links your shaders and newly created "program" together.

Clears out leftover shader data so it doesn't sit uselessly in memory. You could delete these shaders manually by waiting for JavaScript's garbage collector, but this gives more control.

STEP 3: PULL SHADER DATA FROM THE DOM

In the previous listing, gd.core.shader.init() accesses the shader-vertex and shader-fragment scripts you put in index.html. gd.core.shader.get() retrieves and processes your shader by pulling it from the DOM, sending back a compiled package of data or an error. gd.core.shader.init() continues processing and attaches your DOM results to a program. The program sets up vertices, fragments, and color in a store method. Lastly, all the leftover graphics data is deleted. Replace gd.core.shader.get() and gd.core.shader.store() with the next listing in core.js to complete loading your shaders.

Listing 9.11   core.js—Shader retrieval

```
gd.core = {
    shader: {
        get: function(id) {
            this.script = document.getElementById(id);

            if (!this.script) {
                alert('The requested shader script was not found ' +
                    'in the DOM. Make sure that gd.shader.get(id) ' +
                    'is properly setup.');
                return null;
            }

            this.source = "";
            this.currentChild = this.script.firstChild;

            while (this.currentChild) {
                if (this.currentChild.nodeType ===
                    this.currentChild.TEXT_NODE) {
                    this.source += this.currentChild.textContent;
                }
                this.currentChild = this.currentChild.nextSibling;
            }

            if (this.script.type === 'x-shader/x-fragment') {
                this.shader = gd.gl.createShader(gd.gl.FRAGMENT_SHADER);
            } else if (this.script.type === 'x-shader/x-vertex') {
                this.shader = gd.gl.createShader(gd.gl.VERTEX_SHADER);
            } else {
                return null;
            }

            gd.gl.shaderSource(this.shader, this.source);
            gd.gl.compileShader(this.shader);

            if (!gd.gl.getShaderParameter(this.shader,
                gd.gl.COMPILE_STATUS)) {
                alert('Shader compiling error: ' +
                    gd.gl.getShaderInfoLog(this.shader));
                return null;
            }

            return this.shader;
        },
```

No shader script in the DOM? Return nothing and an error.

Returns the compiled shader data after being collected via a while loop.

Tests what kind of shader is being used (fragment or vertex) and processes it based on the results.

Takes all of your shader data and compiles it together.

Compile success? If not, fire an error.

Retrieves vertex data from your shader program for rendering 3D objects later.

Color data retrieval from shader program.

```
store: function() {
    this.vertexPositionAttribute =
        gd.gl.getAttribLocation(
            this.program, "aVertexPosition");
    gd.gl.enableVertexAttribArray(this.vertexPositionAttribute);

    this.vertexColorAttribute = gd.gl.getAttribLocation(
        this.program, "aVertexColor");
    gd.gl.enableVertexAttribArray(this.vertexColorAttribute);
    }
  }
};
```

9.2.3 Creating buffers for shape, color, and dimension

With all that shader data present, you now need to create buffers for shape, color, and dimension. One interesting fact about buffer data is that each object will have its own independent set of buffers.

STEP 4: CREATE SHAPE, COLOR, AND DIMENSION BUFFERS FOR ENTITIES

Core API

To buffer your data, open template.js and append gd.template.Entity.shape(), gd.template.Entity.color(), and gd.template.Entity.indices() to the Entity object with the following listing.

Listing 9.12 template.js—Buffer configuration

Stores created buffer data so you can use it.

At the end of each method you need to record information about the passed array because your dependency sylvester.js requires extra array details.

When creating a shape you'll pass in vertices, and this method will take care of everything else.

Creates buffer data.

Uses float32 to change the array into a WebGL editable format.

A helper to disassemble large packages of color data.

```
gd.template = {
    Entity: Class.extend({
        shape: function(vertices) {
            this.shapeStorage = gd.gl.createBuffer();
            gd.gl.bindBuffer(gd.gl.ARRAY_BUFFER, this.shapeStorage);
            gd.gl.bufferData(gd.gl.ARRAY_BUFFER,
                new Float32Array(vertices), gd.gl.STATIC_DRAW);

            this.shapeColumns = 3;
            this.shapeRows = vertices.length / this.shapeColumns;
        },
        color: function(vertices) {
            this.colorStorage = gd.gl.createBuffer();

            if (typeof vertices[0] === 'object') {

                var colorNew = [];

                for (var v = 0; v < vertices.length; v++) {
                    var colorLine = vertices[v];
                    for (var c = 0; c < 4; c++) {
                        colorNew = colorNew.concat(colorLine);
                    }
                }

                vertices = colorNew;
            }

            gd.gl.bindBuffer(gd.gl.ARRAY_BUFFER, this.colorStorage);
            gd.gl.bufferData(gd.gl.ARRAY_BUFFER,
                new Float32Array(vertices), gd.gl.STATIC_DRAW);
```

```
        this.colorColumns = 4;
        this.colorRows = vertices.length / this.colorColumns;
    },
    indices: function(vertices) {
        this.indicesStorage = gd.gl.createBuffer();
        gd.gl.bindBuffer(gd.gl.ELEMENT_ARRAY_BUFFER,
            this.indicesStorage);
        gd.gl.bufferData(gd.gl.ELEMENT_ARRAY_BUFFER,
            new Uint16Array(vertices), gd.gl.STATIC_DRAW);

        this.indicesCount = vertices.length;
    }
})
};
```

> **Indices is plural for index. In WebGL buffers are used to assemble triangles into a single shape. By using indices you can define the location of a pair of triangles, instead of just one at a time.**

To use the buffer methods you created, you'll need to manually call `this.shape()`, `this.color()`, and possibly `this.indices()` when you create a new entity. More on how to use these new methods when you program run.js later in this chapter. In order to output the created buffer data, you'll need to configure `gd.core.draw()` next.

9.2.4   *Displaying shape data on a screen*

Using `gd.core.draw()`, you'll loop through all of the current entities in `gd.core .storage.all`. For each entity, you'll use a three-step process that spans three code listings, which means you need to make sure each of the next three listings continues from the previous one or the code won't work. Note also that we're now working through the second group of steps.

- Group 2—Working with matrices and drawing shapes
  - Step 1: Use matrices and buffers to visually output information.
  - Step 2: Bind and draw shapes.
  - Step 3: Detect overlap and remove entities.
  - Step 4: Add matrix helpers to simplify matrix interaction.
  - Step 5: Add Vlad Vukićević's WebGL helpers for rotation.

STEP 1: USE MATRICES AND BUFFERS TO VISUALLY OUTPUT INFORMATION

Core API

Let's start step 1 by opening core.js and replacing `gd.core.draw()` with listing 9.13. The listing will clear out the canvas's previous draw data and set the current perspective to draw all entities currently in storage. For all of the entities, it will run their update and rotation logic if it's configured. Be careful with the `for` loop in this listing, because it's continued for two more listings (up to listing 9.15).

Listing 9.13   core.js—Drawing shapes

```
gd.core = {
    draw: function() {
        gd.gl.clear(gd.gl.COLOR_BUFFER_BIT | gd.gl.DEPTH_BUFFER_BIT);

        this.perspectiveMatrix = makePerspective(45, this.horizAspect,
            0.1, 300.0);
```

> **Wipes your WebGL viewport clean to draw a brand-new frame.**

> **Sets the viewing perspective from 1 to 300 units of distance (prevents aspect ratio distortion).**

```
for (var i in this.storage.all) {
    this.loadIdentity();

    this.storage.all[i].update();

    this.mvTranslate(this.storage.all[i].position());
    this.mvPushMatrix();

    if (this.storage.all[i].rotate.axis) {
        this.mvRotate(
            this.storage.all[i].rotate.angle,
            this.storage.all[i].rotate.axis);
    }

}
};
```

Resets and creates a matrix that has ls diagonally and 0s everywhere else[3].

Run the update() before outputting shapes to prevent new entities from showing up in the wrong location for a split second.

Grabs x, y, and z coordinates from your entity to clarify a draw location and pushes it into an array.

If rotate data is present, it will be run here.

Standardized method for pushing the current matrix item to the top of the matrix stack.

Loops through every entity in storage and draws it. The for statement doesn't end in this listing because it's continued in the next two.

STEP 2: BIND AND DRAW SHAPES

With the matrix set up properly and rotation applied, you need to output the buffer information for the current 3D object. Do this by binding 3D data and then outputting it through `gd.gl.vertexAttribPointer()`, which passes along bound buffer data. Use the next listing to continue your `gd.core.draw()` method.

Listing 9.14 core.js—Drawing shapes (continued)

```
gd.core = {
    draw: function() {
        gd.gl.bindBuffer(
            gd.gl.ARRAY_BUFFER,
            this.storage.all[i].shapeStorage);
        gd.gl.vertexAttribPointer(
            this.shader.vertexPositionAttribute,
            this.storage.all[i].shapeColumns,
            gd.gl.FLOAT,
            false, 0, 0);

        gd.gl.bindBuffer(
            gd.gl.ARRAY_BUFFER,
            this.storage.all[i].colorStorage);
        gd.gl.vertexAttribPointer(
            this.shader.vertexColorAttribute,
            this.storage.all[i].colorColumns,
            gd.gl.FLOAT,
            false, 0, 0);

        this.setMatrixUniforms();

        if (this.storage.all[i].indicesStorage) {
            gd.gl.drawElements(
                gd.gl.TRIANGLES,
                this.storage.all[i].indicesCount,
```

Binds ARRAY_BUFFER to your shapeStorage object.

Defines an array of generic vertex attribute data.

Depending on whether or not indices were used, the buffer data needs to be output differently.

Pushes your matrix data from JavaScript to WebGL so the shaders can be properly seen.

---

[3] Weisstein, Eric W., "Identity Matrix," MathWorld, a Wolfram Web Resource, http://mng.bz/CO1M.

```
                    gd.gl.UNSIGNED_SHORT,
                    0);
            } else {
                gd.gl.drawArrays(
                    gd.gl.TRIANGLE_STRIP,
                    0,
                    this.storage.all[i].shapeRows);
            }

            this.mvPopMatrix();                         ←——| Removes an item from the
        }                                                  | current matrix stack.
    }
};
```

NOTE We know it's frustrating that you can't see 3D models by simply refreshing your browser. Bear with us to output 3D models through the engine's draw loop, and we'll show you the awesome result of what you've created.

STEP 3: DETECT OVERLAP AND REMOVE ENTITIES

You've completed your output for 3D objects, but you need to append one more chunk of code to cp.core.draw() with the following listing. It will add optimized collision detection to properly monitor a (friendly) to b (enemy) overlap and clean up your graveyard.

Listing 9.15   core.js—Drawing shapes (continued)

```
gd.core = {
    draw: function() {
            if (this.storage.all[i].type === 'a') {       ←——| Collision detection
                for (var en = this.storage.b.length; en--;) {  | compares a type
                    if (this.overlap(                          | and b type entities
                    this.storage.all[i].x,                     | to minimize logic.
                    this.storage.all[i].y,
                    this.storage.all[i].width,
                    this.storage.all[i].height,
                    this.storage.b[en].x,
                    this.storage.b[en].y,
                    this.storage.b[en].width,
                    this.storage.b[en].height)) {
                        this.storage.all[i].collide(this.storage.b[en]);
                        this.storage.b[en].collide(this.storage.all[i]);
                    }
                }                    |  Closes the for
            }                        |  statement from two
        }                            ←  listings back.
    }

        this.graveyard.purge();   ←——  Deleted elements are dumped out of the graveyard.
    }                                  This is accomplished here instead of in the loop to
};                                     prevent accidentally referencing a nonexistent entity.
```

PROGRESS CHECK!

Now is a good time to check your browser's console for errors other than run.js being missing. If so, you're good to move on to the next section.

STEP 4: ADD MATRIX HELPERS TO SIMPLIFY MATRIX INTERACTION.

For `gd.core.draw()` you'd normally have to write some extremely complex logic to handle matrices for colors and shapes. Instead, you're going to use some prewritten helpers for modelview (http://3dengine.org/Modelview_matrix), perspective (http://mng.bz/VitL), and identity matrices (http://en.wikipedia.org/wiki/Identity_matrix). Append listing 9.16 to your `gd.core` object. Like webgl_util.js, the following chunk of code comes from an unknown source, but you'll find that Mozilla's WebGL tutorials, Learning WebGL, and many other online lessons make use of it.

Listing 9.16 core.js—Matrix helpers

```
gd.core = {
    loadIdentity: function() {
        mvMatrix = Matrix.I(4);
    },
    multMatrix: function(m) {
        mvMatrix = mvMatrix.x(m);
    },
    mvTranslate: function(v) {
        this.multMatrix(Matrix.Translation($V([v[0], v[1],
            v[2]])).ensure4x4());
    },
    setMatrixUniforms: function() {
        var pUniform = gd.gl.getUniformLocation(
            this.shader.program, "uPMatrix");
        gd.gl.uniformMatrix4fv(pUniform, false,
            new Float32Array(this.perspectiveMatrix.flatten()));

        var mvUniform = gd.gl.getUniformLocation(
            this.shader.program, "uMVMatrix");
        gd.gl.uniformMatrix4fv(
            mvUniform, false, new Float32Array(mvMatrix.flatten()));
    }
};
```

Loads up an identity matrix, which is a series of Is surrounded by 0s.

Multiplies a matrix[4].

Runs matrix multiplication and then translation[5].

Sets the perspective and model view matrix.

STEP 5: ADD VLAD VUKIĆEVIĆ'S WEBGL HELPERS FOR ROTATION.

The code in listing 9.17 comes from Mozilla's site at http://mng.bz/BU9f. Mozilla tells us that "these routines were borrowed from a sample previously written by Vlad Vukićević," whose blog you can find at http://blog.vlad1.com. Vlad has created a couple of tools to help with rotation and with pushing and popping data. Append his rotation logic to `gd.core` with the following code.

Listing 9.17 core.js—Vlad Vukićević utilities

```
gd.core = {
    mvMatrixStack: [],

    mvPushMatrix: function(m) {
        if (m) {
```

Your stack will be used to manipulate matrix data with the following methods.

Moves given data to the top of the stack.

---

4 "Matrix multiplication," Wikipedia, last modified April 8, 2013, http://mng.bz/yo4D.
5 "Translation (geometry)," Wikipedia, last modified Feb. 21, 2013, http://mng.bz/2dbB.

```
            this.mvMatrixStack.push(m.dup());
            mvMatrix = m.dup();
    } else {
            this.mvMatrixStack.push(mvMatrix.dup());
    }
},
mvPopMatrix: function() {
    if (! this.mvMatrixStack.length) {
        throw("Can't pop from an empty matrix stack.");
    }

    mvMatrix = this.mvMatrixStack.pop();
    return mvMatrix;
},
mvRotate: function(angle, v) {
    var inRadians = angle * Math.PI / 180.0;

    var m = Matrix.Rotation(inRadians, $V([v[0], v[1],
  v[2]])).ensure4x4();
    this.multMatrix(m);
    }
};
```

> **Pop in JavaScript refers to an array method that removes the last element from an array and returns that value to the caller. Here, mvPopMatrix() is returning an error or removing and returning the last item.**

> **This is the method that fires rotation in cp.core.draw().**

PROGRESS CHECK!

Run index.html now and check your browser's console. You should see the screen shown in figure 9.7, possibly without the missing-file error. If you get additional errors or have trouble with your engine's code as you proceed, you might find it easier and less frustrating to replace the engine files with chapter 9's source code instead of debugging files. Debugging WebGL is a bit of a nightmare because browsers don't have easily accessible graphic monitoring tools.

With the last of the utility helpers in place, you should now feel somewhat comfortable with graphics card communication, comfortable enough to write basic 3D output for a WebGL application at least. Next, we'll take the foundation you created and use it to build your interactive 3D game: Geometry Destroyer.

Figure 9.7   Your code should output the displayed error of "run.js is missing" or no errors at all when running index.html. If you have trouble with the engine files as you proceed, just replace them with the source files from Manning's website. It's a nightmare to debug WebGL because of browsers not having easily accessible graphic monitoring tools.

9.3   Putting it all together: creating Geometry Destroyer

Creating 3D shapes is tough, but you just created (or read through as we created) a 3D engine that will significantly simplify the process. You can create new entities and attach 3D data via matrices; the engine will take care of outputting all the data for you. The engine will also take care of cleaning data out of memory whenever you need to.

> **In this section, you'll build a cool game as you learn to**
> - Write a simple matrix to output shape and color in 3D space
> - Create 3D rotation data and use it with a controller to indicate direction in 2D
> - Create and control entity generations for enemies and particles
> - Use indices to turn triangles into squares for easy matrix creation
> - Draw simple 2D shapes in 3D, plus unique polygons and cubes

As you understand how to create entities, you'll learn about 3D modeling and efficient OOP programming. If you don't have any knowledge about creating 3D shapes or entity management, don't worry; we'll guide you along the way.

> **Prereqs: play the game, grab the code, and test your engine**
> If you haven't done so already, head over to http://html5inaction.com/app/ch9/ and play the game. And make sure you pick up the game's files from http://www.manning.com/crowther2/ by downloading *HTML5 in Action*'s source files.

The work in this section is bundled into three groups of steps:

Group 1—Making your player	Group 2—Outputting enemies	Group 3—Generating particles
■ Step 1: Capture user input. ■ Step 2: Program the heads-up display. ■ Step 3: Create the 2D player entity. ■ Step 4: Animate the player entity. ■ Step 5: Create the player's bullets.	■ Step 1: Create a 3D polygon enemy. ■ Step 2: Create a complex 3D model. ■ Step 3: Generate random enemy properties. ■ Step 4: Resolve enemy collisions. ■ Step 5: Spawn enemies in a controlled manner.	■ Step 1: Create a 3D cube particle. ■ Step 2: Add color, rotation, and index data for cubes. ■ Step 3: Add size, type, and other cube metadata. ■ Step 4: Generate square particles.

Let's dive in to the first group and make your player.

9.3.1   Creating a game interface and control objects

The first thing we'll focus on is setting up the intro screen's non-3D logic, the result of which appears in figure 9.8.

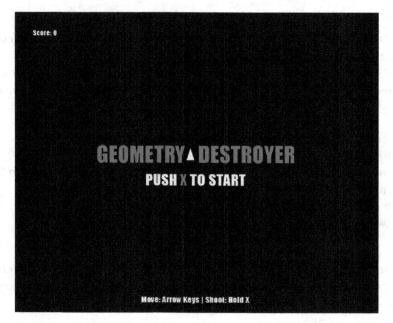

Figure 9.8   The first thing you'll do is set up the intro screen logic. After that, you'll create the triangular player between the words *Geometry* and *Destroyer*, which you haven't seen previously.

STEP 1: CAPTURE USER INPUT

In your js folder, create and/or open run.js in the text editor of your choice. You should notice that it's completely blank. Set up the game's basic input monitor and methods by inserting everything into a self-executing function with the following listing in run.js. Make sure to place all code from here on out in this self-executing function to prevent variables from leaking into the global scope.

Listing 9.18   run.js–Initial game setup

```
(function() {
    gd.core.init(800, 600, function() {
        Ctrl.init();
        Hud.init();
        gd.game.spawn('Player');
    });

    gd.game.size = {
        width: 43,
        height: 32
    };

    var Ctrl = {
        init: function() {
            window.addEventListener('keydown', this.keyDown, true);
            window.addEventListener('keyup', this.keyUp, true);
        },
```

Declares width, height, and game setup logic to fire after loading your engine.

Place all code from here on out inside the self-executing function to prevent variables from leaking into the global scope.

The width and height of the play area in 3D units. Everything is measured from the middle with a Cartesian graph, so this is only half the width and height.

Controller for user input.

```
        keyDown: function(event) {                          Up arrow.
            switch(event.keyCode) {
                case 38: Ctrl.up = true; break;
Down arrow.     case 40: Ctrl.down = true; break;
                case 37: Ctrl.left = true; break;           Left arrow.
Right arrow.    case 39: Ctrl.right = true; break;
                case 88: Ctrl.x = true; break;
                default: break;
            }                                               x keyboard key.
        },

        keyUp: function(event) {
            switch(event.keyCode) {
                case 38: Ctrl.up = false; break;
                case 40: Ctrl.down = false; break;
                case 37: Ctrl.left = false; break;
                case 39: Ctrl.right = false; break;
                case 88: Ctrl.x = false; break;
                default: break;
            }
        }
    };
}());
```

STEP 2: PROGRAM THE HEADS-UP DISPLAY

Controller input is now detectable, and the game engine will launch as expected. But you still need to create the heads-up display (HUD) to manage score and initial setup. You also need the player, but let's start with the HUD by creating a new variable called Hud below Ctrl with the following listing.

Listing 9.19   run.js—Heads-up display (HUD)

```
var Hud = {
    init: function() {                               Begins polygon generation
        var self = this;                             when a players presses X.

        var callback = function() {
            if (Ctrl.x) {
                window.removeEventListener('keydown', callback, true);
                PolygonGen.init();
                self.el.start.style.display = 'none';
                self.el.title.style.display = 'none';
            }
        };

        window.addEventListener('keydown', callback, true);
    },
    end: function() {                                Ends the game by displaying
        var self = this;                            the Game Over screen.
        this.el.end.style.display = 'block';
    },
    score: {                                         Simple method that increments
        count: 0,                                    and tracks a player's score.
        update: function() {
```

```
            this.count++;
            Hud.el.score.innerHTML = this.count;
        }
    },
    el: {                                                      Captures and stores
        score: document.getElementById('count'),              alterable elements
        start: document.getElementById('start'),              for easy reference.
        end: document.getElementById('end'),
        title: document.getElementById('title')
    }
};
```

9.3.2 Creating 2D shapes in 3D

With your HUD and controller built, you can program the player entity, a simple white triangle that can move when certain keyboard keys are pressed. You'll also make it generate bullets whenever a player presses the X key. Figure 9.9 shows the white, triangular player and a single red bullet.

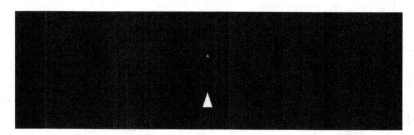

Figure 9.9 Displays the player's ship firing a bullet. Notice that both shapes are 2D but drawn in a 3D environment.

STEP 3: CREATE THE 2D PLAYER ENTITY

Core API Append the next listing after your Hud object to create all of the data required to initialize your player. Most of the initializing information will be stored in variables at the top, so you can easily tweak the player's data in the future.

Listing 9.20 run.js—Player creation

```
gd.template.Player = gd.template.Entity.extend({        Offsets player to line
    type: 'a',                                          up nicely with text.
    x: -1.4,
    width: 1,                          All width and height measurements
    height: 1,                         are equal to one player unit.
    speed: 0.5,
    shoot: true,                       A variable we'll use to decide how
    shootDelay: 400,                   fast a player's position increments.
    rotate: {
        angle: 0,
        axis: [0, 0, 1],               Allows you to only
        speed: 3                       rotate the player in 2D.
    },
```

Can be a value from 0 to 360.

```
init: function() {
    this.shape([
        0.0,   2.0,   0.0,
       -1.0,  -1.0,   0.0,
        1.0,  -1.0,   0.0
    ]);

    this.color([
        1.0, 1.0, 1.0, 1.0,
        1.0, 1.0, 1.0, 1.0,
        1.0, 1.0, 1.0, 1.0
    ]);
},

boundaryTop: function() { this.y = gd.game.size.height; },
boundaryRight: function() { this.x = gd.game.size.width; },
boundaryBottom: function() { this.y = -gd.game.size.height; },
boundaryLeft: function() { this.x = -gd.game.size.width; },

kill: function() {
    this._super();
    PolygonGen.clear();
    Hud.end();
}
});
```

◁─| Creates a triangle by plotting and connecting three different points from the passed array data. Each line of the array plots a point in the format of x, y, and z.

Outputs white for all three points you created with the shape method.

◁── Creates a color for each point you created with the shape method. Each line of this array outputs a color as red, green, blue, alpha.

◁── When the player is destroyed, the HUD and polygon generator (set up later) will be shut down.

3D DRAWING BASICS

 Core API

The most confusing part of creating players is probably the shape() and color() methods. The shape() method assembles the triangle in figure 9.10, and the color() method fills it in with white.

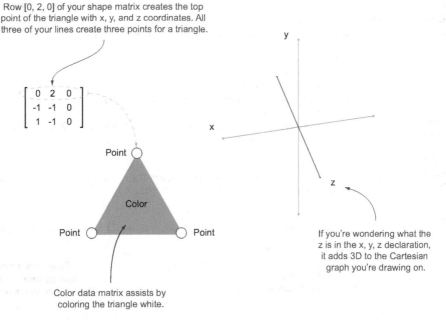

Row [0, 2, 0] of your shape matrix creates the top point of the triangle with x, y, and z coordinates. All three of your lines create three points for a triangle.

$$\begin{bmatrix} 0 & 2 & 0 \\ -1 & -1 & 0 \\ 1 & -1 & 0 \end{bmatrix}$$

Point

Color

Point   Point

Color data matrix assists by coloring the triangle white.

If you're wondering what the z is in the x, y, z declaration, it adds 3D to the Cartesian graph you're drawing on.

Figure 9.10 Diagram on the left shows a triangle comprising three points from the player's matrix data. The right diagram shows a Cartesian coordinate system with x, y, and z.

The single form of the word *vertices* is *vertex*. In math, a vertex of an angle is an endpoint where two line segments meet. Declaring three vertices, you created a triangle, as shown in the previous figure. Adding one more vertex to the triangle creates the square shown in figure 9.11, as you probably guessed.

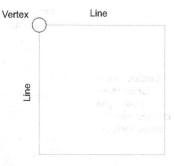

Figure 9.11 Demonstrates where a vertex is located on a square

STEP 4: ANIMATE THE PLAYER ENTITY

Getting back to your `Player` entity, you need to append an `update()` method with the following listing to complete it with movement, rotation, and shooting controls via the keyboard. You're already generating keyboard properties from the `Ctrl` object you integrated earlier.

Listing 9.21   run.js—Player update

```
gd.template.Player = gd.template.Entity.extend({
    update: function() {                          ◄── Update logic fires every time
        var self = this;                              a new frame is drawn.

        if (Ctrl.left) {                          ◄── When pushing left or right,
            this.rotate.angle += this.rotate.speed;   rotation will be triggered
        } else if (Ctrl.right) {                      for the player. Rotation is
            this.rotate.angle -= this.rotate.speed;   automatically applied by
        }                                             the cp.core.draw method
                                                      you set up earlier.
        if (Ctrl.up) {
            this.x -= Math.sin(this.rotate.angle * Math.PI / 180)
                * this.speed;
            this.y += Math.cos(this.rotate.angle * Math.PI / 180)
                * this.speed;
        } else if (Ctrl.down) {
            this.x += Math.sin(this.rotate.angle * Math.PI / 180)
                * this.speed;
            this.y -= Math.cos(this.rotate.angle * Math.PI / 180)
                * this.speed;
        }

        gd.game.boundaries(this, this.boundaryTop, this.boundaryRight,
            this.boundaryBottom, this.boundaryLeft);

        if (Ctrl.x && this.shoot) {
            gd.game.spawn('Bullet', this.rotate.angle, this.x, this.y);   ◄──

            this.shoot = false;
            window.setTimeout(function() {                   Generates a bullet from
                self.shoot = true;                           ship's current location and
            }, this.shootDelay);                             moves it at its current angle.
        }
    }
});
```

Updates the player's position using the current angle.

Prevents the player from going out of the game's boundaries.

Figure 9.12 You should be able to move your player around the screen now. We've moved him from between "Geometry Destroyer" to the upper-left corner. Be warned: You can't shoot bullets with X yet.

PROGRESS CHECK!

At this point, you should be able to move your ship around the page without errors, as shown in figure 9.12. If you press X on the keyboard, though, your application will explode because bullets haven't been configured yet. Let's fix that.

STEP 5: CREATE THE PLAYER'S BULLETS

Create bullets to shoot by appending the following listing after your `Player` entity. Your player will shoot small triangles that destroy enemy entities on collision. `Bullets` will spawn at the `Player`'s position when you pass in parameters through the `init()` method.

Listing 9.22 run.js—Making bullets

```
gd.template.Bullet = gd.template.Entity.extend({
    type: 'a',
    width: 0.6,
    height: 0.6,
    speed: 0.8,
    angle: 0,

    init: function(angle, x, y) {
        this.shape([
            0.0,   0.3,   0.0,
           -0.3,  -0.3,   0.3,
            0.3,  -0.3,   0.3
        ]);

        var stack = [];
        for (var line = this.shapeRows; line--;)
            stack.push(1.0, 0.0, 0.0, 1.0);
        this.color(stack);

        this.angle = angle;
        this.x = x;
        this.y = y;
    },

    update: function() {
        gd.game.boundaries(this, this.kill, this.kill, this.kill, this.kill);
```

Angle is used to determine the movement direction (0 to 360 degrees).

Notice how init() allows the bullet to spawn at an x and y location and then move at the player's current angle.

Alternative method for creating a color matrix. Useful when creating a massive number of points that have the same color value.

```
        this.x -= Math.sin( this.angle * Math.PI / 180 ) * this.speed;
        this.y += Math.cos( this.angle * Math.PI / 180 ) * this.speed;
    },
    collide: function() {
        this._super();
        Hud.score.update();
    }
});
```

Armed with bullets, you should be able to run the game and fly your ship around. Try it out if you'd like. You'll notice that once you fire a bullet, the game fails because you haven't yet created the enemy assets. Let's create those targets next.

9.3.3   Creating 3D shapes and particles

Enemies in Geometry Destroyer are complex and robust because of their dynamic color and spawning points. As you can see in figure 9.13, they explode on contact, shattering into cubes and rectangle particles to create an interesting effect.

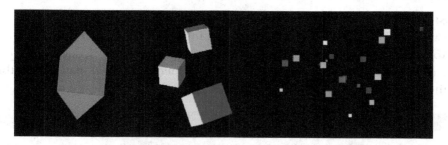

Figure 9.13   Enemies in the game have three major components. First is the large shape shown on the far left. When destroyed, it spawns the next two components: cubes (middle) and particles (far right).

Let's get started with the second group of tasks:

- Group 2—Outputting enemies
  - Step 1: Create a 3D polygon enemy.
  - Step 2: Create a complex 3D model.
  - Step 3: Generate random enemy properties.
  - Step 4: Resolve enemy collisions.
  - Step 5: Spawn enemies in a controlled manner.

STEP 1: CREATE A 3D POLYGON ENEMY

Set up the large `Polygon` first by adding it below `gd.template.Bullet` with the following listing. You're only going to create its base right now; you'll configure its 3D data in the next listing.

> **Listing 9.23   run.js—Polygon base**

```
gd.template.Polygon = gd.template.Entity.extend({
    type: 'b',
```

```
                    width: 7,
                    height: 9,
```

| | Width is the measurement of the shape's span of vertices from left to right, whereas `height` is top to bottom. |

```
                    init: function() {
                        this.randomSide();
                        this.randomMeta();

                        var stack = [];
                        for (var v = 0; v < this.shapeRows * this.shapeColumns; v += 3) {
                            if (v > 108 || v <= 36) {
                                stack.push(this.colorData.pyramid[0],
                    this.colorData.pyramid[1], this.colorData.pyramid[2], 1);

                            } else {
                                stack.push(this.colorData.cube[0], this.colorData.cube[1],
                    this.colorData.cube[2], 1);
                            }
                        }
                        this.color(stack);
                    }
                });
```

Tests if a triangle is being drawn instead of a square. (margin note, pointing to the `for`/`if` lines)

Because you have an insane number of points that need to be colored, you'll have to dynamically create a map of colors instead of writing them by hand. (margin note)

STEP 2: CREATE A COMPLEX 3D MODEL

Core API

You need to add a massive amount of vertex data to finish `gd.template.Polygon.init()` from the previous listing. It comprises a pyramid on the top and bottom, with a cube in the middle. You'll notice a massive array of data is needed to create the 3D model. We recommend copying and pasting this from the downloaded source code; if you don't have that option, we sincerely apologize. Prepend `this.shape()` call from the following listing to the top of `gd.template.Polygon.init()`'s existing code from the previous listing.

Listing 9.24   run.js—Polygon shape `init()` prepend

```
gd.template.Polygon = gd.template.Entity.extend({
    init: function() {
        this.shape([
            0.0,   7.0,   0.0,
           -4.0,   2.0,   4.0,
            4.0,   2.0,   4.0,

            0.0,   7.0,   0.0,
            4.0,   2.0,   4.0,
            4.0,   2.0,  -4.0,

            0.0,   7.0,   0.0,
            4.0,   2.0,  -4.0,
           -4.0,   2.0,  -4.0,

            0.0,   7.0,   0.0,
           -4.0,   2.0,  -4.0,
           -4.0,   2.0,   4.0,

           -4.0,   2.0,   4.0,
           -4.0,  -5.0,   4.0,
           -4.0,  -5.0,  -4.0,
```

Top pyramid's front.

Top pyramid's right.

Top pyramid's back.

Top pyramid's left.

Each middle plate section comprises a side of the polygon's cubic body. The sections comprised two triangles drawn together, which creates a square plate.

```
       -4.0,   2.0,   4.0,
       -4.0,   2.0,  -4.0,
       -4.0,  -5.0,  -4.0,

       -4.0,   2.0,  -4.0,
       -4.0,  -5.0,  -4.0,
        4.0,  -5.0,  -4.0,
       -4.0,   2.0,  -4.0,
        4.0,   2.0,  -4.0,
        4.0,  -5.0,  -4.0,

        4.0,   2.0,   4.0,
        4.0,   2.0,  -4.0,
        4.0,  -5.0,  -4.0,
        4.0,   2.0,   4.0,
        4.0,  -5.0,   4.0,
        4.0,  -5.0,  -4.0,

       -4.0,   2.0,   4.0,
        4.0,   2.0,   4.0,
        4.0,  -5.0,   4.0,
       -4.0,   2.0,   4.0,
       -4.0,  -5.0,   4.0,
        4.0,  -5.0,   4.0,

        0.0, -10.0,   0.0,
       -4.0,  -5.0,   4.0,
        4.0,  -5.0,   4.0,

        0.0, -10.0,   0.0,
        4.0,  -5.0,   4.0,
        4.0,  -5.0,  -4.0,

        0.0, -10.0,   0.0,
        4.0,  -5.0,  -4.0,
       -4.0,  -5.0,  -4.0,

        0.0, -10.0,   0.0,
       -4.0,  -5.0,  -4.0,
       -4.0,  -5.0,   4.0
      ]);
    }
  }
};
```

Each middle plate section comprises a side of the polygon's cubic body. The sections comprised two triangles drawn together, which creates a square plate.

Bottom pyramid parallels the drawing format of the top pyramid, except it's drawn pointing down instead of up.

STEP 3: GENERATE RANDOM ENEMY PROPERTIES

With your polygon's 3D data built, you need to generate speed, rotation, color, and a spawning point so it functions properly. Append `randomMeta()` and `cube()` methods to `gd.template.Polygon` with the next listing.

Listing 9.25   run.js—Polygon shape `init()` prepend

```
gd.template.Polygon = gd.template.Entity.extend({
    randomMeta: function() {
        this.rotate = {
            speed: gd.game.random.number(400, 100),
            axis: [
                gd.game.random.number(10, 1) / 10,
```

Responsible for creating random details about rotation, speed, and color.

```
              gd.game.random.number(10, 1) / 10,
              gd.game.random.number(10, 1) / 10
          ],
          angle: gd.game.random.number(250, 1)
      };

      this.speed = {
          x: gd.game.random.number(10, 4) / 100,
          y: gd.game.random.number(10, 4) / 100
      };

      this.colorData = {
          pyramid: [
              gd.game.random.number(10, 1) / 10,
              gd.game.random.number(10, 1) / 10,
              gd.game.random.number(10, 1) / 10
          ],
          cube: [
              gd.game.random.number(10, 1) / 10,
              gd.game.random.number(10, 1) / 10,
              gd.game.random.number(10, 1) / 10
          ]
      };
    }
});
```

> Generates random color details for pyramids and cubes. Data is processed and arranged by methods in Polygon.init() you already created.

STEP 4: RESOLVE ENEMY COLLISIONS

The last step to create the `gd.template.Polygon` requires you to add methods for generating shape data from a random side and cube particles when it's destroyed. You also need to update logic and collision information. Append your remaining methods to `gd.template.Polygon` with the following listing.

Listing 9.26   run.js—Polygon side, update, and collide

```
gd.template.Polygon = gd.template.Entity.extend({
    randomSide: function() {
        var side = gd.game.random.number(4, 1);

        if (side === 1) {
            this.angle = gd.game.random.number(200, 160);
            var range = gd.game.size.width - this.width;
            this.x = gd.game.random.number(range, -range);
            this.y = gd.game.size.height + this.height;
        } else if (side === 2) {
            this.angle = gd.game.random.number(290, 250);
            var range = gd.game.size.height - this.height;
            this.x = (gd.game.size.width + this.width) * -1;
            this.y = gd.game.random.number(range, -range);
        } else if (side === 3) {
            this.angle = gd.game.random.number(380, 340);
            var range = gd.game.size.width - this.width;
            this.x = gd.game.random.number(range, -range);
            this.y = (this.height + gd.game.size.height) * -1;
        } else {
            this.angle = gd.game.random.number(110, 70);
```

> Determines from which side to randomly spawn a polygon.

```
        var range = gd.game.size.height - this.height;
        this.x = gd.game.size.width + this.width;
        this.y = gd.game.random.number(range, -range);
    }
},

update: function() {
    gd.game.boundaries(this, this.kill, this.kill, this.kill, this.kill,
        (this.width * 2));

    this.x -= Math.sin( this.angle * Math.PI / 180 ) * this.speed.x;
    this.y += Math.cos( this.angle * Math.PI / 180 ) * this.speed.y;

    gd.game.rotate(this);                    ◄──┐  Uses randomly generated
},                                               │  rotate data to make the
                                                 │  polygon slowly rotate.
collide: function() {
    if (gd.core.storage.all.length < 50) {
        for (var p = 15; p--;) {
            gd.game.spawn('Particle', this.x, this.y);
        }
    }

    var num = gd.game.random.number(2, 4);        ◄──  Generates a random
    for (var c = num; c--;) {                           number of cubes at the
        gd.game.spawn('Cube', this.x, this.y);          center of a polygon
    }                                                    upon destruction.

    this.kill();
    }
});
```

Creates a number of particles at the center of a polygon upon destruction. Only occurs if the storage isn't too full to prevent hogging memory.

STEP 5: SPAWN ENEMIES IN A CONTROLLED MANNER

Although you now have a class for polygon entities, you'll need a separate object to generate them. You can create this with a new object called PolygonGen right below gd.template.Polygon with the next listing.

Listing 9.27   run.js—Polygon generator

```
var PolygonGen = {
    delay: 7000,
    limit: 9,                          │  Initiates polygon
                                       │  generation by
    init: function() {        ◄────────┤  creating an interval.

        var self = this;

        this.count = 1;
        gd.game.spawn('Polygon');

        this.create = window.setInterval(function() {
            if (gd.core.storage.b.length < self.limit) {   ◄──┐  Failsafe to prevent
                if (self.count < 3)                             │  too many objects
                    self.count++;                               │  spawning and
                                                                │  potentially
                for (var c = self.count; c--;) {                │  crashing the
                    gd.game.spawn('Polygon');                   │  browser.
                }
            }
        }
```

```
        }, self.delay);
    },
    clear: function() {
        window.clearInterval(this.create);          ◁─── Shuts down
        this.count = 0;                                   polygon
        this.delay = 7000;                                generation.
    }
};
```

Polygons will now generate after you press X on a keyboard for the first time. If you shoot them, they'll fire an error because the game tries to use nonexistent entity templates for cubes and particles. You'll set up those with the next set of tasks:

- Group 3—Generating particles
  - Step 1: Create a 3D cube particle.
  - Step 2: Add color, rotation, and index data for cubes.
  - Step 3: Add size, type, and other cube metadata.
  - Step 4: Generate square particles.

Issues with requestAnimationFrame() and other timers

Your method in `gd.core.animate()` that fires `requestAnimationFrame()` stops running when a user leaves a tab open in the background, unlike JavaScript's traditional timers `setInterval()` and `setTimeout()`, which keep on running. This means coupling animation with traditional timers is generally not a good idea, because traditional timers keep on running in the background. There used to be polyfills that relied on a frame counter in the `draw()` loop, but some implementations of `requestAnimation-Frame()` still update a frame after a couple seconds when a user navigates away from a tab. The most bulletproof way to use traditional and nontraditional timers is to build a custom timer script that checks elapsed time and fires in your `draw` loop. But this subject is complicated, and we don't have the time to cover it here. Instead, we've given the `polygonGen` object a limit to how many enemies it can spawn for a quick patch.

STEP 1: CREATE A 3D CUBE PARTICLE

Core API

Create a new `gd.template.Cube` entity below `PolygonGen` with this listing.

Listing 9.28   run.js—Cube shape

```
gd.template.Cube = gd.template.Entity.extend({
    init: function(x, y) {                    Sets position for x and y with the
        this.x = x;                           parameters passed at spawn.
        this.y = y;

        this.meta();

        this.shape([                          Our shape declaration is using a much
                                              more efficient method than our polygon
            -this.s, -this.s,  this.s,        to create rectangles by using four points
             this.s, -this.s,  this.s,        instead of six. The catch is we need to
             this.s,  this.s,  this.s,        provide a set of indices.
            -this.s,  this.s,  this.s,
```

Front plate; this.s is a reference to a random size generated later in gd.template.Cube.meta().

```
     -this.s, -this.s, -this.s,
     -this.s,  this.s, -this.s,      Back plate.
      this.s,  this.s, -this.s,
      this.s, -this.s, -this.s,

     -this.s,  this.s, -this.s,
     -this.s,  this.s,  this.s,      Top plate.
      this.s,  this.s,  this.s,
      this.s,  this.s, -this.s,

     -this.s, -this.s, -this.s,
      this.s, -this.s, -this.s,      Bottom plate.
      this.s, -this.s,  this.s,
     -this.s, -this.s,  this.s,

      this.s, -this.s, -this.s,
      this.s,  this.s, -this.s,      Right plate.
      this.s,  this.s,  this.s,
      this.s, -this.s,  this.s,

     -this.s, -this.s, -this.s,
     -this.s, -this.s,  this.s,      Left plate.
     -this.s,  this.s,  this.s,
     -this.s,  this.s, -this.s
    ]);
  }
});
```

STEP 2: ADD COLOR, ROTATION, AND INDEX DATA FOR CUBES

You now need to append the gd.template.Cube.init() method with color, rotation, and indices data from the next listing. If you're wondering what indices are, they allow you to draw the sides of a square with four points. Normally, a square's side requires six points to create two triangles—this cuts down on code and makes it easier to maintain.

Listing 9.29   run.js—Cube indices and color

```
gd.template.Cube = gd.template.Entity.extend({
    init: function(x, y) {
        this.indices([
               0,  1,  2,    0,  2,  3,
               4,  5,  6,    4,  6,  7,
               8,  9, 10,    8, 10, 11,
              12, 13, 14,   12, 14, 15,
              16, 17, 18,   16, 18, 19,
              20, 21, 22,   20, 22, 23
        ]);

        this.color([
              [1, 0, 0, 1],
              [0, 1, 0, 1],
              [0, 0, 1, 1],
              [1, 1, 0, 1],
              [1, 0, 1, 1],
              [0, 1, 1, 1]
        ]);
```

Each row of indices assembles the shape coordinates of two triangles into a plate. Each number here represents an index to an indice, not x, y, z coordinates.

We're passing an array of indices for the colors; you previously set up the color method in your template.js file to output large amounts of color data for indices.

```
          if (this.rotate)
              this.rotate = {
                  axis: [
                       gd.game.random.number(10, 1) / 10,
                       gd.game.random.number(10, 1) / 10,
                       gd.game.random.number(10, 1) / 10],
                  angle: gd.game.random.number(350, 1),
                  speed: gd.game.random.number(400, 200)
              };
      }
});
```

STEP 3: ADD SIZE, TYPE, AND OTHER CUBE METADATA

Before gd.template.Cube is complete, you need to add metadata, such as size, type, and other details. Append the following listing to your existing Cube object.

Listing 9.30 run.js—Cube metadata

```
gd.template.Cube = gd.template.Entity.extend({
    type: 'b',
    size: {
        max: 3,                             ◄─┤  You'll use a size object and the meta
        min: 2,                                method to randomly generate a cube's size.
        divider: 1                             This makes size changes easy for when you
    },                                         extend this entity for particles later.
    pressure: 50,                       ◄─┤  Pressure will be used to generate
                                              how much speed a cube has after
                                              exploding out of a polygon.
    meta: function() {
        this.speed = {
            x: (gd.game.random.number(this.pressure, 1) / 100)
               * gd.game.random.polarity(),
            y: (gd.game.random.number(this.pressure, 1) / 100)
               * gd.game.random.polarity()
        };

        this.angle = gd.game.random.number(360, 1);

        this.s = gd.game.random.number(this.size.max, this.size.min)
            / this.size.divider;
        this.width = this.s * 2;
        this.height = this.s * 2;
    },

    update: function() {
        gd.game.boundaries(this, this.kill, this.kill, this.kill,
            this.kill, this.width);

        this.x -= Math.sin( this.angle * Math.PI / 180 ) * this.speed.x;
        this.y += Math.cos( this.angle * Math.PI / 180 ) * this.speed.y;

        if (this.rotate)
            gd.game.rotate(this);
    }
});
```

STEP 4: GENERATE SQUARE PARTICLES

Core API

Finish your game by adding `gd.template.Particle` right after `gd.template.Cube` with the following listing. For awesome special effects, you can turn up the number of particles and turn off the particle limiter in `Polygon.collide()`. Keep in mind that generating lots of particles can cause memory issues and frame-rate drops.

Listing 9.31   run.js—Particle generation

```
gd.template.Particle = gd.template.Cube.extend({        ⟵  Extends the cube logic
    pressure: 20,                                            instead of writing a
    type: 0,                                                 new particle entity
    size: {                                                  from scratch.
        min: 2,
        max: 6,
        divider: 10
    },

    init: function(x, y) {
        this.x = x;
        this.y = y;

        this.meta();                             ⟵  Creates a flat
                                                     rectangle shape
        this.shape([                                 with four points.
             this.s,   this.s,   0.0,
            -this.s,   this.s,   0.0,
             this.s,  -this.s,   0.0,
            -this.s,  -this.s,   0.0
        ]);

        var r = gd.game.random.number(10, 0) / 10,
        g = gd.game.random.number(10, 0) / 10,       Randomly generates a red,
        b = gd.game.random.number(10, 0) / 10;       green, blue color with a
        this.color([                                 constant alpha level.
            r, g, b, 1,
            r, g, b, 1,
            r, g, b, 1,
            r, g, b, 1
        ]);

        var self = this;                         ⟵  Cleans the particle out of
        this.create = window.setTimeout(function() {   memory after five seconds
            self.kill();                               to prevent memory hogging.
        }, 5000);
    }
});
```

Boot up the completed application in your browser, and everything should work correctly. You did it! You created a real 3D game—a basic WebGL engine—and learned foundational 3D programming concepts at the same time. With these tools, you can start using WebGL in your JavaScript projects immediately to create logos, illustrations, and more—especially with robust 3D libraries like three.js.

Figure 9.14 Almost every illustration on the bjork.com home page is drawn in a 2D fashion. When they're moved, you can tell that all the illustrations are 3D.

9.4 Summary

The words *3D application* evoke thoughts of video games and animation that illuminate the mind's eye. Even though you can use WebGL for entertainment purposes, this function makes up a small percentage of what you can do. Some authors have created 3D simulations for various scenarios, such as walking through architecture and operating vehicles. Uses for 3D in-browser can also transcend Canvas's 2D space limitations. For instance, Bjork's website (bjork.com) uses 2D shapes in a 3D environment for an amazing effect (shown in figure 9.14).

Various websites and companies are investing big money in WebGL. It's too powerful to ignore, and as support improves, it will drastically change how websites and mobile devices are programmed, mostly because WebGL will eventually give mobile developers the ability to write one 3D application with graphics acceleration for multiple devices. Therefore, we think it's important for developers to learn more about it now by playing with demos and tutorials.

You'll also be glad to know that WebGL isn't the only API that's evolving the Net; we'll talk about several others, such as the Full-Screen, Orientation, and Pointer Lock APIs in appendix I.

HTML5 and related specifications

It would be odd if you hadn't heard buzzwords such as HTML5, CSS3, and Node.JS used inaccurately, or even incorrectly, at some point. In particular, HTML5 has become a catchall word for emerging web technologies. For example, one of the authors once met a marketer who said, "I can create an SEO-optimized video game with HTML5." At the least, it's important to know what an HTML5 specification is, and what it isn't, to keep you from making a fool of yourself. For appendix A, we'll cover what's officially HTML5 and what isn't.

A.1 The origins of HTML5

You might be surprised to learn that the Worldwide Web Consortium (W3C) didn't advocate HTML5 in the beginning. W3C considered HTML to be dead after HTML4 and was working on XHTML2, continuing the trend of web markup based on an XML syntax. If you thought XHTML1 was strict, the second version promised to take things further. As a result, many members in the W3C felt a need for a change of direction, and the WHATWG (Web Hypertext Application Technology Working Group) was formed to begin work on HTML5.

HTML5 started off as Web Apps 1.0 and Web Forms 2.0, then later merged into a single specification: HTML5. Before long, W3C began to realize that there was merit to the case for HTML and began working on version 5 of HTML (not quite the same as HTML5, it should be noted), taking the work of WHATWG as the starting point for the new standard. For a time, this only added to the confusion. Not only was WHATWG continuing to work on HTML5, but W3C was also working on version 5 of HTML, derived from an earlier version of the HTML5 specification, while it was also continuing work on XHTML2. Confused? We certainly were.

Since that time, XHTML2 finally died, and developers at both WHATWG and W3C worked on the HTML5 specification, with each maintaining a separate version, albeit both overseen by the same editor. Why the need for two separate groups? Politics. For various reasons, some stakeholders in the process can't join WHATWG and others can't join W3C. As a result, both groups continue to work concurrently.

A.1.1 WHATWG vs. W3C

The goal of WHATWG is to continually update the "HTML Living Standard" based on feedback from all stakeholders to maintain a position slightly ahead of current implementations. WHATWG has given up on version numbers and sees the standard as an evolving document. It aims to stay just ahead of the functionality in browsers, providing a forum for everyone to agree on the details of any new feature and documentation of the final implementations.

W3C is sticking with the traditional version-based approach. We can expect HTML5 to be followed by HTML6 and HTML7, all using a snapshot of the WHATWG document as a basis. As a result, W3C has split what exists as one specification at the WHATWG into (currently) eight different specifications so that features can develop at their own pace without holding up the release of standards. You can find a list of the individual specifications at WHATWG's FAQ page: http://mng.bz/dWRb.

Another key difference between the groups is decision making. In WHATWG, the editor has complete control when it comes to making decisions regarding the HTML5 specification. W3C has an HTML Working Group with its own escalation process for making decisions on disputed issues.

W3C has a large number of specifications outside of HTML, and one goal is that all the specs should be compatible. W3C has been focused on XML-based technologies for a number of years, and WHATWG was formed in opposition to the pure XML approach, so this has been the underlying source of the disagreements so far. But despite some heated discussions, the two specs are yet to diverge.

To help you keep the key differences straight, refer to the summary in table A.1.

Table A.1   WHATWG and W3C compared

Topic	W3C	WHATWG
Membership	Mostly paid members with corporate sponsors.	Anyone can join the mailing list.
Editorial process	Editor is subject to strictures of W3C's feedback and review processes.	Editor is "benevolent dictator."
HTML-related specifications managed	8 (derived from WHATWG's 1 spec).	1.
Non-HTML specifications managed	Lots (e.g., CSS, DOM, SVG, XML, RDF).	None.
Release process	Versioned snapshots.	Rolling release, constantly updated.

The real-life interactions of thousands of smart people are, of course, more complex than can be described in a simple table, especially when you remember that many of these people are in both W3C and WHATWG. But this section has given you some useful context if you ever have to dive into a debate on the WHATWG mailing list or the W3C bug tracker over some detail of one of the specs when you're just trying to figure out which browser is "doing the right thing."

A.1.2   So ... what is HTML5 anyway?

We consider a technology an official part of HTML5 if it's part of the WHATWG Living Standard or it's one of W3C's specifications derived from that standard. But many of the technologies, such as CSS3, Geolocation, and the Storage APIs, that partake of the buzzword *HTML5* aren't part of this official definition. In the next section, you'll have a quick review of the HTML5 technologies that are officially HTML5, and in the following section, those that are not.

> #### Does it really matter what is or isn't HTML5?
> The short answer is no! When you're building web apps, you need to pick and choose technologies in the modern web platform based not on which spec they appear in but on whether they do something you need and they work in browsers. Although you may end up in some heated social network debates, you'll receive no explicit punishment for claiming things like Geolocation as a key part of your HTML5 app. As you'll see, even the authors of this book have stretched the definition of HTML5 to include several "unofficial" technologies.

A.2 Popular HTML5 specifications

In this section, we'll discuss the technologies that are part of WHATWG's HTML Living Standard and the HTML5 family of specifications at W3C. Although the WHATWG spec hasn't always been called the HTML Living Standard, we'll use that term to differentiate it from the HTML5 spec at W3C. Each section will mention which specification at the W3C applies and the relevant chapter or chapters in this book.

A.2.1 Semantic markup, forms

HTML5 introduces HTML elements that change how people structure website markup and use form elements. It also gives programmers more control over their markup through attributes such as data. These attributes can hold important metadata inside an HTML element. This is all core HTML stuff and so is in the W3C HTML5 specification.

You can learn about semantic markup and forms in chapters 1 and 2.

A.2.2 Video and sound (multimedia)

In the past, web developers have primarily relied on Flash or another plug-in to provide audio and video support. The HTML5 audio and video elements allow a browser to run both, without any additional configuration. Both use the Media Element API, which means their event systems for toggling playback, sound, stopping, and so on are similar. This is also in the core W3C HTML5 specification.

Audio and video are covered in chapter 8; also check out appendix I for some of the more cutting-edge video technologies.

A.2.3 Canvas and SVG (interactive media)

The Canvas API and SVG give you the ability to create interactive media via JavaScript programming. The first and most popular Canvas API was originally an Apple product from Mac OS X. Developers can create raster-based graphics on the fly inside a <canvas> element with it. Although the <canvas> element itself is covered in the core HTML5 spec, the 2D context (the JavaScript API that lets you draw stuff) is in a separate specification called "HTML Canvas 2D Context." Note that although WebGL allows Canvas to display 3D graphics, the 3D context is not officially part of HTML5 (see section A.3 for details).

SVG is an XML-based language that's been around since 2001. All HTML5 adds is the ability to inject SVG elements into HTML pages (it has always been allowed to inject SVG into XHTML pages), nothing more. It's important to understand that SVG is a piece of HTML5 but not a specification created by it.

Canvas, the 2D context, and SVG are covered in chapters 6 and 7; Canvas is also used in chapter 8 to manipulate live video and in chapter 9 along with the 3D context.

A.2.4   Storage

HTML5 is associated with several storage-based APIs; the ones that are part of the HTML5 specifications are Web Storage and Offline Applications.

At W3C, offline apps are covered in the core HTML5 spec, and session and local storage are covered by the Web Storage spec. Both are discussed in chapter 5.

A.2.5   Messaging

Web Messaging (cross-document and channel messaging), Server-Sent Events, and WebSockets are all core HTML5 technologies. At W3C they are covered by three specs: "HTML5 Web Messaging," "Server-Sent Events," and "WebSockets API." Note that the WebSockets Protocol, which describes the format of the transmitted data, is defined by a specification at the Internet Engineering Task Force (IETF). Messaging is covered in chapter 4 and appendix F.

A.2.6   The XML HTTP Request object

This API has existed in IE since the late 1990s and has been heavily used in web applications since Firefox implemented its version between 2000 and 2002, giving birth to AJAX (Asynchronous JavaScript And XML). But XHR had never been documented in any specification until WHATWG added it to its specifications in 2004. Currently, the XML HTTP Request (XHR) object has a specification all to itself at the W3C. XHR and AJAX are well known and well used, so even though XHR is, strictly speaking, HTML5, we don't cover it specifically in this book.

A.3   Popular non-HTML5 technologies

Some popular specifications and technologies are commonly mistaken for HTML5 because of their intriguing features. Although these new technologies began to emerge around the same time that HTML5 was becoming established and frequently featured in HTML5 Showcase sites and HTML5 books (including this one), they're not HTML5 by the definition given earlier. One good way to describe this group of web development technologies, suggested by Bruce Lawson, is "HTML5 and friends."

A.3.1   CSS3

CSS3 brings several amazing features to web development, such as transitions and 3D transforms. But it's an entirely separate specification from HTML5. There is no specific CSS3 coverage in this book, but CSS will be used to support all of this book's apps.

For a gentle introduction to CSS3, see *Hello! HTML5 & CSS3* by Rob Crowther (Manning, 2012). There's also good information on tools for CSS3 in *Sass and Compass in Action* by Wynn Netherland, Nathan Weizenbaum, Chris Eppstein, and Brandon Mathis (Manning, 2013).

A.3.2 Geolocation

A lot of early HTML5 demos featured the Geolocation API. But this API has never been a part of the HTML Living Standard or the HTML5 family of specifications at W3C.

The Geolocation API has its own specification at the W3C; it's covered briefly in chapter 3.

A.3.3 Storage

We mentioned storage in the previous sections. There are two key storage technologies that aren't part of the HTML5 spec: IndexedDB and the File System API. These are in the Indexed Database API, File API, File API: Directories and System, and File API: Writer specs at the W3C.

Check out chapter 5 for more on IndexedDB and chapter 3 for the File API.

A.3.4 WebGL

The WebGL technology is based on OpenGL. The Khronos Group has taken OpenGL and adapted it for use in web browsers; the result is WebGL. All desktop browsers have support for WebGL. Even Microsoft, after initially being opposed to the technology, has implemented WebGL in IE11.

A.3.5 Node.js

Many people have mistaken the new software platform Node.js (often simply called *Node*) for an HTML5 API. Although it makes use of emerging web-standard technologies and improves the use of many HTML5 APIs, it's not part of any web standard. It runs on Google's V8 JavaScript engine and is primarily sponsored by Joyent. This book covers basic Node usage; for more, check out *Node.js in Action* by Mike Cantelon, TJ Holowaychuk, and Nathan Rajlich (Manning, 2013). Jode.js is also covered in chapter 4 and appendix E.

A.3.6 jQuery and other JavaScript libraries

JavaScript libraries followed along after the last "buzzword fad" on the web: AJAX. The main problem they initially solved was to provide a compatibility layer over the differing browser implementations of the XHR object that underlies AJAX, but each also added its own features. The popular Prototype.js added features and encouraged a style of programming inspired by the Ruby programming language; Dojo did a similar thing except in the style of Python. For many years, the ultimate solution in cross-browser compatibility has been the jQuery library. HTML5 doesn't replace libraries like jQuery, but it should help make them more performant. The extensive effort to standardize browser behavior through the process of building the HTML5 spec will also make the compatibility provided by these libraries less important. Some common JS library features that are replaced by HTML5 are shown in table A.2.

Table A.2   JS Library functionality and modern web platform equivalents

Feature	JS libraries	HTML5 (or related) feature
Selecting elements by class	Nearly all	The `getElementsByClassName()` method was originally introduced in the HTML Living Standard; it's currently in the DOM CORE spec at W3C. The `querySelector()` and `querySelectorAll()` methods are defined in the Selectors API Level 1 spec at the W3C.
Drag and drop	Scriptaculous, jQuery-UI, ExtJS, Dojo, YUI	Added to the HTML Living Standard as a reverse engineering of the IE feature.
Advanced form controls (date pickers, sliders, spinboxes, etc.)	jQuery-UI, ExtJS, Dojo, YUI	New form controls are part of the core HTML5 specification.
Storing arbitrary data on elements	Jquery, Dojo	HTML5 has `data-*` attributes for storing data for scripting.

A.4   Keeping up with the specs

The best way to keep up with the main HTML specification is to follow The WHATWG Blog (http://blog.whatwg.org/). Reading the specification in its raw form can be tedious, to say the least. We find it much easier to read the spec using the edition for web authors, which is available at http://developers.whatwg.org/. This edition doesn't include the technical information targeted at browser vendors and is far easier to read.

For the rest of the specifications there's no central source. Each individual W3C working group has its own blog and/or mailing list. One approach is to keep an eye on the development blogs for the major browsers to find out what new features they're experimenting with:

- *Mozilla Hacks*: https://hacks.mozilla.org/
- *Google Chrome Blog*: http://chrome.blogspot.co.uk/
- *IEBlog*: http://blogs.msdn.com/b/ie/
- *Surfin' Safari*: https://www.webkit.org/blog/
- *Opera Desktop Team*: http://my.opera.com/desktopteam/blog/
- *Opera Mobile*: http://my.opera.com/mobile/blog/

HTML5 API reference

In this appendix, you'll find numerous references that give you a quick overview of various HTML5 and related APIs. We've compiled lists of methods, attributes, and events that should make it easy for you to look up how to use API information when you need it.

The material is broken down into three sections:

- The HTML5 APIs
- Other APIs and specifications, which cover Geolocation and IndexedDB
- The File System API

We begin with the HTML5 APIs.

B.1   HTML5 APIs

In this section, we cover what you need to know for the

- Constraint Validation API
- API for offline web applications
- Editing API
- Drag and Drop API
- Microdata API
- APIs for Web Storage
- Media Element API

B.1.1   Constraint Validation API

The Constraint Validation API defines a series of new attributes and methods, outlined in table B.1, that you can use to detect and modify the validity of a given form element.

Table B.1   Constraint Validation API

Attribute/method	Description
willValidate	Checks if the element validates when the form is submitted.
validationMessage	Holds the error message the user will see if the element is checked for validity.
validity	An object that contains attributes representing the validity states of the element. Each attribute defines a validation error condition. When "getting" an attribute, a value of true is returned if the error condition is true, otherwise false. validity contains the following boolean attributes: • valueMissing (required field but has no value) • typeMismatch (incorrect data type) • patternMismatch (doesn't match required pattern) • tooLong (longer than maxlength content attribute value) • rangeUnderflow (lower than min content attribute value) • rangeOverflow (higher than max content attribute value) • stepMismatch (not a multiple of step content attribute) • customError (has a custom error) • valid (field is valid)
checkValidity()	Checks if the element is valid.
setCustomValidity(message)	Sets a custom error message on the element.

B.1.2   API for offline web applications

The API for offline web applications consists of a collection of events and a number of DOM attributes and methods. Table B.2 lists the events.

Table B.2   Application cache events

Event name	Description
checking	Fires when checking for an update or trying to download the cache manifest for the first time.
noupdate	Fires when manifest has not been modified.
downloading	Fires when the browser is downloading items in the manifest for the first time. Also fires when the browser is downloading items after detecting a manifest update.
progress	Fires once per file as the browser downloads each file listed in the manifest. The event object's total attribute returns the total number of files to be downloaded. The event object's loaded attribute returns the number of files processed so far.
cached	The application is cached and the download is complete.
updateready	Resources have been downloaded and an update is available. The application can use the swapCache method to switch to the new resources.

Table B.2 Application cache events *(continued)*

Event name	Description
obsolete	The manifest was not found and the cache is being removed.
error	The manifest or one of the resources in it was not found, or the manifest changed while the update was in progress, or some other error has occurred, so caching has been canceled.

Table B.3 lists the DOM attributes and methods for offline applications. All apply to the application cache object itself, apart from the ones where an explicit root object is listed.

Table B.3 Application cache API

Attribute/method	Description
window.applicationCache	Returns an application cache object for the active document.
self.applicationCache	Returns an application cache object for a shared worker.
status	Gets the current status of the cache: ■ UNCACHED (numeric value: 0) ■ IDLE (1) ■ CHECKING (2) ■ DOWNLOADING (3) ■ UPDATEREADY (4) ■ OBSOLETE (5)
update()	Starts downloading resources into a new application cache.
abort()	Cancels downloading of resources.
swapCache()	Switches to the newest application cache, if a newer one is available.

The Browser State API is covered in table B.4, though this is less useful than you might think. Deciding whether the browser is online isn't the same thing as being able to connect to the internet or your application. It's merely a reflection of the browser's online mode.

Table B.4 Browser State attributes and events

Attribute/method, event name	Description
window.navigator.onLine	Checks if the browser mode is online (returns true) or offline (returns false).
online	The browser's online status has changed to online.
offline	The browser's online status has changed to offline.

B.1.3   *Editing API*

The Editing API allows you to implement direct editing of HTML pages loaded in the browser. This is commonly referred to as rich-text editing; it enables the web application to use all the formatting options available to HTML. This ability distinguishes rich-text editing from plain-text editing that can be achieved in `textarea` elements and other form inputs.

The Editing API was created by reverse engineering the behavior of IE. The documentation had always been incomplete, so there are many parts of it that exist simply because IE has them rather than because there's a rational explanation for their existence.

All the methods in table B.5 are on the document object; in most cases they will apply to any selected block of text within a `contenteditable` section of the current document.

Table B.5   Editing API

Method	Description
`execCommand(command, showUI, value)`	Executes the command described in the first argument. The `command` argument is a string value. The `showUI` argument is a Boolean value to determine whether or not to show the default UI associated with `command`. The `value` argument is passed to `command`. Not all commands need a `value` argument.
`queryCommandEnabled(command)`	Checks if `command` is supported and enabled.
`queryCommandIndeterm(command)`	Checks if `command` is indeterminate (if the selected text is part active and part inactive).
`queryCommandState(command)`	Returns a Boolean value indicating whether `command` is currently applied to the selected text.
`queryCommandSupported(command)`	Checks if `command` is supported.
`queryCommandValue(command)`	Returns `command`'s value, if it has one.

As you can see, the API isn't much use without a value to enter for `command`. Tables B.6–B.8 list categories of available commands. Pass the command as a string to the methods in table B.6, for example: `execCommand('bold',false,'')`. For more information on these commands, see http://mng.bz/4216.

Table B.6 lists commands for formatting inline elements.

Table B.6   Inline formatting commands

`backColor`	`bold`	`createLink`
`fontName`	`fontSize`	`foreColor`
`hiliteColor`	`italic`	`removeFormat`
`strikethroug`	`subscript`	`superscript`
`underline`	`unlink`	

Table B.7 lists commands for formatting block elements.

Table B.7 Block formatting commands

delete	formatBlock	forwardDelete
indent	insertHorizontalRule	insertHTML
insertImage	insertLineBreak	insertOrderedList
insertParagraph	insertText	insertUnorderedList
justifyCenter	justifyFull	justifyLeft
justifyRight	outdent	

Table B.8 lists commands for other formatting and editing issues.

Table B.8 Miscellaneous commands

copy	cut	defaultParagraphSeparator
paste	redo	selectAll
styleWithCSS	undo	useCSS

B.1.4 Drag and Drop API

The Drag and Drop API is another API that's reverse engineered from the IE implementation. The API has three main parts: the dataTransfer object, the dataTransfer item, and a collection of events. These are covered in tables B.9, B.10, and B.11, respectively. A drag operation will create a dataTransfer object; this will contain one or more dataTransfer items in the items attribute, and you can gain access to both by listening to the events.

Table B.9 dataTransfer object

Attribute/method	Description
dropEffect	This is the type of operation taking place (copy, link, move, none).
effectAllowed	Contains the type of operations allowed (copy, copyLink, copy-Move, link, linkMove, move, all, uninitialized, none).
items	Returns a list of dataTransfer items with the drag data (see table B.12).
setDragImage(element, x, y)	Updates the drag feedback image with the given element and coordinates.
addElement(element)	Adds an element to the list of elements used to render drag feedback.

Table B.9   `dataTransfer` object *(continued)*

Attribute/method	Description
`types`	List of data formats set in the `dragstart` event.
`getData(format)`	Returns the data being dragged.
`setData(format, data)`	Sets the data being dragged.
`clearData([format])`	Removes data of the specified format (or all formats if omitted).
`files`	Returns a list of files being dragged, if any.

Table B.10 lists the attributes and methods of the `dataTransfer` item. The `dataTransfer` item defines an object being dragged to the drop zone.

Table B.10   `dataTransfer` item

Attribute/method	Description
`kind`	This is the kind of item being dragged (string or file).
`type`	This is the data item type string.
`getAsString(callback)`	If the data kind is string, this invokes the callback with the string data as an argument.
`getAsFile()`	If the data kind is file, this returns a `file` object.

Table B.11 lists the drag-and-drop events. When the application listens for these events, it can use the event object to gain access to the `dataTransfer` object or `dataTransfer` items. To access the `dataTransfer` object, use `e.dataTransfer`, where e is an event object. To access `dataTransfer` items, use `e.dataTransfer.items`, where items is a list of `dataTransfer` items.

Table B.11   Drag-and-drop events

Event name	Description
`dragstart`	Fires on the source element when the user starts to drag the source element.
`drag`	Fires on the source element as the user is dragging the source element.
`dragenter`	Fires on the target element when the user drags the source element into it.
`dragleave`	Fires on the target element when the user drags the source element out of it.
`dragover`	Fires on the target element as the user is dragging the source element over it.
`drop`	Fires on the target element when the user drops the source element on it.
`dragend`	Fires on the source element when the user stops dragging the source element.

B.1.5 Microdata API

The Microdata API (table B.12) has one method on the document object and a couple of DOM attributes on elements that have Microdata content attributes (itemscope and itemprop).

Table B.12 Microdata API

Attribute/method	Description
document.getItems([type])	Returns a list of top-level Microdata items. If you're looking for a particular type of Microdata item, such as event items, you can select all event items by specifying 'http://microformats.org/profile/hcalendar#event' as the type parameter. Multiple types can be specified in a space-separated list.
element.properties	Gets the element's attributes (only if it has an itemscope attribute).
element.itemValue	Gets or sets the element's Microdata item value (only if it has an itemprop attribute).

B.1.6 APIs for Web Storage

Web Storage defines APIs on two objects, window.localStorage and window.sessionStorage; see table B.13. The APIs for both of these objects are identical.

Table B.13 localStorage and sessionStorage API

Attribute/method	Description
length	Number of items (key/value pairs) currently stored in the storage area.
key(index)	Gets the name of the key at the given index.
getItem(key)	Gets the value of the item at the given key.
setItem(key, value)	Sets the value of the item at the given key to the value provided.
removeItem(key)	Removes the item at the given key.
clear()	Removes all items in the storage area.

Web Storage also defines an event, storage, that fires when the storage area changes. This event returns a storage event object, which contains attributes to determine what changed; see table B.14.

Table B.14 Storage event object

Attribute/method	Description
key	The key of the item that was modified
oldValue	The previous value of the modified item

Table B.14   Storage event object *(continued)*

Attribute/method	Description
newValue	The new value of the modified item
url	The address of the document that contains the item
storageArea	The storage object in which the change was made

The methods in table B.15 apply to localStorage, sessionStorage, and to cookies created using the document.cookie API. It's available on the window.navigator object.

Table B.15   Another storage method

Attribute/method	Description
yieldForStorageUpdates()	Allows scripts to access storage areas, even if other scripts are currently blocking those areas.

B.1.7   *Media Element API*

The Media Element API, shown in table B.16, is implemented by both the <audio> and <video> elements.

Table B.16   Media Element API

Attribute/method	Description
autoplay	Corresponding DOM attribute to the autoplay content attribute.
buffered	Returns a TimeRanges object (an array of start and end times) that represents the ranges of the media resource that the browser has buffered.
canPlayType(type)	Accepts a MIME type, for example, video/webm, and returns a value indicating whether or not the browser thinks it will be able to play media of that type. The possible return values, in decreasing order of certainty, are 'probably', 'maybe', and an empty string.
controller	The MediaController object associated with the element's mediagroup.
controls	Corresponding DOM attribute to the controls content attribute.
crossOrigin	Reflects the value of the crossorigin content attribute. This setting is for Cross Origin Resource Sharing (CORS). The value can be either anonymous or use-credentials, depending on whether the omit credentials flag should be set or unset in the CORS headers.
currentSrc	The address of the currently playing media.
currentTime	The offset, in seconds, from the start of the media to the point currently playing.

Table B.16   Media Element API *(continued)*

Attribute/method	Description
defaultMuted	Corresponding DOM attribute to the `muted` content attribute.
defaultPlaybackRate	The default playback rate of the media; if this differs from the `playbackRate`, then the user is using fast forward or slow motion.
duration	The playing time, in seconds, of the media (if available).
ended	Boolean attribute that returns `true` if the media has reached the end of playback.
error	If any error has occurred, this attribute will be set to a `MediaError` object, which can be examined for the details.
load()	Resets the media element, clearing any currently playing media and rerunning the media-selection algorithm as if the page had just been loaded.
loop	Corresponding DOM attribute to the `loop` content attribute.
mediaGroup	Corresponding DOM attribute to the `mediagroup` content attribute. Allows the grouping of multiple media elements for synchronized playback.
muted	Boolean value indicating whether or not the current media is muted.
networkState	The state of any interaction between the media element and the network. Returns an integer value from 0 to 3, which corresponds to the constants `NETWORK_EMPTY`, `NETWORK_IDLE`, `NETWORK_LOADING`, and `NETWORK_NO_SOURCE`, respectively.
pause()	Sets the `paused` attribute to `true`, loading the media resource if necessary.
paused	Boolean value indicating whether or not the media is paused.
play()	Sets the `paused` attribute to `false`, loading the media and beginning playback if necessary. If the playback had ended, will restart it from the beginning.
playbackRate	The current effective playback rate; 1.0 is normal speed.
played	Returns a `TimeRanges` object (an array of `start` and `end` times) that represents the ranges of the media resource that the browser has played.
preload	Corresponds to the value of the `preload` content attribute; can have the value `none`, `metadata`, or `auto`.
readyState	The readiness of the element to play media. Returns an integer value from 0 to 4, which corresponds to the constants `HAVE_NOTHING`, `HAVE_METADATA`, `HAVE_CURRENT_DATA`, `HAVE_FUTURE_DATA`, and `HAVE_ENOUGH_DATA`, respectively.
seekable	Returns a `TimeRanges` object (an array of `start` and `end` times) that represents the ranges of the media resource that the browser is able to seek to (if any).

Table B.16   Media Element API *(continued)*

Attribute/method	Description
seeking	Boolean value indicating whether or not the browser is seeking (i.e., loading new data) because the playback position has been skipped forward.
src	Corresponds to the value of the src content attribute.
startDate	If the media has an embedded explicit time (for example, timestamped CCTV footage), this attribute will return the start date. This attribute was previously called startOffsetTime.
volume	Returns the current playback volume as a value between 0.0 and 1.0, inclusive.

B.2   Other APIs and specifications

In this section, we cover the Geolocation API and the IndexedDB specification.

B.2.1   Geolocation API

The Geolocation API methods are defined on the window.navigator.geolocation object. The options argument in the two position-retrieval API methods in table B.17 is a Position Options object and can have any of the attributes defined in table B.18.

Table B.17   Geolocation API

Attribute/method	Description
getCurrentPosition(successCallback, [errorCallback], [options])	Gets the current position of the device, invoking the relevant success callback function when it has been located. If a problem is encountered, the error callback function will be called.
watchPosition(successCallback, [errorCallback], [options])	Monitors the position of the device and invokes the relevant success callback provided as the location of the device is updated or the error callback if there's a problem. Calling this function returns a watch ID, which can be passed to clearWatch to cancel a watch.
clearWatch(watchId)	Clears an existing geolocation watch.

Table B.18   Position Options object

Attribute/method	Description
enableHighAccuracy	Informs the browser that the application would like to receive the maximum possible results. The browser can use this to determine whether it should use a more accurate sensor such as a Global Positioning System (GPS) sensor.
timeout	The maximum length of time (in milliseconds) allowed to pass before the relevant callback function is invoked.

Table B.18 Position Options **object** *(continued)*

Attribute/method	Description
maximumAge	Typically, a device will store position information for a period of time to avoid wasting battery by having the position-detection hardware running constantly. If you're willing to accept slightly out-of-date position data, you can specify an acceptable maximum age in milliseconds in this parameter. If the value is 0 or omitted, the browser must fetch a new position, even if a cached position is available.

When one of the Geolocation API methods invokes a success callback function, it passes a Position object to that function; see table B.19.

Table B.19 Position **object**

Attribute/method	Description
coords	A Coordinates object including the geographic coordinates of the user's location and the estimated accuracy. Further details are shown in table B.20.
timestamp	The time when the user's position was acquired.

coords, an attribute of the position object, lists the device's coordinates, the estimated accuracy of those coordinates, the device's direction of travel, and its speed.

Table B.20 Coordinates **object**

Attribute/method	Description
latitude	Geographic latitude coordinate, in degrees
longitude	Geographic longitude coordinate, in degrees
altitude	The height, in meters, above (approximately) sea level
accuracy	The accuracy of the latitude and longitude values, in meters
altitudeAccuracy	The accuracy of the altitude value, in meters
heading	The direction the device is traveling in, specified in degrees
speed	The device's current velocity in meters per second

B.2.2 *IndexedDB specification*

IndexedDB is a very large specification, approximately 105 printed pages, so there's not room in this appendix to discuss every single attribute, method, and the like. Instead, this section lists only the most important components used in this book. These components have been grouped under their respective IndexedDB interfaces, and presented in a table format. Summaries for each component have been prepared by Joe Lennon and Greg Wanish and are derived from IndexedDB content (http://mng.bz/1M6o) by

Mozilla contributors at the Mozilla Developer Network (MDN) and used under Creative Commons CC-BY-SA (http://creativecommons.org/licenses/by-sa/2.5/). These tables of IndexedDB interfaces are licensed under Creative Commons CC-BY-SA (http://creative commons.org/licenses/by-sa/2.5/) by Joe Lennon and Greg Wanish. See http://mng.bz/ 1M6o for a more complete explanation of the IndexedDB specification.

The object `window.indexedDB` implements the `IDBFactory` interface and enables applications to create, access, and delete an indexed database. Table B.21 lists the methods and attributes for the asynchronous version of the `IDBFactory` interface. The asynchronous version works with or without web workers; no browser at this time supports the synchronous version.

Table B.21 `IDBFactory` **interface**

Attribute/method	Description
`open(name, [version])`	Requests a connection to a database with given `name` and `version` number. If no database with `name` exists, create a database with given `name` and `version` number.
`deleteDatabase(name)`	Requests deletion of a database with given `name`.
`cmp(first, second)`	Compares two keys to determine equality and ordering for IndexedDB operations, such as ordering. Returns a -1, if first key is less than second key; 0, if first key is equal to second key; 1, if first key is greater than second key.

Table B.22 lists the attributes and methods of the `IDBCursor` object. The cursor iterates over object stores and indexes within an indexed database.

Table B.22 `IDBCursor` **interface**

Attribute/method	Description
`source`	On getting, returns the `IDBObjectStore` or `IDBIndex` that the cursor is iterating over.
`direction`	On getting, returns the cursor's current direction of traversal.
`key`	On getting, returns the key for the record at the cursor's position. If the cursor is outside its range, this is `undefined`.
`primaryKey`	On getting, returns the cursor's current effective key. If the cursor is currently being iterated or has iterated outside its range, returns `undefined`.
`update(value)`	Returns an `IDBRequest` object. In a separate thread, uses `value` to update the value at the current position of the cursor in the object store. If the cursor points to a record that has just been deleted, a new record is created with the given `value`.
`continue(key)`	Continues along the cursor's current direction of movement, and finds the next item with a key matching the optional `key` parameter. If no key is specified, goes to the immediate next position, based on the cursor's current direction of movement.

Table B.22 `IDBCursor` interface *(continued)*

Attribute/method	Description
`delete()`	Returns an `IDBRequest` object. In a separate thread, deletes the record at the cursor's position without moving the cursor. Afterward, the cursor's value is set to `null`.

Table B.23 lists the methods and attributes of the `IDBDatabase` object. The `IDBDatabase` serves primarily as a container for indexes and object stores. The `IDBDatabase` object is the only way to get a transaction on the database.

Table B.23 `IDBDatabase` interface

Attribute/method	Description
`createObjectStore(name, [parameters])`	Creates and returns a new object store or index with a given name. `parameters` is an optional object with the following properties:
	`keyPath` Specifies a field in the object as a key. Each object must have a unique key.
	`autoIncrement` If `true`, the object store creates keys automatically via a key generator.
`setversion (deprecated)`	Updates the version of the database. Upon invocation, returns immediately, and, on a separate thread, runs a `versionchange` transaction on the connected database.
`transaction(storeNames, [mode])`	Immediately returns an `IDBTransaction` object and, on a separate thread, starts a transaction. The parameter `storeNames`, an array of strings, identifies the object stores and indexes that are to be accessible to the new transaction. The `mode` parameter defines the new transaction's type of access: `'readonly'` or `'readwrite'`. The default is `'readonly'`.
`version`	The version of the connected database. When a database is first created, this attribute is the empty string.

Table B.24 defines the interface for the `IDBEnvironment` object; it has only a single attribute, `indexedDB`. The `IDBEnvironment` provides access to a client-side database.

Table B.24 `IDBEnvironment` interface

Attribute/method	Description
`indexedDB`	Provides a mechanism for applications to asynchronously access the capabilities of indexed databases.

Table B.25 lists the `IBDIndex` object method, `openCursor`. This method is useful for filtering through an index. The `IBDIndex` provides methods to access an index of a database.

Table B.25 **IDBIndex interface**

Attribute/method	Description
openCursor([range], [direction])	Immediately returns an IDBRequest object, then, on a separate thread, creates a cursor over the specified key range. The optional parameter range specifies the key range of the cursor. The other optional parameter, direction, specifies the cursor's direction of movement through the index.

Table B.26 lists some of the methods for creating indexes and working with the object store. These methods belong to the IDBObjectStore object.

Table B.26 **IDBObjectStore interface**

Attribute/method	Description
createIndex(name, keypath, [parameters])	Creates and returns a new IDBIndex object with given name and keypath. This method can only be called from a VersionChange transaction mode callback. The optional parameters object has the following properties:
▪ unique	If true, the index won't allow duplicate values for a single key.
▪ multiEntry	If true, when the keypath resolves to an Array, the index will add an entry in the index for each array element. If false, the index will add one single entry containing the Array.
index(name)	Returns the name index in the object store.
openCursor([range], [direction])	Immediately returns an IDBRequest object, then, on a separate thread, creates a cursor over the records in the object store. The range parameter specifies the key range of the cursor. If the range is not specified, it defaults to all records in the object store. The direction parameter defines the cursor's direction of movement.
put(value, [key])	Immediately returns an IDBRequest object, then, on a separate thread, creates a clone of the value and stores it in the object store. The value parameter defines the value to be stored. The parameter key identifies the record. If not defined, it defaults to null.

Table B.27 lists the onupgradeneeded event handler used in the My Tasks application. onupgradeneeded is an event in the IDBOpenDBRequest interface that provides access to results of requests to open a database using event handler attributes.

Table B.27 **IDBOpenDBRequest interface**

Attribute/method	Description
onupgradeneeded	The event handler attribute for the upgrade needed event. This event handler is executed when a database's version number has increased.

Table B.28 lists the onsuccess event handler used in the My Tasks application to access the results of an asynchronous request. onsuccess is an event in the IDB-Request interface that provides access to results of asynchronous requests to databases and database objects using event handler attributes. Reading and writing operations on a database are executed with a request.

Table B.28 `IDBRequest` **interface**

Attribute/method	Description
onsuccess	The event handler attribute for the success event.

Table B.29 shows the method of the IDBKeyRange object used to search for keys within the index created for the My Tasks database. The IDBKeyRange interface defines a range of keys.

Table B.29 `IDBKeyRange` **interface**

Attribute/method	Description
bound(lower, upper, [lowerOpen], [upperOpen])	Creates and returns a key range with upper and lower bounds. If optional parameter lowerOpen is false (the default value), then the range includes the lower bound of the key range. If optional parameter upperOpen is false (the default value), then the range includes the upper bound value of the key range.

B.3   *File System API*

The File System API is massive; it will change how people think about managing web application data. In this section, we cover directory-based APIs within the File System API, as well as Blob data APIs. The following tables will give you some references and shortcuts for better managing your file data.

Table B.30 lists attributes associated with a File object.

Table B.30   File API

Attribute/method	Description
name	The name of the file
size	The size of the file in bytes
type	The MIME type of the file

Table B.31 lists attributes and methods associated with the FileList object. A File-List object is returned by the files property of the HTML <input> element.

Table B.31   FileList API

Attribute/method	Description
length	Number of files in the list.
item(index)	Gets the file at the given index (zero-based).

Table B.32 lists attributes and methods associated with the FileReader object. A File-Reader object lets web applications asynchronously read the contents of files (or raw data buffers) stored on the user's computer, using File or Blob objects to specify the file or data to read.

Table B.32   FileReader API

Attribute/method	Description
abort()	Aborts reading the file
readAsArrayBuffer(blob)	Reads the contents of the blob (which is either a File or a Blob object) into an array buffer.
readAsDataURL(blob)	Reads the contents of a Blob or File object and returns a data: URL to it.
readAsText(blob, [encoding])	Reads the contents of a Blob or File object into a text string if the optional encoding parameter is specified (e.g., 'ISO-8859-1' or 'UTF-8'); then the string will be encoded using that character set.
error	If an error occurs, it will be loaded into this property.
readyState	The state of the file read operation (0 = EMPTY, 1 = LOADING, 2 = DONE).
result	This will be populated with the file's contents when a read operation has been completed. The format of the result will depend on the method used to read the file.

Table B.33 lists events associated with the FileReader object.

Table B.33   FileReader events

Event name	Description
abort	Fires when the read operation is aborted.
error	Fires when an error occurs while reading the file.
load	Fires when the read operation has successfully completed.
loadend	Fires after onload or onerror, regardless of whether the operation was successful.

Table B.33   FileReader events (*continued*)

Event name	Description
loadstart	Fires when the read operation is about to start.
progress	Fires periodically during the read operation.

Table B.34 lists methods associated with the FileWriter object. A FileWriter object can perform multiple write actions, rather than just saving a single Blob.

Table B.34   FileWriter API

Attribute/method	Description
seek(offset)	Sets a specific file location at which the next write will occur.
truncate(size)	Alters the length of the file to the size passed in bytes.
write(data)	Writes the input data to a Blob object.

Table B.35 lists the methods associated with the FileSaver object which has methods to write a Blob object to a file.

Table B.35   FileSaver API

Constructor/attribute/method	Description
FileSaver(data)	Creates a FileSaver object with Blob data.
abort()	Terminates file saving.

Table B.36 lists the events associated with the FileSaver object which has events to monitor the progress of writing a Blob to a file.

Table B.36   FileSaver events

Event name	Description
writestart	Fires when starting a writing event.
progress	Fires repeatedly while file is being written.
write	Fires when a file is being written to.
abort	Fires when file writing is canceled.
error	Fires in response to an error or an abort.
writeend	Fires when writing to a file has ended.

Table B.37 lists the methods associated with the FileEntry object. A FileEntry object has methods to write and inspect the state of a file.

Table B.37 FileEntry API

Constructor/attribute/method	Description
createWriter(success, error)	Creates a new FileWriter associated with the file that FileEntry represents. If successful, calls function success; otherwise calls function error.
file(success, error)	Returns a file that represents the current state of the file that the FileEntry represents. If successful, calls function success; otherwise calls function error.

B.3.1 Directory-based APIs within the File System API

The File System API contains APIs to read directory entries in a directory. It also contains APIs to create, read, look up, and recursively remove files in a directory. Directory entries are objects that describe either a file or subdirectory. A directory entry contains attributes defining the entry's status as a file or subdirectory, the pathname to the entry, and the filesystem containing the entry.

Table B.38 lists the methods for the directory entry object. This object represents a directory entry in a filesystem. It includes methods for creating, reading, looking up, and recursively removing files and subdirectories in a directory.

Table B.38 DirectoryEntry API

Constructor/attribute/method	Description
createReader()	Creates a new DirectoryReader object to read the directory.
getDirectory(path, [options], [success], [error])	Creates or looks up a directory depending on set options. Successful creation or location is handled by the success callback; any errors will cause the error callback to be executed.
getFile(path, [options], [success], [error])	Creates or looks up a file depending on set options. Successful creation or location is handled by the success callback; any errors will cause the error callback to be executed.
removeRecursively(success, [error])	Deletes a directory and all contents; may only partially delete a directory if an error occurs. Successful creation or location is handled by the success callback; any errors will cause the error callback to be executed.

Table B.39 lists the only method for the DirectoryReader object.

Table B.39 DirectoryReader API

Attribute/method	Description
readEntries(success, error)	Allows you to read the next block of entries from the current directory, with a successful read being handled by the success callback and errors being handled by the error callback.

B.3.2 Blob data APIs

A `Blob` is an object of immutable data. `Blobs` are usually used to store the contents of a file. Part of the File API is inherited from the Blob API. Table B.40 lists the methods and attributes of a `Blob`.

Table B.40 `Blob` interface

Constructor/attribute/method	Description
`blob([array], [attributes])`	Creates a `Blob` object without `BlobBuilder`. The array can be any number of `ArrayBuffer`, `ArrayBufferView` (typed array), `Blob`, or `DOMString` objects, in any order. `attributes` is an object that can specify the media type and line endings in the `type` and `ending` properties, respectively.
`size`	Size in bytes of `Blob`'s data; read only.
`type`	MIME type of the `Blob`'s data.
`slice([start], [end], [type]`	Returns a specific chunk of `Blob` data, from offset `start` to offset `end` with MIME type `type`.

Table B.41 lists the methods for the `BlobBuilder` object. The `BlobBuilder` provides a way to construct `Blob` objects by calling one or more append methods on the `BlobBuilder` object. This API has been deprecated.

Table B.41 BlobBuilder API

Attribute/method	Description
`append(ArrayBuffer)`	Appends the `ArrayBuffer` to the `Blob`.
`append(Blob)`	Appends the `Blob` parameter to the `Blob`.
`append(data, [endings])`	Appends the string `data` to the `Blob`. The `endings` parameter specifies how strings containing \n are to be written out. This can be `'transparent'` (endings unchanged) or `'native'` (endings changed to match host system convention).
`getBlob([contentType])`	Returns the `Blob` object that's the result of all the append operations. If specified, the content type will be set on the returned `Blob`. This operation will also empty the `BlobBuilder` of all data.
`getFile(name, [contentType])`	Returns a `file` object with an optional content type.

appendix C
Installing PHP
and MySQL

To make the SSE Chat application from chapter 4 work, you'll need to set up a web server with PHP and MySQL. This combination is available free from various online providers, but setting up your own local install will allow you to experiment more freely. In this appendix we'll walk you through setting up PHP and then MySQL on Windows 7 and Mac OS X Mountain Lion.

C.1 Installing PHP on Windows 7

In this section you're going to download and install PHP and get it working with Windows's built-in web server component, Internet Information Services (IIS).

C.1.1 Configuring Windows 7 IIS

IIS is not installed by default in Windows 7 but can be added through the Control Panel option Turn Windows Features On and Off. Follow three steps to install IIS:

1 Open Control Panel and use the search feature to locate the Turn Windows Features On and Off option. Double-click it, and you'll see a dialog box like the one shown in figure C.1.

In figure C.1 the functionality is divided into a tree of options. A check mark shows that the feature and all its subfeatures are installed. A blue square indicates that the feature, but only some of the subfeatures, are installed. Selecting a feature with subfeatures will select the default set of subfeatures; this isn't necessarily *all* of the subfeatures. In the figure you can see that Application Development Features is selected, but only six of the seven subfeatures are selected.

Figure C.1 Adding the IIS components to Windows 7

2 Ensure that the options for IIS, World Wide Web Services, and, under the Application Development Features section, CGI are all selected. Selecting IIS will automatically select World Wide Web Services but not the CGI feature. Make sure you expand the tree and select the CGI feature explicitly.

3 After you make all your changes, click OK. There will be a short delay while the new features are installed.

C.1.2 Downloading PHP

PHP installers for Windows are available from http://windows.php.net/download/; look for the links that say "Installer." To follow along with us, use the latest 5.3 version (5.3.16 at the time of writing, see figure C.2), which has an Installer option. The installer will do a lot of automatic setup for you, so it's the better option even if it's not the most recent version on the page.

One other feature you should notice on the download page is that the Windows binaries are available in Thread Safe and Non Thread Safe varieties. The difference is only relevant if you want to integrate PHP with Apache; for installing PHP with IIS, you want the Non Thread Safe version, so download that now.

After clicking the link, you should have a file called php-5.3.16-nts-Win32-VC9-x86.msi (or a similar name with a larger version number) to use in the next step.

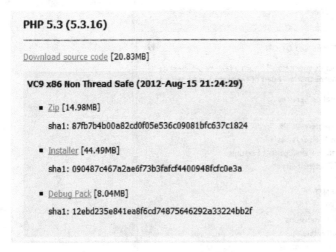

PHP 5.3 (5.3.16)

Download source code [20.83MB]

VC9 x86 Non Thread Safe (2012-Aug-15 21:24:29)

- Zip [14.98MB]

  sha1: 87fb7b4b00a82cd0f05e536c09081bfc637c1824

- Installer [44.49MB]

  sha1: 090487c467a2ae6f73b3fafcf4400948fcfc0e3a

- Debug Pack [8.04MB]

  sha1: 12ebd235e841ea8f6cd74875646292a33224bb2f

Figure C.2   The download page at php.net; use the latest 5.3 version to follow along as you read.

C.1.3   Installing PHP

Now that you have the installation files downloaded you're ready to install PHP by following these steps:

1 The MSI file you downloaded in C.1.2 will do most of the work for you. There are only two steps, which we'll walk you through, where you have to make decisions. Double-click the file to start, and accept the license agreement and the default file location.

2 For IIS configuration, select the option IIS FastCGI, which appears in the first decision screen, as shown in figure C.3. Note that this is why we had you take special care to select the CGI option earlier.

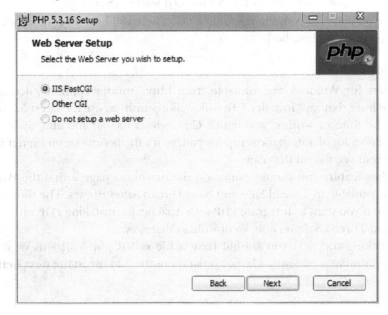

Figure C.3 Selecting the web server configuration in the PHP setup

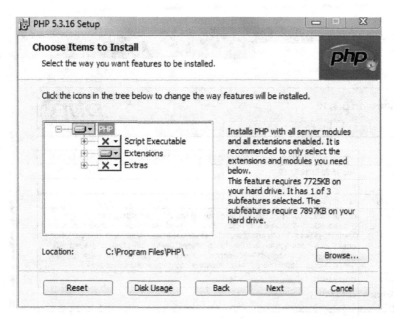

Figure C.4 Select the PHP components to install

3 When you see the next decision screen (figure C.4), accepting the defaults should be fine, but just in case, you want both PHP and Extensions selected.

Continue to the end of the installer, and you'll have a working PHP installation. As a final step, let's check that everything is working.

C.1.4 Confirm PHP is installed

IIS by default will serve files from the directory C:\Inetpub\WWWRoot\.

1 Create a file in that directory called index.php. Add the following code to it:

```
<?php phpinfo(); ?>
```

2 Load the URL http://localhost/index.php in your web browser. You should see a page like the one shown in figure C.5.

When it comes time to run chapter 4's SSE Chat application, you can make this work in a similar way; copy the entire working folder into C:\Inetpub\WWWRoot\, then browse to http://localhost/sse-chat/index.php (substitute sse-chat for whatever name you gave your working directory). Now that you have PHP installed, it's time to move on to setting up MySQL.

C.2 Installing MySQL on Windows 7

MySQL also has a convenient MSI-based installation process, which will take care of everything for you. In this section you'll walk through downloading and installing the database and client tools and then creating a database for use with the sample application in the book.

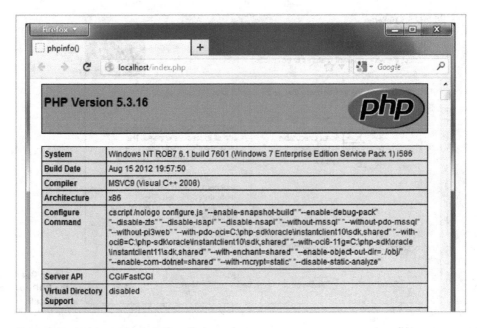

Figure C.5   PHP is successfully installed.

C.2.1   Downloading MySQL

MySQL can be downloaded from http://dev.mysql.com/downloads/. The Download button is hard to miss because it's prominently displayed in the middle of the page, as you can see from figure C.6.

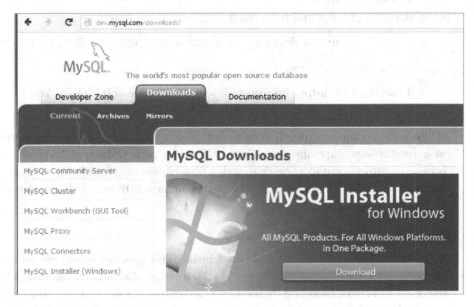

Figure C.6   The Download button is very prominent on the MySQL website.

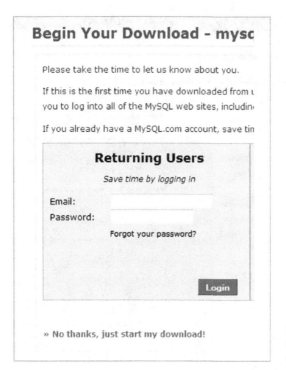

Figure C.7   Click the "No thanks" link at the bottom of the page to download without registering.

1   Click the button to download.

2   On the next page, you'll be presented with an option to create an account (figure C.7). You don't have to do this, although you can if you want to. To start the download, just click the link at the bottom that says, "No thanks, just start my download!"

C.2.2   Installing MySQL

In this section, you'll install the MySQL server:

1   You should now have an MSI file called mysql-installer-community-5.5.27.3.msi, except you'll have a more recent version number; double-click it to start.

2   Although you should be able to accept the defaults at every step to get a working installation, the next few steps highlight a few of the screens involved to help you stay on track. When you get to the Setup Type screen, shown in figure C.8, make sure the option Developer Default is selected.

Selecting the Developer Default option will install all the necessary tools to run and manage a local database instance.

3   When you get to the Configuration page, shown in figure C.9, you don't have to change the defaults, but you should consider whether you really want your MySQL Server available to anyone on your local network. If you want only local connections allowed, deselect the option Enable TCP/IP Networking. If you

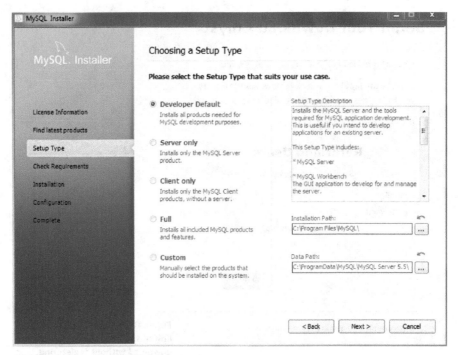

Figure C.8   Choosing the MySQL setup type

Figure C.9   The MySQL installer Configuration page

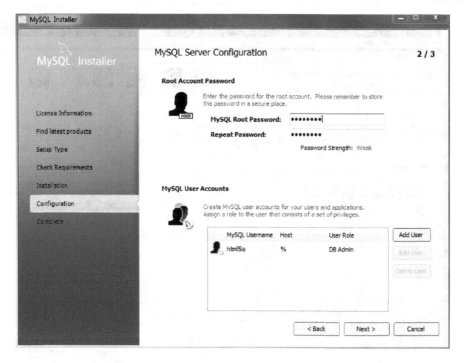

Figure C.10   Setting the root password

spend a lot of time connected to public Wi-Fi networks, you should definitely deselect this option.

Figure C.10 shows the next key configuration step, setting the root password. Although it's important to set a strong password, it's also important to set a memorable one. If you forget this password, you won't be able to access the database server. If you deselected the option to allow network access in the previous screen, then the password strength is less of an issue. On this screen you can also create other user accounts and assign them to various administrative roles within the database server. This isn't necessary to get anything in this book working but shouldn't break anything if you'd like to add some.

4   Enter a password, and click Next until the installer has finished.

5   At the end of the process, the installer will ask if you want to launch MySQL Workbench now; click Yes before proceeding to the next section. This is a tool for managing databases and running scripts; in the next section you'll use it to create a database you can use for the SSE Chat application.

C.2.3   Creating a database and running scripts

Having a database server available is only half the battle; you also need to create a database on that server for your app to use. In this section you'll create a database and

Figure C.11   The home page of MySQL Workbench

add the required structures for the chapter 4 SSE Chat app by running the chat.sql script provided in the code download for that chapter. Before you start, make sure you can see the MySQL Workbench welcome screen shown in figure C.11.

The first task is to connect to your new database server. Double-click the local instance in the leftmost box on the Welcome screen, under the heading Open Connection to Start Querying. You'll then be asked to enter your root password, as shown in figure C.12.

Figure C.12   The enter root password dialog box

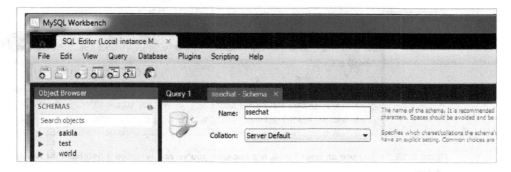

Figure C.13 Creating a database

Type in the password you set earlier and click OK. You'll be taken to the SQL Editor screen. In the left pane you'll see a list of databases (MySQL Workbench calls them Schemas), and on the right is a text editor to use to enter queries.

The second task is to create a database. On the toolbar you'll see an icon of a yellow cylindrical object with a plus sign in front of it; it's the third icon from the left.

1. Click that third icon, and you should see the create database dialog box shown on the right side of figure C.13.
2. Enter a suitable name like ssechat. Click the Apply button toward the bottom of the screen. Confirm that the script is being run, as shown in figure C.14, which will create the database for you.
3. Open the chat.sql file from the chapter 4 code download; the File menu has all the usual options for this sort of thing.
4. Run the script on the database you've just created by selecting the Execute (All or Selection) option from the Query menu. This will set up the tables required for the app.

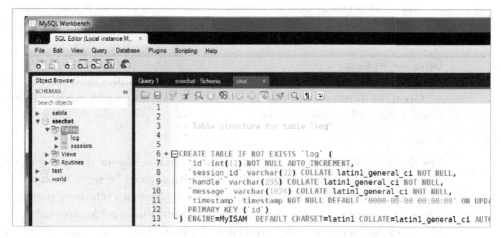

Figure C.14 The chat.sql file open in the MySQL workbench

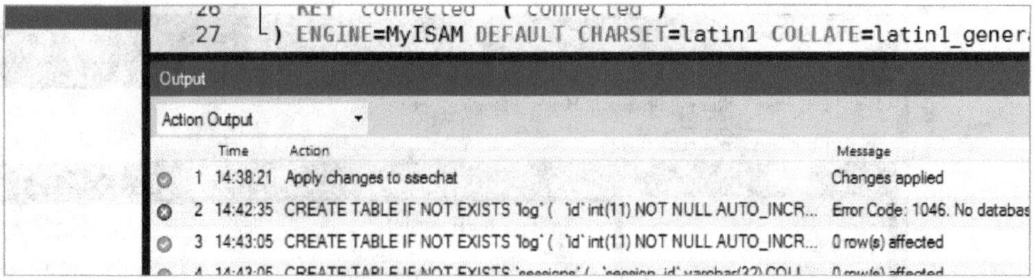

Figure C.15   If you see an error 1046, it's because you've not selected a database for running the query.

Note that if you see an error 1046 like the one shown in figure C.15, this is because the database isn't selected.

If you get that error, double-click the database name in the left pane and run the script again.

You now have PHP and MySQL set up and working on your Windows 7 machine.

C.3   Installing PHP and MySQL on Mac OS X Mountain Lion

All recent versions of Mac OS X come equipped with Apache and PHP. By default, Apache is not running, nor is it configured to load PHP when it runs. To get everything running, you'll need to follow along with a few steps.

C.3.1   Configuring Apache and PHP

To get PHP running on your computer you must first edit a couple of Apache configuration files. By default, these files are hidden from the Finder, so the easiest way to access them is through the Terminal application. Don't worry if you're not familiar with the Terminal and command line in OS X; just follow along and you should be okay.

> **NOTE**   For brevity, when we display the command line we'll simply use $ to represent the prompt. Any bold text is text that you'll type in, and any non-bold text is what will appear in the Terminal.

USING THE TERMINAL

The Terminal app can be found in the Applications/Utilities folder on your system.

Open the Terminal and you'll be presented with a greeting message followed by a prompt that looks similar to this:

```
MacBook:~ scott$
```

The first part of the prompt, MacBook, is the hostname of your computer; this will most likely be different on your computer. (The hostname can be set to whatever you'd like in the Computer Name: text field of the Sharing System Preference pane.) After the colon (:) is your current path. The path represents what folder you are currently in. Most likely, when you start the terminal you're in the Home directory (/Users/*YourUsername*); Terminal abbreviates a user's Home directory with the ~ symbol. After that the prompt shows you your username (which won't be scott unless that's actually your user-name) followed by the $ prompt and a cursor awaiting your input.

Our first Terminal command will take you to the location where the Apache con-figuration files are stored:

```
$ cd /etc/apache2/
```

This will take you to the apache2 folder where the configuration files are kept. (Note that after you type this command the ~ in the prompt changes to apache2.) It does this with the cd (change directory) command, which tells the terminal to go to a spe-cific directory.

Next, let's look at the files in this directory:

```
$ ls -FG
```

You should get a response showing the following:

```
extra/        magic        original/      users/
httpd.conf    mime.types   other/
```

The ls (list directory) command lists the contents of a directory. The -FG part is flags that add features to the basic ls command. In this case the -F adds symbols to special files (in this case the trailing / for subdirectories) and the -G adds color to special files. These two are slightly redundant, but they make the listing prettier.

At this point, your first step is to edit the httpd.conf file. This is the master Apache configuration file.

EDITING APACHE CONFIGURATION FILES

Editing the httpd.conf file involves a few tricks. By default, only a superuser (aka root) can edit this file; for this reason most graphical text editors (including any downloaded through the App Store) will refuse to save any changes to this file (see fig-ures C.16 and C.17)

> **NOTE** Some graphical text editors will allow you to unlock and edit files like httpd.conf, but such capabilities aren't allowed in applications found in the App Store. For example, BBEdit, which is available in the App Store, will allow you to edit httpd.conf, but if you purchase the App Store version you'll need to download an additional file from the BareBones website to enable this feature.

"httpd.conf" is locked for editing and you may not be able to save your changes. Do you want to unlock it?

"httpd.conf" is currently locked because you are not the owner of the file and do not have write permission.

☐ Do not show this message again

Don't Unlock   Unlock

Figure C.16 When you try to edit httpd.conf in most text editors, you'll first get a warning saying the file is locked.

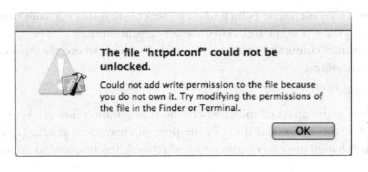

Figure C.17 If you try to unlock httpd.conf, in most text editors you'll get another warning saying that it can't be unlocked here.

So, if there are many roadblocks to editing the httpd.conf file, how do you go about it? It's not too difficult from the Terminal app using sudo along with a command-line text editor.

> **NOTE** The sudo (switch user and do) command is available to any user on Mac OS X with Admin rights. Most users have Admin rights to their Mac. But if a business, school, parent, or untrusting spouse provided your computer for you, you may not have Admin rights. If this is the case, you can't continue on your own; rather you should bug the person who provided you your computer incessantly until they either give you Admin rights to your system or set all of this up for you.

To begin, though, we'll test out sudo and create a backup copy of httpd.conf just in case, all at the same time with the following:

```
$ sudo cp httpd.conf httpd.conf.orig
Password:
```

After typing this command you'll be prompted to enter your system password to complete the command. Also, if this is the first time you've used sudo, you'll be given a warning about the dangers of using sudo inappropriately. Upon successfully typing in your password, you can run the ls command, and you should see a new httpd.conf.orig file listed. If not, something went wrong (check the previous note about being Admin).

Assuming you were able to create a copy of httpd.conf, you should be ready to go, assured that even if you do something horribly wrong, you can recover using your backup file. So begin the editing with

```
$ sudo nano httpd.conf
```

Now, because you recently ran the sudo command to create your backup, you may not be prompted again for your password. sudo will remember you for short periods of time between sudo commands, so you don't need to enter your password every time you run the command.

This command will open the httpd.conf file in the nano text editor with superuser permissions, allowing you to edit and save the file. As a result, nano will take over your terminal screen, which should now look something like this:

```
GNU nano 2.0.6                    File: httpd.conf

#
# This is the main Apache HTTP server configuration file.  It contains the
# configuration directives that give the server its instructions.
# See <URL:http://httpd.apache.org/docs/2.2> for detailed information.
# In particular, see
# <URL:http://httpd.apache.org/docs/2.2/mod/directives.html>
# for a discussion of each configuration directive.
#
# Do NOT simply read the instructions in here without understanding
# what they do.  They're here only as hints or reminders.  If you are unsure
# consult the online docs. You have been warned.
#
# Configuration and logfile names: If the filenames you specify for many
# of the server's control files begin with "/" (or "drive:/" for Win32), the
# server will use that explicit path.  If the filenames do *not* begin
# with "/", the value of ServerRoot is prepended -- so "log/foo_log"
# with ServerRoot set to "/usr" will be interpreted by the
# server as "/usr/log/foo_log".

                          [ Read 500 lines ]

^G Get Help  ^O WriteOut  ^R Read File ^Y Prev Page ^K Cut Text   ^C Cur Pos
^X Exit      ^J Justify   ^W Where Is  ^V Next Page ^U UnCut Text ^T To Spell
```

Now your primary goal in this file is to set up and enable PHP. To do this you need to scroll down to the directive that loads the PHP module. By default this should be on line 117. You can use the Ctrl+Shift+_ keyboard shortcut to invoke the `Enter line number, column number:` command in nano and enter 117 to go directly to line 117. Alternatively, just scroll down using the down-arrow key until you reach the part of the file that looks like this:

```
LoadModule alias_module libexec/apache2/mod_alias.so
LoadModule rewrite_module libexec/apache2/mod_rewrite.so
#LoadModule perl_module libexec/apache2/mod_perl.so
#LoadModule php5_module libexec/apache2/libphp5.so
#LoadModule hfs_apple_module libexec/apache2/mod_hfs_apple.so

<IfModule !mpm_netware_module>
```

The line that reads `#LoadModule php5_module libexec/apache2/libphp5.so` is the line you're interested in. Once you're there, place the cursor in front of the # at the beginning of the line and delete it (with the Delete key). That's it. Now hit Ctrl+X to exit. Upon exiting you'll be asked if you want to save the buffer (geek speak for "save the file"). Press Y for yes, then Enter to accept httpd.conf as the name you want to save it as. Finished!

> **NOTE** nano is one of the command-line options for text editors available to Mac OS X users. You could also choose to use vi (or vim) or emacs, both of which are significantly more powerful then nano, but both also present a much steeper learning curve, one that isn't appropriate for this discussion. If you already know and wish to use one of these other text editors, it'll work just fine.

Now, to make sure everything works right, start Apache (or restart it) with the following command:

```
$ sudo apachectl graceful
```

> **NOTE** Prior to Mountain Lion you could control Apache by selecting the Web Sharing option in the Sharing System Preference pane. This, to much criticism, was removed for Mountain Lion. Apple feels that if you really must run a web server, you'd be better served by loading OS X Server ($19.99) from the App Store.

If you inadvertently created any errors in your httpd.conf file, you may receive an error here. If so, compare your httpd.conf file to your httpd.conf.orig backup and see if there are any changes other than removing the # from the PHP LoadModule line.

If you see nothing, you're probably in good shape. Try opening http://localhost in a web browser. If you get a web page that by default says "It Works!" you're in good shape; Apache is running.

SERVING WEB FILES FROM YOUR OWN SITES DIRECTORY

There's one more configuration step for files so you can easily create and serve web pages from a Sites folder in your Home folder. The first thing is to go to your Home folder in the Finder (once you're in the Finder, the Command+Shift+H keyboard shortcut will take you directly to your Home folder) and create a new folder called Sites. This is where you'll create your web files.

> **NOTE** The editing of the httpd-userdir.conf file isn't necessary on OS X prior to Mountain Lion.

Now upon restarting Apache (with the apachectl graceful command), Apache will immediately recognize your folder, but if you try to access it through a web browser, you'll get an error. The reason for this is Apache has very restrictive default directory settings as a security precaution. To override this for user directories you need to edit the httpd-userdir.conf file. To open the file for editing, use this command:

```
$ sudo nano /etc/apache2/extra/httpd-userdir.conf
```

You may or may not be prompted for your password depending on when you last used sudo.

Once the httpd.userdir.conf file is open, scroll to the bottom and add the following:

```
<Directory "/Users/*/Sites/">
    Options Indexes FollowSymLinks MultiViews
    AllowOverride None
    Order allow,deny
    Allow from all
</Directory>
```

Exit nano as you did before saving the revised httpd.userdir.conf file.

In short, this bit of code tells Apache that it has permission to look and serve content from any user's Sites folder.

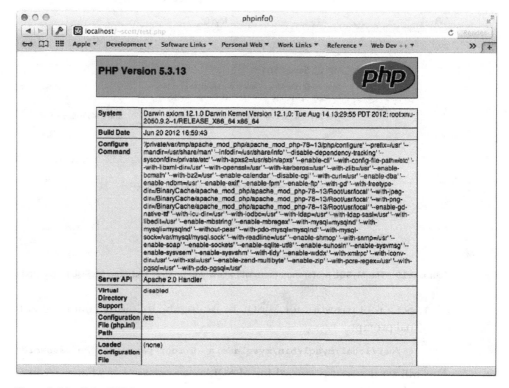

Figure C.18 **If the PHP info page shows up, Apache is configured and running properly.**

To test everything and make sure it all works, type the following at the terminal prompt:

```
$ echo "<? phpinfo() ?>" > ~/Sites/test.php
$ sudo apachectl graceful
```

Then point your web browser to http://localhost/~user/test.php (where *user* is replaced by your username). The resulting web page should look like figure C.18.

C.3.2 *Installing MySQL on Mac OS X*

The easiest way to get MySQL up and running on your Mac is as follows:

1 Go to the MySQL website and download the latest version of MySQL community edition (http://www.mysql.com/downloads/mysql). If you're running Mountain Lion (which is a 64-bit OS), then the appropriate version to download is the X86, 64-bit version of MySQL in DMG format. Once the disk image is downloaded, open it and right-click the MySQL installer package and select Open. This will install MySQL into your /usr/local/ directory. For convenience, right-click the MySQL.prefPane item on the disk image, and select Open. This will install a preference pane, allowing you to control MySQL from the System Preferences (see figure C.19).

2 Start MySQL (click the Start MySQL Server button in the Control Panel).

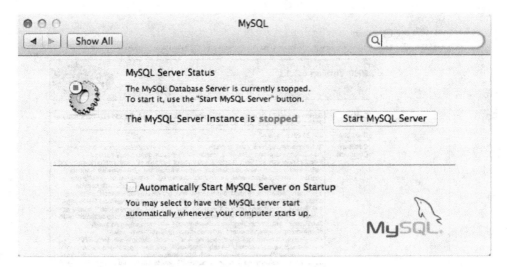

Figure C.19 The MySQL preference pane will allow you to start and stop MySQL as needed.

3 Set a root password for MySQL by issuing the following command at the terminal prompt:

```
$ /usr/local/mysql/bin/mysqladmin -u root password "newpassword"
```

This will set the root password for MySQL to *newpassword* or whatever you put in the quotes (remember it!).

That completes the basic configuration of MySQL (easy!). Now you can invoke the MySQL client from the command prompt using

```
$ /usr/local/mysql/bin/mysql -u root -p
```

and entering your password when prompted.

C.3.3 *Getting MySQL and PHP to play nice together*

There's one frustrating issue with getting PHP and MySQL to play nice together in Mac OS X: the location of mysql.sock. mysql.sock is a Unix socket file that allows bidirectional communication between MySQL and any other local application. In the case of our sample application, we want PHP and MySQL to talk to each other, but if you look at the PHP info (using your test.php web page from before), you'll see that PHP is looking for mysql.sock in /var/mysql, whereas the actual mysql.sock file is by default in /tmp/. What to do?

There are four ways to fix this. Read through the options and decide which is the sanest approach for you.

- Create the /var/mysql directory (sudo `mkdir` /var/mysql) and create a symbolic link from /tmp/mysql.sock to /var/mysql/mysql.sock (with: sudo `ln -s` /tmp/mysql.sock /var/mysql/mysql.sock). This method is easiest but a bit of a hack.

- Edit the /etc/php.ini file (it may not exist, in which case just `sudo cp /etc/php.ini.default /etc/php.ini`) so that `pdo_mysql.default_socket=/tmp/mysql.sock` (by default line 1065), `mysql.default_socket = /tmp/mysql.sock` (by default line 1219), and `mysqli.default_socket = /tmp/mysql.sock` (by default line 1278). This method is the easiest *real* way.

- Edit (or create) /etc/my.cnf, adding the following lines: `[mysqld] socket=/var/mysql/mysql.sock [client] socket=/var/mysql/mysql.sock`. This will tell MySQL to create its socket where Mac OS X's default PHP is looking for it. Next, you also need to create the /var/mysql directory *and* `sudo chown mysql /var/mysql` it, or MySQL won't start because it won't be able to create the socket. (Various sample my.cnf files can be found in /usr/local/mysql/support-files.) This method isn't too bad, but it could cause issues with other MySQL clients that look for the socket in /tmp/mysql.sock.

- Recompile `php` for your version of MySQL. This method, although a pain, isn't a terrible idea; it's actually the best fix although clearly neither fast nor easy.

Pick the way that works for you and do it. When you've finished, your computer will be ready to serve up MySQL-driven, PHP-based web apps—including the sample app in chapter 4.

appendix D
Computer networking primer

The client-server model is the foundation of the web: Your browser is the client, servers sit out in the internet cloud, and computer networking is how they talk to each other. JavaScript can only do so much by itself; most web applications are still built around the communication back to the web server. The fundamentals of computer networking—and terminology like headers, latency, throughput, and polling—are covered in most undergraduate computer science programs, but because web development attracts people from a broad range of backgrounds, this appendix assumes you've not been through a program like that. Here, we'll introduce you to the following concepts:

- The basics of computer networking
- The overhead of headers
- Two important network performance metrics: latency and throughput
- Polling versus event-driven communications
- Server-side choices for event-driven web applications
- The WebSocket protocol

Along the way, you'll also briefly review the hacks used in HTML4 to avoid the particular performance trade-offs inherent in the fundamental web protocol, HTTP. For starters, if you're not sure what *real-time web development* even means, this appendix will provide some context.

D.1 The basics of computer networking

Computer networks have both hardware and software components. Physically, they're wires, fiber optics, or radio waves, but in software they're defined by what's

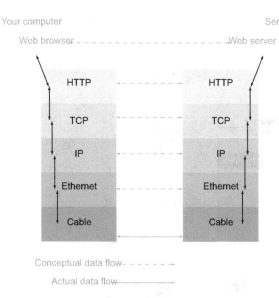

Figure D.1 A network stack.
Conceptually, each layer
communicates directly with its
counterpart on another computer.
In reality, the data flow is down the
stack, across the physical wires,
and back up the other stack.

called a *protocol*. The physical wires transmit pure bits of data, zeros and ones; it's the protocols that give those bits wider meaning.

· To keep life simple, the software protocols are divided into layers. At the "bottom" of the stack are things like Ethernet, which is a protocol for pushing bits along wires by dividing them into packets. Above that sit protocols like the Internet Protocol (IP), which can deal with routing messages across several Ethernet connections. On top of this are protocols such as the Transmission Control Protocol (TCP), which deals with keeping track of which messages have been sent, which have been received, when to consider a message lost and repeat it, and what order they should all be in when they arrive. It's only once you get above TCP that you hit protocols like HTTP, which was designed specifically for passing web pages around.

When writing a web server it's not necessary to consider how to communicate with different types of network hardware. It doesn't need different methods for sending messages across Ethernet or Wi-Fi. All it needs to know is how to describe HTTP requests to the TCP layer of the local network stack.

Figure D.1 shows this arrangement in pictorial form.

This arrangement allows communication to be conceptually simple. Applications that want to talk HTTP only need to know about HTTP and not all the other layers. But this simplicity doesn't come without cost. Each layer needs to add some information to what's being transmitted—this information generally can be referred to as *headers*, and you'll learn more about them in the next section.

D.2 *The overhead of headers*

Figure D.2 focuses on exactly what's going on at the interchange between the layers, when data needs to be passed from an application over HTTP and down the network

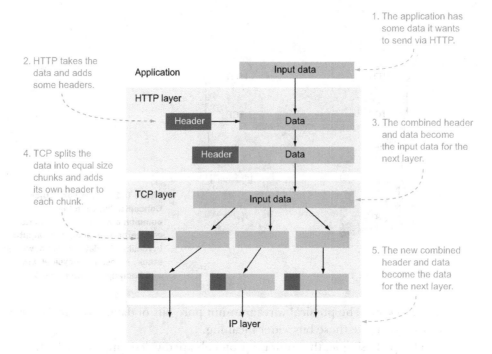

1. The application has some data it wants to send via HTTP.

2. HTTP takes the data and adds some headers.

Application

Input data

HTTP layer

Header → Data

3. The combined header and data become the input data for the next layer.

Header   Data

4. TCP splits the data into equal size chunks and adds its own header to each chunk.

TCP layer

Input data

5. The new combined header and data become the data for the next layer.

IP layer

Figure D.2   Each layer adds header information and passes the data down the stack.

stack. At each stage, a small amount of information is added to allow the receiving layer to understand what the data is and what it's for.

The HTTP, TCP, and later IP layers each add a different type of header information. The TCP and IP header information is binary data. In binary data each of the headers can be represented by the minimum number of bits—if there are only four possible values, then only 2 bits need to be used. HTTP headers are plain text, which makes them easy to read but more verbose. The smallest possible theoretical header is a single-character label, a colon, and a single-character value. In ASCII encoding this adds up to 24 bits. Most labels and values are made up of several letters, and each HTTP request has several headers attached, with the result that most HTTP requests attach between 0.7 and 2 kilobytes of headers. This is one of the disadvantages of HTTP for data communication. If a single chat message needs to be sent, and the message is only 20 or 30 bytes, it needs to be sent with all this extra data.

In network performance terms we talk about *throughput* (or bandwidth): the amount of data that the server can send per second. If the server is limited to a throughput of 10 kilobytes per second, then it can deliver around 10 HTTP responses per second. If it only had to send the chat data, it would be able to send about 330 chat messages. From a slightly different point of view, an application based on thousands of users receiving small, real-time updates will need 33 times as many servers if you send that data over HTTP than if you're just sending the chat data.

Throughput is only one measure of network performance. In the next section you'll consider the other key factor, latency.

D.3   *Network performance metrics: latency and throughput*

Throughput, the amount of raw data that can be transferred in a given time period, is only one aspect of networking performance. The other key factor is *latency*: the time it takes for a single bit of data to travel between two computers. Latency is important when you expect to have a lot of requests, and those requests depend on one or more of the previous requests completing.

In the previous section you learned that all the extra headers used by HTTP impact the throughput. You have every right to wonder, then, why bother with them. One reason is to improve latency. All of those headers include information about caching. This allows a browser to only download a resource, such as an image or a style sheet, a single time and then reuse the cached version for every other page that uses it. For any users who visit more than one page on your site, this means fewer network requests and therefore lower latency.

For transferring small and largely independent portions of data, all of these extra headers are a waste. The data is unique; otherwise, there's no point sending it, which means you've nothing to gain from caching.

That's not the only problem with using HTTP for data transfer. What if the client only wants to check to see if there's new data available, a process known as *polling*? Each poll will come with all the baggage of those HTTP headers. Polling can be inefficient to start with, which makes it a poor choice for real-time applications. The next section will examine this issue in more detail.

D.4   *Polling vs. event-driven*

The phrase "real-time web" has become fashionable in recent years. Although it's based on a number of trends, the real-time web embodies a shift from the traditional client polling approach in web applications to a more *event-driven* approach. Instead of clients deciding when to ask the server if there's new information, the server sends new information to the client when it's ready.

Event-driven approaches are far more efficient than polling. This section will demonstrate that point with a series of timeline diagrams. Figure D.3 illustrates an optimum case for polling.

Even with the optimum polling solution you'll still have polls when there's no data, and for other polls data will be available for nearly the full length of time between polls. And the optimum polling solution is hard to achieve. The average chat room will have busy periods and quiet periods, and when those occur depends on the confluence of schedules of people living thousands of miles apart. It's more likely the application will spend more time in the degenerate cases (see figure D.4).

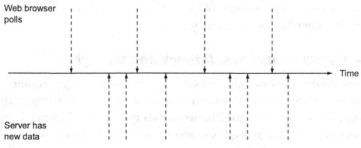

Figure D.3   The optimum case for polling: new data is available regularly, and the frequency of the new data being available is similar to the number of polls.

The solution is to switch from polling to event-driven communication, as illustrated in figure D.5. Then the server, which knows when the information is available, is in charge of when information is delivered.

Event-driven communication is clearly more efficient because it exactly matches the frequency of communication with the frequency of the availability of new data. With no built-in support for event-driven messaging, web developers who wanted to avoid the use of plug-ins have resorted to two HTML/JavaScript hacks to simulate it: long polling and the forever frame.

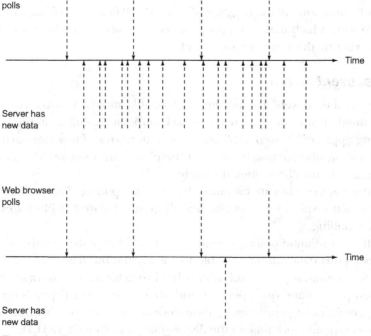

Figure D.4   The worst cases for polling: top—when new data is available far more frequently than it's polled for; bottom—when polling happens far more frequently than there's data available.

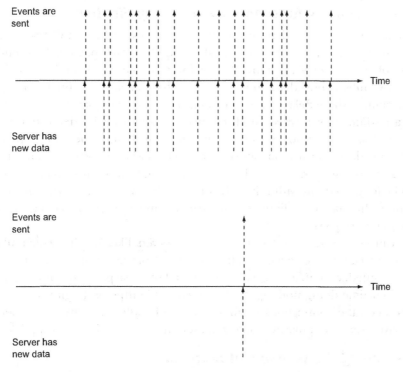

Figure D.5 Having event-driven communication means data is sent exactly as often and exactly when it becomes available. Data is received without any wasted requests or delays.

Long polling allows for an increased chance of instantaneous updates by being purposefully slow in responding to a request. Instead of responding to a request immediately, the server holds the connection open and waits until there's new data. As soon as the browser receives the new data, another long poll is initiated.

The *forever frame* is a way of loading a web page slowly. The web page is loaded into a hidden iframe element. Instead of delivering all the content as quickly as possible, the server sends a chunk at a time, as updates become available. In the main page, the iframe is repeatedly scanned for new content.

Long polling approximates event-driven communication, but each request still requires a full set of HTTP headers. The forever frame approach requires the headers to be sent only once, but it still requires a lot of messing around in client code to check the contents of the frame to see if they've been updated.

Server-sent events (SSE) work along the same lines as forever frames, except the browser has a convenient API that's similar to the cross-document and channel-messaging APIs you've already seen.

D.5   Server-side choices for event-driven web applications

The two new event-driven, client-server APIs in HTML5 are SSEs and WebSocket. Event-driven, client-server approaches are ideal for applications that need to send small amounts of data quickly to many clients; for example, stock-trading applications, where a few milliseconds' delay in updating can have measurable financial impact, or network gaming where delays (or lag) can make the game unplayable.

On a traditional web server, each connection is allocated a dedicated thread or process (a flow of execution within a program), which suits the model where each connection is data-intensive but short lived, such as when a web page and its linked resources are being downloaded. Event-driven communication expects the connections to be long lived but with relatively little activity. When each thread is assigned a connection, the maximum limit is soon reached and the server becomes unable to respond to new requests.

This can be a problem for traditional web servers like Apache, which allocate a process or thread per connection. The number of processes or threads that can be created is limited, even if, as is usually the case, all of those processes or threads spend most of their time doing nothing. Servers such as Lighttpd and nginx share the processes between the connections to allow them to handle a far larger number; these servers have risen in popularity along with event-driven, real-time web applications.

D.6   Understanding the WebSocket protocol

The WebSocket protocol allows bare-bones networking between clients and servers with little overhead—certainly far less overhead than the previously more common approach of attempting to tunnel other protocols through HTTP. With WebSockets it's possible to package your data using the appropriate protocol, the eXtensible Messaging and Presence Protocol (XMPP) for chat, for example, but benefit from the strengths of HTTP, which, like MasterCard, is accepted nearly everywhere.

D.6.1   WebSocket protocol vs. WebSocket API

The specifications for WebSockets are split into two parts. The WebSocket protocol describes what browser vendors and servers have to implement behind the scenes; it's the protocol used at the network layer to establish and maintain socket connections and pass data through them. The WebSocket API describes the interface that needs to be available in the DOM so that WebSockets can be used from JavaScript.

The Internet Engineering Task Force (IETF) maintains the specification for the WebSocket protocol. This is the same organization that manages the specifications for HTTP, TCP, and IP.

WHATWG maintains the specification for the WebSocket API in concert with W3C, the same as for the HTML5 specification itself.

D.6.2   *The WebSocket protocol*

Like parts of the HTML5 specification, the WebSocket protocol spent many months under heavy development, but unlike HTML5, the versions that the client and server are using need to match for everything to work.

The WebSocket protocol describes, in detail, the exact steps a client and server take to establish a WebSocket connection, exchange messages, and ultimately close the WebSocket. To make a node, or any web server, accept WebSocket connections, you need to implement the WebSocket protocol. In this section you'll get an overview of how that protocol works. The following listing is a set of HTTP headers that the browser will send to the server in order to initiate a WebSocket connection.

Listing D.1   The WebSocket handshake

This header is a base64-encoded string (decoded, this one reads "the sample nonce"). The decoded string must be 16 bytes long. It will be transformed by the server and returned to the browser for security verification in listing D.2.

The format is intentionally modeled after HTTP requests; to web servers, routers, proxies, and other web infrastructure this request should look like a normal HTTP request.

```
GET /chat HTTP/1.1
Host: server.example.com
Upgrade: websocket
Connection: Upgrade
Sec-WebSocket-Key: dGhlIHNhbXBsZSBub25jZQ==
Origin: http://example.com
Sec-WebSocket-Protocol: chat.example.com, chatplus.example.com
Sec-WebSocket-Version: 13
```

These headers indicate to the server that you're expecting an upgrade from HTTP to WebSocket.

The WebSocket protocol version the web browser is expecting; for hybi-I7 the version is I3 because hybi-I3 was the last version where a noncompatible change was made.

The list of subprotocols the browser understands; the protocol the application will be using across the Web Socket—these are application-specific and the whole header is optional.

This tells the server where the script making the WebSocket request originated, allowing cross-domain requests to be blocked if necessary.

A typical server response is shown in the next listing.

Listing D.2   The server response

The web server announces that it has accepted the upgrade request.

```
HTTP/1.1 101 Switching Protocols
Upgrade: websocket
Connection: Upgrade
Sec-WebSocket-Accept: s3pPLMBiTxaQ9kYGzzhZRbK+xOo=
Sec-WebSocket-Protocol: chat.example.com
```

The upgrade headers are echoed back.

Response to the Sec-WebSocket-Key header in listing D.I. The string 258EAFA5-E9I4-47DA-95CA-C5AB0DC85BII is appended to the value; it's hashed with SHA-I and then base64-encoded again and placed in this field.

Of the subprotocols listed by the client, this is the one the server understands.

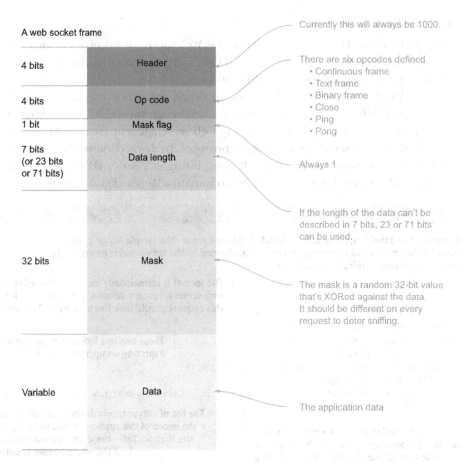

Figure D.6   Diagram of a WebSocket frame—the non-data parts take up only 48 bits, equivalent to six characters.

Once the handshake is complete, data exchange can begin. The messages in WebSockets are sent in what are referred to as frames. Figure D.6 shows the structure of a frame. Frames are a lightweight container for the data with minimal binary headers. The overhead per message is only 6 bytes.

D.6.3   *WebSocket browser support*

Although the protocol is well-defined, let's review further complications. The WebSocket protocol was only finalized in spring 2012. Before that, seven different versions of it had seen some browser support. Table D.1 shows the different versions and the browsers that support each of them.

Table D.1 lists only the versions where noncompatible changes were made. But you can see from the numbers in the table that there have been many versions of the specification, up to version 76 when the specification was still maintained by WHATWG (hixie-76), which then became the initial version of the IETF-maintained specification.

Table D.1 WebSocket protocol versions and browser support

WebSocket protocol version					
hixie-75	4				5.0.0
hixie-76 / hybi-00	6	4 (disabled)		11 (disabled)	5.0.1 (and iOS5)
hybi-06			8/9 (add-on)		
hybi-07		6			
hybi-09			8/9 (add-on)		
hybi-10	14	7	10 (DP1)		
hybi-17 / RFC 6455	16	11	10	12.50	6.0, iOS6

It has since seen 17 further revisions before finally being released as RFC 6455. The client passes the version it understands in the initial request (listing D.1). On the server side you can decide whether or not to support the version the client understands. Obviously, the more versions you choose to support, the more work you have to do on the server.

appendix E
Setting up Node.js

This appendix is provided for readers who need to set up Node.js for the chapter 4 application. You might be wondering why we chose Node.js. There are several alternative web servers that are much better suited to WebSockets than the traditional choices of Apache or IIS (IIS8 will have built-in WebSocket support). These servers share connections between threads, taking advantage of the mostly idle nature of event-driven connections. In chapter 4, you'll be using Node.js for two reasons:

- It uses JavaScript, which you're already familiar with.
- It has an easy-to-use library implementing the WebSocket protocol.

This appendix will walk you through installing and setting up Node.js for the chapter 4 application. You'll also learn how to build basic web applications with Node.js and how to use the Node Package Manager (NPM). NPM lets you easily install modules to extend the functionality of Node. You'll also create a simple application to confirm that the modules are installed correctly.

E.1 Setting up Node.js to serve web content

Node.js is an event-driven web server based on the V8 JavaScript engine, which is part of the Google Chrome browser. The basic process for installing Node is to download the source code and compile it. For Linux and Unix users, this isn't an unfamiliar approach, but this may come as a bit of a shock to Windows users. For Windows, a prebuilt binary is available from the installation page: https://github.com/joyent/node/wiki/Installation.

Even if you're using the prebuilt binaries, the prerequisites mentioned on the installation page are still required because they're used in the installation of modules (which you'll look at in E.2). Unfortunately, the installation page doesn't do a very good job of explicitly stating the requirements for each platform; table E.1 summarizes the prerequisites for all the major platforms.

Table E.1   Node.js prerequisites by platform

Platform	Prerequisites
Linux	GCC 4.x.x; GNU make 3.81 or newer; Python 2.6 or 2.7
Unix/BSD	GCC 4.x.x; GNU make 3.81 or newer; Python 2.6 or 2.7; libexecinfo
Mac	Xcode 4.5; GNU make 3.81 or newer; Python 2.6 or 2.7
Windows	Visual Studio 2010 or Visual C++ 2010 Express; Python 2.6 or 2.7

Once you've installed your prerequisites correctly you can get started. This appendix will walk you through a few simple example Node applications, which will confirm that your installation is correct and let you see how common web application scenarios are handled in Node.

E.1.1   Create a Node Hello World application

In this section you'll build, in two steps, the traditional Hello World application shown in figure E.1. You'll generate a page entirely dynamically using JavaScript.

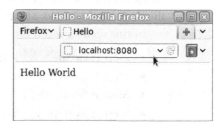

Figure E.1   Node says "Hello World."

STEP 1: CREATE A NODE APPLICATION

The first listing is a simple Hello World application for Node, as shown in figure E.1. Create a file called app.js in your working directory and place this code into it.

Listing E.1   Node Hello World

```
var http = require('http');      ◄─┐  Most functionality in Node is implemented through a
                                      system of modules; here the built-in http module is loaded.

http.createServer(function(request, response) {   ◄─┐
    response.writeHead(200);
    response.write("<!DOCTYPE html>");   ◄─             The http module has a create
    response.write("<html>");                          server method, which is passed
    response.write("<head>");                          a handler function that will be
    response.write("<title>Hello</title>");            called when requests are made.
    response.write("</head>");
    response.write("<body>");                  The response itself is a simple
    response.write("Hello World");             web page; each line is explicitly
    response.write("</body>");                 written into the response.
    response.write("</html>");
    response.end();                   ◄─┐  After the server is created, it's set to listen on
}).listen(8080);                  ◄─      port 8080; any requests to http://localhost:8080
                                          will now be passed to the handler function.
```

The end() method indicates that the content is complete.

STEP 2: RUN A NODE APPLICATION

After you've created your app.js file you should be able to start Node. Issue a command like the following from your shell or command prompt, making sure you're in your working directory (you may need to log off and back on for the Node folder to be added to your path):

```
node app.js
```

This command will start Node running in the current directory using the file app.js to determine behavior. Start the Node server with the command shown previously. Once the Node server is running, point your browser at http://localhost:8080/ and re-create figure E.1.

E.1.2   Serving static files with Node

Node is a bare-bones web server, which means many things you might take for granted with more traditional web servers won't happen in Node, unless you write code to make them happen. For instance, Node won't transparently transfer any static files that happen to be sitting in the execution directory. If you want a file called index.html to be sent to the browser in response to a request, it's up to you to detect the requested URL, locate the file, and then send it in response.

In this section you'll create, in four steps, a static file and serve it with Node:

- Step 1: Create a static file.
- Step 2: Load a file from a disk.
- Step 3: Send the file to the browser.
- Step 4: Run the application.

The end result will look identical to what you achieved in the previous section, but the architecture will be improved because your display rendering is separated from your application logic.

STEP 1: CREATE A STATIC FILE
The next listing is a simple index.html file—place it in a new working directory.

Listing E.2   A static index.html file

```
<!DOCTYPE html>
<html>
<head>
    <title>Hello</title>
</head>
<body>
Hello world
</body>
</html>
```

STEP 2: LOAD A FILE FROM A DISK
Now that you have a static HTML file, you need to load it from a disk. Node has a built-in module for reading files from a disk called fs. You can use the fs.readFile() method to load a file. Create a new app.js file in your working directory and add the code from the following listing.

Listing E.3 An app.js file that reads a file from a disk

```
var http = require('http');
var fs = require('fs');                                    To read from the filesystem,
                                                           the fs module is needed.
http.createServer(function(request, response) {
    fs.readFile('./index.html', function(error, content) {    Two parameters
        //Code to handle the file goes here                   are required for
    });                                        In the next    readFile(), a path to a
}).listen(8080);                               step you'll fill file and a function that
                                               in this code.  will be called after the
                                                              file has been read.
```

STEP 3: SEND THE FILE TO THE BROWSER

After the `readFile()` function has completed, your callback function will execute; you need to check that the file was read successfully and send it to the browser. You can use the same `http` module methods from section E.1.1 to do this. Replace the comment in listing E.3 with the code in the following listing.

Listing E.4 Sending the file to the browser in app.js

```
if (error) {
    response.writeHead(500);              If there's an error reading the file,
    response.end();                       it will be handled gracefully here...
} else {
    response.writeHead(200,
        { 'Content-Type': 'text/html' });    ...otherwise, send
    response.end(content, 'utf-8');           the file to the user.
}
```

STEP 4: RUN THE APPLICATION

Just as in the last example, start your application from the co

```
node app.js
```

Point your browser at http://localhost:8080/ and   the Hello World page.

Serving static files isn't interesting in and of i   namic files, as in section E.1.1, isn't practical either; in a real ,   nt your web designers attempting to edit HTML and CSS insi   ication logic. You need to be able to mix static content with t   ation logic, and you'll look at that in the next section.

E.1.3 Serving mixed static and dynamic content with Node

In this section you're going to create an HTML template file with placeholders that will be replaced with dynamic values when the page is requested.

STEP 1: CREATE A STATIC TEMPLATE WITH PLACEHOLDERS

The index.html template is shown in the next listing. It's identical to the previous index.html file, apart from the added placeholder for the dynamic variable. Create a new working directory and place this index.html file into it.

Listing E.5   A simple template index.html

```html
<!DOCTYPE html>
<html>
<head>
    <title>Hello</title>
</head>
<body>
Hello world {0}
</body>
</html>
```

{0} is a placeholder for your dynamic content.

STEP 2: MIX DYNAMIC CONTENT INTO YOUR TEMPLATE

The following listing inserts dynamic values into a static template file using the standard JavaScript `String.Replace` function. Create an app.js file in your working directory and add this code to it.

Listing E.6   Mixing static and dynamic content in app.js

```javascript
var http = require("http");
var fs = require("fs");
var inc = 0;

http.createServer(function(request, response) {
    fs.readFile('./index.html', function(error, content) {
        if (error) {
            response.writeHead(500);
            response.end();
        } else {
            response.writeHead(200, { 'Content-Type': 'text/html' });
            response.end(
                content.toString().replace(/\{0\}/g,++inc),
                'utf-8'
            );
        }
    });
}).listen(8080);
```

The file is loaded as before.

A simple dynamic page is implemented by replacing all instances of {0} with the value of a pre-incremented inc.

STEP 3: TEST IN THE BROWSER

Start Node with your new app.js file as you did in the previous examples, and load the page in the browser. Each time the page gets refreshed in the browser, the variable should get incremented once. You can expect the number on the page to increase by one with every page load. Let's try it in real time in a few browsers. Figure E.2 shows the results.

You may be scratching your head at this result—we certainly did. Chrome's Network tab in its developer tools shows only a single request, so why does the variable get incremented twice? The answer is that Chrome makes an additional request that it doesn't tell you about for `favicon.ico`. In case you're not familiar with it, `favicon.ico` is the standard name for the little icon that appears alongside the URL in the address bar. Because your Node server is configured to respond to every request with

Each time the page is
loaded in Firefox, the
variable increments once.

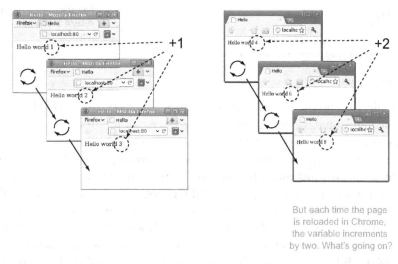

But each time the page
is reloaded in Chrome,
the variable increments
by two. What's going on?

Figure E.2 **The results of reloading the simple dynamic page in Firefox and Chrome**

the same HTML file, it sends that file in response to the request for favicon.ico, too. This results in the variable being incremented twice.

To stop this from happening, you need a way to route requests for different URLs to different server responses. This is called *routing* and will be the subject of the next section.

E.1.4 Routing: serving different files for different URLs

Routing is the matching up of the URL requested by the browser with the appropriate response from the server. The following listing demonstrates a simple approach.

Listing E.7 Simple routing app.js example

```
var http = require("http");
var fs = require("fs");
var inc = 0;

http.createServer(
function(request, response) {
    if (request.url === '/index.html' || request.url === '/') {
        fs.readFile('./index.html', function(error, content) {
            if (error) {
                response.writeHead(500);
                response.end();
            } else {
                response.writeHead(200, { 'Content-Type': 'text/html' });
                response.end(
```

Only respond with the file to requests for index.html or the default document.

```
                    content.toString().replace(/\{0\}/g,++inc),
                    'utf-8'
            );
        }
    });
} else {
    response.writeHead(404);
    console.log(request.url + ' not found');
}
}).listen(8080);
```

For any other request, return a 404 not found error.

The example increments the variable only once for every page reload in Chrome, because the index.html is sent only to explicit requests for it or for the root document.

In this section, we've provided a low-level understanding of how Node handles web applications. In real life, you don't want to spend hours figuring out how to do things such as sending each individual file to your users, or slicing up your data to fit into WebSocket frames, or keeping up with all the changes in the specification. To avoid repeatedly doing the boring stuff in Node.js, you need more modules. But the modules you'll need aren't included as standard with Node like http and fs that you've already used. In the next section, you'll learn how to go above and beyond the standard set of modules by downloading third-party modules using the Node Package Manager (NPM).

E.2   Easy web apps with Node modules

In the previous section, you explored several functions that need to be performed in Node in order to create real web applications: placing dynamic content inside static files (or templating) and mapping requests at different URLs to appropriate handlers (or routing). But you also need to handle WebSocket requests. That was the point of installing Node in the first place. If you looked at the explanation of the WebSocket protocol in appendix D, you know that handling WebSockets involves a lot of slicing and dicing of binary data. This is hardly the use case for which JavaScript was designed. You don't want to spend all your time dealing with low-level stuff like that when you could be writing applications. All of this can be more easily accomplished in Node by taking advantage of third-party modules. In this section we'll set you up with the following modules:

- *Director*—for routing
- *Mustache*—for templating
- *WebSocket-Node*—for the WebSocket protocol

You can easily manage modules with the NPM script. Because modules have become fundamental to using Node, NPM, once a handy add-on, now comes as part of the main Node.js distribution.

It's easy to install the modules; Node looks for them in the node_modules directory of the current directory. This will be the same place where your app.js file is

Figure E.3 Application file
layout with modules installed

located, so make sure you're in that directory before installing modules. Then, run
these commands:

```
npm install director
npm install mustache
npm install websocket
```

Modules are now installed local to your application, and you have a file structure like
that shown in figure E.3.

Now you're going to create an application
that's going to try loading all three of these modules and show a message if it is successful. This
will tell you the modules have been installed
correctly. The result is shown in figure E.4.

The following listing is the app.js file in figure E.3. Create a new working directory and
add app.js to it. When you run it with Node,
it'll attempt to load all the modules you've
installed and create a simple page.

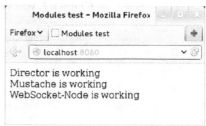

Figure E.4 If you see this page,
everything is working correctly.

Listing E.8   An app.js using Director, Mustache, and WebSocket-Node

```
var http = require("http");
var director = require("director");          When installed with NPM, add-on
var mustache = require("mustache");          modules are referenced in the
var WebSocketServer = require('websocket').server;   same way as built-in modules.

var template = '<!DOCTYPE html>\n'           Instead of emitting the markup
          + '<html>\n'                        directly, we'll use this variable to
          + '<head>\n'                        store a template for mustache.
          + '<title>Modules test</title>\n'   In later examples you'll load the
          + '</head>\n'                        template from disk.
          + '<body>\n'
          + 'Director is {{director_status}}<br>\n'
          + 'Mustache is {{mustache_status}}<br>\n'
          + 'WebSocket-Node is {{socket_status}}\n'
          + '</body>\n'
          + '</html>';
```

```
var dict = {
    'director_status': director.http.Router ? 'working':'broken',
    'mustache_status': mustache.to_html ? 'working':'broken',
    'socket_status' : typeof WebSocketServer !== 'undefined'
                    ? 'working':'broken'
};

var html = mustache.to_html(template,dict);

http.createServer(
    function(request, response) {
        response.writeHead(200);
        response.write(html);
        response.end();
    }
).listen(8080);
```

This object restores the results of a few simple tests, which confirm all the modules loaded correctly.

Mustache is the only module this example uses.

If everything has gone according to plan, you should see a page similar to that shown in figure E.4 when you fire up Node and browse to port 8080.

Now that you know everything is installed correctly you're ready to build your first WebSocket application. If you came to this appendix from the build prerequisites (section 4.2) in chapter 4, you can head back to that chapter and continue with the build.

appendix F
Channel messaging

Channel messaging is similar to cross-document messaging (see chapter 4) except instead of one message channel per window, it allows multiple channels to be created. This is useful if you want to build the page out of a number of loosely coupled, event-driven, independent components. Rather than adapt them all to share a single cross-document messaging interface and ensure they don't clash with each other's internal API for message formats, each component can have its own set of private channels.

Channel messaging   4   ~   10   11   5

In the next few pages you'll build a simple test bed by setting up a page that loads a document from a different domain. You can easily fake running multiple domains from your own computer, and in this section you'll walk through setting up two pages on your computer that run from different domains. One page will load the other in an iframe, and you'll use channel messaging to communicate between the two. Figure F.1 shows the test bed after channel messaging has occurred. You can use the textboxes to create the messages, and any message received will be added to the document.

You can build the example by following these five steps:

- Step 1: Install a local development web server.
- Step 2: Set up a cross-domain test environment.
- Step 3: Create the example pages.
- Step 4: Add JavaScript to the first page.
- Step 5: Add JavaScript to the second page.

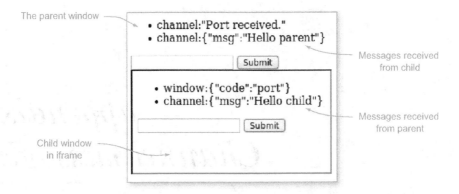

Figure F.1   A simple channel-messaging example, such as the one you'll build in chapter 4's listings 4.5 and 4.6

STEP 1: INSTALL A LOCAL DEVELOPMENT WEB SERVER

You'll need to be able to serve web pages from your local machine. In other words, you need to have a web server. If you already have one, please skip ahead; otherwise, follow along, and we'll review some easy options:

Windows	Microsoft Visual Web Developer Express comes with a built-in web server. You can easily create a web application project and place the files you create in the next section within it. See the download pages at http://mng.bz/gu1b for further details.
Mac	Go into System Preferences > Sharing, and check the Web Sharing box. The default folder is /Library/WebServer/Documents/.
Linux	Most Linux distributions come with Python already installed, and Python includes the `SimpleHTTPServer` module. To start it, open a command prompt and set the current directory to the one containing your files; then issue the command `python -m SimpleHTTPServer 8000` to start a server listening on port 8000.

STEP 2: SET UP A CROSS-DOMAIN TEST ENVIRONMENT

To experiment with messaging between scripts in different domains, you need to have multiple domains available. The easiest way to do this is to fake some domains by editing the hosts file on your computer. On Windows this file is usually found at C:\Windows\System32\drivers\etc\hosts (note the lack of a file extension; also note that this is a system file, so run your editor as administrator); on Mac OS X and Linux it'll be found at /etc/hosts. Opening that file in a simple text editor should reveal some lines like the following:

```
127.0.0.1 localhost
```

Add your fake domains to the end of the line starting 127.0.0.1:

```
127.0.0.1 localhost domain1.com domain2.com
```

Now you can browse to http://domain1.com and http://domain2.com, and the pages will be served from your local web server.

STEP 3: CREATE THE EXAMPLE PAGES

First, you'll need two pages in your working directory. Call them example-1.html and example-2.html, and add the markup shown in the following listing to the body section. This markup is even simpler than the cross-document messaging example in chapter 4 because JavaScript will add the iframe.

Listing F.1 Channel messaging/example-1.html body content

```html
<ul id="log"></ul>
<form id="msgform">
    <input type="text" id="msg">
    <input type="submit">
</form>
```

STEP 4: ADD JAVASCRIPT TO THE FIRST PAGE

Now you need to add code to initiate the messaging.

Channel messaging works by creating a pair of ports. A port is a generic object that allows messaging. It supports the postMessage method and onmessage event that you're familiar with from cross-document messaging. Anything sent to one port will appear as output from the other port; in HTML5 terms they're described as *entangled*. This is by analogy to *quantum entanglement*: two particles that, no matter what distance separates them, change simultaneously. One of the ports is then sent to another script context. This could be a script in another document or window or a web worker. Listing F.2 shows the details. The code from listing F.2 should go in a <script> block after the form in example-1.html (you could add it in the head element, but then you'd need to wrap it in a function and execute it on the load event). As you can see, the channel-messaging API is similar to the cross-document messaging API you looked at in chapter 4.

Listing F.2 Channel messaging/example-1.html JavaScript

As with cross-document messaging, the second parameter is the domain the message is getting passed to.

```javascript
var f = document.getElementById('msgform');
var m = document.getElementById('msg');
var l = document.getElementById('log');

var channel = new MessageChannel();

var w = document.createElement('iframe');
document.body.appendChild(w);
w.setAttribute('src','http://domain2.com/example-2.html');
var sendPort = function() {
    w.contentWindow.postMessage({"code":"port"},
            'http://domain2.com',
            [channel.port2]);
}
w.addEventListener('load', sendPort, false)
```

For convenience, several global variables are set up; if this was more than a single-page example, it would be better to wrap this whole listing in a reusable object.

The MessageChannel constructor returns a pair of entangled ports.

Create an iframe element and load a document into it.

Here's the familiar postMessage function; the first argument is a string. The value used here isn't necessary, but it'll allow for easy detection in the other page.

The new parameter for channel messaging is an array of port objects; the second port from the MessageChannel is passed.

There's no point in sending the port if the document isn't loaded, so wait for the load event before sending the port.

```
var channel_message = function(e) {
    var li = document.createElement('li');
    li.appendChild(
        document.createTextNode(
            'channel:' + JSON.stringify(e.data)
        )
    );
    l.appendChild(li);
}
channel.port1.onmessage = channel_message;      ◀─
var send_message = function(e) {                ◀──
    var s = {};
    s.msg = m.value;
    channel.port1.postMessage(s);
    m.value = '';
    e.preventDefault();
}
f.addEventListener('submit', send_message, false);  ◀─
```

The first port of your channel is now entangled with the port sent to the other document, so to receive the messages you need to listen to the onmessage event.

Reversing that, if you use postMessage on the first port, the message will appear on the second port in the other document.

The send_message function is bound to the form's submit event to allow the user to send messages to the other document.

STEP 5: ADD THE JAVASCRIPT TO THE SECOND PAGE

Now you need to set up the second page to allow it to receive the port and then send and receive messages through it. The code from the next listing should go in a `<script>` block after the form in example-2.html.

Listing F.3 Channel messaging/example-2.html JavaScript

```
var f = document.getElementById('msgform');
var m = document.getElementById('msg');
var l = document.getElementById('log');
var port;                                         ◀──
var receive_port = function(e) {                  ◀──
    var d = typeof e.data === "string"
                    ? JSON.parse(e.data)
                    : e.data;
    if (d.code == "port") {                       ◀──
        port = e.ports[0];
        port.postMessage("Port received.");
        port.onmessage = function(e) {
            var d = typeof e.data === "string"
                            ? JSON.parse(e.data)
                            : e.data;
            var li = document.createElement('li');
            li.appendChild(
                document.createTextNode('channel:' + d)  ◀──
            );
            l.appendChild(li);
        }
        var send_message = function(e) {
            var s = {};
            s.msg = m.value;
            port.postMessage(s);
            m.value = '';
            e.preventDefault();
        }
```

Several global variables are set up, but this time there's no need to create a new MessagePort. Instead, a variable is created to store the port that will be sent to this window.

This function will be used when you're passed a message from another document.

Store a reference to the port in the global variable.

The convention is that if there's a message code of "port," then you should grab the attached port and use it for messaging. You don't have to use "port"; anything else would work as well, but it's here that you would start to define an API for clients.

Let the caller know the port has been received.

Attach a handler to the port message event.

Any messages received will be logged.

<table>
<tr><td>

Set up the form so the user can send messages back through the port.

</td><td>

```
        f.addEventListener('submit', send_message, false);
    }
    var li = document.createElement('li');
    li.appendChild(document.createTextNode('window:' + d));
    l.appendChild(li);
}
window.addEventListener('message', receive_port, false);
```

</td><td>

The fact that a message event has been handled is logged for the benefit of your audience.

The receive_port handler is bound to the window.

</td></tr>
</table>

Now you're ready to try to re-create figure F.1. If you've been following along, the URL should be similar to http://domain1.com:8000/example-1.html. The port number (8000) might be different, depending on which local web server you used; refer to the documentation for details.

appendix G
Tools and libraries

It's important to know what tools and libraries are available for developers looking to leverage HTML5 APIs. These can save time and make your projects less buggy. In this appendix, you'll find out about several tools for mobile and HTML5 applications.

G.1 Tools for mobile web applications

If you're an experienced web application developer, you'll probably be familiar with web and JavaScript frameworks that make your life easier when it comes to ensuring cross-browser compatibility with your code, or that reduce your workload by giving you access to UI widgets and components. If so, you may have been wondering if there's any such framework for mobile web applications. Fortunately, the answer is yes, and there's a decent choice of frameworks on offer, including:

- jQuery Mobile
- Sencha Touch
- Dojo Mobile
- Jo

These frameworks provide a means of building mobile web applications that leverage HTML5 to create a native app experience. They all feature a set of rich UI components that mimic native mobile UI features such as lists, navigation bars, toolbars, tab bars, form controls, carousels, and more. Each also provides a data abstraction layer that makes it easier to interact with HTML5's storage features, which are covered in chapter 5. All of these frameworks can be used in tandem with frameworks, such as PhoneGap, for deploying mobile web applications as native apps on various platforms.

G.2 Tools for HTML5 applications

This section covers things that you'll find useful when developing HTML5 applications. It includes tools within browsers, development versions of browsers, and external tools and scripts to make your life easier.

G.2.1 Firebug, Chrome/Safari developer tools, Dragonfly, IE developer tools

When developing HTML5 applications, your development environment will primarily consist of a text editor or integrated development environment (IDE) and a web browser. Every web developer should at least have a copy of the latest versions of the major browsers:

- Apple Safari
- Google Chrome
- Microsoft IE
- Mozilla Firefox
- Opera

In addition to installing the major web browsers, you should ensure that you have the available relevant tools to make your life easier. All of the major browsers now include a suite of web developer tools. These tools are vital when it comes to testing, debugging, and analyzing the performance of your web pages and applications. The features provided by these tools include the following:

- Console output
- JavaScript debugging
- Element and property inspection
- Network activity and traffic analysis
- JavaScript performance profiling
- On-the-fly element styling and manipulation

G.2.2 Browser development versions

In addition to the release (or stable) versions of browsers your users have right now, you should also consider installing one or more of the development versions. Development versions of browsers are where the testing of new features happens, so they allow you to try out new standards as they're being finalized and also test your web applications in the next version of the browser.

Table G.1 lists the major browsers and where to get development versions of them.

Table G.1   Browsers and their development versions

Browser	Development Versions
	• Chrome Beta: https://www.google.com/landing/chrome/beta/ (can't be installed side by side with stable or dev versions) • Chrome Dev: http://mng.bz/XKev (can't be installed side by side with stable or beta versions) • Chrome Canary: https://tools.google.com/dlpage/chromesxs (can be installed side by side with stable, beta, or dev versions)
	• Firefox Beta: https://www.mozilla.org/en-US/firefox/beta/ • Firefox Aurora: https://www.mozilla.org/en-US/firefox/aurora/ • Firefox Nightly: http://nightly.mozilla.org/
	Internet Explorer has a much slower release cycle than the other major browsers, so there isn't a regular snapshot available. Check http://ie.microsoft.com/testdrive/ for information on any beta versions or release candidates available.
	Opera: Beta and alpha versions are called Opera Next; get them here: http://www.opera.com/browser/next/ Whether a particular Opera Next release is a beta or an alpha depends on how close to the next release they're getting; closer to release and they'll be betas.
	Safari: There are no beta releases of Safari as such, but you can download a nightly version of the WebKit rendering engine that powers Safari and use it within your existing Safari install: http://nightly.webkit.org/

The different browsers' development versions each use their own terminology. Table G.2 will help you to understand what to expect from each version.

Table G.2   Development version terminology

Term	Description
Beta/Release Candidate	Mostly stable and approaching release, updated once every week or two
Dev/Aurora/Alpha	Not guaranteed to be stable, updated once a week or more
Nightly/Canary	Cutting edge and unstable, updated every night

G.2.3   HTML5 Shiv

HTML5 Shiv is a shim (a small, compatibility-focused library) for enabling support for HTML5's new elements in older versions of IE. That it's called HTML5 Shiv rather than HTML5 Shim is an accident of history, but it does serve to differentiate it from the large number of shims that have arisen around HTML5 in recent years. Download the latest version from https://github.com/aFarkas/html5shiv or use Modernizr (described in the next section), which includes the Shiv.

G.2.4   Modernizr

One of the problems with using HTML5 is the lack of consistent browser support for the various features defined in the specification. For example, the new autofocus attribute for input elements works in Firefox4 but not in Firefox3.6. Safari4 didn't have support for WebSockets; these were introduced in Safari5. With the ever-expanding set of features in HTML5, and the ever-changing state of browser support among the major vendors, it would be exhausting trying to maintain a list of which browser supports which feature.

You can use JavaScript to easily detect if the visitor's browser supports a particular feature. For example, to check if they have support for offline applications, you'd use the following code:

```
!!window.applicationCache
```

This statement will evaluate to true if the HTML5 application cache is supported or false if it is not. Unfortunately, not every HTML5 feature is detected in the same way. Local storage is also implemented as a property of the window object. As such, you might expect the following to work:

```
!!window.localStorage
```

This will work in many places, but if you try to use it in a debugging tool like Firebug, it will raise a security exception. Instead, you can consistently use the following statement:

```
'localStorage' in window
```

To detect some features, you have to go to much more trouble than the previous approach. Let's take the <canvas> element as an example:

```
!!document.createElement('canvas').getContext
```

This code basically creates a dummy <canvas> element and calls the getContext method on it. The double-negative prefix on this statement will force the result of this expression to evaluate to either true or false, in this case informing you of whether or not the browser supports the <canvas> element.

As a final example, let's look at how you'd detect one of the new HTML5 form input element types, in this case the date type:

```
var el = document.createElement('input');
el.setAttribute('type', 'date');
el.type !== 'text';
```

Pretty ghastly stuff, huh? Of course, you could wrap this in a function to make it reusable, but writing functions for each and every HTML5 feature would be painstaking. Thankfully, there's a JavaScript library named Modernizr that does all this for you.

To use Modernizr, grab the minified JavaScript source file for the library from http://www.modernizr.com, and include it in your HTML document by adding it to the <head> section:

```
<script src="modernizr-1.7.min.js"></script>
```

You'll also need to add a `class` attribute to your document's `<html>` element, with the value `no-js`, as follows:

```
<html lang="en" class="no-js">
```

You can now use Modernizr to detect support for various HTML5 features. Let's see how you'd use it to detect the four features we detected earlier in this section:

```
Modernizr.applicationcache //true if offline apps supported
Modernizr.localstorage //true if local storage supported
Modernizr.canvas //true if canvas supported
Modernizr.inputtypes.date //true if date input type supported
```

We're sure you'll agree that this is much easier to remember and read. Modernizr also adds a host of CSS classes to the `<html>` element of your document to indicate if a particular feature is available in the visitor's browser. This allows you to serve up different styles to users based on whether their browser supports a given feature. For further information on the Modernizr library, visit the project's website at http://www.modernizr.com.

G.2.5 HTML5 Boilerplate

If you're building an HTML5 application from scratch, there's quite a lot to watch out for. Ensuring your app is cross-browser compatible, supporting caching in an efficient manner, optimizing for mobile browsers, performance profiling, unit testing, writing printer-friendly styles—these are just a sample of the various complexities that come with the territory when building modern web applications.

Rather than learning about and catering to all of these issues individually, wouldn't it be nice if you could get up and running quickly using a template that takes care of all of this for you? This is exactly what the HTML5 Boilerplate does. The following is just a snippet of the features the Boilerplate includes:

- Modernizr
- jQuery (hot-links to a Google-hosted file for performance, with a local fallback)
- Optimized code for including Google Analytics
- Conditional comments to allow for Internet Explorer–specific styling
- CSS reset, printer-friendly styles
- Google-friendly robots.txt file
- .htaccess file jam-packed with site-optimization goodness

We highly recommend using HTML5 Boilerplate as a starting point for all of your HTML5 applications. As the creators of the Boilerplate point out, it's Delete-key friendly, so if you don't want to include anything that comes as part of the Boilerplate, you can remove it. The latest version of the project also supports custom builds, allowing you to include only those parts that you really need. For further information and to download the HTML5 Boilerplate, visit the project's website at http://html5boilerplate.com.

G.2.6 *jsFiddle*

Sometimes you may want to try out HTML, CSS, and JavaScript code quickly and store it as a snippet that you can return to at some point in the future. To do this on your own machine, you'd need to open a text editor, create one or more text files (if you want to separate the HTML, CSS, and JavaScript elements), save the files, and open them in a browser. If you wanted to share the snippet, you'd need to upload the files to a web server, and the person you're sharing with must use their browser's View Source feature to see the code behind it. This is, quite frankly, a bit of a pain. Wouldn't it be great if there were an integrated solution that allows you to enter HTML, CSS, and JavaScript code and view the results in a single window? How awesome would it be to be able to save that snippet so that when you share it, the recipient sees the same view as you?

There is a nifty little web application named jsFiddle that provides all of this functionality. Not only that, but it also gives you a really simple way to include various JavaScript libraries, tidy up your markup, check the validity of your JavaScript code with JSLint, test AJAX requests, and much more besides. A screenshot of jsFiddle in action is shown in figure G.1.

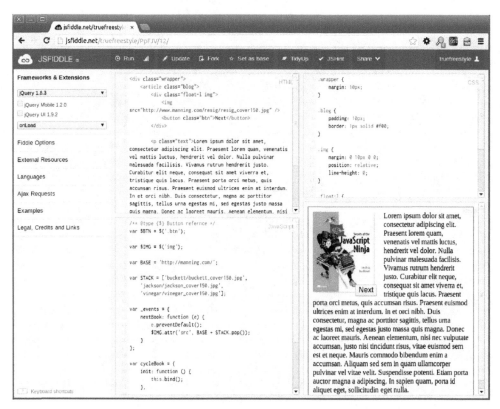

Figure G.1 The jsFiddle web app allows you to quickly write HTML, CSS, and JavaScript code and see a preview of the result, all in a single browser window.

To use jsFiddle, simply visit http://jsfiddle.net—you don't even need an account. Check out the examples to get an idea of some of the neat things you can do with this excellent tool.

G.2.7 *Feature support websites*

For information on the current implementation status of new features, there are a couple of useful websites:

- http://caniuse.com/
- http://html5test.com/

appendix H
Encoding with FFmpeg

You can convert video between container formats and re-encode the audio and video streams within them using several different utilities. In this appendix you'll concentrate on FFmpeg, a command-line tool. Let's review several good reasons for using this tool:

- It's open source and freely downloadable.[1]
- It's available for all the major client and server platforms: Windows, OS X, and Linux.
- Command-line tools lend themselves to scripting, if you have to process many videos.
- It can be called from server-side code.

Let's also look at disadvantages:

- You may be unfamiliar with command-line tools if you've mainly used Windows OSes.
- The sheer flexibility of FFmpeg means it has a confusing plethora of options and configurations.

In this appendix, we'll do our best to walk you through using FFmpeg, but if you're planning to do serious video work, you'll need to get down to the nuts and bolts. If you're only interested in playing around with the video element itself, you can just stick with an easy-to-use tool such as Miro Video Converter (http://www.mirovideoconverter.com/).

---

[1] FFmpeg is free, but you may be required to pay a licensing fee to the MPEG-LA if you use it to encode h264 video.

H.1   How to get FFmpeg

If you don't have FFmpeg, the first thing you need to do is to install it. FFmpeg is primarily distributed as source code. Fortunately, several helpful developers have produced binary versions of it for all the major platforms. Check the officially sanctioned downloads on the website for Windows binaries: http://ffmpeg.org/download.html. If you have a Mac, go here: http://ffmpegmac.net.

If you run Linux, or your server does, FFmpeg will almost certainly be available through one of your standard repositories (although possibly in the non-free section). Note that to do any encoding, you'll also need libraries to supply the codecs (like MP4 or OGG). On Linux, you'll download them using the same package manager you used to install the main binary, but Windows and Mac users may have to do a bit of extra work.

> **NOTE**   If you have problems with the examples in this section, we recommend using a virtual machine and installing one of the popular Linux distributions on it. The examples in this chapter have been tested with Fedora 17 using FFmpeg version 0.10.4 recompiled from the source RPM to enable FAAC.

H.2   Finding out what codecs were used on source video

The first useful thing you can do with FFmpeg is investigate which codecs have been used on your source video. Following is an example command line:

```
ffmpeg -i VID_20120122_132134.mp4
```

This code will produce a whole load of output describing what options your FFmpeg binary was built with, but at the end you should see something like what's shown in the following listing.

Listing H.1   Output from the `ffmpeg -i` **command**

Summarizes the entire content—video and audio.

Stream #0.1 is the audio stream, AAC encoded.

```
Input #0, mov,mp4,m4a,3gp,3g2,mj2, from 'VID_20120122_132134.mp4':
  Metadata:
    major_brand    : isom
    minor_version  : 0
    compatible_brands: isom3gp4
    Duration: 00:00:11.59, start: 0.000000, bitrate: 3259 kb/s
      Stream #0.0(eng): Video: h264, yuv420p, 720x480, 3014 kb/s, PAR
  65536:65536 DAR 3:2, 30.01 fps, 90k tbr, 90k tbn, 180k tbc
      Stream #0.1(eng): Audio: aac, 16000 Hz, mono, s16, 95 kb/s
```

Describes the container format; in this case it includes a number of equivalent file extensions.

Stream #0.0 is the video stream, h264 encoded.

For comparison, the next listing shows the output from a file recorded on a "proper" HD video camera.

Listing H.2   Output from the `ffmpeg -i` **command**

```
Input #0, mpegts, from '00003.MTS':
  Duration: 00:00:46.59, start: 0.332544, bitrate: 13305 kb/s
  Program 1
```

This time the container format is mpegts.

```
    Stream #0.0[0x1011]: Video: h264, yuv420p, 1920x1080 [PAR 1:1 DAR
 16:9], 50 fps, 50 tbr, 90k tbn, 50 tbc
    Stream #0.1[0x1100]: Audio: ac3, 48000 Hz, 5.1, s16, 384 kb/s
```

This time the second stream is AC3 (Dolby Digital).

The first stream is again an h264-encoded video, but this time it's 1080p HD.

H.3   *Determining container formats and supported codecs*

A couple of other useful commands allow you to check what formats and codecs your version of FFmpeg has available. To see a list of available container formats, issue this command:

```
ffmpeg -formats
```

The hyphen indicates a parameter. What comes immediately after the parameter is the parameter name. In the previous command line the parameter is formats; in the command line at the start of the section the parameter is i, for input file, followed by the data for that parameter. Here it is again to remind you:

```
ffmpeg -i VID_20120122_132134.mp4
```

To see the list of supported codecs, issue this command:

```
ffmpeg -codecs
```

Now that you've learned the basics, the next few sections will cover converting to several key video formats. Note that all of the listings that follow show each ffmpeg option on a line by itself for clarity, but when you type the commands into the terminal, they should all be on a single line.

> **Recompiling FFmpeg to add codec support**
>
> As mentioned in the previous note, the examples in this chapter have been tested with Fedora 17 using FFmpeg version 0.10.4 recompiled from the source RPM to enable FAAC. This was necessary because the Fedora version of FFmpeg doesn't support AAC by default. Although this may sound scary, it's a straightforward process on Linux; check out this blog post for a description of the process we followed: http://mng.bz/hF3O.
>
> On Windows and Mac, you may have to search around for a build of FFmpeg that supports all the required codecs.

H.4   *Encoding to MP4/h264 with AAC*

The videos you're using in this appendix are already MP4 containers with h264 video and AAC audio. This means for the application you don't need to know how to convert files to this format. In fact, because h264 is a lossy format, re-encoding the files to MP4 at the same resolution will lower the quality. But in real applications it's likely your source video is in a different format or is at least an HD recording (for example, 1080p is 1920px by 1080px resolution), and one of your key targets will be iOS devices, where all those extra pixels will be wasted. Fortunately, FFmpeg allows you to re-encode a video at a lower resolution in the same way you would re-encode to a different format. A command line for encoding to MP4 with h264 and AAC is shown in the following listing. Again, although it's shown across multiple lines for clarity, you should type it into your command prompt in a single line.

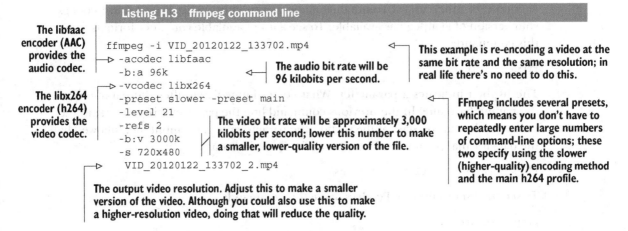

Listing H.3   ffmpeg command line

The libfaac encoder (AAC) provides the audio codec.

The libx264 encoder (h264) provides the video codec.

```
ffmpeg -i VID_20120122_133702.mp4
  -acodec libfaac
  -b:a 96k
  -vcodec libx264
  -preset slower -preset main
  -level 21
  -refs 2
  -b:v 3000k
  -s 720x480
  VID_20120122_133702_2.mp4
```

This example is re-encoding a video at the same bit rate and the same resolution; in real life there's no need to do this.

The audio bit rate will be 96 kilobits per second.

The video bit rate will be approximately 3,000 kilobits per second; lower this number to make a smaller, lower-quality version of the file.

FFmpeg includes several presets, which means you don't have to repeatedly enter large numbers of command-line options; these two specify using the slower (higher-quality) encoding method and the main h264 profile.

The output video resolution. Adjust this to make a smaller version of the video. Although you could also use this to make a higher-resolution video, doing that will reduce the quality.

The input video can be any format that FFmpeg supports. If you have a non-MP4 video, replace the filename (after the `-i`) with your video.

H.5   Encoding to MP4/h264 with MP3

Converting from AAC audio to MP3 isn't a common requirement for web development, but it does allow us to demonstrate another useful feature of FFmpeg. As you already know, h264 is a lossy codec, so re-encoding h264 at the same resolution will reduce quality. But sometimes you may want to re-encode the audio—how can you do that without reducing the quality of the video? Our next listing has the answer—again, type it into your command prompt on a single line.

Listing H.4   ffmpeg command line

```
ffmpeg -i VID_20120122_132134.mp4
  -acodec libmp3lame
  -b:a 96k
  -vcodec copy
  VID_20120122_132134_3.mp4
```

Re-encode the audio to MP3 using the libmp3lame codec.

Use the copy codec so the video stream is copied across unchanged.

You can use the copy codec for several tricks like this. It's also useful if you want to convert between container formats without re-encoding either the audio or video streams.

H.6 Encoding to WebM/VP8

It's likely that WebM will be your second most required format after MP4. With MP4 and WebM format videos, you'll have more than 80% of desktop browser users supported and significant mobile platforms, including iOS and Android. The next listing shows the command line for converting to the WebM format, using its associated VP8 video codec and Ogg audio.

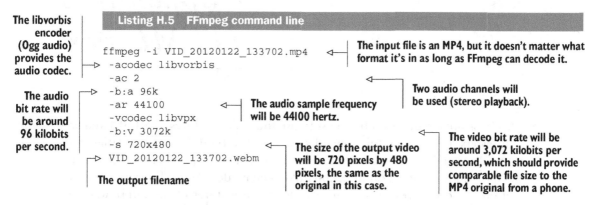

The libvorbis encoder (Ogg audio) provides the audio codec.

The audio bit rate will be around 96 kilobits per second.

Listing H.5 FFmpeg command line

```
ffmpeg -i VID_20120122_133702.mp4
  -acodec libvorbis
  -ac 2
  -b:a 96k
  -ar 44100
  -vcodec libvpx
  -b:v 3072k
  -s 720x480
  VID_20120122_133702.webm
```

The input file is an MP4, but it doesn't matter what format it's in as long as FFmpeg can decode it.

Two audio channels will be used (stereo playback).

The audio sample frequency will be 44100 hertz.

The video bit rate will be around 3,072 kilobits per second, which should provide comparable file size to the MP4 original from a phone.

The size of the output video will be 720 pixels by 480 pixels, the same as the original in this case.

The output filename

H.7 Encoding to Ogg/Theora

Every browser that supports Ogg/Theora also supports WebM, which means most of the time it'll be technically unnecessary to create an Ogg/Theora version of your video. But if you want to support the older versions of those browsers or you prefer the Ogg/Theora format for ideological reasons, your best bet is to download ffmpeg2theora. This is a command-line tool based on the FFmpeg libraries that works out all of the correct video encoding settings: http://v2v.cc/~j/ffmpeg2theora/.

Binaries are available for all the major OSes. It's similar to FFmpeg in how you use it; an example command is shown here.

Listing H.6 Use ffmpeg2theora to convert to Ogg/Theora video

```
ffmpeg2theora
  --optimize
  --deinterlace
  -v 7.8
  -F 30
  -x 720
  -y 480
  -A 96
  -c 2
  -H 44100
  -o VID_20120122_132134.ogv
  VID_20120122_132134.mp4
```

The video quality—this was chosen by trial and error to give a similar file size to the original.

The frame rate—ffmpeg2theora uses the input frame rate if you leave off this parameter.

Size of the video.

Audio bit rate.

Number of audio channels.

Audio sample rate.

Output filename.

appendix I
HTML next

This book concentrates on how best to use the major features of HTML5 available in browsers right now. In this appendix, we'll look at HTML5 capabilities that aren't yet finalized and are under heavy development in a browser's beta versions, such as video captioning, media capture, and full-screen modes. You'll also learn about several proposed features so you can plan for these features of the future web platform, such as peer-to-peer connectivity (for example, for video conferencing) and rotation lock (so that games on mobile devices don't keep flipping between landscape and portrait modes).

Specifically, we'll cover the following:

- Accessing and sharing media
- Providing subtitling and captions for media
- Capturing mouse events outside the bounds of an element
- Expanding elements to full screen
- Measuring orientation to control animation
- Locking the pointer to the center of the screen.

I.1   Accessing and sharing media devices

Many devices where HTML5 is expected to be used come equipped with built-in cameras, but until now you've needed to use Flash or write a native application to get access to them. One of the goals of the HTML5 spec was to build an open application platform to replace native apps in common use cases. With this in mind a W3C working group has been set up to produce standards for real-time media access and communication (http://www.w3.org/2011/04/webrtc/). The charter of this group specifically mentions six deliverables, summarized in table I.1 alongside pointers for the features we'll discuss in this section.

Table I.1 Deliverables of the Web Real-Time Communications Working Group

	Deliverable	Being worked on?	In this appendix?
1.	API functions to explore device capabilities; e.g., camera, microphone, speakers	In scope for the Device APIs & Policy Working Group	Not covered
2.	API functions to capture media from local devices (camera and microphone)	In scope for the Device APIs & Policy Working Group, experimental implementations available	Covered in section I.1.1
3.	API functions for encoding and other processing of those media streams		Not covered
4.	API functions for establishing direct peer-to-peer connections, including firewall/NAT traversal	Being worked on at the IETF, experimental implementations available	Discussed in section I.1.2
5.	API functions for decoding and processing (including echo canceling, stream synchronization, and a number of other functions) of those streams at the incoming end		Not covered
6.	Delivery to the user of those media streams via local screens and audio output devices	Part of the HTML5 specification work, experimental implementations available	Covered in chapter 8

In this section you're going to learn about the experimental implementation for point 2 in table I.1, getUserMedia(), as well as discuss point 4, which, in concert with getUserMedia(), will allow the creation of web applications for telephony and video conferencing.

I.1.1 Grab input with getUserMedia()

The getUserMedia() function allows you to grab a media stream from the user's device and use it within the browser. The current focus is on audio and video streams, since the elements to output those already exist in HTML5, but there's no reason why other sources of data couldn't be accessed in the future and handled with the File API (see chapter 3) or new elements.

Opera, Google, and Mozilla have already implemented a significant chunk of the functionality targeted by the working group thanks to getUserMedia(). You will, of course, need a PC or laptop with a webcam. You could also use your mobile phone or tablet device, but then you'd need some way of making the files you create on your computer available over the network your device is on. This might involve setting up a local web server and possibly fiddling around with your firewall and router settings to allow access to it, or if you already have a web server online, you could upload your files to that.

In this section, to demonstrate how to use getUserMedia(), you're going to modify the video telestrator jukebox code from chapter 8 to accept video input from your camera. Figure I.1 shows what you're going to be finishing up with—a live video stream that you can telestrate.

The method signature for getUserMedia() is shown in the first listing. It follows the pattern of accepting an array of options along with callback functions, similar to the Geolocation API (see chapter 3).

Listing I.1   getUserMedia() **method signature**

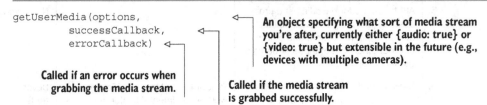

Figure I.1   **Author Rob Crowther after tweaking the code from the video telestrator application in chapter 8 to incorporate a live video stream. With the live video stream appearing on the browser, Rob was then able to telestrate, or draw, additional features on his face, perhaps to impress a potential client during a video meeting.**

---

[1] In Firefox 19 you need to set media.enabled to true in about:config to turn on the experimental support.

The following shows practical code for making `getUserMedia` work in Opera and Chrome. It will grab a video stream from the camera and pipe the output directly into a video element. The annotations indicate where this code fits in the finished code (index-8.html) from chapter 8.

Listing I.2 `getUserMedia` working in Chrome, Opera, and Firefox

Request a video stream. In older examples you'll see a simple string 'video' passed; the current syntax is to pass in an object.

Find this line in the finished code from chapter 8; the new code goes after it. You can remove the change_video() function and binding.

Called if it all goes horribly wrong.

Currently Opera has implemented an unprefixed version of getUserMedia in the beta version, whereas Chrome and Firefox have a prefixed version.

Everything below is conditional on support existing in the user's browser.

Called if the video stream is grabbed successfully.

Chrome supports the File API; in that browser you have to pass the stream through createObjectURL.

In Opera and Firefox, attach the stream directly to the video element.

```javascript
var context = canvas[0].getContext('2d');
navigator.getUserMedia =
    navigator.getUserMedia ||
    navigator.mozGetUserMedia ||
    navigator.webkitGetUserMedia;
if (navigator.getUserMedia) {
    navigator.getUserMedia({ video: true },
                           successCallback,
                           errorCallback);
    function successCallback(stream) {
        console.log('success');
        if (window.webkitURL) {
            v.src = window.webkitURL.createObjectURL(stream);
        } else {
            v.src = stream;
        }
        v.play();
    }
    function errorCallback(error) {
        console.error('An error occurred: [CODE ' + error.code + ']');
        return;
    }
} else {
    console.log('Native web camera streaming (getUserMedia)
                is not supported in this browser.');
}
```

Now that you have the stream in the video element, everything else functions as before. The `canvas` element grabs frames from the video, mixes them with the telestrator graphics, and outputs the whole thing.

Being able to let a user display a picture of themselves is a cool gimmick. You can probably see how this could be extended to more practical applications such as snapping photos for entrance badges. But the main goal of this functionality is to allow you to share a video stream across the internet, enabling such applications as video chat. The plan for the future is to combine `getUserMedia()` with peer-to-peer communication protocols. This will enable the creation of video conferencing and telephony applications within the browser; the next section briefly discusses the standard aimed at achieving this, WebRTC (Web Real Time Communication).

I.1.2 Peer-to-peer media connections with WebRTC

The WebRTC specification is focused on initiating a peer-to-peer connection between two browsers and allowing them to send media streams to each other; a common application of this would be internet telephony or video chat. Google and Mozilla have recently announced their initial implementations of this standard in the development versions of Chrome and Firefox. The following listing shows an excerpt from the Mozilla blog post announcing the availability of the feature,[2] to give you an idea of how the final standard will work.

Listing I.3 Initiating a peer-to-peer video chat with WebRTC

```
function initiateCall(user) {
  navigator.mozGetUserMedia({video:true, audio:true},    ◄──┤ The same getUserMedia
  function(stream) {                                           function you were using
    document.getElementById("localvideo").mozSrcObject = stream;   in the previous section.
    document.getElementById("localvideo").play();
    document.getElementById("localvideo").muted = true;       Firefox object
    var pc = new mozRTCPeerConnection();         ◄──          that creates a
    pc.addStream(stream);                                     PeerConnection.
                                           ◄──┐ Local stream is added to
                                              │ the PeerConnection object.
    pc.onaddstream = function(obj) {
      document.getElementById("remotevideo").mozSrcObject = obj.stream;
      document.getElementById("remotevideo").play();
    };
                                                   A connection is initiated
    pc.createOffer(function(offer) {        ◄──    by sending an offer via
      pc.setLocalDescription(offer, function() {   an intermediate server
        peerc = pc;                                using a standard HTTP
        jQuery.post("offer", {                     POST request.
          to: user,
          from: document.getElementById("user").innerHTML,
          offer: JSON.stringify(offer)
        },
        function() { console.log("Offer sent!"); }
        ).error(error);
      }, error);
    }, error);
  }, error);
}
```

An addstream event will be fired when the remote client connects; the remote stream will be part of the object parameter.

Because there's no stable support for this feature in current browsers, we won't go into further detail at this point. Instead, in the next section you'll look in detail at another experimental feature that's complementary to audio playback: subtitling and captioning.

---

[2] Maire Reavy and Robert Numan, editor, "Hello Chrome, it's Firefox calling!", Mozilla Hacks.Mozilla.org, Feb. 4, 2013, http://mng.bz/kbLL.

I.2   Media text tracks: providing media subtitles and captioning

Grabbing webcam and microphone input isn't the only experimental feature in the works for HTML5 media; another potentially very useful feature is text tracks. The central feature of text tracks is to provide subtitles and captioning for hearing-impaired users. All that boils down to is a file format for describing bits of information associated with time spans and a means of presenting that information within the browser. With an API, this sort of structure could be useful in all sorts of ways if you want things to happen in your pages at certain times during playback of media. For example, if your page contained both a video of a presentation and a widget showing the slides from the presentation, then you might want the slideshow widget to automatically switch to the next slide in time with the video.

Fortunately, HTML5 provides such an API. In this section you're going to learn how to use text tracks and the Text Track API by adding subtitles to one of the videos used in chapter 8. Figures I.2 and I.3 show the basic idea: subtitles overlaid on the video corresponding to the current action.

To make this work you'll need Chrome 18 or later, and you should enable the track element in the about:flags page; in more recent versions of Chrome (24 and later),

Figure I.2   On the playing video, the caption reads "PASS."

Figure I.3   Later on the playing video, the caption reads "INTERCEPTION."

it's enabled by default. The file index-3.html from the chapter 8 code will be used as the basis for your experimentation here.

Text Track API   18   N/A   10   N/A   N/A

Local web server required

If you try to run any of the examples in this section directly from the filesystem (with a `file:///` URI), then Chrome will fail to load the Text tracks because of cross-domain security restrictions. In order to make them work, you'll need to either run a local web server (see appendix F where this is discussed) or upload them to an online server.

I.2.1   *Adding a text track to the videoText*

Tracks come in cue files, files containing a series of timestamped cues (the word comes from theater and film/television; think of an actor onstage waiting for a cue to deliver a line). Chrome supports the WebVTT (Web Video Text Tracks) file format for cue files; a sample for you to use is shown in the following listing. To keep things simple in the long run, save this in a file with a name similar to the video file associated with it, such as VID_20120122_133036.vtt.

Listing I.4   VTT Captions VID_20120122_133036.vtt

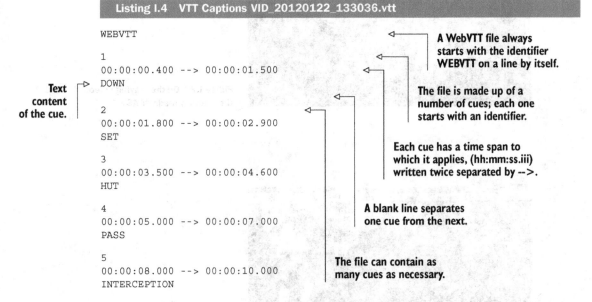

To associate the WebVTT file with a `<video>` element, add a `<track>` element, as shown in the next listing. Use the index-3.html file from chapter 8's code download;

then you can drop the video element shown in the listing in place of the one already in that file and save it with a new name.

Listing I.5   index-vtt-1.html, video element with a captions track

```
<video controls
       width="720" height="480">
    <source src="videos/VID_20120122_133036.mp4" type="video/mp4">
    <source src="videos/VID_20120122_133036.webm" type="video/webm">
    <track src="tracks/VID_20120122_133036.vtt"
           kind="captions"
           default>
    Your browser does not support the video element, please
    try <a href="videos/VID_20120122_133036.mp4">downloading
    the video instead</a>
</video>
```

The kind of track this is. See more on kinds of tracks in section F.2.2.

The <track> element; it should go after any <source> elements but before any other content.

Use this track as the default.

And that's all there is to it. With these two additions you can now play the video to re-create the screenshots from the introduction. Check the file index-vtt-1.html in the code download for the complete listing.

I.2.2   Adding multiple text tracks

Things get more fun when you add multiple <track> elements. The kind attribute in listing I.5 can be set to several different values depending on the purpose of the timed track. A full list is shown in table I.2.

Table I.2   Values for the kind attribute

Kind	Description
subtitles	Transcription or translation of the dialogue, suitable for when the sound is available but not understood (e.g., because the user doesn't understand the language of the media resource's audio track). Overlaid on the video.
captions	Transcription or translation of the dialogue, sound effects, relevant musical cues, and other relevant audio information; suitable for when sound is unavailable or not clearly audible (e.g., because it's muted or drowned out by ambient noise, or because the user is deaf). Overlaid on the video; labeled as appropriate for the hearing-impaired.
descriptions	Textual descriptions of the video component of the media resource, intended for audio synthesis when the visual component is obscured, unavailable, or not usable (e.g., because the user is interacting with the application without a screen while driving, or because the user is blind). Synthesized as audio.
chapters	Chapter titles, to be used for navigating the media resource. Displayed as an interactive (potentially nested) list in the user agent's interface.
metadata	Tracks intended for use from script. Not displayed by the user agent.

In this section, you're going to build a simple UI for switching from captions to subtitles to descriptions. Figure I.4 shows video with the caption selected; figure I.5 shows

Figure I.4   Video with captions selected

Figure I.5   Video with subtitles selected

the subtitles after clicking the middle button. The third button, for descriptions, you'll deal with in the following section.

For this to work you'll need additional WebVTT files. Listings I.6 through I.8 show the files you need for the captions, subtitles, and descriptions. Note that the long filenames are provided in code comments.

Listing I.6 Captions	Listing I.7 Subtitles	Listing I.8 Descriptions

`//`
`VID_20120122_133036-`
`captions.vtt`
	`//`
	`VID_20120122_133036-`
	`subtitles-enGB.vtt`
		`//`
		`VID_20120122_133036-`
		`description.vtt`

`WEBVTT`	`WEBVTT`	`WEBVTT`

`1`
`00:00:00.400 -->`
`00:00:01.500`
`Players line up`
	`1`
	`00:00:00.400 -->`
	`00:00:01.500`
	`DOWN`
		`1`
		`00:00:00.000 -->`
		`00:00:04.000`
		`A rugby field in`
		`Oxfordshire, American`
		`Footballers get ready`
		`for the play`

`2`
`00:00:01.800 -->`
`00:00:02.900`
`Offense gets ready`
	`2`
	`00:00:01.800 -->`
	`00:00:02.900`
	`SET`
		`2`
		`00:00:04.000 -->`
		`00:00:08.000`
		`The ball is snapped,`
		`the quarterback drops`
		`back to pass`

`3`
`00:00:03.500 -->`
`00:00:04.600`
`The ball is snapped`
	`3`
	`00:00:03.500 -->`
	`00:00:04.600`
	`HUT`
		`3`
		`00:00:08.000 -->`
		`00:00:09.000`
		`The pass is thrown`
		`wide of the receiver,`

`4`
`00:00:05.000 -->`
`00:00:07.000`
`It's a pass`
	`4`
	`00:00:05.000 -->`
	`00:00:07.000`
	`PASS`	

```
5                           5                           a defender makes the
00:00:08.000 -->            00:00:08.000 -->            interception
00:00:10.000                00:00:10.000
It's picked off             INTERCEPTION                4
                                                        00:00:09.000 -->
                                                        00:00:12.000
                                                        The defender sets off
                                                        with the ball, the
                                                        offensive players in
                                                        pursuit
```

Now add the files to the `<video>` element in multiple `<track>` elements, as shown in the following listing.

Listing I.9   `<video>` element with multiple `<track>` elements

> As before, <track> elements come after <source> elements and before any other content.

```
<video controls
       width="720" height="480">
    <source src="videos/VID_20120122_133036.mp4" type="video/mp4">
    <source src="videos/VID_20120122_133036.webm" type="video/webm">
    <track src="tracks/VID_20120122_133036-captions.vtt"
       kind="captions"
       default
       label="Captions">
    <track src="tracks/VID_20120122_133036-subtitles-enGB.vtt"
       kind="subtitles"
       srclang="en-GB"
       label="English Subtitles">
    <track src="tracks/VID_20120122_133036-description.vtt"
       kind="descriptions"
       label="Text Description">
    Your browser does not support for video element, please
    try <a href="videos/VID_20120122_133036.mp4">downloading
    the video instead</a>
</video>
```

> Each track can also have a label; in the future it is envisaged user agents will offer a UI for selecting between tracks using this label.

> The kind attribute differentiates the tracks.

> If the track is of kind subtitles or captions, then the srclang attribute allows the browser to select the correct one based on the user's language preferences.

Next, you'll need buttons to hang the functionality from. Just as you did in chapter 8, add a `<menu>` to the page under the `<video>` element that looks like the following code.

Listing I.10   A `<menu>` for choosing the text track

```
<menu>
    <button>Captions</button>
    <button>Subtitles</button>
    <button>Descriptions</button>
</menu>
```

Finally, you need code that makes actions happen when the buttons are clicked. You can reuse the menu-handling function from chapter 8 with appropriate changes to reflect the new functions. The code is shown in the next listing.

Listing I.11   Changing the track shown with JavaScript

```
$('menu').bind('click', function(event) {
    var action = $(event.target).text().trim();
    var p = $('#player video:first-of-type')[0];
    switch (action) {
        case 'Captions':
            p.textTracks[0].mode = "showing";
            p.textTracks[1].mode
                               = "hidden";
            p.textTracks[2].mode = "hidden";
            break;
        case 'Subtitles':
            p.textTracks[0].mode = "hidden";
            p.textTracks[1].mode = "showing";
            p.textTracks[2].mode = "hidden";
            break;
        case 'Descriptions':
            p.textTracks[0].mode = "hidden";
            p.textTracks[1].mode = "hidden";
            p.textTracks[2].mode = "showing";
            break;
    }
    return false;
});
```

Use the text of the button to determine the action.

You can get at the text tracks through the textTracks array on the <video> element.

In this case, you know which tracks are which, so you can access them directly. You could use the kind attribute or any other DOM methods to work out which is which.

Whether or not the track is displayed is determined by the mode property of the track (more on this in I.2.3).

DISABLED, HIDDEN, and SHOWING are available as properties of TextTrack (see table I.3).

The complete listing is available as index-vtt-3.html in the book's code download.

If you experiment with this latest listing, you'll note that clicking the Descriptions button doesn't do anything. This is because tracks of kind `description` aren't intended for visual display but for aural accompaniment. But this does give us an opportunity to experiment with the rest of the Text Track API. In the next section you'll use the API to extract the text content from the `description` track.

I.2.3   The Text Track API

You got a glimpse of the Text Track API in section I.2.2, where you used the `mode` attribute. In this section, you'll go into more depth, covering reading individual cues from a track and listening to events that are fired when the active cue changes. To begin, you will use the API to grab text from the `description` track you added in section I.2.2. Figure I.6 shows the basic idea; when the Descriptions button is clicked, content from the track is shown.

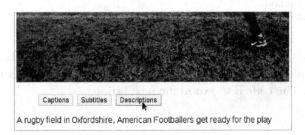

Figure I.6   JavaScript has been used to extract the text content of the normally invisible `description` track and display it on the screen.

Before you dive into the code, review table I.3, which lists the properties and methods of the Text Track API.

Table I.3 The Text Track API

Name	Type	Description
kind	String property	The kind of text track, corresponds to the `kind` attribute.
label	String property	A human-readable label, corresponds to the `label` attribute.
language	String property	The language of the track, such as en-US, corresponds to the `srclang` attribute.
mode	Integer property	The mode of the track: DISABLED (the track will not be loaded), HIDDEN (the track will be loaded but not displayed), or SHOWING (the track will be loaded and displayed if appropriate).
cues	Array property	An array containing the individual cues from the track.
activeCues	Array property	An array containing the cues that apply to the current point in the media.
addCue()	Method	Add a cue to the cues array.
removeCue()	Method	Remove a cue from the cues array.

The property you need here is the `activeCues` array, or a set of cues that should be displaying currently. Displaying the text from the active cue of the `description` track is as simple as grabbing the first element of the array and using the `text` property, as shown in the following listing. Replace the last case in the `select` statement in listing I.11 with this one.

Listing I.12 Display the active cue

```
case 'Descriptions':
    p.textTracks[0].mode = "hidden";        ← The mode property
    p.textTracks[1].mode = "hidden";          seen in listing I.10.
    p.textTracks[2].mode = "showing";                              The activeCues
    $('#desc').html(p.textTracks[2].activeCues[0].text);  ←       array is made up
    break;                                                         of TextTrackCue
                                                                   objects.
```

As you might guess from listing I.12, the cue objects have their own API. Each cue is of type `TextTrackCue`; a complete list of properties is shown in table I.4.

Table I.4 The TextTrackCue API

Attribute/method	Type	Description
track	TextTrack	The track to which this cue belongs.
id	string	Unique identifier for the cue.
startTime	double	The time the cue starts.

Table I.4   The TextTrackCue API *(continued)*

Attribute/method	Type	Description
endTime	double	The time the cue ends.
pauseOnExit	boolean	Returns `true` if the media will pause at the end of the cue.
vertical	string	Returns a string describing the `TextTrack` writing direction. Either empty (horizontal), `"rl"` for vertical growing left, or `"lr"` for vertical growing right.
snapToLines	boolean	Returns `true` if the cue is set to render at a point that's a multiple of the height of the starting line plus the starting point or `false` if its position is a point at a percentage of the overall size of the video.
line	long (or "auto")	Returns a number giving the position of the line or `"auto"` if there are multiple cues.
position	long	A number giving the position of the text of the cue within each line, to be interpreted as a percentage of the video
size	long	A number giving the size of the box within which the text of each line of the cue is to be aligned, to be interpreted as a percentage of the video.
align	string	`"start"`, `"middle"`, `"end"`, `"left"`, or `"right"`.
text	string	The text of the cue.
getCueAsHTML()	DocumentFragment	Returns the text of the cue as HTML.

There's a working version of this code in index-vtt-4.html in the code download in case you don't want to piece it together from the snippets here. If you load it, play the video and click the Descriptions button a few times; you should see the descriptions appear below the video. But you'll also probably see the odd error message like that shown in figure I.7.

The error in figure I.7 can have two main causes:

- There isn't a cue available for the current time.
- The text track hasn't loaded yet.

Figure I.7   An error trying to access the currently active cue in the text track

Determining whether there is a cue currently available follows the normal rules of JavaScript; simply do a test like if (typeof p.textTracks[2].activeCues[0] !== 'undefined') before attempting to access the text property. In most real-life cases, you'll do this as a matter of course. But it's clearly the second issue that's the problem here because our description cue file has no gaps in its time coverage. One approach to solving the second issue would be to listen for the load event of the text track, something we'll discuss further in the next section when you learn about events. In the meantime, we'll look at two alternative approaches to solving the second issue:

- Loading all the text tracks in advance
- Checking to see if the text track has loaded

LOADING THE TEXT TRACKS IN ADVANCE

Unless the default attribute is applied to the track, it will be in the default mode of DISABLED. For the browser to load the tracks, you need to set them to either HIDDEN or VISIBLE. It's easy enough to do this in the ready event you already have in your code, as shown in the following listing.

Listing I.13　Adjust the document `ready` event

```
$(document).ready(
    function() {                                         ← The document ready event
        $('.playlist').bind('click', change_video);       you're already using.
        var p = $('#player video:first-of-type')[0];
        p.textTracks[0].mode = "hidden";      ←  The three new lines are added here. If
        p.textTracks[1].mode = "showing";        you have more than three tracks, you
        p.textTracks[2].mode = "hidden";         might consider using a loop instead.
```

Find the complete working example in the index-vtt-4a.html file.

CHECKING TO SEE IF THE TRACK IS LOADED

Text tracks have a ready state similar to other dynamically loadable objects (for example, XMLHTTP requests). The complete list of values for text tracks is shown in table I.5.

Table I.5　Track `readyState` values

State	Value	Description
NONE	0	The track has not been loaded.
LOADING	1	The track is in the process of being loaded.
LOADED	2	The track has been loaded.
ERROR	3	Attempting to load the track led to an error.

Clearly, all you now need to do is check that the readyState of the track is 2 before you attempt to access the text property. The next listing shows an updated descriptions case for the menu-handling function.

Listing I.14   Check the track ready state

```
case 'Descriptions':
    p.textTracks[0].mode = "hidden";
    p.textTracks[1].mode = "hidden";
    p.textTracks[2].mode = "hidden";
    var t = v.find('track[kind="descriptions"]');
    if (t[0].readyState == 2) {
        $('#desc').html(p.textTracks[2].activeCues[0].text);
    }
    break;
```

Use standard jQuery to get the descriptions track.

The ready state is available on the track element.

Find the complete working example in the index-vtt-4b.html file.

I.2.4   *Using TextTrack events*

Although the examples in the previous sections show some useful techniques and allow you to explore the API, it's more in keeping with JavaScript to deal with text tracks in an event-driven style. The track element has a load event that allows you to call a function when loading is complete in the same way you've done hundreds of times before. Because we have limited space here, you're not going to do that right now; instead, you're going to learn about an event that's specific to timed tracks: cuechange.

The cuechange event is fired every time a new cue is to be displayed. If you handle the cuechange event, then instead of showing the current description whenever the user clicks the Menu button, you can instead show the descriptions at the appropriate time. The following listing updates the switch statement in the menu handler to attach an event to the description track's oncuechange property when the Descriptions button is clicked.

Listing I.15   Listening to the cuechange event

```
switch (action) {
    case 'Captions':
        p.textTracks[0].mode = "showing";
        p.textTracks[1].mode = "hidden";
        p.textTracks[2].oncuechange = null;
        $('#desc').html('');
        break;
    case 'Subtitles':
        p.textTracks[0].mode = "hidden";
        p.textTracks[1].mode = "showing";
        p.textTracks[2].oncuechange = null;
        $('#desc').html('');
        break;
    case 'Descriptions':
        p.textTracks[0].mode = "hidden";
        p.textTracks[1].mode = "hidden";
        $('#desc').html(p.textTracks[2].activeCues[0].text);
        p.textTracks[2].oncuechange = function() {
            if (typeof this.activeCues[0] !== 'undefined') {
```

If the captions or subtitles are playing, remove the oncuechange event handler.

When the user clicks the Descriptions button, attach an oncuechange handler.

```
                $('#desc').html(this.activeCues[0].text);
            }
        };
        break;
}
```
The body of the handler is the same code you were using already.

Now when the user clicks the Descriptions button, the descriptions will be updated automatically as the cues change. Grab file index-vtt-5.html to try it for yourself.

Although you've used the API to read the descriptions in this section, a more common use would be to perform an action at a particular time with the media. If you refer to table I.2, you'll note that the last kind of track is metadata. This can be used for any kind of data you want to use from within your scripts; for example, you could have a series of cues populated with data in JSON format.

Before we move on to other things, let's take a look at styling the cues as they appear on the video.

I.2.5   Styling text tracks

Text tracks can contain simple markup. Typographical elements like <b> and <i> are allowed. Figure I.8 shows an updated captions file in action.

The new version of the captions file is shown in the following listing.

Figure I.8   Captions using the `<i>` element

Listing I.16   A cue file with simple formatting

```
WEBVTT

1
00:00:00.400 --> 00:00:01.500
<i>Players line up</i>

2
00:00:01.800 --> 00:00:02.900
<i>Offense gets ready</i>

3
00:00:03.500 --> 00:00:04.600
<i>The ball is snapped</i>

4
00:00:05.000 --> 00:00:07.000
<i>It's a pass</i>

5
00:00:08.000 --> 00:00:10.000
<i>It's picked off</i>
```

In the future it will also be possible to style the cues in CSS using the ::cue pseudo; unfortunately, Chrome hasn't yet implemented this.

That's enough media APIs and features for now. For the remainder of this chapter, you're going to learn about experimental APIs that will be particularly useful for games or mobile devices (or games on mobile devices!).

I.3 APIs for gaming and mobile

This section groups together a set of HTML5 APIs that are targeted at gaming, with particular reference to gaming on mobile devices. In this section you will

- Build a test bed, which you'll use to explore the APIs
- Target mouse events at a single element with `setCapture`
- Expand an element to full screen
- Replace mouse events with touch events
- Replace mouse events with orientation events
- Use the vibration and battery APIs
- Use the pointer lock API to enable immersive experiences

I.3.1 Preparing a test bed—the return of Wilson

We need something with which to demonstrate all these APIs, so initially you're going to build a simple canvas app (see chapter 6 for background), which draws an object that will then follow the mouse around the screen. You'll use this as the basis for all the experiments until the end of the appendix, so it's worth spending time understanding how to put it together even if the techniques are familiar to you.

Your starting point for API exploration is a Wilson head, which follows your mouse pointer around. The result is shown in figure I.9.

The process for creating this test bed is as follows:

- Step 1: Create a basic page with a <canvas> element.
- Step 2: Create a function that draws an image at a particular position on the canvas.
- Step 3: Detect and record mouse movement.
- Step 4: Update the position of the image each time the animation is updated.

Gaming and mobile testbed

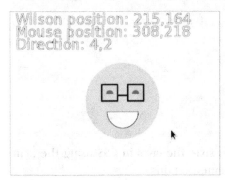

Figure I.9   We have a Wilson following our mouse pointer! Debugging information displays in the background showing the values of important variables.

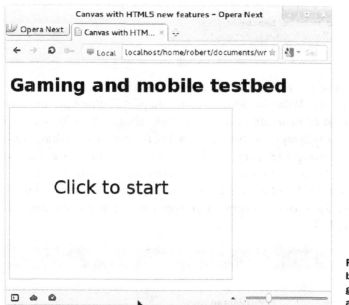

Figure I.10 A simple test bed for exploring APIs for gaming and mobile applications

STEP 1: CREATE A BASIC PAGE WITH A CANVAS ELEMENT

To start, you need a simple HTML5 document like the one shown in figure I.10.

The code for figure I.10 is shown in the following listing. In addition to the code in this listing, you'll need the requestAnimationFrame polyfill from https://gist.github.com/1579671 that you used in chapter 8. It's also in the code download.

Listing I.17 Example app page framework

```
<!DOCTYPE html>
<html>
<head>
    <meta charset="utf-8">
    <title>Canvas with HTML5 new features</title>
    <script>
    function go() { }
    function draw_welcome(){
        var canvas = document.getElementById('canvas');
        canvas.width = 400;
        canvas.height = 300;
        if (canvas.getContext) {
            var ctx = canvas.getContext('2d');
            ctx.font = "24pt sans-serif";
            ctx.fillText('Click to start ',
                canvas.width/2-120,
                canvas.height/2);
        }
    }
    window.addEventListener("load", draw_welcome, false);
    </script>
</head>
```

The go() function, which will be doing most of the setup in this and later sections.

Function to display a welcome message when the page loads.

Attach the function to the load event.

```
<body>
    <h1>Gaming and mobile testbed</h1>
    <canvas id="canvas" onclick="go()"></canvas>
</body>
</html>
```

STEP 2: CREATE A FUNCTION TO DRAW AN IMAGE AT A PARTICULAR POSITION

Our image will be the Wilson character from chapter 7, this time in canvas form. Because you'll need to maintain state information about where Wilson is, what he's aiming for, and how quickly he's moving toward it, the function to draw Wilson will be part of an object. Listing I.18 shows the initial version of this. It's a long and mostly irrelevant listing as far as the new features are concerned, but the rest of the examples won't work without this bit of code, so you need it. There's no need to understand it thoroughly. This code should go between the go() function and the draw_welcome() function in listing I.17.

Listing I.18   The `wilson` object

```
var wilson = {
    x: 0,                        ←──┐  Variables to store
    y: 0,                           │  the current state
    target_x: 0,                    │  of Wilson.
    target_y: 0,
    v_x: 0,
    v_y: 0,
    draw: function (canvas) {
        var tl_x = wilson.x - 70;        ←──┐  For ease of use, you're
        var tl_y = wilson.y - 70;           │  storing the center point,
        if (canvas.getContext){             │  but the drawing code
            var context = canvas.getContext('2d');   │  works from the top-left
            context.beginPath();                     │  corner down, so calculate
            context.arc(tl_x + 70, tl_y + 70,        │  the offset here.
                    70, 0, 2 * Math.PI, false);
            context.fillStyle = 'yellow';
            context.fill();
            context.beginPath();
            context.arc(tl_x + 45, tl_y + 57,
                    7, 0, 1 * Math.PI, true);
            context.moveTo(tl_x + 100,tl_y + 57);
            context.arc(tl_x + 95,tl_y + 57,
                    7, 0, 1 * Math.PI, true);
            context.fillStyle = '#777777';
            context.fill();
            context.beginPath();
            context.arc(tl_x + 70,tl_y + 90,
                    30, 0, 1 * Math.PI, false);
            context.lineTo(tl_x + 100,tl_y + 90);
            context.fillStyle = '#ffffff';
            context.fill();
            context.stroke();
            context.fillStyle = 'black';
            context.lineWidth = 3;
```

```
        context.lineJoin = 'round';
        context.lineCap = 'round';
        context.beginPath();
        context.moveTo(tl_x + 30,tl_y + 40);
        context.lineTo(tl_x + 30,tl_y + 70);
        context.lineTo(tl_x + 60,tl_y + 70);
        context.lineTo(tl_x + 60,tl_y + 40);
        context.lineTo(tl_x + 30,tl_y + 40);
        context.moveTo(tl_x + 60,tl_y + 60);
        context.lineTo(tl_x + 80,tl_y + 60);
        context.moveTo(tl_x + 80,tl_y + 40);
        context.lineTo(tl_x + 80,tl_y + 70);
        context.lineTo(tl_x + 110,tl_y + 70);
        context.lineTo(tl_x + 110,tl_y + 40);
        context.lineTo(tl_x + 80,tl_y + 40);
        context.stroke();
    }
  }
}
```

STEP 3: DETECT AND RECORD MOUSE MOVEMENT

Next, record the mouse movement. The function in the following listing will add an event listener to the <canvas> element, which updates the wilson object when mouse movement is detected. Add this code directly after the wilson object you added in listing I.18.

Listing I.19   Listen to mouse events and update Wilson's target position

```
function get_mouse_pos(obj, evt){            Calculate the mouse position
    var top = 0, left = 0;                   relative to the top left of a
    while (obj && obj.tagName != 'BODY') {   given element.
        top += obj.offsetTop;
        left += obj.offsetLeft;
        obj = obj.offsetParent;
    }
    var mouseX = evt.clientX - left + window.pageXOffset;
    var mouseY = evt.clientY - top + window.pageYOffset;
    return { x: mouseX, y: mouseY };
}
function follow_mouse() {                                Set up the event
    var canvas = document.getElementById('canvas');      listener to capture
    var context = canvas.getContext('2d');               mouse movement.
    canvas.addEventListener('mousemove', function(evt){
        var mousePos = get_mouse_pos(canvas, evt);
        wilson.target_x = mousePos.x;
        wilson.target_y = mousePos.y;
    }, false);
};
```

Note that you're not making any attempt to update the canvas within this handler. You want all drawing to happen in the requestAnimFrame loop to minimize resource usage, so this function simply records the position and exits. If the browser is ready to make use of the position, it will; otherwise, it will be replaced by the next mousemove event.

STEP 4: UPDATE THE POSITION OF THE IMAGE EACH TIME THE ANIMATION IS UPDATED

So now you need a function to be called each animation frame to move Wilson toward the current mouse position. The two functions in the listing that follows should be added to the wilson object so that you can use them later.

Listing I.20   Move Wilson toward the target position

Calculates how far to move the current position to the target position; the farther away, the faster it will move.

If the previous calculation produced an invalid number, use zero.

If the motion is 0 but the points don't yet match, move I pixel in the correct direction.

```
get_v: function(t,c) {
    var v = Math.floor(Math.sqrt(t*2) - Math.sqrt(c*2));
    if (isNaN(v)) { v = 0; }
    if (v == 0 && c != t) { v = (t - c) / Math.abs(t - c); }
    return v;
},
update_xy: function() {
    wilson.v_x = wilson.get_v(wilson.target_x,wilson.x);
    wilson.v_y = wilson.get_v(wilson.target_y,wilson.y);
    wilson.x += wilson.v_x;
    wilson.y += wilson.v_y;
    if (isNaN(wilson.x) || wilson.x < 0) { wilson.x = 0; }
    if (isNaN(wilson.y) || wilson.y < 0) { wilson.y = 0; }
},
```

Update the x and y velocities.

Add the velocity to the current position.

Check that the bounds haven't been exceeded in some way.

The code in the previous listing is a bit rough and ready, but it will produce a fairly natural-looking deceleration toward the target point everywhere but at the edges without your having to worry about mapping floating point numbers into an integer coordinate space. When you write your killer gaming app based on this sample, you should definitely spend a little more time on it!

Now you're ready to hook the various components together in the go() function. Replace your go() function from listing I.17 with the version in the following listing.

Listing I.21   Draw Wilson

```
function go() {
    var canvas = document.getElementById('canvas');
    canvas.width--;
    canvas.width++;
    if (canvas.getContext) {
        var context = canvas.getContext('2d');
        wilson.x = canvas.width/2;
        wilson.y = canvas.height/2
        wilson.target_x = wilson.x;
        wilson.target_y = wilson.y;
        wilson.draw(canvas);
        follow_mouse();
        (function anim_loop(){
            requestAnimFrame(anim_loop);
            canvas.width--;
            canvas.width++;
            wilson.update_xy();
```

Clear the canvas.

Set Wilson's draw point to be the midpoint of the canvas.

Draw Wilson.

```
                         wilson.draw(canvas);
            }) ();
        }
    }
}
```

Now that you have a basic example application in place, let's look at some APIs!

I.3.2   *The Mouse Event Capture API: continuing movement beyond the bounds of an element*

The first API you're going to look at is Mouse Event Capture, comprising the `set-Capture()` and `releaseCapture()` methods. The problem this API is trying to solve is that mouse events immediately stop the moment the mouse pointer moves outside of the element where they're being captured. The problem is illustrated in figure I.11.

> **NOTE**   The Mouse Event Capture API is not yet part of any standard, but that's more because no one has decided where to put it than that it's not useful or won't be standardized. The HTML5 and W3C recommendation requirement of "two compatible implementations" has already been met. It's possible it will appear in the DOM Level 3 specification.

Mouse Capture	N/A	4	5.5	N/A	N/A

Figure I.11   **Although the mouse pointer has moved to the right, Wilson has not followed because the pointer movement occurred outside of the bounds of the element.**

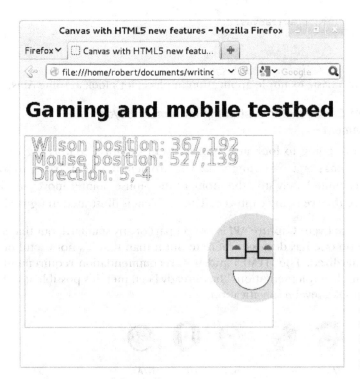

Figure I.12 With the capture events API Wilson continues to follow the pointer when it leaves the element or even the browser window.

This is obviously annoying behavior if your user is controlling a game with their mouse, because as soon as the mouse pointer leaves the element, the game piece they're manipulating will stop responding. Figure I.12 shows the difference when `setCapture()` is used (you'll just have to trust that I did the same thing with the mouse pointer—or download the sample code and try it for yourself).

The next listing shows how you could use the event capturing API to work around the issue. It's a replacement for the `follow_mouse()` function you implemented in the previous section.

Listing I.22 Following the mouse with `setCapture()`

```
function follow_mouse() {
    var canvas = document.getElementById('canvas');
    var context = canvas.getContext('2d');
    function mouse_down(e) {
        e.target.setCapture();
        e.target.addEventListener("mousemove",
                        mouse_moved, false);
    }
    function mouse_up(e) {
        e.target.removeEventListener("mousemove",
                        mouse_moved, false);
    }
    function mouse_moved(evt){
        var mousePos = get_mouse_pos(canvas, evt);
```

> The setCapture() method needs to be called inside a mousedown event.

> The movement-tracking function is the same as before except it's now a declared function instead of an anonymous one.

```
            wilson.target_x = mousePos.x;
            wilson.target_y = mousePos.y;
        }
    canvas.addEventListener('mousedown', mouse_down , false);
    canvas.addEventListener('mouseup', mouse_up , false);
};
```

For best results here, implement additional bounds checking on Wilson's movement; otherwise, he'll leave the canvas at the right or bottom.

If you comment out this line, then mouse events will continue to be captured by the canvas after the mouse button is released.

That's all you need to know about capturing mouse events on an element, but there's an alternative approach you might want to consider. Instead of attempting to capture mouse movement as it moves outside the element, you could make the element take up the full screen. You'll learn about the Full-Screen API in the next section.

I.3.3   *The Full-Screen API: expanding any element to full screen*

The Full-Screen API allows any element to expand to take up the entire screen. The element will be the only thing displayed; no browser chrome will be visible. Figure I.13 shows Wilson in full-screen mode in Firefox12. The text "Press ESC at any time to exit fullscreen" will fade out after a few seconds; it's added as a security measure so that it's obvious to users that they've entered full-screen mode. Otherwise, a nefarious script could simulate their entire desktop in order to steal passwords and other personal information.

A summary of the Full-Screen API is shown in table I.6.

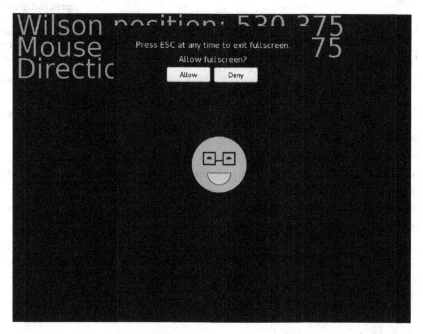

Figure I.13   Wilson entering full-screen mode in Firefox with the user information overlay showing

Table I.6   The Full-Screen API

Property/event name	Type	
requestFullscreen()	Method	Ask for an element to go to full screen.
fullscreenEnabled	Read-only boolean	Is the page currently in full-screen mode?
fullscreenElement	Read-only enabled	If full screen is enabled, this property will be set to the element that's full screen.
fullscreenchange	Event	The fullscreenEnabled state has changed.

Full-Screen API	15	9	N/A	N/A	N/A

ENTERING FULL-SCREEN MODE

Entering full-screen mode is quite straightforward, even accounting for experimental browser implementations. Undo any changes you made to your example in section I.3.2, and then place the code from the following listing at the top of your go() function.

Listing I.23   Request FullScreen for the <canvas> element

```
function go() {
    var canvas = document.getElementById("canvas");
    if (canvas.requestFullScreen) {
        canvas.requestFullScreen();
    } else if (canvas.mozRequestFullScreen) {
        canvas.mozRequestFullScreen();
    } else if (canvas.webkitRequestFullScreen) {
        canvas.webkitRequestFullScreen();
    }
}
```

The browser has implemented the standard.

requestFullScreen must be called from an event handler. In this case the go() function is being called from a click event, so you're okay.

Mozilla's experimental implementation.

Chrome's experimental implementation.

STYLING THE FULL-SCREEN BACKGROUND

If you try your new example in both Firefox and Chrome, you'll immediately notice a compatibility issue: Firefox defaults the full-screen background to black; Chrome defaults it to white. Fortunately, this problem can be overcome with CSS. Check out the following listing, which uses the experimental :full-screen pseudo class to set a consistent background color.

Listing I.24   Set CSS styles that only apply in full-screen mode

```
canvas:-moz-full-screen {
    background: #006;
    outline: none;
}
canvas:-webkit-full-screen {
    background: #006;
    outline: none;
```

```
}
canvas:fullscreen {
    background: #006;
    outline: none;
}
```

EXITING FULL-SCREEN MODE

Now that the full screen has a pleasant dark-blue background in all browsers, the next issue to consider is what happens when the user exits full-screen mode by hitting Esc. In a more complex app, you may want to pause an activity or take the opportunity to switch to a different mode of interaction. To do this, listen to the `fullscreenchange` event. Our next listing has some example code.

> **Listing I.25   Add a listener to the `fullscreenchange` event**

```
document.addEventListener("fullscreenchange", function () {
    console.log(document.fullscreen);
}, false);
document.addEventListener("mozfullscreenchange", function () {
    console.log(document.mozFullScreen);
}, false);
document.addEventListener("webkitfullscreenchange", function () {
    console.log(document.webkitIsFullScreen);
}, false);
```

Feel free to experiment with these events further; we're not going to go into any more detail. In the next section, you're going to jump to mobile; to get full advantage you should have an iPhone or Android device handy.

I.3.4   *The Device Orientation API: controlling on-screen movement by tilting a device*

The Device Orientation API delivers events to your web page that correspond to the movement of the device. The device can be rotated around three axes; have a look at figure I.14.

Device Orientation API	7/A3	3.6	N/A	N/A	iOS4.2

Alpha   Beta   Gamma

Figure I.14   The directions of motion used in the Device Orientation API. (Based on diagrams at https://developer .mozilla.org/en/DOM/ Orientation_and_motion_data_ explained.)

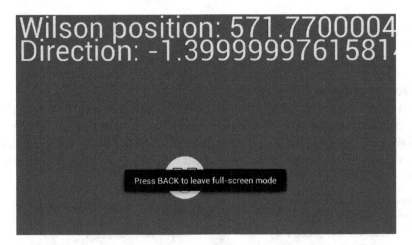

Figure I.15   Full-screen mode in Firefox Android version, using device orientation to control Wilson

Figure I.15 shows Wilson in full-screen mode on an Android device being controlled by the Device Orientation API, although the angle of the device is hard to tell from a flat screenshot!

So how do you take advantage of the Device Orientation API? It all depends on the deviceorientation event. The following listing adapts the now inaccurately named follow_mouse() function to listen to this event. For this listing to work, you'll need a device with a built-in accelerometer such as an Android or iOS phone or tablet.

Listing I.26   Update the follow_mouse() function to use device-orientation data

Rotation around the y-axis in degrees ranging between -90 and 90.

A flag indicating whether the orientation returned is in the context of earth's coordinate frame or relative to the device.

Rotation around the z-axis in degrees ranging between 0 and 360.

Rotation around the x-axis in degrees ranging between -180 and 180.

Plug the beta and gamma rotation directly into the wilson object's velocity properties.

```
function follow_mouse() {
    var canvas = document.getElementById('canvas');
    var context = canvas.getContext('2d');
    function handleOrientation(orientData) {
        var absolute = orientData.absolute;
        var alpha = orientData.alpha;
        var beta = orientData.beta;
        var gamma = orientData.gamma;
        wilson.v_x = -1 * beta;
        wilson.v_y = gamma;
    }
    window.addEventListener("deviceorientation",
                            handleOrientation, true);
};
```

Because of the slightly different approach in setting the velocity—with mouse events you're aiming at a target; with orientation events you're linking the velocity directly to the angle—the update_xy() function in the `wilson` object also needs updating. The following listing has the code.

Listing I.27   Update Wilson's X and Y positions

```
update_xy: function(canvas) {
    wilson.x += wilson.v_x;
    wilson.y += wilson.v_y;
    if (isNaN(wilson.x) || wilson.x < 0) { wilson.x = 0; }
    if (isNaN(wilson.y) || wilson.y < 0) { wilson.y = 0; }
    if (wilson.x > canvas.width) { wilson.x = canvas.width; }
    if (wilson.y > canvas.height) { wilson.y = canvas.height; }
},
```

No need to calculate the velocity; use it directly.

The bounds of Wilson's movement are no longer limited to the bounds of mouse movement in the element, so add a check to keep him in view.

FUTURE IMPROVEMENTS: LOCKORIENTATION

If you play with this example on your mobile device, you'll probably notice a minor annoyance: Everything is set up assuming landscape mode, but as you rotate the device, it's very easy to flip the orientation to portrait mode. At the moment your only option is to detect the orientation change and adjust your code to deal with both portrait and landscape modes. But plans are afoot to provide web apps with the same ability to lock orientation that native apps get. Unfortunately, experimental implementations aren't yet available.

I.3.5   The Vibration API: accessing a mobile device's vibration function

Mobile devices offer alternative methods for feedback as well as the alternative methods for input you looked at in the preceding sections. The Vibration API is a proposal from Mozilla to provide access to a mobile's built-in vibration function. You can adapt the example from section I.3.3 to vibrate when Wilson hits the edges of the screen by adjusting the update_xy() function again, as shown in the next listing.

| Vibration API | N/A | 11 | N/A | N/A | N/A |

Listing I.28   Vibrate when screen edges are reached

```
update_xy: function(canvas) {
    wilson.x += wilson.v_x;
    wilson.y += wilson.v_y;
    if (isNaN(wilson.x) || wilson.x < 0) {
        wilson.x = 0;
        navigator.mozVibrate(50);
    }
    if (isNaN(wilson.y) || wilson.y < 0) {
        wilson.y = 0;
        navigator.mozVibrate(50);
    }
```

Vibrate for 50 milliseconds.

```
    if (wilson.x > canvas.width) {
        wilson.x = canvas.width;
        navigator.mozVibrate(50);        ◁─┐
    }                                        ├─ Vibrate for 50
    if (wilson.y > canvas.height) {          │  milliseconds.
        wilson.y = canvas.height;            │
        navigator.mozVibrate(50);        ◁─┘
    }
},
```

The Vibration API can also create a pattern if you pass it an array rather than a single number. The values are again times in milliseconds, but now they alternate between vibrating and not vibrating. The following listing shows an example of this.

Listing I.29   Vibrating in a pattern

```
navigator.mozVibrate([100,    ◁─┐
              ┌─▷     100,       ├─ Vibrations.
   Pauses.   │       200,    ◁─┘
              └─▷     200]);
```

I.3.6   Battery API: adjusting application processing based on battery life

The Battery API allows you to adjust how much processing your app does depending on the state of the battery. In a real app, you could avoid doing any heavy processing or reduce the number of network connections when the battery is low. In our example app, there isn't much opportunity to cut back processing, so you're just going to draw less of Wilson as the battery level drops. Figure I.16 shows the end result in Firefox on an Android phone.

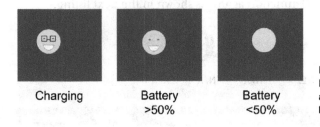

Charging   Battery   Battery
                  >50%   <50%

Figure I.16   By integrating the Battery API, you can make your app do less work as the charge level drops.

The Battery API consists of four properties and four events. See the summary in table I.7.

Table I.7   The Battery API

Property/event name	Type	Description
charging	Read-only boolean	Is the power connected?
chargingTime	Read-only double	Seconds remaining until the battery is charged.

Table I.7 The Battery API *(continued)*

Property/event name	Type	Description
dischargingTime	Read-only double	Seconds remaining until the battery is discharged.
level	Read-only double	A value between 0.0 and 1.0 representing the current battery charge level, where 1.0 is full.
chargingchange	Event	The value of charging has changed.
chargingtimechange	Event	The chargingTime has changed.
dischargingtimechange	Event	The dischargingTime has changed.
levelchange	Event	The level has changed.

In this example you're just going to take advantage of the charging and level properties. The following table shows the browser compatibility; this API will work on mobile devices but also laptops.

Battery API	20	10	N/A	N/A	N/A

For this example, you can either continue working with the code from the previous section or, if you don't have access to a mobile phone, you can use the code from section I.3.3 as a starting point. The changes required to the draw() function are shown next.

Listing I.30 Using the battery object in the draw function

```
draw: function (canvas, battery) {
    var tl_x = wilson.x - 70;
    var tl_y = wilson.y - 70;
    if (canvas.getContext){
        var context = canvas.getContext('2d');
        context.beginPath();
        context.arc(tl_x + 70, tl_y + 70,
                70, 0, 2 * Math.PI, false);
        context.fillStyle = 'yellow';
        context.fill();
        if (battery.charging
            || (!battery.charging
                && (battery.level > 0.5))) {
            context.beginPath();
            //...
    }
}
```

The battery object is passed into the draw function so the browser-compatibility code can be all in one place.

Always draw the yellow circle.

If the battery is charging...

...or the battery isn't charging and...

...the battery charge level is above 50%, then draw the eyes and mouth.

This code is the same as before and has been elided for brevity.

```
        if (battery.charging) {
            context.fillStyle = 'black';
            //...
        }
    }
}
```

←— **Draw only the glasses if the battery is charging.**

←— **This code is the same as before and has been elided for brevity.**

As the annotation mentions, the battery object needs to be passed in, which necessitates a small change in the go() function. The next listing shows the code for getting a reference to the battery status and passing it to wilson.draw().

Listing I.31 Passing the battery object to the draw() function

```
var battery = navigator.battery ||
              navigator.mozBattery ||
              navigator.webkitBattery;
wilson.draw(canvas, battery);
```

That's enough mobile excitement for now; in the next section you're going back to the desktop and the Pointer Lock API, a necessary component of most 3D games.

I.3.7 The Pointer Lock API: tracking mouse motion instead of pointer position

Pointer lock may sound like it's another way of doing setCapture, but it's targeted at a different use case. Whereas setCapture allows you to continue tracking the mouse pointer position even when it moves outside the target element, pointer lock takes the pointer position out of the equation entirely. Instead of tracking the position of the mouse pointer, it tracks motion from the mouse itself. The difference is that the pointer position is limited by the bounds of the screen; the mouse can carry on moving. This is crucially important in immersive games like first-person shooters, where the mouse is used to orient the player. Figure I.17 shows an example taken from http://media.tojicode.com/q3bsp/; note that the mouse pointer doesn't even appear.

The Pointer Lock API involves only a few properties, methods, and events. A summary is shown in table I.8.

Table I.8   The Pointer Lock API

Property/event name	Type	Description
requestPointerLock()	Method	Ask for the pointer to be locked.
pointerLockElement	Read-only element	If the pointer is locked, this property will be set to the element that requested it.
pointerlockchange	Event	The pointer lock status has changed.
pointerlockerror	Event	There was an error requesting pointer lock.

Figure I.17 Pointer lock in action along with WebGL; note that the mouse pointer isn't visible.

The Pointer Lock API has experimental implementations in Chrome (with the `--enable-pointer-lock` command-line switch) and Firefox.

Pointer Lock API	18	14	N/A	N/A	N/A

To experiment with the Pointer Lock API, you're going to need a world to explore. Although ideally you'd create your own 3D world, that would take quite some time (please refer to chapter 9 if you'd like to give it a go). In the meantime, you can fake a world with a panoramic photograph. A suitable large image is included in the code download. The following listing shows where you can add the image.

Listing I.32 Add a background image to canvas

```
<canvas id="canvas" onclick="go()">
    <img src="panorama.jpg" id="panorama">
</canvas>
```

You'll take this image and add it as a background to the <canvas> element. Because the image is 9073 pixels wide, it should stretch across more than a single screen on all but the largest of displays. Figure I.18 shows the initial screen in Firefox 14.

The first requirement is a function to draw a correctly scaled slice of the image on the canvas, as shown in listing I.33.

Figure I.18   Wilson exploring a London park

Listing I.33   Draw a segment of the background image

```
function draw_background(canvas,image,x_offset) {
    var scale = canvas.height / image.height;
    var x = x_offset * scale;
    var slice = canvas.width / scale;
    var ctx = canvas.getContext('2d');
    ctx.drawImage(image,
            x, 0, slice, image.height,
            0, 0, canvas.width, canvas.height);
}
```

Calculate a scaling factor to match the image to the canvas height.

Use the scaling factor to convert the offset into a screen length.

Use the scaling factor to convert the screen width into an image offset so you can grab a correctly scaled slice of the image.

The next listing shows the code to activate the Pointer Lock API. This code should go at the top of the go() function.

Listing I.34   Request pointer lock when the mode changes to full screen

```
canvas.requestPointerLock = canvas.requestPointerLock     ||
                            canvas.mozRequestPointerLock  ||
                            canvas.webkitRequestPointerLock;
function on_full_screen() {
    canvas.requestPointerLock();
    follow_mouse();
}
document.addEventListener("fullscreenchange",
                          on_full_screen, false);
document.addEventListener("mozfullscreenchange",
                          on_full_screen, false);
```

Map the different custom implementations to a single function.

The request for a pointer lock must be made inside a fullscreenchange event.

```
document.addEventListener("webkitfullscreenchange",
                          on_full_screen, false);

function pointer_lock_change() {
    if (document.pointerLockElement === canvas ||
        document.mozPointerLockElement === canvas ||
        document.webkitPointerLockElement === canvas) {
      console.log("Pointer Lock was successful.");
    } else {
      console.log("Pointer Lock was lost.");
    }
}
document.addEventListener("pointerlockchange",
                          pointer_lock_change, false);
document.addEventListener("mozpointerlockchange",
                          pointer_lock_change, false);
document.addEventListener("webkitpointerlockchange",
                          pointer_lock_change, false);

function pointer_lock_error() {
    console.log("Error while locking pointer.");
}
document.addEventListener("pointerlockerror",
                          pointer_lock_error, false);
document.addEventListener("mozpointerlockerror",
                          pointer_lock_error, false);
document.addEventListener("webkitpointerlockerror",
                          pointer_lock_error, false);
```

The <pointerlockchange> event will be fired when the request is made; you can test for success of the request by checking the document.pointerLockElement.

The <pointerlockerror> event will let you investigate any errors that may occur.

Next, you need to update the follow_mouse() function again, as shown in the following listing. The Pointer Lock API adds two additional properties to a mouse event: movementX and movementY. These can be used in a similar way to the orientation events in section I.35.

Listing I.35 Follow the mouse movement

```
function follow_mouse() {
    document.addEventListener("mousemove", function(e) {
        wilson.v_x = e.movementX       ||
                     e.mozMovementX    ||
                     e.webkitMovementX ||
                     0;
        wilson.v_y = e.movementY       ||
                     e.mozMovementY    ||
                     e.webkitMovementY ||
                     0;
        offset += wilson.v_x;
    }, false);
};
```

I.4   Summary

In this appendix you've had a glimpse of the future of HTML5. A lot of effort is directed toward accessing device capabilities (webcams, microphones, orientation sensors, and so on) as well as toward building seamless gaming and application experiences (full-screen and pointer lock) to rival native applications. As these standards are finalized and implementations mature over the next few years, we should see a lot of exciting new web applications. Now that you've read this appendix (and the rest of this book), you should be well equipped to take an active role in developing the World Wide Web of tomorrow!

appendix J
Links and references

In this appendix, you'll find a chapter-by-chapter list of many of the links to useful resources, articles, and demos strewn throughout *HTML5 in Action*. Links for each chapter start with important applications and references for building your apps. Near the bottom of each link list, you may also find interesting tidbits such as fun links, live demos, and extra libraries for future projects.

Chapter 1: Introduction

- *Modernizr*—http://modernizr.com/
- *Remy Sharp's HTML5 Shiv (included in Modernizr)*—http://remysharp.com/2009/01/07/html5-enabling-script/
- *WHATWG*—www.whatwg.org/
- *Hello! HTML5 and CSS3*—www.manning.com/crowther/
- *ARIA Attributes*—http://mng.bz/6hb2
- *Google's Microdata Vocabulary*—http://schema.org/
- *Is This HTML5?*— http://mng.bz/PraC

Chapter 2: Forms and validation

- *Webshims Lib*—http://afarkas.github.com/webshim/demos/
- *H5F*—https://github.com/ryanseddon/H5F
- *Webforms2*—https://github.com/westonruter/webforms2
- *html5Widgets*—https://github.com/zoltan-dulac/html5Forms.js
- *Modernizr Polyfills*—http://mng.bz/cJhc

Chapter 3: Working with files on the client side

- *File API*—www.w3.org/TR/FileAPI/
- *File Writer API*—www.w3.org/TR/file-writer-api/

- *File System API*—www.w3.org/TR/file-system-api/
- *Geolocation API*—www.w3.org/TR/geolocation-API/

Chapter 4: Messaging

- *Apache*—http://apache.org/
- *PHP*—http://php.net/
- *MySQL*—http://dev.mysql.com/
- *jQuery*—http://jquery.com/
- *Node.js*—http://nodejs.org/
- *Connect*—https://github.com/senchalabs/connect
- *Mustache*—http://mustache.github.com
- *WebSocket-Node*—https://github.com/Worlize/WebSocket-Node
- *EventEmitter.js*—https://github.com/Wolfy87/EventEmitter
- *Polyfills EventSource.js*—http://mng.bz/ahX0

Chapter 5: Web storage and working offline

- *Offline API (in HTML5 spec)*—http://mng.bz/5u67
- *IndexedDB*—www.w3.org/TR/IndexedDB/
- *Web SQL (deprecated)*—www.w3.org/TR/webdatabase/

Chapter 6: 2D Canvas

- *HTML5 Canvas Cheat Sheet*—http://mng.bz/5r65.
- *explorercanvas*—http://code.google.com/p/explorercanvas/
- *Game Physics guide*—http://gafferongames.com/game-physics/
- *playtomic*—https://playtomic.com/
- *MDN window.requestAnimationFrame*—http://mng.bz/D14s
- *requestAnimationFrame for polyfills*—http://mng.bz/h9v9
- *JavaScript Madness: Keyboard Events*—http://unixpapa.com/js/key.html
- *Sketchpad*—http://mudcu.be/sketchpad/
- *Rome: 3 Dreams of Black*—http://ro.me
- *ImpactJS*—http://impactjs.com/

Chapter 7: SVG

- *Official SVG page*—www.w3.org/Graphics/SVG/
- *W3C SVG animation*—www.w3.org/TR/SVG11/animate.html
- *Canceling animation requests*—http://mng.bz/3Eq1
- *Raphael.JS*—http://raphaeljs.com/
- *Svgweb*—http://code.google.com/p/svgweb/
- *SVG a element*—http://tutorials.jenkov.com/svg/a-element.html
- *svg-edit*—https://code.google.com/p/svg-edit/

Chapter 8: Video and audio

- *FFmpeg*—http://ffmpeg.org
- *FFmpeg Mac Version*—http://ffmpegmac.net/
- *FFmpeg2theora*—http://v2v.cc/~j/ffmpeg2theora/
- *Image Filters with Canvas*—http://mng.bz/3OsN
- *Playback Rate Bug*—https://bugzilla.mozilla.org/show_bug.cgi?id=495040

Chapter 9: WebGL

- *WebGL Cheat Sheet*—http://blog.nihilogic.dk/2009/10/webgl-cheat-sheet.html
- *OpenGL ES Shading Language Reference*—http://mng.bz/1TA3
- *Introduction to 3D graphics*—http://mng.bz/STHc
- *Simple JavaScript Inheritance*—http://ejohn.org/blog/simple-javascript-inheritance/
- *Sylvester*—http://sylvester.jcoglan.com/
- *Wolfram Identity Matrix explanation*—http://mathworld.wolfram.com/IdentityMatrix.html
- *Opera's Introduction to WebGL*—http://mng.bz/4Lao
- *MDN 2D WebGL content and WebGL utilities file*—http://mng.bz/2585
- *MDN WebGL rotation*—http://mng.bz/O5Z2
- *MDN WebGL tutorials*—https://developer.mozilla.org/en/WebGL
- *Joe Lambert's Request polyfill*—http://mng.bz/3epb
- *Learning WebGL*—http://learningwebgl.com
- *three.js*—https://github.com/mrdoob/three.js/
- *Copperlicht*—www.ambiera.com/copperlicht/
- *IEWebGL*—http://iewebgl.com/
- *Secrets of the JavaScript Ninja*—www.manning.com/resig/
- *X-Wing WebGL app*—http://oos.moxiecode.com/js_webgl/xwing/
- *Vlad Vukićević's blog*—http://blog.vlad1.com

index